Some Day Your
Witch Will Come

Some Day Your Witch Will Come

KAY STONE

WAYNE STATE UNIVERSITY PRESS

Detroit

12 11 10 09 08   5 4 3 2 1

Library of Congress Cataloging-in-Publication Data
Stone, Kay F., 1939–
   Some day your witch will come / Kay Stone.
      p. cm. — (Series in fairy-tale studies)
   Includes bibliographical references and index.
   ISBN-13: 978-0-8143-3286-3 (pbk. : alk. paper)
   ISBN-10: 0-8143-3286-2 (pbk. : alk. paper)
   1. Fairy tales—History and criticism.   2. Symbolism in fairy tales.
   3. Psychoanalysis and fairy tales.   4. Women—Folklore.   I. Title.
   GR550.S76   2008
   398.209—dc22

                                    2007047525

Published with the assistance of a fund established by Thelma Gray
James of Wayne State University for the publication of folklore and
                         English studies.

∞ The paper used in this publication meets the minimum requirements
   of the American National Standard for Information Sciences—
Permanence of Paper for Printed Library Materials, ANSI z39.48-1984.

                  Designed by Isaac Tobin
         Typeset by The Composing Room of Michigan, Inc.
                  Composed in Bulmer MT

In memory of
Grace Lousara (Jones) Mitchell
May 1911–May 1991
and
Glenn Allen Mitchell
July 1904–August 1995

who introduced me to fairy tales

Contents

II

FAIRY TALES AND STORYTELLING

III

FAIRY TALES AND DREAMS

Foreword

Modern fairy-tale studies were born in the 1970s. In the midst of the cultural turmoil brought about by the student movement, feminism, the civil rights movement, the war in Vietnam, and the Watergate Scandal, scholars had rediscovered, of all things, the fairy tale. It was not an impulse to escape the era's conflicts that drew scholars to the genre and its magical world. Rather, it was the recognition that fairy tales played an important role in cultural conflict and the debate over social values. While some critics of traditional fairy tales warned exclusively of their outdated ideologies and complicity in promoting repressive politics, others insisted that the fairy tale's special form of enchantment offered a way out of cultural chaos and a return to the moral certainty of the past. When expressed in the extreme, these polarizing views of the fairy tale's meaning and importance generated a great deal of excitement and controversy, but they fell short of grasping the protean nature and real potential of the genre. Ultimately, the most useful and responsible scholarship produced during the 1970s and the decades that followed came from scholars who recognized the genuinely problematic role of fairy tales and sought to understand it by pursuing research that was open to nuance and complexity. The most important research came from scholars who sought relentlessly to comprehend why we tell fairy tales and how we use them to understand and shape our lives.

Kay Stone is one of these scholars. Speaking as both scholar and story-teller—as folklorist and performing artist—Stone brings a dual perspective that offers nuanced insights into the stories that she has both studied and performed. As a result, her essays on the fairy tale published over three decades still speak to us today and tell their own story about the trajectory of fairy-tale scholarship.

Stone first made her mark in a pivotal essay published in 1975 called "Things Walt Disney Never Told Us." This memorably titled essay was her entry into the growing body of feminist fairy-tale scholarship that had received its impetus from a debate in the early 1970s between Alison Lurie and Marcia Lieberman. What Stone brought to the discussion was the perspective of a newly minted folklorist who was not driven by ideology and whose knowledge was not limited to a small selection of canonical tales. While much of the feminist critique revolved monotonously around the stereotypical portrayal of women as either passive or evil, Stone's careful investigation revealed that women in fairy tales have a much more interesting profile. Looking carefully into the corpus of classical tales and searching beyond it in a broader representation of tales, she found examples that offered positive, aggressive heroines.

This finding was significant and provocative in its own right, underlining as it did the need for both a more careful examination of canonical tales and a wider search for lesser-known stories about women. However, Stone's most important contribution came from her interest in the way readers actually respond to fairy tales. Drawing on interviews she had conducted for her dissertation "Romantic Heroines in Anglo-American Popular Literature" (Indiana University, 1975), she uniquely illuminated the question of gender in fairy tales in ways that allowed her work to rise above the kind of speculation about the sociocultural effects of fairy tales that characterized other feminist scholarship. While Stone's research confirmed that the passive heroines of childhood's classic tales do influence readers, her interviews also revealed that through the fascinating work of selective memory, women sometimes turn heroines whom they once experienced as passive into heroines who are active. Pursuing her rich data and stimulating methodology, Stone was ultimately able to demonstrate—as she does in "The Misuses of Enchantment" (1985)—that the romantic ideals and problematic images of women in fairy tales can actually prompt female readers to struggle critically with questions of identity, to reinterpret classical stories, and to reclaim the genre for themselves. Stone's foundational scholarship, then, shows that fairy tales—even those with stereotypical characters—are full of surprising possibility and that the responses of individual readers and listeners can transform tales in ways that transform lives.

The potential for fairy tales to be transformed and to transform those who engage them is fundamental to all of Stone's work. As Stone developed her own identity as both folklorist and storyteller, she began looking even more deeply into the creative process and the relationship between the storyteller's life and the stories he or she narrates. This dimension of her scholarship paralleled not only the North American storytelling revival but also the growing interest among folklorists in the context of storytelling and the role narrative plays in an individual's life. Using techniques similar to those she had used in the study of women and fairy tales, Stone's work on fairy tales and storytelling mines the experiences of urban storytellers with fascinating results. These inward explorations give us, to paraphrase from one of her titles, "journeys into the heart of the story" by revealing how performers select and transform traditional tales in the context of their personal lives. These journeys of transformation for both tale and teller shed light once again on the extraordinary and often unexpected ways that traditional tales can be reclaimed by performers and their audiences.

The emphasis throughout Stone's work on personal responses to fairy tales made it inevitable that her scholarly exploration of storytelling would take an autobiographical turn, as it does in essays such as "Fire and Water" and "In My Mother's Garden." We should also not be surprised that the trajectory of Stone's personal and scholarly journey—which from the beginning has sought to understand the production and reception of fairy tales—would ultimately focus on the inner workings of the creative process and the relationship of fairy tales and dreams. In the hands of a less talented folklorist and writer, these introspective journeys might not be as instructive and compelling as they are. As it is, however, Stone's essays blend perfectly the voices of the scholar and storyteller, producing engaging explorations that generate confidence in the transforming power of storytelling and in the fairy tale's remarkable potential to reshape individual lives.

DONALD HAASE
Series Editor

Preface

I was enthusiastic when I was invited to submit a proposal for a retrospective anthology of my writing for the Series in Fairy-Tale Studies, published by Wayne State University Press. It seemed to be the proverbial dream-come-true—my own work, chosen by me, and with no editing required, only introductory comments for each piece. After thirty years I am more crone than princess, so I chose the witch to guide me on this journey, playing on Snow White's song of yearning for her prince in my title, "Some Day Your Witch Will Come."

In my initial enthusiasm I gathered copies of the articles and book chapters I wanted to include, created a table of contents dividing the work into sections that made sense, and wrote a prospectus. As always, the planning phase of the project was delightful and everything looked promising. All was in place. However, this dream gradually darkened as I began to reread and comment on my early work, which seemed so long ago, so dated, and so unrelated to what I was doing now. I felt like the familiar fairy tale antagonist who unknowingly names her own doom, thinking that she's going to get the prince but getting boiled in oil or meeting some similar fate instead. When I invited the crone, I should have expected that she would most certainly come.

Fortunately for me, I had a helper to get me through the forests. Much of the earliest work had to be retyped. Janet Regehr, a friend who offered to do this, saw the articles with fresh eyes. She was inspired to reread the Grimm tales I mentioned, in both English and German, and to question me about the Grimms, about Charles Perrault, and, of course, about Walt Disney. In answering Janet's questions, I remembered that much of what seemed old to me might be new to other readers, and it is such readers that I kept in mind as I described, in personal rather than scholarly terms, how each article came into being, and how my ideas gradually evolved.

The result is this anthology selected from my major writings, beginning with the first published article in 1975 and ending with chapters from my 2004 book, *The Golden Woman: Dreaming as Art.* I hope to show the evolution of my ideas, beginning with reviewing the position of women in folktales, gradually shifting from studying stories into exploring the actual telling of them, and finally, with a leap like an enchanted frog, looking at creative connections between folktales, dreams, and biographies as artistic creations. Despite the seeming disparity, there are connecting threads that persist all the way from 1975 to 2004. I suppose that might be obvious to others, but it was a surprise to me, since my three phases seemed to be quite distinct, each one being almost a rejection of the previous period. But I can now see how each separate piece, and all of them together, reveal my abiding fascination with the process of oral creativity and with the people themselves—those who responded to my early queries about what they remembered of fairy tales, and later, tellers and their intimate connections with stories and dreamers with their dreams. Each article reveals the connecting warp of these ideas, and each also weaves its own pattern on this warp.

Since my writing falls into three broad periods, I organize chapters into three sections, aware of the power of the number three in fairy tales. Section 1, Fairy Tales and Women, includes five articles selected from early work, beginning with "Things Walt Disney Never Told Us." Section 2, Fairy Tales and Storytelling, includes eight articles that explore tellers and their tales in the contemporary "storytelling revival" movement. Several of these include full story texts and the accompanying comments of the tellers. Three of the eight are adapted from my first book, *Burning Brightly: New Light on Old Tales Told Today.* Section 3 includes four pieces, opening with my first attempt at linking fairy tales and dreams from *Marvels & Tales: Journal of Fairy-Tale Studies,* followed by three chapters from *The Golden Woman.* These needed slight modifications since book chapters often do not stand easily on their own, being part of a whole fabric. Each of the four deals with specific stories and dreams and includes comments from the various dreamers.

As a retrospective, the anthology reveals how ideas and approaches evolve over a lengthy career, much as an artistic retrospective reveals the personal development of a painter or sculptor. Rereading three decades of writing led me to wonder about creative thinking in all kinds of human endeavor. This curiosity propelled me through the work of trying to bring overall order to the articles and chapters, seeking a balance between objective and subjective approaches.

Placing these pieces all together in a single volume makes them available to readers interested in fairy tales and the telling of them, whether they be general readers, students, or scholars. It is a delight to be able to present something that might be of use to others engaged in their own studies, and to make available some of my lesser known work.

Acknowledgments

It is a joy to publicly recognize many who have been part of the creation of this book. Since all of the storytellers' names already appear in both text and index, I will not repeat them here, but I express my sincere appreciation for their artistic skills. I do acknowledge the five tellers whose story texts and commentaries are included here: Stewart Cameron, Susan Gordon, Marvyne Jenoff, Joe Neil MacNeil, and Marylyn Peringer.

For the friends who agreed to copy edit chapters, I apologize for giving them so much work to do. Very little slipped by the eagle eyes of Jane Cahill, Morgana Graham, Katherine Himelblau, Maureen and Ron McIntosh, and Iris and Brian Rountree. There were many gems that slipped right through spellcheck. My three favorites were: "Snot White" instead of "Snow White," "the none-year-old girl" instead of "the nine-year-old girl," and "Cloning Ceremony" instead of "Croning Ceremony." Thank you all for catching these.

Since my earlier pre-computer chapters had to be retyped, I am indebted to Janet Regehr, who not only did the typing, but also questioned and commented as she read. Her curiosity spurred me on when I was ready to give it all up.

I am grateful to Donald Haase, who first encouraged me to put all this writing together; to Annie Martin, Kathryn Wildfong, and Carrie Downes Teefey of Wayne State University Press, who kept me going; to the anonymous readers, whose suggestions offered me good guidance; and to copyeditor Sue Breckenridge, who found things that everyone else missed.

And, as always, I am thankful to Rachel Stone, in Winnipeg, and Nathaniel Stone, in Toronto, for their continuing interest in my writing. Daniel Stone read, commented, indexed, and made me laugh. A lot.

Introduction

SOME DAY YOUR WITCH WILL COME

I wrote much of the commentary on these articles while sitting at the kitchen table with a strange companion, a whimsical witch of natural cypress wood that my mother gave me to celebrate the completion of my dissertation. What a fine eye she had. I had always seen the piece as an ancient robed Chinese woman with a complex hair arrangement. I looked again, thirty years later, and saw what my mother had seen—the witch herself. I suppose one needs to be closer to cronehood in one's own life to know her more fully. The bent old figure seems to be pondering something as she hunches there in her pale brown wooden robe. I even saw the suggestions of a face for the first time, musing rather than menacing, and the high hair arrangement became the hat of a witch. She stayed on my table to remind me of my original purpose, which was to try to make sense of three decades of work that began with a dissertation in the folklore program at Indiana University.

I never intended to write a doctoral dissertation of any sort, much less articles and books focusing on fairy tales. I was going to be a graphic artist but was sidetracked by anthropology and geography, and finally folklore. How, then, did I come to write a dissertation on women in folktales in 1975 and a book on dreaming as an art three decades later, with much essay writing in between? It was a long journey, and I present the evidence in this collection.

1

I am now, as I was not in the beginning, a teller of tales—not a liar, as this term is often intended to mean, but not a rhetorician, either. I left that behind when I retired from the academic world in 1998. So I put my comments in a narrative rather than a rhetorical form that will, I hope, bring all of these separate pieces into perspective as creative expressions. Each article speaks for itself, unedited except for necessary corrections, even when editing would have been an improvement. The joy of any kind of retrospective is to catch the flow of thought and creativity, like watching a river develop from its first tiny mountain rivulets into the greater watercourses on their way to the sea. And that is what remains with me from all those years of studying geography: water runs downhill. The folktale equivalent, I believe, is that when you call the witch, she *will* come. And I have done so.

I should have known that the title I chose for the book, *Some Day Your Witch Will Come,* would unleash a lot of negative power, and a great deal of hard confrontations from all those critical voices inside that are so familiar from all of my previous writing. The Crone, after all, is not a fairy godmother but an aggressive and quite uncompromising challenger. She wants to get to the heart of things and, if necessary, to bring about transformations that might not be to your liking. And she will not go away once she has been called up.

For example, there is an unfinished manuscript, "And She Lived Happily Ever After," that I hid under piles of other writing in the bottom drawer of the file cabinet in my Winnipeg basement. It has been down there since the late 1970s, when I gave up trying to transform my dissertation into a readable book. Others had managed to write their own books on women in fairy tales, but I could not bring mine to fruition. I discovered all too belatedly that I am more of an essayist than a writer of books, and so the manuscript remained where it was, and in fact still is. Both of the books I did eventually complete are, in keeping with my essay-writing bent, filled with freestanding chapters that connect satisfactorily. They are filled with descriptions of what I learned from the people who shared stories and dreams with me, and short on theory, and some of these chapters have found their way into this present book.

As I reread my work it sometimes seemed that I had changed my path altogether. In the beginning I saw the majority of folktale heroines as downtrodden or downright hopeless, but gradually learned that this view was cramped, opinionated, and shallow. Traditional oral tales have spiraling levels of meaning that tend to be obscured by the flatness of the two-dimensional page and by subjective literary and psychological approaches of interpretation—including my own. I began to get a hint of their personal depths right from the beginning, when I interviewed children and adults for my dissertation, but I did not pay sufficient attention to dissenting responses at that time because they did not yet make sense to me. I had neither the frame of reference nor the experience I needed to understand that it was possible to regard even a heroine who lost everything—not only her home and family but also her hands—as heroic. It took a very long time to learn that, and a lot of listening to other people who had a more flexible view of "heroic" than I did.

I also learned from the stories themselves. One in particular, the Grimm tale "Frau Trude," taught me a great deal. When I was a scholar of fairy tales, this cautionary tale about a girl who is destroyed in Frau Trude's fire for being too curious seemed utterly without promise. Becoming a teller of tales allowed me to see other possibilities in the story, one of them being a re-view of Frau Trude as challenger rather than destroyer. She will be one of my guides as I proceed here, and she is certainly ready at any moment to toss me into her fireplace if I do not treat her properly, if I fail to recognize her in her true form.

The living world of fairy tales burst upon me dramatically at age five, and set me on a path I would not understand until decades later. In 1944 I sat with my sister Janet and my Aunt Val watching the Disney version of *Snow White and the Seven Dwarfs*. The experience was so immediate that I can still hear Snow White's clear, small voice singing, "Some day my prince will come," but it is the stepmother/queen whose image has stayed with me for all these decades. In retrospect, I see how strongly affected I was by the opposed images of these two women, the "good" girl and her "bad" stepmother, and also the stark contrast between the beautiful queen and the ugly hag she turns herself into. Obviously I was not conscious of the deeper implications as I sat there in the theater, but something was brewing.

I was certainly aware, in the way children are, that Janet was the "good" and the pretty girl in our family and that I was something else—perhaps not bad nor ugly, though I thought so for years, but certainly not obedient. After all, I was an older sister, which colored my responses to reading fairy tales in which the older sister was anything but obedient. It was not Snow White who held my attention but the stepmother/queen/hag, so much so that I still retain a relatively clear vision of her Janus-like face as handsome woman and ugly hag. This film and my own self-image set me up for a rejection of fairy tales as "happily ever after" stories from early on. But I still devoured them, perhaps looking for one that was different. It took me a few decades to succeed in that quest.

3

More by accident than design, I found myself beginning research for a doctoral dissertation on fairy tale women, with only my childhood biases to guide me.

Since the Grimm tales still held a strong place in my imagination and, I assumed, in the imagination of many others, I decided to begin with them. I had not even looked at a fairy tale for decades, and was surprised to find the stories fresh and surprising, not quite what I had expected. There were indeed some crones, like Frau Holle, who were not destructive, and even a few princesses who were not pretty and passive, but they were definitely in the minority. I expanded my reading to other popular collections, notably the stories of Charles Perrault and Andrew Lang, and even Hans Christian Andersen, since his early written stories were based loosely on folktales.

Eventually I began to ask my friends and then my family casual questions about what they remembered. Their responses were so interesting and varied that I began to do formal interviews with people of various ages and backgrounds. I heard how many of them, some who could barely remember specific stories, had been deeply moved negatively or positively in their early years. Almost all claimed to have left the tales behind, yet some could recall their favorites with both clarity and emotion. Their comments reinforced my observations that in the popular collections the "good" girls were most often victims, and the "bad" older women were most often aggressive villains. Fathers were largely absent, which somehow absolved them of guilt. This was my limited understanding when I began my research in 1973. I had much to learn.

I reread Betty Friedan's *The Feminine Mystique* and Simone de Beauvoir's *Second Sex* to see what they had to say about fairy tale women, but their remarks were much too general. They did not cite specific stories, but referred only to popular heroines like Cinderella and Sleeping Beauty as negative stereotypes without exploring the actual stories. It was exciting to read Marcia Lieberman's challenging article on heroines in Lang's fairy books, "Some Day My Prince Will Come." She did indeed look at specific stories, and she gave some idea of how passive heroines dominated Lang's books, though they did not seem to be in control over their own lives in the stories. I incorporated this new information into my interview questions. But I still did not have the whole story.

Of the very few people writing about fairy tales at the time I was doing my research in the early 1970s, none had any idea that there were other collections of traditional stories. Though some of these books were popular enough to appear on library shelves (not always in the children's rooms), such books seemed to be largely disregarded by or even unknown to people writing about fairy tales and folktales. These included the now widely read "Jack Tale" books of Richard Chase (*Jack Tales, Grandfather Tales*), rewritten from his gathering of southern mountain folktales, and the more scholarly collections of tales by Katharine Briggs in England; by Marie Campbell, Vance Randolph, Leonard Roberts, and Emelyn Gardner in the United States; and Arthur Huff Fauset in Canada. Since I was only beginning to discover these collections myself, I was hardly surprised that neither scholars nor those I was interviewing had knowledge of them.

In the interviews, I wanted to find out what fairy tales or characters were remembered, whether there were any favorites, and whether anyone could recall women who did not fit the popular stereotype of the passive princess. Oh yes, many responded—the witches and stepmothers. I heard this often when I began to interview small groups of girls (three to five in a group) from ages nine to fifteen. I tried to include boys but found none that would admit to having read fairy tales, though children's librarians assured me that they did. I also continued to question individual adults, and here I did succeed in finding three men who could recall at least something about fairy tales. Once again I found myself on an unexpected path, because these interviews revealed things about fairy tales and people's responses to them that would echo throughout my published work. In fact, almost everything I published from the 1970s on has included the voices of others, not just my own ideas and opinions. I just kept asking questions, about heroines, about witches and crones, about heroes, anything that would open the flow of memories for those I queried. Sometime in the late 1980s I began to change my own mind, allowing another stream to develop that carried me away from my own stereotypes about passive women in opposition to aggressive crones.

My change of heart and mind and my interest in further explorations of fairy tales led me gradually to look at them as *told* stories and not just as book stories. I was just beginning to tell stories outside of my university lectures, and I was surprised to learn that a "storytelling revival" had been developing since the late 1970s. Other people were also telling stories—in schools and libraries, but increasingly on concert stages as well. I explored two major national festivals, one in the small town of Jonesborough, Tennessee, and one in the major Canadian city of Toronto. I began to talk to tellers who favored fairy tales, many of whom had been trained in the "library tradition" described in historical detail by Richard Alvey (*Historical Development*). Gradually I moved toward formal interviews with performers in order to discover how and why they learned stories, why they thought these were still relevant, and what, in their opinion, *was* "the storytelling revival." In this initial work the folkloristic "purist" bias was strong. I did not really consider performing artists as true oral narrators, since most of them learned their stories from books and often performed them verbatim. Was this "legitimate" storytelling? I was intrigued enough to continue questioning, first the few narrators who grew up in a living oral tradition, like Ray Hicks from Beech Mountain, North Carolina (his family provided Richard Chase with many tales), Donald Davis from Waynesville, North Carolina, Joe Neil MacNeil from Cape Breton Island, Nova Scotia, and Cree narrator Nathaniel Queskekapow from the Norway House Reserve in Manitoba.

But what about all the others who made up the majority of the festival performers, those nontraditional tellers who learned their stories from books? Many of them felt very strongly that they were keeping storytelling alive by their actions, and some even called themselves "traditional oral tellers" without understanding what this meant in folkloric terms. As far as I knew, there were only two others at the time, Joseph Sobol and Charlotte Ross, who were looking at this new "revival" with academically trained eyes, but they had not yet written much, and their focus was on the American South. I decided to investigate the smaller and slower growing Canadian scene, concentrating on the Toronto area because it was the most developed in the 1980s. I was aware of the disdain folklorists in general held for the very people Sobol, Ross, and I were investigating. Just how strong this bias was became painfully clear to me when I attended a prestigious academic conference that attempted to bring together folklorists and performing storytellers. I was optimistic, and so were the organizers. I had one foot in each camp, and looked forward to seeing if bridge-building was possible. I discovered to my dismay that few on either side wanted to cross the bridge, and very little communication took place. To use another image, I had put my toe in to test the water and found it cold. This discouraged me from revealing my new interest in academic contexts, and for a few years I published only in the non-academic storytelling publications: *Appleseed Quarterly* from the Storytellers School of Toronto and *The Storytelling Journal* from the National Association for the Preservation and Perpetuation of Storytelling (NAPPS at that time, later changed to NSA, National

Storytelling Association) in Jonesborough. The flexibility of this kind of writing allowed me to explore more freely, and to find the directions I might take in investigating the performers who were part of the "revival" and the process of their development as storytellers.

In 1986 I was asked to write an article on contemporary storytelling for an innovative book on fairy tales by scholar Ruth Bottigheimer. My contribution, "Oral Narration," was a stumbling early effort to make academic sense of what I was trying to do, and I almost did not include it here because it seemed antediluvian compared to my later flood of work. But, since this is a retrospective, this early effort is included here in all its awkwardness.

My second attempt to look at contemporary storytelling from a broader perspective, "Social Identity in Organized Storytelling," was written eleven years later. What was I doing in the decade between these two articles? I was struggling to write an academic book on storytelling as a legitimate topic of research for folklorists. This became *Burning Brightly: New Light on Old Tales Told Today.* At the same time, Joseph Sobol was reworking his doctoral dissertation, a detailed account of the development of American storytelling centered on the "national" activities in Jonesborough, Tennessee ("Jonesborough Days"). We exchanged complaints and information as we continued. By the time we both finished our books in 1998, his barely two months after mine, the academic world had relaxed enough that there were now a number of masters' theses and even a few doctoral dissertations being done on contemporary storytelling.

I took early retirement in 1998, the year that my book was published, and regarded this as my final work of academic writing. I had already begun a project just for the fun of it, an exploration of dreams as they related to folktales. I even put together a modest hundred-page manuscript for an experimental honors course at the University of Winnipeg, little knowing that this would eventually become a full book on dreaming as an art. Since I had no reason to hurry, I spent the next several years doing more interviewing and discovering that it is pure joy to ask people about their dreams. The result was *The Golden Woman: Dreaming as Art,* from which the final chapters of this present book arise.

My work has led me into adventurous paths all along. The earliest writing challenged stereotypes held by readers and academics alike. For example, the master of folktale scholarship, Stith Thompson, paid little attention to heroines beyond pointing out their stereotypical passivity. Similarly, master narrative scholar Linda Dégh preferred hero tales in her Hungarian collection because "those of the abused heroine follow the well-known pattern of the European versions" (*Folktales of Hungary* xxx). In other words, hero tales were proudly national, but heroine tales were too similar to be anything more than general. Looking at these observations in a more positive way, we might regard heroine tales as universal, and hero tales as merely national—though I do not think that is what Thompson and Dégh had in mind. My early work on women and fairy tales disputed such views and provided both specific tale analyses and valuable interview responses. This in itself was not controversial, since narrative scholarship was already well respected in the field of folklore. Though I was often passing through dark forests, the path was clear and became even more so when more scholars like Karen Rowe, Maria Tatar, Jack Zipes, and Ruth Bottigheimer, among others, focused attention on fairy tales and women.

In contrast, my work on nontraditional storytelling took me into even darker forests where the path was not at all clear, and sometimes not even visible. This path attracted antagonists who denigrated nontraditional telling as unworthy of scholarly attention. I had some sympathy for the princess who was put into that hundred-year sleep and was surrounded by a fierce and thorny hedge. But I stayed awake, and eventually the hedge came down and everything came back to life when I finally completed *Burning Brightly*. In contrast, *The Golden Woman* was never intended to be an academic book. In fact, I even challenged myself to see if I could write an entire book without a single explanatory note, and I succeeded. Yet all of my work, even the casual articles on storytelling written for popular journals, arose from my careful training as an academic folklorist specializing in traditional narratives.

All of the separate pieces gathered here reveal the slow progress from the more traditional academic writing of my early work to less formal writing in later publications. Because they were written separately, there are many overlaps in ideas and examples. Also, I draw on some of the same interview material more than once, since the memorable voices of many of those I spoke with in the early 1970s have followed me into the present. It is not entirely accurate, then, to divide these writings into three periods, since there are also some chronological overlaps: I had begun to write about the new storytelling movement while I was still very much immersed in fairy tale women, and by the time

Burning Brightly was completed, I was already writing articles on dreams and folktales. Nevertheless, the three sections do give an overall picture of how the spiraling path of my work developed over three decades.

Looking back, it seems to me that my long journey echoes those of fairy-tale princesses and crones themselves. It is in this spirit that I offer *Some Day Your Witch Will Come.*

I

Fairy Tales and Women

1

Things Walt Disney Never Told Us

(1975)

My first published article grew from my initial participation in one of the early feminist panels at the 1974 annual meeting of the American Folklore Society and was published in the first collection of feminist folklore, *Women and Folklore* (1975), edited by Claire Farrer. It was a joy to write, since it had a sharper tone in discussing the mistreatment of women in folktales, not only in the stories themselves but in the reworking of these tales by the Grimms and Disney. Also, I enjoyed playing with Freudian symbolism in the tales, and much to my surprise ended up seeing the power of some of this imagery, especially in the tales centering on girls who were punished for looking up into chimneys and boys who saved themselves by cutting down their own beanstalks. Whatever the article lacked in experience and maturity was balanced by the enthusiasm and energy that fuelled my early writing. It encapsulated the basic ideas of the dissertation in a more digestible form, being freer in style and content.

The article made clear my sharp contrast between passive and assertive heroines, though I did not describe all four categories established in the dissertation (Persecuted, Moderate, Tamed, Heroic). There was also very strong emphasis on others' failures to consider heroines available in the more interesting collections from British and North American sources. Both readers and critics tended to look only at the popular works of the Grimms, Perrault,

Lang, and Andersen. This was important enough to compel me to return to it in many future writings.

My stand against passive heroines in these popular collections was so strong that I commented on the few women I interviewed who disagreed with me as having "performed a fascinating feat of selective memory" by transforming passive heroines into active ones in their memories of fairy tales. I would eventually perform my own "fascinating feat" by seeing their point in later writings.

The following item appeared recently in the *Winnipeg Free Press* on April 14, 1972:

> In Pittsburgh, Pennsylvania, a burglar lost his shoe as he fled from the home of Mrs. M., age 43. Patrolmen arrested R. T., age 20, who was sitting shoeless in a nearby bar. Authorities said a shoe matching the one found in the M. home was discovered behind the bar.

The headline read, "Police Use Cinderella Approach." This brief example is only one of many that illustrate the popularity of fairy tale heroines in North America. They have become household words as well as "household tales," due to the unintentional efforts of the Grimms and the very intentional efforts of Walt Disney.

Despite the wide appeal of such heroines, they have received little scholarly discussion. Stith Thompson's definition of the term *Märchen* begins by stating that the genre is "characterized by such tales as 'Cinderella,' 'Snow White,' or 'Hansel and Gretel'" (*The Folktale* 8), but then he goes on to consider only the exploits of *Märchen* heroes. Lord Raglan does not include a single heroine in his international survey of twenty-one heroic characters (*The Hero*). Linda Dégh explains that she has excluded most heroines from her Hungarian collection because they are much the same throughout Europe, and it is only the heroes who take on national coloring (*Folktales of Hungary* xxx). In North America, where oral forms of the *Märchen* are not abundant and where the Grimm tales are read mainly by or to children, heroines have been virtually ignored by scholars, though non-academic writers have been more responsive.[1]

In attempting to correct this imbalance in attention I have surveyed both popular and scholarly collections in English and have asked dozens of women to recall their childhood memories. Almost all of those interviewed were completely unfamiliar with Anglo-American heroines, most of whom appear in scholarly collections not often found in children's sections of libraries. All, however, could easily recall tales popularized through the numerous Grimm translations and the Disney films. These tales are so thoroughly accepted that one woman I interviewed during my dissertation research even referred to the Grimm stories as "English fairy tales," because her German-born mother told her "real" German tales.

What have the Grimm translations offered to North American children? Of the total of 210 stories in the complete edition, there are 40 heroines, not all of them passive and pretty. Many translations offer no more than twenty-five tales, and only a few heroines are usually included. Most of them run the gamut from mildly abused to severely persecuted. In fact, a dozen docile heroines are the overwhelming favorites, reappearing in book after book from the mid-nineteenth century to the present. These are, in order of their popularity: "Sleeping Beauty," "Snow White," "Cinderella," "Rapunzel," "The Frog Prince," "Hansel and Gretel," "Rumpelstiltskin," "King Thrushbeard," "The Little Goose Girl," "Red Riding Hood," "Frau Holle," and "The Six Swans." Heroines in "Cinderella" and "Frau Holle" succeed because of their excessive kindness and patience; the women in "Sleeping Beauty" and "Snow White" are so passive that they have to be reawakened to life by a man; and the innocent heroines of "The Little Goose Girl" and "The Six Swans" are the victims of scheming and ambitious women.

The villains are not always women, however. A girl is forced by her father to accept a grotesque suitor in "The Frog Prince" and another is married off to a greedy king by her father in "Rumpelstiltskin." Still another father is encouraged to mutilate his daughter in order to save himself in "The Girl without Hands." Though this tale is not as popular as the others, it is sufficiently well known to have inspired author Joyce Carol Oates's novel, *Do with Me What You Will*. The title is taken from the girl's words to her careless father.

Some Grimm heroines do show a bit of spirit, but they are not usually rewarded for it. In "The Clever Peasant Lass" the girl is threatened with abandonment by her boorish husband, and the proud daughter in "King Thrushbeard" is humbled by both her father and her unwanted husband. Only Gretel in "Hansel and Gretel" is allowed a brief moment of violence in order to save herself and her brother. No other popular Grimm heroines destroy the villain.

The passivity of these heroines is magnified by the fact that their stories jump from 20 percent in the original Grimm collections to as much as 75 percent in many children's books. In this sense the fairy tale, a male-oriented genre in Europe (both by tale and by teller), becomes a female-oriented genre in North American children's literature.

But if the Grimm heroines are, for the most part, uninspiring, those of Walt Disney seem barely alive. In fact, two of them hardly manage to stay awake. Disney produced three films based on *Märchen* ("Sleeping Beauty," "Snow White," and "Cinderella"). All three had passive, pretty heroines, and all three had female villains, thus strongly reinforcing the already popular stereotype of the innocent beauty victimized by the wicked villainess. In fact, only half of the Grimm heroine tales have female villains, and among the Anglo-American tales, only one-third. Yet even Stith Thompson believes otherwise; he states that: "for some reason, to the composer of folktales, it is the woman of the family who is nearly always chosen for the part of the villain" (*The Folktale* 113).

But Walt Disney is responsible not only for amplifying the stereotype of good versus bad women suggested by the children's books based on the Grimms, he must also be criticized for his portrayal of a cloying fantasy world filled with cute little beings existing among pretty flowers and singing animals. Though *Newsweek* calls him a "Master of Fantasy" in fact Disney removed most of the powerful fantasy of the *Märchen* and replaced it with false magic.

In brief, then, the popularized heroines of the Grimms and Disney are not only passive and pretty, but also unusually patient, obedient, industrious, and quiet. A woman who failed to be any of these could not become a heroine. Even Cinderella has to do no more than put on dirty rags to conceal herself completely. She is a heroine only when properly cleaned and dressed.

In contrast, *Märchen* heroes can be slovenly, unattractive, and lazy, yet their success will not be affected. The Grimms' "Hans-my-Hedgehog" has a hero who actively exploits his grotesque shape in order to gain power, wealth, and—of course—a beautiful wife. The hero of "The Little Red Ox," unlike the passive sister in "One-Eye, Two-Eyes, Three-Eyes," does not docilely accept his fate; he kills his stepmother instead of the helpful ox and rides boldly away. The many youngest-son tales known as "male Cinderellas" almost always have heroes who, unlike the female Cinderella, do not seem to be the least bothered by their unfavored position. One of these, in the Grimms' "The Youth Who Wanted to Learn What Fear Is," is clearly described as dull and stupid, in contrast to his clever and industrious brother. He is seen as a burden to the family because he does everything wrong. Not exactly the typical Cinderella. The only resemblance between this hero and Cinderella is that he wins in the end because he proves to be more courageous than his brother, not because he sits at home awaiting the arrival of a princess.

Heroes succeed because they act, not because they are. They are judged not by their appearance or inherent sweet nature but by their ability to overcome obstacles, even if these obstacles are defects in their own characters. Heroines are not allowed any defects, nor are they required to develop, since they are already perfect. The only tests of most heroines require nothing beyond what they were born with: a beautiful face, tiny feet, or a pleasing temperament. At least that is what we learn from the translations of the Grimm tales, and especially from the films of Walt Disney.

In contrast, a number of significant Anglo–North American collections give voice to oral narrators who do not confine themselves to passive princesses, judging from the 186 heroines found in the collections of Katharine Briggs, Marie Campbell, Fauset, and the multiple listings for Randolph and Leonard Roberts. There are even women who express a national coloring apparently lacking in European heroines. Katharine Briggs's *A Dictionary of British Folktales* has a female version of "Jack and the Beanstalk," for example, and the American collections feature several heroines well suited to tough pioneering life. They do not always rely on sympathetic fairy godmothers or overprotective dwarfs, nor do they always await the last-minute arrival of the hero. And, as already mentioned, they are more often aggravated by male villains than by the familiar wicked stepmother. Of the 186 heroine tales, only 62—exactly one-third—have exclusively female villains. Of the male villains, many are angry or abusive fathers, murderous lovers, and jealous husbands.

Among the four books of Ozark tales collected by Vance Randolph, we find women who destroy the threatening male villains, and also a girl who does not need her father to convince her that frogs make interesting bedfellows.[2] Leonard Roberts introduces a number of similarly assertive Kentucky heroines who do not fit European stereotypes. The heroine of "Bully Bornes," Roberts's version of "Cupid and Psyche," marries a prizefighter instead of a more obvious beast, and she is not intimidated by his brutal treatment (*South*

60–63). In the same book, "The Little Girl and the Giant" features a mother and daughter who cooperate in escaping from a giant and destroying him (45–46). The Randolph and Roberts collections, and others also, offer a number of versions of "Cinderella" that would have made Disney's hair curl.

Four British heroines from the Briggs collection are outstanding. The heroine of "Kate Crackernuts" (*Dictionary* 344), a story similar to "The Twelve Dancing Princesses," not only rescues a prince from nocturnal fairies but also cures the beautiful stepsister deformed by the heroine's own jealous mother. The heroine in "Mossycoat" leaves home voluntarily to escape an unwanted suitor—with the encouragement of a loving mother, not because of the threats of an incestuous father (416). Unlike many of her counterparts, she is not only unintimidated by her jealous fellow-workers, but actually bewitches them into silence. Still another heroine in the Briggs collection, in "Tib and the Old Witch," leaves home in protest over her father's rejection of her lover (522). She is not locked into a tower as in the Grimms' "Lady Madelaine," nor is she forced to choose against her will as in the Grimms' "King Thrushbeard." Tib does not return home, but instead lives happily and adventurously ever after.

Even more aggressive is the heroine of "Mally Whuppie" (*Dictionary* 400). Like Tib, Mally leaves home, abandoned by parents with too many children, and takes two younger sisters with her. She protects them from a giant and wins husbands for them *before* she wins one for herself. She succeeds in answering a king's challenge to return and steal the giant's three treasures. Unlike Jack in "The Boy Steals the Giant's Treasures," she succeeds in doing so without killing the giant. She even prevents him from unknowingly destroying his own wife. A more violent Kentucky variant, "Polly, Nancy, and Muncimeg," is found in Roberts *Up Cutshin and Down Greasy* (119–23). Here the heroine is in competition with her sisters, who want to kill her, and more violent toward the giant's family; Muncimeg does not destroy him, but does allow his wife to drown when the woman insists on taking her place in the sack.

In none of these tales do we find the stereotyped conflict between the passive, beautiful woman and the aggressive, ugly one. Most of the active heroines are not even described in terms of their physical attributes; Mally Whuppie is even praised by the king as "a clever cutty" (402). Like heroes, these heroines are judged by their actions. Though most do marry, their weddings are no more central to the tale than is the concluding marriage of most heroes. Some husbands are even won as passive prizes in the same way that princesses are won by heroes in many tales. Most importantly, active heroines are not victims of hostile forces beyond their control but are, instead, challengers who confront the world rather than waiting for success to fall at their pretty feet. Unfortunately, heroines of this sort are not numerous in oral tales and do not exist at all in any of the Grimm tales or the Disney films.

Female aggressiveness in not the only aspect of heroine tales that is unfamiliar to most of us. Sexuality in fairy tales seems to be limited to Jack's beanstalk.[3] Overt sexual references, if they even find their way into original collections, rarely appear in children's books. Translations of the Grimms, for example, usually omit the fact that Rapunzel's initial encounter with the prince resulted in twins. The Grimms' "other" Cinderella, "All Kinds of Fur," is usually left out altogether, since the heroine is forced to leave home to avoid her father's threats of an incestuous marriage. A "Disney version" of this tale is difficult to imagine, for Disney found even the more passive Grimm version of "Cinderella" unsuitable for children, and used the more innocuous Perrault version instead.

Other sexual references are more subtle. We must look closely to discover that it is at puberty that Rapunzel is locked in a tower, Snow White is sent out to be murdered, and Sleeping Beauty is put to sleep. Such heroines have their freedom severely restricted at a time in life when heroes are discovering full independence and increased power. Restrictions on girls at puberty, in contrast to the increased freedom their brothers enjoy, possibly explain the intensely sympathetic reaction many women have to such passive heroines in fairy tales. This was emphasized by a school guidance counselor whom I interviewed in Winnipeg in 1973. In the specific tales mentioned, this restriction reflects anxiety about competition with other women that increased sexuality offers. It might also be seen as a protection for the heroine herself, who must remain pure for the one man who will eventually claim her. The restriction of women at puberty can also be interpreted as a reaction of men to the threat of female sexuality.[4]

Though female symbols in general have certainly been considered by Freud, Jung, and a handful of other scholars, they still lack a familiar name, and, compared with phallic symbols, have received practically no attention from folktale scholars.[5] As Freud notes, female symbols are those that suggest the possibility of either entry or entrapment. These would include rooms and houses, ovens, jugs and bowls, and forests and flowers. Such symbols do not appear randomly and without meaning. They take their significance from the context in which they are used; thus it is not necessary to interpret every house, for example, as a female symbol. Occasionally the symbolism is obvious, such as the hero's plucking of the enchanted flower in "The Girl as Flower." Other references are more obscure, like the fitting of Cinderella's slipper or, in some variants, her ring.[6]

Both male and female symbols can be portrayed positively or negatively, reflecting either desire or anxiety. In this sense Jack's powerful beanstalk leading to a treasure contrasts sharply with the imposing tower in "Rapunzel" or with the dagger used to murder Bluebeard's wives in some versions of the story. Similarly, the lovely enchanted flower presents quite a different image than does the threatening witch's hut or the magic forest, both of which trap unwary male travelers. It is Hansel, one remembers, who is trapped first in the witch's hut and then in her cage.

Sexuality is also portrayed as harmful to the heroine herself. There are many symbolic hints that women should not become too familiar with their own bodies. Bluebeard's wives are murdered for looking into forbidden rooms, and Sleeping Beauty is punished with near death from a sharp object for doing so. Other heroines are threatened with death for breaking a taboo against looking into a fireplace in variants of "The Kind and the Unkind Girls," and little girls are murdered by their stepmothers for breaking jugs in several variants of "The Juniper Tree."

Sexual imagery of this sort would not be obvious to most children (or to most adults, for that matter), but some writers feel that fairy tales do satisfy a more general psychological need, at least for North American children. They suggest that children might view themselves as the helpless underdogs who eventually triumph over the powerful witches and ogres representing their parents.[7] Bettelheim and Heuscher focus on the psychoanalytic power of folktales and touch on erotic elements. Berne devotes much of his book, *What Do You Say after You Say Hello,* to "story scripts" that might mark the direction our lives take. Similarly, Hornyansky emphasizes that North American children are still avid readers of fairy tales, possibly because of such identification: "The stories they want to hear last thing at night are 'Sleeping Beauty,' 'Red Riding Hood,' 'Cinderella,' 'Snow White,' 'Jack and the Beanstalk,' and that crowd: stories full of princes, princesses, giants, wicked witches, wolves, dwarfs, and other persons not normally encountered" ("The Truth of Fables" 121).

Hornyansky mentions only one hero tale, thus underlining the observation made earlier in this paper that the large number of heroine tales in fairy tale books indicates that these are most likely intended for girls. It does not seem an exaggeration to say, as feminist writer Marcia Lieberman does in "Some Day My Prince Will Come," that fairy tales may serve as "training manuals" in passive behavior, and adds that "Millions of women must surely have formed their ideas of what they could or could not accomplish, what sort of behaviour would be rewarded, and of the nature of reward itself, in part from their favorite fairy stories. These stories have been made the repositories of the dreams, hopes, and fantasies of generations of girls" (385).

Psychologist Eric Berne, mentioned above, felt that fairy tales offered not only dreams and hopes but actual programs for behavior. Your favorite fairy tale may parallel and inform your attitudes and acts. Berne is particularly eloquent on this topic in chapters 3, 12, and 13 of *What Do You Say after You Say Hello*.

Rather than accepting these views uncritically, I interviewed women of varying ages and backgrounds.[8] All had read fairy tales, almost all could name several favorite heroines but rarely any heroes, and most of these tales were from Disney or the Grimms. Many admitted that they were certainly influenced by their reading of fairy tales. Some had openly admired the lovely princesses and hoped to imitate them, especially their ability to obtain a man and a suburban castle without much effort. An eleven-year-old told me, "I thought I'd just sit around and get all this money. I used to think 'Cinderella' should be *my* story." Another admirer of Cinderella, a nine-year-old, said, "I wouldn't want to marry a prince, but maybe somebody *like* a prince."

Others reluctantly admired the passive princess because there were few alternative images, but they did not expect to imitate either her attributes or her material successes. Said a twenty-nine-year-old: "I remember the feeling of being left out in fairy stories. Whatever the story was about, it wasn't about *me*. But this feeling didn't make me not interested in them—I knew there was something I was supposed to do to fit in but I didn't. So I thought there was something wrong with *me*, not with the fairy stories." Similarly, a twenty-four-year-old told me that she had really expected to bloom one day as Cinderella had done, but she was still waiting.

Many of those who admired the passive princess, either openly or reluctantly, recognized her image in various forms of popular entertainment, notably in romantic tales on television and in comic books, magazines, and novels read almost exclusively by women. Even women who had shaken the persistent princess in their daily lives returned to her in fantasy through such popular materials. The woman who mentioned feeling left out in fairy stories said she had to force herself to stop buying romantic magazines: "They depressed me and made me feel confused. There was something about them— something like the victimized fairy tale women—that I didn't want to see in myself."

Many informants under the age of fifteen (the post-Disney generation) were not so impressed with the passive heroines of Disney and the Grimms. Some of them found them boring and stopped reading fairy tales altogether, such as the young woman who said that she "never liked those lily-white princesses," and added, "the poor thing, so beautiful and helpless. She's got a long wait for that prince." Others who liked the fantasy world of the *Märchen* claimed they compensated for the lack of interesting heroines by reading about heroes, but they could rarely name even one.

Still others performed a fascinating feat of selective memory by transforming relatively passive heroines into active ones. Several were mentioned (including the persecuted sister of "The Maiden Who Seeks Her Brothers," found in the Aarne-Thompson index, *The Types of the Folktale* [hereafter AT] 451), but the best remembered was Gretel, who pushed the witch into the oven. In fact, this is her *only* aggressive act, and it seems almost accidental in comparison with the ever-confident Hansel. He does not even lose hope when he is caged but devises the fake finger to fool the witch into delaying his death. Yet not surprisingly it is the tearful Gretel who is remembered by girls in search of active heroines, for Gretel is indeed aggressive when compared to most of the Grimm heroines and all of the Disney heroines. However, when compared to the Anglo-American heroines mentioned earlier, she seems far less heroic. We see through her what we have lost by taking our own heroines from Grimm and Disney rather than from the tales of our own heritage.

Among the informants, whether they admired Cinderella or found her boring, whether they felt heroines like Gretel were active or were not, there was general agreement that considerably more diversity would have been welcome. Many reacted favorably to a radically reinterpreted version of the archetypical fairy tale of "The Dragon-Slayer." Instead of waiting to be rescued, an unintimidated princess destroys her own dragon and leaves the men to clean up the remains. While those who listened to the story did enjoy it, they did not feel that it was a fairy tale. They were correct. It was an authored story by Jay Williams, titled *The Practical Princess*. Still, those I interviewed, even the men, were interested to hear that there were traditional heroines, and Anglo-

American ones at that, who were equally as impressive as Williams's dragon-slaying princess—and that Cinderella herself did not always wait for a rescuing prince in some versions.

Walt Disney neglected to tell us that Cinderella's freedom does not always end at midnight.

2

Fairy Tales for Adults

WALT DISNEY'S AMERICANIZATION
OF THE *MÄRCHEN* (1980)

The title I chose for my previous article soon came to haunt me; I became popularly known as "The Disney Woman." Five years later I was invited to contribute a short biographical entry on Walt Disney for the German publication *Enzyklopädie des Märchens,* and I saw this as a way to move beyond my own biases. While I had little interest in Disney himself, I was curious to see if I could discover how decisions were made in the making of his three fairy tale films: *Snow White and the Seven Dwarfs* in 1937, *Cinderella* in 1950, and *Sleeping Beauty* in 1959. [*Beauty and the Beast* was released in 1991, well after this article was written.] I had also had five more years of experience in research and writing, and in university teaching; these all contributed to making this a stronger and more convincing article. Since it was based on actual research and not opinion, my prejudices are somewhat mitigated, but certainly not abandoned. The fact that the article was being prepared for a festshrift, *Folklore on Two Continents* (Burlakoff and Lindahl), honoring my mentor, Linda Dégh, provided additional energy.

My work at the archives of Walt Disney Productions in Burbank, California, drew on the production transcripts for the first two films, *Snow White and the Seven Dwarfs* and *Cinderella.* There were no comparable notes for *Sleeping Beauty,* a pity since it would have been interesting to compare this film with the other two. Disney had died by this time and there was no indi-

cation of who was guiding the artists. I was unable to discover how the characters and plot line developed for *Sleeping Beauty,* which departed widely
from the French source.

Though this article was certainly a more even-handed treatment of the
Disney films than "Things Walt Disney Never Told Us," I still faulted Disney
for moralizing the stories by exaggerating the differences between good and
evil women, trivializing them with charming secondary characters of all sorts
(dwarfs are anything but charming in many fairy tales), and most of all by emphasizing the romantic aspects of the fairy tales over everything else. I still saw
Walt Disney Productions as presenting fairy tales primarily as "the secular
myth of the modern age—the love story," and concluded with a statement of
my own position: that the "happily ever after" meaning of fairy tales was not
about finding one's prince or princess, but about finding oneself. This observation would weave in and out of much of my future writing. Still, my experience at the Disney archives allowed me to see more objectively how the
medium of any creativity is indeed its message, as we will see in a later chapter here.

A friend complained recently that she would soon have to give up Disney films
since her children were growing too old for her to accompany them. She was
surprised when I suggested she go alone, but later she realized that Disney's
"family" films are equally entertaining for adults and children. His fairy tale
films in particular have remained so successful that they are re-released periodically. Certainly these would not be shown today if they appealed only to
children. Their continuing success reveals something about adult reactions to
fantasy and about Disney's understanding of these reactions.

Walt Disney's interest in fairy tales was evident in his earliest cartoons,
done in Kansas City, Missouri, in the 1920s. He produced six films there,
among which are three stories he reworked later in his career: *Little Red Riding Hood* became *The Big Bad Wolf* in 1934; *Jack and the Beanstalk* became
Mickey in Giantland in 1933 and *Mickey and the Beanstalk* in 1947; *Cinderella,*
considered but not completed for a Silly Symphony in 1934, was released as a
full-length feature in 1950.

Comparing his first crude cartoons with the later ones, we can see Disney's
development as an interpreter of fairy tales. The earliest pieces parody the

stories through the use of broad humor and deliberately absurd modernizations. In his earliest *Cinderella*, for example, the heroine goes to the ball in a garbage can transformed into a "Tin Lizzie." The later films are somewhat more serious and considerably more sophisticated. The giants who confront Mickey Mouse in the two versions of "Jack and the Beanstalk" have a menacing quality barely disguised by their silly stupidity. In neither film are they destroyed, however, as they are in the traditional tale. Disney was not yet ready for a real villain. Disney came closer with "The Big Bad Wolf," who nevertheless remained a humorous character who—like Mickey's Giants—was not destroyed.

Mickey Mouse starred in two other folktale-inspired films, *The Brave Little Tailor* in 1938 and *The Sorcerer's Apprentice* in 1940.[1] Appropriately, Mickey portrayed a typical folktale hero who was humorous rather than heroic, succeeding by his wits rather than his strength. In more ways than one he symbolized Disney's own fairy tale–like ascent from a poor, unknown young artist to the king of the "Magic Kingdom."

The great success of his short folktale cartoons, and particularly of Mickey Mouse, encouraged Disney to attempt a full-length feature based on a popular fairy tale. Instead of continuing the pattern of the unpromising hero who has wits rather than courage, Disney decided on a long-suffering heroine. "Snow White" was already one of the most popular fairy tales, judging by its frequent appearance in fairy tale books, but Disney's project was still referred to by many as "Disney's Folly." Few believed that a cartoon based on a children's story, no matter how popular, would appeal to a general film audience. Not even Disney was fully prepared for the stunning success of the elaborate *Snow White and the Seven Dwarfs*, finally released in 1937 after four years of careful planning. In it he portrays his first uncompromisingly vicious villain, and allows her to be destroyed. After this success he was encouraged to begin production of a long and equally popular series of full-length cartoons, among them two more based on fairy tales, *Cinderella* in 1950 and *Sleeping Beauty* in 1959.

Disney's three full-length fairy tales bear little resemblance to his earlier crude works. He now had hundreds of artists who painstakingly created the thousands of handsome drawings necessary for an animated film. He also had a more mature view of the tales and admonished his artists to take the tales seriously. "As we do it, as we tell the story, we should believe it ourselves. It's a 'once upon a time' story, and I don't think we should be afraid of a thing like that."[2] Such a statement is unnecessary for children, many of whom already believe in the tales. It is adults who must be encouraged to believe in them.

Literate societies usually distinguish between sophisticated and popular forms of literature and often place folktales very firmly in the popular sphere. Popular writing, of course, is not always taken seriously except by sociologists and psychologists, so folktales are not highly regarded. Furthermore, fairy tales in particular are thought of as "children's reading," a further demotion by smug adult standards. What adults no longer value is considered suitable for children. J. R. R. Tolkien says eloquently in *Tree and Leaf* that old furniture, like fairy tales, ends up in the nursery "because the adults do not want it and do not mind if it is misused" (34). In this kind of thinking, who but a child could believe in witches and dragons, or most ridiculous of all, living happily ever after? And who but a child would always expect the small and weak to be treated fairly, not with the justice of a complex legal system or with the "eye-for-an-eye" justice of the Old Testament, but with a natural justice in which villains chose their own punishment or are punished by unknown forces?

Still, if Disney had been interested solely in appealing to children, his major fairy tale films would probably not be available today. Disney was thus adventurous in insisting that his artists and script writers believe in the "once upon a time" stories. He also intuitively understood that a successful storyteller had to adapt tales to an audience varied in age and interests.

Adults have always been an important part of the Disney audience. His earliest Mickey Mouse and Silly Symphony shorts were seen by adults who were waiting for the main feature. His longer cartoons, even though aimed more specifically at children, had an eager adult audience as well. Disney was able to develop a means of realizing his stories that satisfied the differing interests and expectations of both age groups. In the case of the fairy tales children could enjoy the amusing dwarfs, fairies, and various animals, the touches of magic, the clear representation of good and evil, and the ensuing punishments and rewards, just as they did in the traditional tales already familiar from books.

Disney's contribution was in reinterpreting the fairy tales in a way that would appeal to adults as well as to children, in this century, on this continent. Disney chose three already-popular fairy tales in which bad and good women clash. Having chosen them, he found the heroines rather dull and made them more interesting. It was a conscious decision on his part. "I'd make Cinderella a sparkling, alive girl, even going so far as to give her a few human weaknesses. In this way we can prove that Cinderella really did live and that she still lives in

the heart of every young girl who dreams" (Disney, "*Cinderella* Notes").
A month later he added, "There is one thing certain, we wish Cinderella to
have a certain strength of character quite unlike the fairy story version of the
heroine."

Disney certainly succeeds in transforming the passive, pretty princesses of
the original tales. Snow White is not a naive seven-year-old as in the Grimm
tale, but an appealing teenager ready for romance; a girl who is not frightened
by the dwarfs, but who instead takes over their untidy household in an efficient
American manner. Thus she becomes the mother rather than the child. Disney's heroine in *Cinderella* is alluring even in her rags, and shows consider-
able spirit and even occasional humor in dealing with her mean stepfamily.
Similarly, the heroine in *Sleeping Beauty* does not simply fall asleep as in the
Perrault version of the tale.[3] Instead, she cheerfully grows up in the cottage of
the three good fairies, and boldly wanders alone in the forest where she meets
her future prince democratically dressed as a woodsman. All three Disney
heroines sing romantic songs, carry on daily activities, and in general come to
life in a way that involves the audience in their fates.

The heroes in these three stories are also transformed from the originals:
they traditionally appear only in the closing lines, but Disney gives them a
fuller role in the story. He also plays down their royal background. The prince
in *Snow White,* for example, is described in an early planning session as "a
Doug Fairbanks type, about 18 years old," with a horse who is "like Tom Mix's
horse Tony, the prince's pal" (Disney, "*Snow White* Notes"). Cinderella's
suitor is "just a nice boy that was nice to her" (Disney, "*Cinderella* Notes").
The prince in *Sleeping Beauty* meets his love in ordinary clothes, and falls in
love with her even though she herself is in peasant dress. They are both prepared to oppose their parents' plan for a royal wedding, not realizing that they
are themselves the prince and princess for whom the wedding is planned. In
this film the prince takes a fully active role, even destroying the wicked fairy
who has cursed his beloved. Interestingly, Disney had originally planned such
a role for the prince in *Snow White,* but did not develop the idea.[4]

Disney balances his All-American girls and boys with melodramatically
menacing villains. They do not tie the heroines to railway tracks as in early
American films and later parodies, but they are equally cruel and vindictive.
These women are everything that the heroines are not—coldly calculating,
ambitious, sadistic, and not at all romantically inclined. And most important
in a Disney film, they are not popular with small, cuddly animals, dwarfs, or

good fairies. Disney is so committed to this narrow view of ambitious women that in *Sleeping Beauty* he creates a villain where there is none. The traditional fairy is not necessarily evil, just angry at being ignored; and she disappears from the story immediately after her curse is pronounced. In *Cinderella*, Disney lays the whole blame for Cinderella's suffering on the stepmother: "I feel that the stepsisters are under a domineering mother. They are spoiled brats, but it's the mother who is forcing them" ("*Cinderella* Notes"). In the original tale she has far less power.

The heroines, heroes, and villains carry the main action of the folktales, but in Disney's films there are also secondary characters who provide the humor and who at times steal the scene from the major actors. Disney uses the dwarfs and the non-predatory animals in *Snow White,* the mice and other animals in *Cinderella,* and the silly fairies in *Sleeping Beauty* to lighten the dark side of these tales. They are placed between the antagonists who in the original tales are meant to meet head on, with no humorous mediators to soften the collision. The dwarfs in *Snow White* and the mice in *Cinderella* interfere directly with the action of the story. The former are involved in the death of the wicked queen, and the latter steal the key which releases Cinderella from her attic prison. The fairies in *Sleeping Beauty* are less successful—though no less active—in their attempts to intervene. The prince himself must defeat the wicked fairy and rescue his beloved. But the good fairies have the last word: the closing scene shows the princess's dress changing from pink to blue and back again as the fairies argue over the appropriate color. In addition to comic relief, these secondary characters also extend the plot of the original tales. None of these stories could have sustained feature-length treatment without the development of such characters.

Disney is quite successful in his Americanization of the old European tales. He makes the heroines and heroes more interesting, adds humor, subtracts magic, and downplays royalty. The changes Disney makes are similar to those made by traditional American storytellers, who also had to adapt European tales to the new demands of this continent. American fairy tale heroines, for example, are often more aggressive than those we read about in Grimm's fairy tales. In one tale a girl and her mother confront and destroy a giant ("Polly, Nancy, and Muncimeg" in Roberts, *Up Cutshin* 119), and in another one a sister successfully completes an impossible task and rescues her less successful older sisters ("Three Girls with Journey Cakes," in Campbell, *Tales from Cloud Walking* 140). Many tales also display a rough native humor, particularly those featuring a lazy hero who brags his way to success and then must prove his exaggerated bravery.[5]

The king of the European tales is often demoted to a commoner by North American tellers. In one oral tale I heard in Winnipeg the "king" was a mayor, and in another he was a rich storekeeper. Often the magic of the original tale is downplayed in the North American variants. For example, the beast in "Beauty and the Beast" may be simply a man in a fur coat, or even a beastly prize fighter.[6] Despite these changes, however, the American fairy tales do not lose their basic force, for protagonists must still test their selflessness or cleverness against the materialism and cynicism of powerful antagonists, often without the help of amusing dwarfs, fairies, and friendly animals.

While in some ways Disney parallels traditional storytellers in North America by making some of his characters more resourceful, his particular use of cuteness, sentimentality, and humor dominates his films. He diminishes both magic and royalty by poking fun at them, and allows his amusing secondary characters to take over the stories at times. The dwarfs in *Snow White* are funny—almost pathetically so—rather than powerful and a bit frightening as they are in the traditional story. The fairy godmother in *Cinderella* and her relatives in *Sleeping Beauty* are absent-minded bunglers rather than convincing sorceresses. And in *Snow White* even the wicked queen jokes with her raven at the conclusion of her transformation of herself and the apple, this softening one of the most powerful scenes of the film. Disney had a fine touch for the sinister, but developed absurdly cute characters who overcome any sense of real evil.

With these subtle shifts in plot and character, Disney focuses attention on the romantic aspects of fairy tales. What he believes in, then, is the secular myth of the modern age, the love story.[7] The opening comment of a *Snow White* planning session states that, "of the various angles discussed about the meeting of Snow White and the Prince, the one chosen to be worked on is the 'romantic angle'" ("*Snow White* Notes"). By the simple ploy of introducing his princes and princesses to each other early in the stories, Disney effectively accomplishes his romantic ends. In the traditional stories the princes appear only at the end. In the folktale versions of "Snow White" and "Sleeping Beauty" the heroines have literally never seen the prince before, and in "Cinderella" she has only danced with him. Thus they cannot spend their time daydreaming and singing songs about their princes, as do their Disney counterparts.

Other sentimental touches not found in the folktales are the interplay between Snow White and the individual dwarfs, who in the original tale were not
named or provided with amusing personalities; between Cinderella and the
mice; and between Sleeping Beauty and the three fairies. Also, in *Snow White,*
by having the wicked queen die before the wedding and by having Snow
White awakened with a kiss, Disney emphasizes love rather than conflict. In
the original the queen is invited to the wedding and is forced to dance to her
death in red-hot shoes, thus diverting attention away from romance and focusing it on justice done. Traditionally the prince does not give Snow White
"love's first kiss," but carries her coffin off to his castle as a conversation piece.
When his servants slip and the apple-bite is bounced out of her throat, Snow
White awakens.

With *Cinderella,* Disney's romanticizing task was easier. He rejected the
more brutal Grimm version for the already sentimentalized French concoc-
tion of Charles Perrault.[8] All he had to do was add a few cute, helpful animals,
and he had a ready-made love story, complete with the familiar injunction of
modern parents to be home before midnight. In the Grimm tale there is no
fairy godmother, no pumpkin coach or transformed mice, no curfew or glass
slipper. And the stepsisters are as beautiful as the heroine, though "vile and
black of heart" (Manheim 84). Thus the conflict is not between mother and
daughter, or between beauty and ugliness, but between selflessness and
selfishness. As in "Snow White," the villains in the Grimm version also attend
the heroine's wedding, and are rewarded by having their eyes pecked out by
vengeful doves. One can certainly understand why Disney did not choose this
version, since its brutal passages are sometimes even edited out of fairy tale
books. It probably was not brutality that caused the folk version to be rejected,
but rather its lack of sentimentality. The heroine seems less interested in finding her prince than is the heroine in the Perrault tale.

Disney not only wanted his romantic stories to be taken seriously, but to be
taken literally. He has already told us that he wanted to "prove that Cinderella
did live and that she still lives in the heart of every young girl who dreams"
("*Snow White* Notes"). Similarly, the 1959 press book for *Sleeping Beauty*
claims that Disney studio researchers discovered "that the teenage Princess
Aurora [the heroine's name in the Disney version] was once a reigning flesh
and blood beauty of medieval courts." In other words, "girls who dream: can
really expect to meet their prince and live happily ever after in Disney's Magic
Kingdom; or as a nine-year-old told me, 'I wouldn't like to marry a prince.

Maybe somebody like a prince'" ("Romantic Heroines" 326).[9] Disney cannot be blamed for forcing a literal interpretation on his audience, for it was one already accepted by many of its members, male and female. For example, one girl in a group of nine-year-old girls I interviewed in 1974 said she had not seen the Disney film and knew the story from books; "I'm sort of like Cinderella," she said. "I vacuum a lot! But I don't clean the fireplace" (344). A twenty-five-year-old was less lighthearted: "I figured Cinderella was pretty lucky . . . I really figured life would be like that. You just sit around and wait, and something fantastic is going to happen. You go to the right dance and you've got it made. But it never happened" (273). An eleven-year-old was a bit more hopeful: "I used to like Cinderella, like it should be my story. She started off very poor and then she got rich and very successful, and I used to think of myself that way. I thought I'd just sit around and get all this money" (348).

These reactions concentrate on the happy endings, on the rewards the heroine gets for her virtuous behavior, and on her good luck. The Cinderella of these viewers is an unhappy teenager who is longing for a handsome, rich young man (with a fancy sports car as a coach) to rescue her from her restrictive family. She wants to live happily ever after in a suburban castle and go to dances whenever she likes without having to worry about midnight curfews. What she will do when her initial passion for the prince wears off is another question. One psychologist assures us that she will continue her passionate affairs with other princes (Berne, *What Do You Say* 95).

Disney accurately portrays the popular view of fairy tales as love stories in these three films. Because these films are so carefully and beautifully done and thus continue to survive through periodic re-releases, Disney's initial reflection of popular values becomes something more. In giving back to the audience what it already believes, Disney is magnifying rather than merely reflecting. True love must continue happily ever after, because Disney agrees, and portrays it so compellingly. Leslie A. Fiedler, in *Love and Death in the American Novel*, seems to agree when he observes that: "Certainly, there is no one in our world to whom the phrase 'they lived happily ever after' is meaningless or unclear; for us the 'happy ending' is defined once and for all: after many trials, the sacred marriage" (46).

Marriage vows, of course, promise "till death do us part." A romantic film, *Heaven Can Wait,* is a modern gothic romance in which love at first sight is combined with reincarnation, thus carrying love even beyond death.

Fairy tales, like dreams, are deceptively simple. The surface story covers layers of meaning available to astute tellers and listeners. This is what has kept the folktale alive from the dim past up to the present; its differing layers of meaning make it relevant to listeners of any age and any level of understanding. Both child and adult can interpret a story superficially or profoundly, and can react on the level of their own understanding and experiences. What modern, literate adults consider simple tales might be unconsciously symbolic, psychological representations of real, everyday conflicts. For a child, giants and witches are as frighteningly real and as unpredictable as their own parents, and the unpromising hero or heroine who somehow overcomes all obstacles might seem very much like themselves. These conflicts are symbolic rather than literal, as frequently noted by psychologists, psychiatrists, and even by astute readers.[10] A grandfather of nine, interviewed for my dissertation, reflected on his childhood reading and its meaning to him: "I liked all these stories I read when I was young because in that time of life you can't accomplish anything much by yourself. And if you're also the youngest and trampled on, you really need to have impossible dreams and to read impossible stories like fairy tales" (337).

Similarly, in an interview with a group of fifteen-year-old girls, one girl stressed the metaphorical power of fairy tales by suggesting that some experiences might happen, but "not in the same way as in the stories" (367).

Modern readers can comprehend this deeper level of meaning in a fairy tale, and also in legends and myths. As a Cree elder, George Head, tried to explain to a non-native collector about Cree legends: "These are really false stories but they got true meaning" (Bauer iv). Similarly, Canadian literary critic Northrop Frye comments: "The child should not 'believe' the story he is told; he should not disbelieve it either, but should send out imaginative roots into the mysterious world between the 'is' and the 'is not' which is where his own ultimate freedom lies" (166).

Thus you might miss the richness and depth of the tales if you interpret them literally, as did the disappointed women quoted earlier—or if you see them only as children's reading. The deeper message of these stories is that the "Magic Kingdom" cannot exist literally in the external world; it exists in the imagination, not as a wishful romantic fantasy but as a meaningful narrative that can reflect your own struggles to find true identity and overcome internal stepmothers, giants, and dragons who challenge this process.

The best of the traditional tales deal with the clash of opposites—good and evil, cleverness and brute strength, humility and arrogance. Such clashes cannot be resolved without struggling to find and hold one's identity. Both protagonists and villains are engaged in the struggle. Snow White's stepmother wants to be the fairest in the land, a fairy tale version of "the fastest gun in the west," and equally impossible to maintain. Cinderella's stepmother wants to extend her own power through the social advancement of her daughters. The evil fairy of the folk "Sleeping Beauty" is furious because she is slighted by the parents; she shows her strength by attempting to destroy the innocent child, just as the other stepmothers mean to destroy, physically or psychologically, their unwanted stepdaughters.

Their stepdaughters, by contrast, are not interested in being the fairest in the land or the most socially accepted; they are not even primarily interested in winning a handsome prince. Their view of the world is not materialistic, as is that of their antagonists. They are concerned with overcoming the cynicism and aggression of their opponents, and with developing a sense of self that does not depend on riches, beauty, or social standing. In order to do so they must submit to threats and humiliations, to imprisonment in towers, or to unnatural sleep. The princes who appear at the end are not lovers but helpers, and the concluding marriage is not romantic but moralistic. The heroine, helped by the hero, thwarts the cynical forces so determined to prevent her awakening and developing. In the end, she is free and mature enough to establish her own domain. This is true of heroes as well, of course.[11]

Disney's versions retain the basic plot and characters, but shift the delicate balance of the traditional tales. In emphasizing their romantic aspects, he changes the relations between protagonist and antagonist as well as between heroine and hero. The main role of the Disney antagonist is to keep apart the heroine and hero, who must then overcome the villain and live happily every after. Disney heightens the conflict between the young, beautiful, and pure heroine and the old, coldly handsome, and vicious villainess. It is not a Freudian conflict between mother and daughter, because fathers play no great roles in these three tales. It is an open battle between the good, unambitious little girl and the bad, ruthlessly aggressive bitch, a favorite character of Disney's; his male villains are rarely as hellishly horrifying. The heroine is totally lacking in ambition. She seems quite willing to sing through her troubles while awaiting the inevitable prince to rescue her from her unpleasant situation. The right clothes, the right place, the right boyfriend, will make her a queen forever, since one day her prince *does* come. It is no wonder that such a heroine, whether in "Cinderella" or "Snow White" or "Sleeping Beauty," still "lives in the heart of every young girl who dreams." As de Rougemont notes in *Love in the Western World:* "All young people breathe in from books and periodicals, from stage and screen and from a thousand daily allusions, a romantic atmosphere in the haze of which passion seems to be the supreme test that one day or other awaits every true man or woman, and it is accepted that nobody has really lived till he or she 'has been through it'" (277).

His observation is supported by the continuing popularity of the love story in countless forms in North America. It is certainly no coincidence that popular writer Eric Segal calls his two creations *Love Story* and *A Fairy Tale.*

It is pleasant to think of life as a romance which continues happily ever after, one in which the supreme test is falling in love. Our willingness to believe this fantasy accounts in large part for the popularity of Disney's fairy tale films with adults. His richly visual films amuse us, but they do not challenge us. In contrast, the traditional stories speak more forcefully to all ages, but particularly to adults. These tales deal with mysterious magic and with real and frightening conflicts with one's self—conflicts not simply resolved with the appearance of a lover. The "happily ever after" meaning of the fairy tale is not about finding one's prince or princess, but finding one's self. You will not find that in Disneyland.

3

The Misuses of Enchantment

CONTROVERSIES ON THE SIGNIFICANCE
OF FAIRY TALES (1985)

In another five years I had moved even further away from a narrow bias against fairy tale heroines. In this chapter, originally written for a gathering of feminist articles in *Women's Folklore, Women's Culture,* edited by Rosan Jordan and Susan Kalčik, I explored how others have interpreted these stories as either problem-solving or problem-creating. The title of the article played on Bruno Bettelheim's popular and now controversial book, *The Uses of Enchantment.* Bettelheim was a writer who considered gender irrelevant in fairy tales, which he saw as problem-solving sources of psychological development. Feminist critics, of course, took the opposite view, claiming that fairy tales provided highly problematic models for readers, especially girls and women. In general, the writers on either side of this issue based their assumptions on hypothetical rather than actual readers. I was curious to see how these positions played out in the interviews from my dissertation. These actual readers, not surprisingly, supported both positions, indicating that personal interpretation might have more significance than theoretical observations. I suggested that the true power of fairy tales was found precisely in this flexibility, that they are always and ever open to new reactions and interpretations at any stage of life. I admitted that for some readers fairy tales had the possibility of not being inherently sexist at all, which is exactly what Alison Lurie suggested in her article "Fairy Tale Liberation." While this is quite a reversal of my earlier views, I still insisted that the "gender of both reader and protagonist is indeed significant in this struggle." That is, the struggle to become a human being on one's own terms.

Little did we realize while reading our childhood fairy tales how controversial these seemingly simple and amusing stories were. Adults were enthusiastically engaged in determining whether such tales were damaging because of their violence or irrationality, or whether they instead furnished powerful fantasies for developing psyches. The battle over the significance of fairy tales has been raging in various forms for some time. As early as the 1700s we find a writer of children's stories referring to fairy tales as "frolicks of a distempered mind," a sentiment still very much alive today (Kiefer 87).[1]

In recent times the battle has spread to a new front, where opposing forces clash over the issue of sexual stereotyping. There are those who feel that fairy tales are unsuitable because they reinforce sexist stereotyping for both boys and girls, others who feel that fairy tales challenge such stereotyping, and still others who insist that these stories have neither a negative nor a positive impact in terms of gender. Because a major premise of folklorists studying women's folklore has been that gender is indeed significant in terms of interaction between people and material, I would like to examine the arguments in this controversy and describe actual rather than theoretical connections between fairy tales and their readers, both male and female.

I have found no clear statements on sexism in fairy tales from the suffragist movement of past decades, probably because feminist efforts then were devoted to legal and economic problems. Writers from more recent decades, however, have expressed themselves clearly on the issue of sexual stereotyping in all forms of literature. Simone de Beauvoir complains that "everything still encourages the young girl to expect fortune and happiness from some Prince Charming rather than to attempt by herself their difficult and uncertain conquest" (126). She mentions "Cinderella," "Snow White," and "Sleeping Beauty" as the stories most widely read and therefore most persuasive in their influence. Bullough and Bullough, in *The Subordinate Sex*, provide a scenario for a modern heroine who has read the stories carefully: "The most obvious example of this today is the beautiful girl with the right measurements who catches the attention of a rich sponsor and simply by being female in a male-dominated society can advance far beyond her own social origins. Men, on the other hand, are more likely to have to earn their status through hard work" (53).

These observations cited from Beauvoir and from Bullough and Bullough appear in the context of much longer works dealing with the broader problem of male-female roles. In 1972, however, we find a lengthy article devoted to the impact of fairy tales in sexual stereotyping. After examining tales in a number of Andrew Lang's fairy-tale books, Marcia Lieberman states: "Millions of women must surely have formed their psycho-sexual self-concepts, and their ideas of what they could or could not accomplish, what sort of behavior would be rewarded, and of the nature of the reward itself, in part from their favorite fairy tales. These stories have been made the repositories of the dreams, hopes and fantasies of generations of girls" (385).

Lieberman's pointed remarks are a reaction to the positive comments of Alison Lurie, who felt that the fairy tale "is one of the few sorts of classic children's literature of which a radical feminist would approve" ("Fairy Tale Liberation" 42). She emphasized that the bulk of the tales portray strong and positive women: "These stories suggest a society in which women are as competent and active as men, at every age and in every class. . . . The contrast is greatest at maturity, where women are often more powerful than men. Real help for the hero or heroine comes most frequently from a fairy godmother or wise woman; and real trouble from a witch or wicked stepmother" ("Fairy Tale Liberation" 42).

Stith Thompson, in his classic work, *The Folktale,* also seems to define *Märchen* (fairy tales) in terms of heroines when he states that "What they are all trying to describe [as fairy tales] is such tales as 'Cinderella,' 'Snow White,' or 'Hansel and Gretel'" (8). Similarly, another folktale scholar, Max Lüthi, reminds us that a great many of the Grimms' fairy tales have heroines, that fairy tales are most often told by women, and that "today children learn fairy tales mainly from their mothers, grandmothers, aunts, and female kindergarten and grade school teachers" (*Once Upon a Time* 136). He concludes from this: "The woman is assigned a privileged position, not only by social custom; in art and literature, as well, she has occupied a central position since the time of the troubadours and the Mariology of the late Middle Ages. In painting and in the novel, she has been the subject of persistent interest and loving concern" (136).

Lurie, Lüthi, and Thompson all emphasize that fairy tales demonstrate the power of women simply because these stories are dominated by women, both as protagonists and narrators. None of them mentions that most of the heroines are pretty and passive rather than powerful. Thompson and Lüthi almost immediately move on to describe the tales with male protagonists only, and Lurie apologetically observes: "Even in the favorite fairy tales of the Victorians it is only the young girls who are passive and helpless. In the older generation, women often have more power and are more active than the men" ("Witches and Fairies" 6). More power, yes—and most often it is of a kind destructive to both heroines and heroes, because the older women are often wicked stepmothers or witches.[2]

The favorable reactions noted above make an interesting contrast to the reaction of a young mother who did not want her daughter to read fairy tales precisely because they are so dominated by women and because the so-called "privileged position" emphasized by Lüthi is really a very restricted one (Minard, *Womenfolk* vii). Her comment inspired Rosemary Minard to compile a collection of traditional tales with active heroines, because she felt these stories were too valuable to give up. In contrast to Lüthi and Lurie, Minard observes: "Many of us . . . are . . . concerned today that *woman* be recognized as a full-fledged member of the human race. In the past she has not often been accepted as such, and her role in the traditional literature reflects her second-rate position. Fairy tales abound with bold, courageous, and clever heroes. But for the most part female characters, if they are not witches or fairies or wicked stepmothers, are insipid beauties waiting for Prince Charming" (viii).

Minard's relatively modest statement was sharply attacked by Susan Cooper, who objected both to "that uncomfortable title" and to "the motive behind the collecting": "It's a false premise: an adult neurosis foisted upon children. I don't believe little Jane gives a damn that Jack the Giant Killer is a boy. Lost in the story, she identifies with him as a *character*, just as little John shares Red Riding Hood's terror of the wolf without reflecting that, of course, she's only a girl" (8).

Cooper, a writer of science fiction/fantasy rather than an expert on either fairy tales or neuroses, expresses an opinion shared by many scholars who are interested in the psychological interpretation of fairy tales. For example, Marie-Louise von Franz, in discussing the Jungian *animus/anima* concept, proposes that the real function of the fairy tale for both females and males is gaining individuation, "the attainment of that subtle rightness which is the far-away goal the fairy tale put before us" (*Problems of the Feminine* 194).

N. J. Girardot, for example, examines the story of "Snow White" in support of his view that fairy tales are essentially nonsexist. He suggests that many fairy tales echo the general outlines of *rites de passage,* thus offering listeners the possibility of a religious experience during which they can recognize "that life itself is a story, a story told by God or the gods, to accomplish the happy passage of men and women through a dark and dangerous world" ("Initiation" 300). He feels that the difference between male and female acts in fairy tales is superficial and deceptive: "Heroes and heroines in fairy tales, more so than in epic and saga, do not ordinarily succeed because they act, but because they allow themselves to be acted upon—helped, protected, saved, or transformed—by the magic of the fairy world" (284).[3] In Girardot's opinion, fairy tales reflect the struggle for maturity and enlightenment, and both hero and heroine are engaged equally in this struggle. The manner in which they "allow themselves to be acted upon" might be different in degree, but not in its basic essence. Both seek an awakening rather than a mate in his opinion.

Bruno Bettelheim makes an even more forceful statement in his lengthy and detailed comment on fairy tales, *The Uses of Enchantment.* I reproduce the following passage in full to avoid possible misrepresentation:

> Recently it has been claimed that the struggle against childhood dependency and for becoming oneself in fairy tales is frequently described differently for the girl than for the boy, and that this is the result of sexual stereotyping. Fairy tales do not render such one-sided pictures. Even when a girl is depicted as turning inward in her struggle to become herself, and a boy is aggressively dealing with the external world, these two *together* symbolize the two ways in which one has to gain selfhood: through learning to understand and master the inner as well as the outer world. In this sense the male and the female heroines are again projections onto two different figures of two (artificially) separated aspects of one and the same process which everybody has to undergo in growing up. While some literal-minded parents do not realize it, children know that, whatever the sex of the hero, the story pertains to their own problems (*Uses* 226).

Like Girardot, Bettelheim feels that gender is irrelevant in the tales' ultimate significance for young readers, and he suggests that only misguided adults fail to see beneath the surface. Children, he maintains, react unconsciously and positively, regardless of any possible surface stereotyping of the characters.

We can assume from the intensity of the statements both attacking and supporting fairytales that these stories are regarded as meaningful for both children and adults rather than as merely quaint and amusing. Moreover, fairy tales apparently have the power to affect readers deeply, either negatively or positively, in ways that other forms of children's literature generally do not. The fact that these multilevel stories are usually read early in life when a child is struggling to find a place in the world, and a sexual identity, can be used to support the arguments of both proponents and opponents of fairy tales.

Thompson, Lüthi, and Lurie seem to feel that fairy tales offer strongly positive images for both boys and girls; Girardot and Bettelheim suggest that gender differences are less important than the psychological significance of the tales; Beauvoir, Lieberman, and Minard insist that significant differences in heroes and heroines exist and that these are important because they contribute to differential socializing of boys and girls in contemporary Western society.

While the authors discussed here argue that fairy tales are either negatively or positively significant, none has given the readers themselves much of a voice. Even the mother concerned about sexism described in Rosemary Minard's book speaks *for* her daughter. Bettelheim does occasionally refer to some of his patients, but only to support his own views. The others speak only in general terms about the effects and the meanings of fairy tales for a hypothetical and therefore silent audience. In the following section I will draw on the reactions of readers of various ages and backgrounds, both male and female. Their varied responses demonstrate that there is no single truth about either the meaning or the impact of fairy tales that is applicable to all readers, but there are some definite patterns.

For several years I questioned people informally and formally about their memories of and reactions to fairy tales. Formal interviews were conducted with forty-four people individually and in small groups.[4] Of these forty-four, twenty-three were girls between the ages of seven and seventeen. Only six of the total number were males, ranging in age from nine to sixty-eight. This small number of male respondents is a result of the inability of male informants *of any age* to recall fairy tales at all. Many males, questioned informally, could not even remember clearly if they had ever read fairy tales. With females, on the other hand, I found that all could remember clearly having read and re-acted to fairy tales, and several in different age groups accurately recalled specific stories—even when they had disliked and rejected them. At first I assumed that boys simply did not read these stories, but parents, teachers, and librarians assured me that they did. The mother of a nine-year-old boy, who had just claimed he had no favorite fairy tales, told me she had read him his favorite, "Jack and the Beanstalk," only the night before. She suggested that he was embarrassed to admit that he read "those girls' stories." Another nine-year-old boy was willing to admit that he had read such stories but that he had since rejected them, for exactly the reason suggested: "I like that one ['Jack and the Beanstalk'] a lot better than those other stories, like 'Snow White' and 'Cinderella.' Those are all girls' stories. They're about girls and not boys. I like the ones with boys a lot better because they're not boring, like the girls' ones. The only one I like with a girl in it is 'Molly Whuppie,' because she does things, sort of like Jack." The story he mentions is a Scottish tale that was, at that time, included in some third grade readers in Winnipeg. In it, a girl saves herself and her sisters from a giant and then steals his treasures. In other words, another variant of his favorite story. But at least he gives the girl credit.

In a class essay by a student-teacher in a fifth grade class, one of my folklore students (male) described the same pattern of boys rejecting and girls accepting fairy tales. He suggested that this was, at least in part, because of the dominance of heroines in popular collections. But his description of boys' and girls' reactions indicates that the situation is more complex than boys rejecting and girls identifying with protagonists because they are female, since the boys seem to have forgotten the tales altogether.

> In the winter of 1978, while discussing fairy tales with a group of grades five and six students, an interesting phenomenon arose. When the discussion centered on the subject of "Cinderella," it became apparent from student remarks that there was a definite difference between boys' and girls' attitudes to the story. The boys' remarks, "It's boring," or "It's a kids' story," reflected a definite lack of interest. The girls, however, said it was one of their favorites. In fact, the majority of girls seemed to feel that some day their prince *would* come and they too would live happily ever after. From this difference in attitudes I am theorizing that fairy tales like "Cinderella," while being enchanting and entertaining in their own right, also serve another purpose entirely. (Spiller n.p.)

Apparently the female-dominated tales extolled by Lurie and Lüthi fail to retain the interest of male readers as they mature. We cannot know for sure whether boys consciously reject them because they are viewed as girls' stories, or whether choices were made on the basis of the passivity or aggressiveness of protagonists rather than strictly on the basis of gender. We cannot even be certain whether this was a conscious decision, or whether boys did work through childhood problems in the way that Bettelheim suggests, thus leaving enchantment with no further uses for them. In any case, the pattern for girls and for boys is clearly different.

A few girls and women seemed to agree with males in their rejection of heroines who were too passive to be interesting, but these readers did not give up fairy tales. They attempted to compensate for disappointing heroines in other ways. A nine-year-old, for example, decided that she preferred heroes to heroines: "My favorite people now are boys named Jack. I remember 'Cinderella' too, but I didn't like it as much as some others. The ones with boys in them are more exciting. They usually go out and do things. 'Cinderella' doesn't have that."

A twelve-year-old reported that she had usually identified with the older sisters "who never got anything and made stupid mistakes like not giving bread to the birds in the woods." Negative as such characters were, they were more interesting to her than "the ones who just sit by the fireside and never do anything, and then one day blossom into beautiful girls." Similarly, a thirty-one-year-old woman observed: "I certainly identified with the women in the stories, but the ones I remember are the ones where the woman was dominant—like in 'The Snow Queen,' where the woman is sort of all-powerful. She may be meant to be a negative figure, but I didn't see her that way. But looking back, I suppose it was the boys who had the action and did things in most of the stories."

While choosing the active but negative women in fairy tales provided these readers with a less passive model, it did not free them from the knowledge that these women were punished in the end for their aggressiveness. The woman just quoted, for example, stated later in the interview: "I wanted to be beautiful like in the stories but I didn't think I was or would be. It just seemed ridiculous. So I was more inclined to the stories where ghastly things would happen to bad little girls. I hated them but I read them over and over." The twelve-year-old admitted that, as an older sister herself, she was frustratingly aware that in her life, as in fairy tales, it was the younger sister "who got all the goodies."

43

These sentiments are more clearly expressed by a twenty-nine-year-old mother who said: "I remember a feeling of being left out in the fairy stories. Whatever the story was about, it wasn't about me. But this feeling didn't make me not interested in them. I knew there was something I was supposed to do or be to fit in there, but I couldn't do it, and it bothered me."

Others were more definite about why they felt left out, and clearly resented the apparent fact that boys "went out and did things" and girls did not. Said one fifteen-year-old: "I don't think it's really fair that in all the fairy tales it's usually the princess who's locked away. Or someone's bartering her off. In the ones with boys—I only remember 'Jack and the Beanstalk'—Jack being a boy meant that he had more curiosity. I don't think I could imagine a girl being Jack, in that kind of story."

Some echoed the sentiments of the thirteen-year-old who was annoyed by the disparity between heroines and heroes (whom she called "Big Joe Tough") and insisted; "You know, there are some girls who can cope with things better than boys can!"

Not all females felt restricted by the seemingly narrow choice of models offered by fairy tale heroines. I would like to examine one especially popular story, "Cinderella," in greater depth to see how both the acceptance and the rejection of fairy tales on the basis of gender relate to the observations of the writers quoted in the first section of this chapter. The issues raised here revolve around the possibilities of fairy tales as either problem-solving stories, as Bettelheim and Girardot suggest, or as problem-creating stories, as feminist writers insist.

While the Cinderella story is found orally in all parts of the world, most North American readers will be familiar with only two versions, from two printed sources. The first of these and by far the most popular is Perrault's 1697 reworking, complete with fairy godmother, pumpkin coach, and glass slipper. The less popular but more dynamic Grimm version has a more resourceful heroine who does without fairy godmothers and coaches and who makes her own curfew. She does not reward her sisters at the end, as does the Perrault heroine, but neither is she responsible for their mutilation, which occurs first at their own hands (cutting off pieces of their feet to force them into the slipper) and then from the vengeful doves, who blind them for their treachery. Apparently this popular story expresses an entire range of hopes, fears, and possibilities for both narrators and audiences.

Here is one example: Folklorist Michael Taft sent me twenty-seven versions of "Cinderella" written by students in his folklore class at Memorial

University in Newfoundland. "They had no prior warning of the assignment and I gave them half an hour to complete this in-class assignment," he told me. Not a single student failed to re-create the story in detail, and their versions all contained the fairy godmother and the glass slipper. Taft unfortunately does not indicate the gender of the students, but presumably male students responded as well as female students. I had similar responses from several of my own folklore classes at the University of Winnipeg, and also from most of those I interviewed: the more passive variant was strongly favored in the books, and thus by readers.

Like most good folktales, "Cinderella" functions on a number of levels of meaning and has several possible interpretations even at a surface level. In the Grimm version, Cinderella's stepsisters equal her in beauty but are "vile and black of heart" (*Complete Grimm's* 121). More significantly, they are interested in getting ahead and hope to do so by marrying the prince. They do not consider their stepsister a serious competitor, although their mother is more perceptive on this score. Cinderella herself is not primarily interested in meeting the prince or in gaining any material benefits—her handsome clothing cannot be purchased at any price since it comes from the doves; she wishes to escape the confines of her painfully narrow existence. She is rewarded with magic objects because she follows precisely the instructions of her dying mother, and wins the prince at least in part because she is not a man-chaser, as are her stepsisters. One interpreter of the tale insists that the prince is merely a symbol for Cinderella's well-deserved freedom and that marriage is not at all the point of the story (Kavablum). In any case, her marriage signifies that she has managed to reject her subservient position and to take action in getting herself to the outside world, and that she has demonstrated her acceptance of maturity by entering into marriage.

Among those interviewed, only three theorized about the possible psychoanalytic significance of the "Cinderella" story. A sixty-eight-year-old male said: "I liked all these stories because in that time of life [childhood] you feel you can't accomplish anything by yourself. And if you're the youngest and trampled on, like Cinderella, you really need to have impossible dreams and read impossible fairy tales."

A seventeen-year-old female added, "You can take the stories like 'Cinderella' from two points of view, for the very serious aspect or for the face value. It depends on what you want at the time. That's what you get out of it." Similarly, a fifteen-year-old girl noted that she didn't expect to see fairy godmothers, witches, dragons, or giants walking on the street, but knew people who took similar roles in real life. For these readers, gender is indeed of little importance, because they are reacting to the tales on an abstract level. The sixty-eight-year-old male, for example, identified Cinderella as an early favorite of his because as a child he identified with her feeling of powerlessness, though his later preferences were for heroic fairy tales, epics, and myths. The two girls mentioned above also did not feel that the sex of the protagonist was significant to them, though they all noted in their interviews that there was a definite difference between heroes and heroines.

For other readers, however, "Cinderella" was interpreted more literally as a model for feminine behavior as well as a depiction of the rewards to be gained. A ten-year-old girl, for example, stated: "Cinderella is my favorite. She's a happy person, when she gets away from her family. People could live like that, like Cinderella. I guess I'd like to live like that, like the happy part. And I wouldn't want to marry a prince, but maybe somebody *like* a prince."

The emphasis here is not on the unpleasant aspects of Cinderella's ordeal, but on her rewards, and on the fact that she "gets away from her family." Here we meet a modern Cinderella, a model for the maturing girl who dreams of escaping with her boyfriend from her restrictive family situation, acquiring a fine wardrobe, a steady income (from her "prince," not from her own efforts), and a suburban castle, all of which will presumably allow her to live happily ever after with glamour and material comfort. One girl in a group of eleven-year-olds said, "I really liked 'Cinderella.' Yeah, when I was about five I guess I wanted to grow up and be a princess, or something like that." Her friend added: "I used to like 'Cinderella' too, like, it should be my story. She starts off very poor and then she gets rich and very successful, and I used to think of myself that way. I thought I'd just sit around and get all this money."

The eleven- and twelve-year-old girls described by the fifth-grade student-teacher quoted earlier were less cynical (or perhaps just less defensive about romantic fantasies), for they had not yet rejected the happily-ever-after ending promised by "Cinderella." In contrast to the ten-year-old who still expects to marry "someone *like* a prince," the eleven-year-olds seem to be more realistic. However, their responses reflect the fact that they have only recently stopped reading fairy tales (few children read them beyond the age of ten, if my sampling is any indication) and are on the defensive about "childish" things. More significantly, older women who might have expressed the same somewhat cynical tone at an earlier age were not so certain upon reconsidering their reactions. For example, a twenty-six-year-old mother of two, now divorced, said somewhat whimsically: "I figured Cinderella was pretty lucky. First I felt sorry for her, and then she went to the dance and got the guy, and I thought this was going to apply to my life. I really figured you just sit around and wait, and something fantastic is going to happen. You go to the right dance and you've got it made! It was definitely 'Cinderella' I liked best. She was gorgeous. I was homely, and I kept thinking it would happen to me too, that I'd bloom one day. But it's never happened. I'm still waiting!"

These readers who identify with Cinderella are definitely interested in the dance and in the prince. One of my university students comments: "My favorite fairy tales were the romantic ones, like 'Cinderella,' 'Snow White,' and 'Sleeping Beauty.' The romantic, 'prince and princess live happily ever after' ones. I easily put myself in the princess' role, waiting for Prince Charming."

Thus the message of the Cinderella story that seems to be most relevant for modern girls and women concerns the rewards one is supposed to receive for being pretty, polite, and passive; the primary reward, of course, is marriage, and marriage to not just anyone but to a "prince," someone who can provide status and the material benefits of the beautiful life. In Winnipeg I talked with Anne Bowden, who was preparing a book on the history of marriage in Manitoba in 1984. She observed that the wedding, as the high point of a girl's life, seems to be a post–World War II phenomenon. She agreed that girls easily identified with the "happily ever after" conclusion of many fairy tales that end in marriage and suggested that many girls have never thought beyond the wedding ceremony. Nor, apparently, did Cinderella.

As Simone de Beauvoir asks, "How, indeed, could the myth of Cinderella not keep all its vitality?" (126). For girls looking for a prince of a man to marry, the message of the tale shifts from Cinderella's growing independence and maturity to the rewards she receives and how she receives them. In this kind of narrow interpretation, success for the female comes from being beautiful and from sitting around and waiting. It is ironic that Cinderella, the ultimate in humility and selflessness, becomes for such readers a woman who uses her beauty and personality to gain material success—and at the expense of other women. In this interpretation, there is little difference between Cinderella and her stepsisters, except that she is more "feminine": unlike her openly ambitious sisters, she masks her real hopes for the future by "just sitting and waiting" for everything to turn out happily ever after for all eternity.

Another aspect of the story commented on by readers was the competition between the women, a competition our society seems to accept as natural.

Some of the sisters I interviewed reacted to this conflict, which they reluctantly accepted as inevitable. One thirty-two-year-old still recalls her sibling relations clearly: "I always felt my sister was making it more than I was. She was blond, blue-eyed, and as a child this was always commented upon. She was the sweet baby girl. I suppose those fairy stories with elder sisters are the ones I have identified with most."

A twelve-year-old (quoted earlier) agrees: "You know, being the oldest daughter like me is sort of . . . well, I didn't want to be a princess, or anything, but I didn't want to be the bad one, either." This supposed inevitability of female competition is commented on by a junior high school guidance counselor: "It's just amazing! The conflicts that occur between girls at this stage are even greater than the conflicts between the boys. . . . I don't know why, for sure, but I guess they're preparing to compete for male attention even when they don't know it."

It would be simplistic to blame fairy tales for encouraging females to see their lives primarily in terms of competing for and winning male attentions, when many other aspects of North American culture reinforce this same ideal. The popular interpretation of the Cinderella story can be identified in disguised form in popular magazines and books, in films, and on television. Psychologist Eric Berne has suggested that one's favorite fairy tale, reinforced by other aspects of culture, could set a lifelong pattern of behavior. "The story will then be his script and he will spend the rest of his life trying to make it come to pass" (95). Despite the masculine pronoun intended to encompass all humanity, Berne provides only female examples when it comes to fairy tales. He describes two "scripts" in detail, one of which is Cinderella, to whom he devotes an entire chapter. Her story, he says, is adopted by women who feel themselves to be unjustly treated or generally unrecognized for their better qualities. They learn to put on a sweet outer personality to improve their chances of getting more recognition and may, when they succeed, taunt other women whom they have bested. Such women, according to Berne, might be unable to give up the exciting game of "Try and Catch Me," first played with the prince and later continued with various adulterous lovers (238).

Berne might be exaggerating in suggesting such a firm connection between stories like "Cinderella" and later behavior, but it would be a mistake to pass fairy tales off as mere "child's play." If one agrees that childhood is a critically impressionable time of life, especially in terms of forming sexual identity, and if popular fairy tales consistently present an image of heroines that emphasize their beauty, patience, and passivity, then the potential impact of such tales cannot be ignored. Certainly some who once favored Cinderella will later find her irrelevant, but many others will continue unconsciously or consciously to strive for her ideal femininity—or will be annoyed with themselves for failing to attain her position. The remarks of a twenty-nine-year-old woman indicate that the fairy tale model undermined her desire for independence: "I couldn't really say whether the impact of stories is stronger when you're an adolescent or when you're younger, but the impact in both cases was harmful to me, I think, because instead of making me feel confident or able to develop my strengths or anything, they made me feel there was something in me I had to stamp out."

A thirty-six-year-old mother of four felt that fairy tales were good stimulation for the imagination but also encouraged impossible expectations, especially for girls:

> I never felt I would ever fit in, but I wanted to. There was a nice romantic thing about fairy tales that was misleading, just like Sunday school was misleading. I identified with them very much. Now I know they didn't relate much to people I knew then . . . well, on the other hand, the men seemed to be able to handle themselves, but the women didn't. Lots of things came together to prevent them. Outside forces controlled their lives, so the only way they could solve it was with some kind of magic. It doesn't say anywhere in the fairy tales I remember that if they just got off their ass and thought about their situation they could maybe do something, except for the ones who were already aggressive and mean.

Several others of various ages mentioned the emphasis on beauty and expressed disappointment in their own inability to measure up. As one woman astutely observed: "I was troubled by the fact that these women were, first of all, very beautiful, and second, virtuous enough not to care about it. So it was sort of a double insult to those of us who worried about our appearance."

Does it all matter? It would be simplistic, as noted earlier, to credit fairy tales with full power as a socializing force, when everything from early nursery rhymes, school texts and other books, television and movies, and personal contacts contribute to our particular system of differential socialization for girls and boys. Still, many adult female informants felt that fairy tales in particular had definitely affected their lives to some degree, and "Cinderella" in particular was the story remembered best. Why "Cinderella," and why such a materialistic interpretation of a story in which the main point is that Cinderella is *not* materialistic, or even man-hungry? Judging by the comments of these respondents, Cinderella *seems* to present the clearest image of our idealized perfect woman—beautiful, sweet, patient, submissive, and an excellent housekeeper and wife. She also represents the female version of the popular rags-to-riches story that can be found at all levels of North American culture, one which assures us that the small can become great and that we all have a chance to do so. For only one example, here is a 1973 *Newsweek* article describing the "Cinderella Story" of the British model, Twiggy: "Once upon a time, back in the 1960s, a wisp of a Cockney lass named Lesley Hornby parleyed her beanstalk figure and wide-eyed air into fame and fortune as Twiggy, one of the world's most photographed fashion models. She became an international celebrity and a movie star. There haven't been many real-life Cinderella stories to match it—and if the slipper fits that well, why not wear it? The Twig is turning into Cinderella in her stage debut, when she will play the fairy-tale heroine in pantomime."

Certainly, if the slipper fits, it is likely to be worn, but it should not be forced. In a thoughtful book that predates Bruno Bettelheim, psychiatrist Julius E. Heuscher emphasized this aspect of the story in his lengthy exploration of myths and fairy tales: "Finally, Cinderella is the individual who is able willingly to restrict her enjoyment of the prince's palace and feast, until she has grown sufficiently, until the slipper fits perfectly" (55).

But for many women, the slipper does not fit, though they try to wear it anyway. And that is why it does matter how and why readers, male and female, interpret and reinterpret fairy tales that they feel were significant to them as children. The few males who mentioned "Cinderella" concentrated solely on the fact that she was a mistreated and powerless person who later obtained status and power. Women, however, concentrated on Cinderella's innate goodness, on her mistreatment at the hands of her own family (a familiar complaint for adolescents of both sexes), her initial lack of beauty and proper clothing, followed by her "blooming," and finally the rewards she received for at last being recognized as the ideal female, in contrast to her ambitious stepsisters.[5] Many of the women who remembered her story recognized, either early or late, that the shoe did not fit. For example, a twenty-eight-year-old divorced mother of three complained: "I remember 'Cinderella' and 'Snow White.' Now I don't think they show the ideal woman—at least not for me, or for my daughter, but I liked them at her age [nine]. It's too glamorous. A man is supposed to solve all your problems. I thought this would be the answer to what I'd been growing up and waiting for. What a bunch of bullshit! Fantasy is okay, but not if it puts patterns into kids' heads about what to expect from life." This woman's statement, made in response to a simple query concerning what she remembered about fairy tales in general, returns us to the issues raised in the first section of this chapter. She responded personally as a girl, and continues to respond as a woman, to heroines rather than heroes in fairy tales. Furthermore, she now views her initial positive response to these tales as problem-creating rather than as problem-solving.

Perhaps her response reflects only the surface of meaning and neglects the psychoanalytic level emphasized first by Bettelheim and then by Girardot, who insist that the "real" meaning of the tales cannot be taken from the surface story alone. Perhaps as a young child she, like other children, unconsciously reacted to this deeper meaning, but was later distracted from it by the other aspects of socialization and her responses to them. In any case, emphasis on the surface level of these stories by this reader and others has been carried into later life, even though fairy tales may no longer be read or even clearly remembered. Furthermore, it is females and not males who continue to be troubled by the view of women presented in fairy tales. It would seem, then, that gender is indeed significant, both in the protagonists of fairy tales and for the readers. Still, the question of the importance of gender is not a simple one.

Bettelheim's observation that fairy tales help certain children work through certain problems at certain times of their lives is undoubtedly correct, though it is difficult to demonstrate this precisely because the working-out process is an unconscious one. For males, fairy tales apparently cease to function at an early age, but for many females these stories continue to function on some level well past childhood. Whatever positive functions the tales have for girls in their early lives apparently become less positive for them in later life. The fact that all the adult females I questioned easily recalled fairy tales both generally and specifically seems to indicate this. That a girl at the age of seven, perhaps, may react to fairy tales as initiatory rites, as Girardot suggests, or as psychoanalytically valid, as Bettelheim suggests, does not prevent them from later interpreting the same tales as literal models for ideal female behavior in later years.

The emphasis on ideal female beauty, passivity, and dependence on outside forces suggested in the fairy tales is supported by Western culture in general. The women and girls who felt uncomfortable with this model, or even those who challenged it, were not fully certain that they had the right to do so. Even when they felt they did not fit in, they did not give up the tales that on the surface suggested they *should* fit in. Similarly, even those who claim to have accepted the ideal feminine model at some time in their lives were defensive. These women often claimed that they had envied and admired Cinderella at an early age, leading one to assume that this was no longer so—but these readers generally did not clearly admit that they had indeed rejected their earlier model of behavior. Often women who said they still felt that the fairy tales projected a positive model for women expressed some doubts about the universal truth of such a model—especially with regard to their own real or hypothetical daughters. A thirty-one-year-old mother of two sons and one daughter, for example, told me: "I guess I would say that the image of stories like 'Snow White' and 'Cinderella' would be good for a little girl. I gave my daughter a fairy tale book for Christmas once, I think. But then when you get down to it, maybe Cinderella and Snow White were too goody-goody. Everyone's doing things to them and they never say anything. Not exactly like real life!"

I am not suggesting that men cease to be concerned with the problem of ideal masculine roles, but that they cease to use fairy tales as a model, while women who have not read these stories since they were children have not left them completely behind. Even when they think they have done so, as did the mother above, they are still struggling with the problem of female roles as they are presented in fairy tales, if not for themselves then projected onto their daughters (or onto other females). The surface message of popular tales like "Cinderella," "Snow White," and "Sleeping Beauty" is that nice and pretty girls have the problems of life worked out once they have attracted and held Prince Charming. Girls and women who have felt that, in some way, they cannot or will not fit themselves into this idealized role, into an image that does not suit their individual characters and needs, still cannot free themselves fully from the fairy tale princess. Her power is indeed strong.

Thus fairy tales, as they are presented through popular collections in which passive heroines outnumber more active heroines or heroes, do not continue to function in the problem-solving manner ideally suggested by Girardot and Bettelheim. For many females they become instead problem-creating as "a purveyor of romantic aechetypes," discussed by Karen Rowe in

"Feminism and Fairy Tales" (357). In this myth love conquers all, and one who is not loved is not complete. While there are certainly male versions of this "myth," fairy tales generally do not figure in them. Thus gender does indeed seem significant in terms of readers' reactions to fairy tales. Males and females at some stage of their lives (and not only as the "literal minded adults" conjured up by Bettelheim) clearly view fairy tale heroines as providing different kinds of idealized behavior, and both males and females react to these differences in different ways. Most importantly, females continue to react to them even when they consciously feel that the problem was left behind in childhood. For women, the problem-creating aspect of the tales is the attempted identification with the ideal woman, or the guilt if one fails to identify with her, and the expectation that one's life will be transformed dramatically and all one's problems solved with the arrival of a man. Females who once reacted strongly to the problem-creating aspect might continue to interpret their responses at various ages, but often without solving the problem. Life is not a "happily ever after" affair for either males or females, nor can anyone else make it so, regardless of how princely they might be. Certain women understand this as well as males, but they are often still held back rather than released.

But if women remember fairy tales, consciously or unconsciously, they can reinterpret them as well. It is the possibility of such reinterpretation that gives hope that women can eventually free themselves from the bonds of fairy tale magic, magic that transforms positively at one age and negatively at another. Such reinterpretation, conscious or unconscious, can occur at any age, of course. I offer here a spontaneous and conscious reworking of "Cinderella" by the nine-year-old girl who earlier claimed that she preferred the character of Jack to Cinderella. Despite her rejection, she did not give up "Cinderella," but came back to the story later in the interview and re-created it in a more pleasing manner for herself. "With 'Cinderella,' I think I'd make it more exciting. Like the prince comes with the slipper, and the mother won't let him try it on Cinderella. Then Cinderella came in and saw it was her slipper. So at night she went to the prince's palace when he was sleeping and got the slipper. And maybe she didn't marry him but got a lot of money." This girl is coming to grips with a problem. She revises for herself a story she dislikes but cannot abandon.

Such personal reworkings, whether conscious or unconscious, are bound to have more impact than those imposed by well-meaning adaptors. For example, concerned psychologist Richard Garner attempted to make the Cinderella story more rational by having his "Cinderelma" reject the prince and palace life, set up her own dress shop, and fall for the printer next door. However, his ending is even more unrealistic than the original: "They never seemed to get bored with one another. They never seemed to get tired of doing things together. In time, they married and had children and lived together until the end of their days" (Garner 96).

In contrast to Garner, Julius Heuscher reminds us, echoing observations of other scholars, that the dynamic possibilities of such stories in meaning and impact, understanding and response, are richly varied: "The fairy tale is not static, is not a rigid image of an immutable situation. It is subject to all kinds of modifications which depend on the psychological make-up of the narrator [and audience] as well as on his [their] cultural environment" (389).

While fairy tales are not inherently sexist, many readers receive them as such. This study indicates that girls and women find in fairy tales an echo of their own struggles to become human beings. Thus gender, both of the reader and of the protagonist, is indeed significant in this struggle.

4

Feminist Approaches to the Interpretation
of Fairy Tales

(1986)

One year later I had broadened my review of feminist writing even further for this contribution to the anthology *Fairy Tales and Society,* edited by Ruth Bottigheimer. It was based on the talk I gave at a conference on fairy tales held at Princeton in 1984. Here I offered perspectives that were built on what I had written earlier in "The Misuses of Enchantment." I identified three basic positions taken by feminist commentators at this point: the earliest writers critiqued the unequal position of women in life and in fairy tales; the next generation viewed women as separate but superior; the third saw women and men as potentially equal, though changes would be needed in male biases for this potential to become actual. I noted that so much of feminist writing in all three categories focused on the same stereotypical heroines again and again, so much so that some feminist views had themselves become stereotyped. I again urged writers to consider other sources in their reflections, especially more recent collections of British and North American tales. While some had begun to include heroines from world mythology and folklore to emphasize the distinctive qualities of feminine and masculine, they still had not discovered heroines closer to home.

All writers, myself included, seemed to agree that fairy tales were un-love stories, either because the happily-ever-after ending was untrue, or because it was about finding one's own self-love rather than romantic love with another.

I was challenged by writers who praised heroines I had labeled as passive and abused, finding in them heroic sources of inner strength and resourcefulness that did not rely on a rescuer. My own change of heart would become increasingly obvious in future writing, especially when I began to focus on storytellers and their interpretations.

In the end, I suggested that fairy tales were deep enough to bear the weight of all possible interpretations, no matter how contradictory, and that every approach could add perspective to our understanding of this rich literature.

The *Märchen* has lent itself to a variety of literary, psychological, and sociological interpretations based on the examination of printed texts. Feminist writers have been attracted to the *Märchen* by its popularity as a genre of children's literature. Initially it was viewed, in its form as the well-known fairy tales (primarily selected tales by the Grimms, Charles Perrault, Hans Christian Anderson, and Andrew Lang), as an unfortunate source of negative female stereotypes.[1] The passive and pretty heroines who dominate popular fairy tales offer narrow and damaging role-models for young readers, feminists argue. Thus much writing has been a sharp critique of the genre.

In early feminist writing (1950s and 1960s) the *Märchen* was uncritically considered as one of the many socializing forces that discouraged females from reaching their full human potential. Few writers from this period focused exclusively on the *Märchen* since it was only one of many sources of stereotyping. Thus critical descriptions tended to be vague and generalized. Both Betty Friedan and Simone de Beauvoir, for example, refer to generalized "Cinderellas" and "Sleeping Beauties" who were urged to wake up and take charge of their own lives rather than wait for "Prince Charming" to act for them (Friedan 118, 292; de Beauvoir 126, 128, 158, 163). A much later book, boldly titled *Fairy Tales and Female Consciousness* by Barbara Waelti-Walters, took the generalized approach to its logical extremes with its overly vague images of "the fairy tale princess" as well as the author's insistence that future generations must be protected from the negative effects of fairy tale stereotyping. The author seemed to be unaware that feminist scholarship had been examining the problem for three decades, and had gone beyond her imprecise imagery.

Later feminist work has examined *Märchen* in more detail. An article written in 1972, for example, reached its conclusions on the damaging passivity of heroines only after an examination of all the heroines in Andrew Lang's multi-volume fairy books. Marcia Lieberman insisted, using ample literary evidence, that the fairy tale romance with its "happily ever after" ending has "been made the repositories of the dreams, hopes, and fantasies of generations of girls" (385). Similarly, Karen Rowe, in "Feminism and Fairy Tales" referred to specific tales (though not such a wide sampling) in attempting to demonstrate connections between fairy tales and popular romantic stories in books and magazines. Once again "Prince Charming" appeared as the villain for whom girls foolishly waited, in both fairy tales and romantic stories. Rowe viewed such tales as problem-creating rather than problem-solving. She thus challenged writers like Bruno Bettelheim who saw fairy tales as gender-free stories that could help children of both sexes solve their problems and define themselves as human beings.

In addition to challenging gender-stereotyping through critiques, feminist writers also responded by offering more aggressive heroines. In *The Practical Princess* and *Petronella,* original stories by Jay Williams, we meet princesses who slay their own dragons and rescue spoiled princes from magicians. Other writers offered reworked traditional tales culled from lesser-known international collections in which heroines assumed more active roles. Among these were Minard's *Womenfolk and Fairy Tales* and Phelps's *The Maid of the North: Feminist Folktales from around the World.* Such writers felt that the availability of strong and enterprising women would counterbalance stereotypic passive princesses and offer a new paradigm for female consciousness.

Feminist writings discussed thus far have been concerned with the effects of gender-stereotyping and have justifiably aimed their criticism at popularly known tales. In so doing they tend to attack the same heroines—notably Cinderella, Snow White, and Sleeping Beauty—again and again, until the feminist view of such heroines has itself become a stereotype. Even Rosemary Minard and Ethel Phelps, despite their attempts to introduce more challenging figures, failed to discover active heroines closer to home. Several twentieth-century gatherings of Anglo-American tales feature heroines who take responsibility for their own destiny.[2] While these collections are not obscure and inaccessible, they are little known outside of folkloric circles. And because many feminist folklorists have concentrated on other forms of verbal expression, the potential connections between these little-known tales and their popular counterparts have not developed in feminist scholarship.[3]

When I began examining *Märchen* heroines in the early 1970s, I attempted to expand the sample of tales to include lesser-known Anglo-American collections and to contrast their heroines with those of popular collections. I accepted the feminist stereotype of popular princesses and challenged it with more aggressive heroines, further supporting my views with interviews in which contemporary readers discussed the degree to which they felt themselves negatively affected by narrow female images.

My approach, along with that of other feminists, came under attack by critics who pointed out that only the surface story was being considered and deeper levels of meaning ignored. Even as these critiques were being formulated, a new feminist view of *Märchen* heroines was beginning to emerge. Feminists agreed that earlier studies ignored the subtle inner strength of heroines. Cinderella, for example, emerged as resourceful rather than remorseful, but not aggressively opportunistic like her sisters. Leah Kavablum insisted that Cinderella really gains freedom from kitchen and fireside, and that her "prince" is symbolic for inner strength. She reminds readers that Cinderella's slipper in Freudian symbolism is her own vagina, and thus her regaining of it establishes her as an independent woman.

Other feminist writers have reworked old stories in new ways to emphasize unrecognized aspects of feminine strength. Angela Carter's *The Bloody Chamber*, for example, reinterprets ten versions of beauty/beast tales beginning with "Bluebeard." Similarly, the poems of Anne Sexton and the stories of Tanith Lee attempt to re-view *Märchen* women both negatively and positively.

In the critiques and the rewritten stories, *Märchen* women, both as heroines and as secondary characters, were set in irreconcilable opposition to male characters. Thus many *Märchen* were no longer regarded as romantic tales about living happily ever after, but instead as dealing with the inner development of the unique female persona. Men could only be a hindrance in this development, or at best (as in Kavablum's *Cinderella*) symbolic of attainment.

A third view of women and of heroines emerged in feminist writings of the late 1970s. Here women were seen as necessarily separate from, but not inherently antagonistic to, men. Feminist critiques were expanded to include *Märchen* heroines and mythic figures together, since the separation of myth and tale was now regarded as artificial and misleading; both myth and tale intertwined the separate realities of the liminal and numinous worlds. Many such works attempted to offer the missing voices of female deities and challenging witch/wisewoman figures in *Märchen*. In *The Book of Goddesses and*

Heroines, for example, Patricia Monaghan listed and described hundreds of major and minor deities and folktale personages from around the world. She noted in her introduction that some of these had previously been described only as "votive figures." In another A-to-Z collection, *The Woman's Encyclopedia of Myths and Secrets,* Barbara Walker agreed that female figures had often been presented too negatively. In describing Pandora and her box, for example, she noted that it "was not a box but a honey-vase, *pithos,* from which she poured out blessings" (12). Ignoring the limited erotic imagery of the honey-box, Walker presented Pandora, like Eve, as a bringer of knowledge to the world rather than as a trouble-maker.[4] I note that Walker's compendium is an uneven work with some entries ("Cinderella" as only one example) that are immoderate.

Similarly, Sylvia Brinton Perera, in *Descent of the Goddess,* interpreted the renewed interest in goddesses and heroines as essential for redeeming "our own full feminine instinct and energy patterns," and which, she insisted, had been regarded by patriarchal religions "as a dangerous threat and called terrible mother, dragon or witch" (7). Her broadly defined study included *Märchen* protagonists like Cinderella and secondary figures like Baba Yaga as descendants of supernatural and divine figures.

An even more detailed examination of myth and *Märchen* as paradigms for inner growth is found in Marie-Louise von Franz's *Problem of the Feminine in Fairytales,* published a decade earlier than the Monaghan and Perera works, but limited to a strict Jungian interpretation. As a Jungian analyst, she was able to present concrete connections between the feminine in traditional literature and in the actual living world of women. Using Jung's concepts of anima and animus she insisted that women come to terms with their masculine force as well as with the dark side of their feminine force. It is precisely this dark side that women had been taught to ignore and repress, according to many feminist writers. Von Franz also suggested that men develop familiarity with their feminine forces, but she did not comment on the fact that the dark sides of their masculine forces already have full expression. In the opinion of von Franz and other Jungians, full individuation for both females and males was encouraged by understanding myth and *Märchen* and other forms of archetypal expression such as dreams. As a Jungian rather than a feminist, von Franz was too moderate. She did not fully acknowledge the additional difficulty women faced in attaining individuation in a male world.[5]

In a more radically challenging examination of femininity and fairy tales, *Kiss Sleeping Beauty Good-Bye,* Madonna Kolbenschlag demonstrated clearly and concisely how the feminine mystique existed negatively and positively. She, too, saw the need for both women and men to understand their conflicting feminine and masculine forces and to open themselves to transformation and transcendence. Kolbenschlag agreed with other feminist mythologists that a new language had to be learned fully by both women and men if human culture was to continue growing. In her concluding chapter, "Exit the Frog Prince," she warned that if the feminine voice continued to be silent, or unheard when spoken, then women might have to separate themselves from men in order to develop fully. In her imaginary letter to the frog prince, she wrote: "My own anger and depression finally forced me to transform my life. What will it take to transform yours? Is rejection the only way to open your eyes? Do I have to leave you, abandon you to your self-serving universe? If we go our separate ways, there will be pain and loss. The tapestry of relationships that we have woven with our lives will be rent" (199–200).

Feminists have often favored the weaving and spinning image for its connection with these traditional female occupations, and also for its optimistic images of connecting and creating positive patterns. A book by folklorist/anthropologist Marta Weigle, *Spiders and Spinsters,* interwove an impressive amount of material on women and folklore. Weigle's underlying assumption was that women are naturally separate because they perceive and react to the world differently from men, and consequently express their perception and reaction differently. Her book attempted to do the same. As she put it, simply, "for the most part, the voices assembled here spin and weave their own story" (ix). She arranged these voices with connecting comments that interwove but did not bind material to restrictive strands of narrow interpretation or theory.

Weigle and others expressed the challenging realization that the feminine voice was indeed different from the masculine, but suggested that this voice was not absolutely limited to women. We make a serious error in equating "female" with "feminine" and "male" with "masculine." The most recent feminist writers have insisted that new perceptions of female and male are needed by all human beings if we are to break the magic spell of gender stereotyping.[6]

Three differing assumptions have underlain the development of feminist writing in general, and in their approaches to *Märchen* and myth specifically. The earliest feminists saw women as artificially separated from and wrongly considered unequal to men; the next generation of writers insisted that women were naturally separate from men and rightly superior; and many recent writers consider both women and men as naturally separate but potentially equal—if men shape up. The *Märchen* has been examined from all three approaches, and feminist reactions have ranged from sharp criticism to firm support of the images of women presented in them. Early writers, unhappy with the images they perceived as reflected in the *Märchen,* insisted that the mirror was at fault, while later writers pointed out that other images could be perceived in the same mirror. If we care to look again at both *Märchen* and myth we might see that they offer flexible paradigms for positive transformations—female *and* male. Eve was the first consumer of the fruit of knowledge, and she shared this dangerous delight with Adam.

5

Three Transformations
of "Snow White"

(1988)

This piece arose from a talk I presented at a University of Illinois international conference honoring Jacob and Wilhelm Grimm, held in 1986. It was reprinted in James McGlathery's 1988 anthology, *The Brothers Grimm and the Folktale*. I played devil's advocate to myself by trying to show more even-handedly how the requirements of new media necessitated and perhaps even justified transformations, both by the Grimm brothers and by Walt Disney Productions. My focus was on the story of "Snow White." To place my perspective into a fuller context, I considered various oral texts collected by Steven Swann Jones ("The Construction") and compared these with the written texts of the Grimms and with the Disney film version. I proposed that each of these did, in its own way, have a variety of "texts" to draw from if the various Grimm editions and the lengthy planning transcripts I explored in the archives of Walt Disney Productions were considered.

Even in this academic article, focusing on a single story and its treatment in three specific media, I still managed to include another voice—that of my then five-year-old son. His personal re-formation of Snow White over the period of several days was, in retrospect, a foreshadowing of the work I would do eventually with non-traditional narrators. They, like my son, were committed to the innate "truth" of the stories they strove to bring into new light through individual understanding. Here, I try to show how this is equally true for the Grimm and Disney versions of Snow White.

———

The story of "Snow White" became popular with readers at the first publication of tales by the Grimm brothers in 1812 and retained its favored position as the German tales were translated into other languages. Thus it was already an obvious choice for the Disney brothers (Walter and Roy) when they chose their first feature-length cartoon in the early 1930s. The story is now so widely known in North America that we tend to forget that it did not originate with either the Grimms or the Disneys, but in oral tradition.

The intention here is to examine the necessary transformations of a story — in this case "Snow White" — in the differing media of oral composition, print, and film. My emphasis is on process rather than on content, as I wish to show as objectively as possible how alterations are a natural result of transformation from one medium to another. While it may seem obvious that contextual change results in content modification, both Grimms and Disneys have been castigated for altering this tale in order to meet the needs of new expressive forms intended for new audiences. The Grimms, for example, reworked traditional stories for an urbane audience of readers unfamiliar with oral material. Scholars have criticized their modifications as inappropriate and also as dishonest, since they claimed to be offering genuine traditional tales "straight from the lips of the peasants." Linda Dégh's critique, for example, specifies the embellished editing that included "polishing of rough edges" as well as combining narratives to make "one perfect tale out of several less complete variants" ("Grimms' *Household Tales*" 83–103).[1]

The Disney brothers also intended to reach a new audience with the now-familiar Grimm material by reinterpreting the story from printed into filmed form. While they made no false claims as to their source, the final film carried Walt Disney's name in place of the Grimms (Walt Disney Presents *Snow White and the Seven Dwarfs*).

The apparent dishonesty of both the Grimm and Disney brothers has fascinated scholars and popular writers for decades. The Disneys have long been reproached for tampering with the Grimm tale,[2] but only recently have the Grimm modifications and misrepresentations become more widely known beyond the narrow walls of academe. For example, John Ellis, in *One Fairy Story Too Many*, mounts an enthusiastic attack on the Grimms for their alterations and false claims; folklorist Alan Dundes frankly identifies the Grimm tale collection as "fakelore," a concept originated by Richard M. Dorson to distinguish material falsely claiming origins in genuine folk tradition. Dundes states: "It does seem sacrilegious to label the Grimms' celebrated *Kinder und Hausmärchen* as fakelore, but to the extent that oral materials are rewritten, embellished and elaborated, and then presented as if they were pure, authentic oral tradition, we do indeed have a *prima facie* case of fakelore" ("Nationalistic" 9). Dundes goes on to urge folklorists not to reject fakelore as unworthy of serious attention but instead to "study it as folklorists, using the tools of folkloristics" (15–16). I accept this challenge. Including the Disneys in such an approach allows me to compare the final Grimm and Disney versions of "Snow White" as well as examples of oral variants.

In recent years folklorists have attempted to clarify the vibrant relations between text, texture, and context in order to more clearly reveal the intricate craftsmanship of verbal arts. Alan Dundes provides the classic explanation of these terms in his essay, "Text, Texture, and Context." By text here, I mean the basic story of "Snow White." Texture is the specific language (visualization, in the case of film) of a particular story; context is any relevant personal, social, historical, and other influences. There might be countless oral texts of "Snow White," each with its own texture and context. The storytelling event, or actual verbal composition of a story, is extremely sensitive to immediate contexts that might motivate changes in texture. Thus "Snow White" in oral tradition is multi-textural and multi-contextual. There is no single "original" or "authentic" oral text. The story would never be told in precisely the same words even by the same person. A unique context for each telling produces different textures, and thus a variety of oral texts.

Print and film, on the contrary, take on a final form combining text and texture in an unchanging unity. Also, the contexts of creating and of receiving are separated so that the readers of the story and the viewers of the film did not share directly and simultaneously in the creation of "Snow White." Thus this particular story in print and film is rigid in text and texture and has no inherent context except when actually created and then received. Unlike oral variants, the printed and filmed tale of "Snow White" can exist indefinitely in storage, quite free of direct human context.

In considering content I find the literary concept of open and closed texts valuable in exploring "Snow White" variations.[3] A closed text is one that carefully develops details and connections, leaving readers or viewers little chance for active participation and interpretation. An open text, on the other hand, presents itself in such a way that a full story is told without elaborating every detail of plot, character, motivation. Thus receivers can take a more active role by making their own connections, by "filling in the gaps." The open or closed nature of the text is influenced by the medium in which it exists. In general, told stories have more possibility for openness than do those in printed and filmed media.

It seems to be current folk wisdom that "the medium is the message." This oft-quoted observation formulated by Marshall McCluhan emphasizes the critical role any medium plays in determining the message of its content. In his *Understanding Media: The Extensions of Man* he states: "In a culture like ours, long accustomed to splitting and dividing all things as a means of control, it is sometimes a bit of a shock to be reminded that, in operational and practical fact, the medium is the message. This is merely to say that the personal and social consequences of any medium—that is, of any extension of ourselves—results from the new scale that is introduced into our affairs by each extension of ourselves, or by any new technology" (7). While his own message is not always easy to understand, he does articulate his basic concept in terms that folklorists can easily comprehend. He explains that his observation that the medium is the message "can, perhaps, be clarified by pointing out that any new technology gradually creates a totally new human environment. Environments are not passive wrappings but active processes" (vi). In other words, he is not looking at a medium as a product but rather as a process. McCluhan meant to challenge interpreters who rely on content alone to discover the "message" of a story. Like folklorists who see context as a critical creative force, McCluhan insists that the message or meaning can be found in the actual process of creation and dissemination rather than in its textural content.

The story of "Snow White" would naturally be altered as it passed from one medium to another. The Grimms could not have furnished an aesthetically powerful printed version of the oral tale any more than the Disneys could have produced a faithful filmed version of the printed Grimm text. The difficulties of accurate translation can be felt in films which have laboriously attempted to reproduce a complex novel, or in careful transcripts of oral texts recorded by professional folklorists. This problem of shifting artistic products from one medium to another has bedeviled folklorists for generations. In maintaining accuracy of transcription from oral to printed forms, textural and contextual impact must often be sacrificed.[4]

The basic story of a girl's blossoming, apparent death, and miraculous rebirth may persist no matter how it is expressed, but its particular concrete manifestations must vary according to the medium of its expression.

"SNOW WHITE" IN ORAL, PRINTED, AND FILMED MEDIA

If we consider any medium of narrative creativity as a bridge of communication between creators and receivers, and understand that the structure of any bridge determines the traffic it can bear, then the dynamic concept of "message" or meaning can be seen to extend well beyond content. Each medium has its own requirements and potentials for communication, and each—as McCluhan observes—creates a new environment in which the communication takes place.

The fullest and most direct bridge of communication would be the orally composed story of "Snow White." In this context both creators and receivers participate simultaneously in the storytelling event, while print and film split the experience of artists and audiences. Much folklore scholarship focuses on the importance of examining stories in their full oral context.[5] The oral bridge in performance contexts allows a constant flow of two-way traffic back and forth, while the bridges of print and film permit only separated flows of traffic, first one way and then the other. In other words, the audience has a far greater opportunity to take part in the telling of a story than is possible while reading a book or viewing a film. This alone could not help but influence the formation of a story in any particular medium.

Since both the Grimm and Disney versions could not have come into being without orally composed interpretations of "Snow White," let us begin with a consideration of verbal creativity.

"Snow White" in Oral Tradition

Stories created verbally are continually fluid and adaptable according to time and place, tellers and listeners, and other contextual factors. Some folklorists describe this vibrancy as "emergent quality," meaning that the precise text of any story emerges at the actual event of its telling.[6] At the same time, these stories maintain a firm stability that has allowed them to exist for uncountable years of ongoing narration and recreation. Narrated tales balance between traditional stability and individual innovation so long as they remain in oral currency. No one story can be considered original in the sense of either primacy or individual innovation. Every traditional teller of "Snow White" is as original as any other. The concept of original and authoritative texts is applicable only to print or film.

The oral story of "Snow White" has been examined by folklorist Steven Swann Jones, who searched through more than one hundred traditional texts from printed collections of European, African, Asian, and New World tales. He chose to focus on 24 representative texts in order to demonstrate precisely how "Snow White" manages to exhibit both stability and variability. As he observes: "It is remarkable that a story should travel such great distances, be told by many different peoples, and undergo apparent changes and yet remain recognizably the same tale. I suggest that folktales such as 'Snow White' are not simply muddied or muddled up the more they are retold by subsequent tellers" (Jones 218). He identifies distinctive formalistic elements that provide the unique pattern of "Snow White." To simplify his detailed enumeration, these begin with the heroine's expulsion from home, the various threats on her life culminating with apparent death, and her rescue and reawakening.

Jones finds this elemental narrative pattern in all texts he surveys, though of course the exact expression or texture varies from story to story. For example, a Norwegian variant has a giant's daughter prick her finger and, inspired by red blood on white snow, wish for a daughter with pure white skin and red lips; a Celtic tale features a jealously beautiful queen named Silver-Tree who threatens the young heroine Gold-Tree; an Icelandic heroine named Vildridr Fairer-than-Vala escapes to a small house carved of stone and inhabited by only two dwarfs. Each of these texts is equally authentic in terms of its contribution to the larger generalized story-type of "Snow White" (AT 709). It matters not a bit if the French-Canadian "Le Miroir Qui Parle" ("The Speaking Mirror") is different in detail than the Louisiana story of "King Peacock." They are both authentic and easily recognizable variants of "Snow White."

Unfortunately we do not know, since the Grimms do not tell us, how many oral texts might have been available in Germanic oral tradition at the time of their collecting activities. We can only assume that the potential variety of details would have provided them with a wealth of material for their single printed text of "Snow White."

The oral medium, then, provides a potentially direct bridge between tellers and listeners that encourages the ongoing recreation of the story in an infinite variety of emergent texts, each with unique texture and context.

"Snow White" in the Printed Medium

Stories composed in writing tend to become fixed and unchanging, and authors and readers no longer share simultaneously in the creative event as discussed previously. When texts become attached to specific creators, the notion of originality in the dual senses of primacy and uniqueness come into play. Because a single text titled "Snow White" was included in the Grimm collections, and because the collection itself was original in both meanings of the word, we arrive at the concept of "the Grimm version" as the "authentic" variant of "Snow White" (excluding oral sources).

If the Grimms had either drawn directly from oral tradition (as they claimed) or completely fabricated their tales, then we might indeed expect to find only one authoritative text for this story. However, the brothers combined both oral and written traditions to produce a new literary form. Apparently they were sincerely committed to recreating what they conceived as a pre-Christian Teutonic literature. Alan Dundes's article on "fakelore," cited earlier, suggests that countries with a weak sense of nationhood, as Germany was in the early nineteenth century, sometimes produced a consciously composed literature deliberately passed off as genuine "folklore."[7]

The Grimms responded to the forces of romantic nationalism by fashioning a unique genre. Interestingly, they offer several variant texts of "Snow White," altering the story somewhat in each of their seventeen editions from 1812 to 1856. The earliest known text is in a 1810 manuscript sent to Clemens Brentano, but never published.[8] Here the handsome queen is the girl's natural mother, who first wishes for her and is then dismayed by her ever-increasing beauty. It is the mother herself who takes Snow White to the forest on the pretext of picking flowers and abandons her there. Except for some changes of wording the basic story is the one already familiar to us, until we reach the death-rebirth motif at the conclusion. Here it is Snow White's father who finds and removes the coffin, and then orders his royal physicians to revive her by tying her body to ropes connected to the four corners of a room. After this surprising climax we find the more familiar marriage to a prince and the queen's dance of death in heated iron shoes (David and David 303–07).

In the first published edition of 1812 the natural mother is still the villain, but this time she orders her huntsman to destroy Snow White in the forest, and return with her lungs and liver as proof. The escape to the dwarfs' house and the three attempts on her life are unchanged, but this time the prince himself carries away the coffin. Two of his disgruntled servants accidentally revive Snow White when they strike her in anger, thus dislodging the apple.

With each edition other minor changes were made, until the final text, which became the "authoritative" version, separated the good and bad aspects of the queen into independent story characters. Since the wording of the various texts is much the same we cannot assume that different oral sources are represented, since these would employ variant wording. Instead it is clear that literary editing is at work. Thus the Grimms have not actually provided the variety of texts that might exist in actual oral tradition, but offer only revisions of one basic text. It is possible that some of the revisions were inspired by additional oral sources encountered over their decades of work, but we cannot know this because none of their original manuscripts before 1809 remain in existence.

The Grimms unknowingly demonstrate the communication problems that can arise when we have only a printed document removed from the context of its creation. As the story was increasingly edited by a single writer it became more his story and less the peoples' story. And we, long trained to accept only one text as "original," consider the Grimm version of "Snow White" as authoritative. We have no prior printed text that challenges it. But in its transformation from oral to printed media it has lost its emergent quality, despite the appearance of variety in the Grimm editions. Separated from the actual context of composition—here in time as well as in space—we no longer experience the multi-textural advantages of narration. "Snow White" in print becomes frozen into the wording of the 1856 edition.

The medium of print offers a narrower bridge of communication than does narration. Artistic traffic moves in two separate streams, from the authors to the book and then from the book to the readers. There can be no direct interchange, but only subordinate reactions.

"Snow White" in the Filmed Medium

Films create an even greater separation of makers and viewers, giving the latter even less possibility for interaction. Both story listening and story reading give us the opportunity to provide our own visual, oral, emotional, and other elaborations, but film provides these all ready-made for our consumption.

The Disney film in particular is exquisitely explicit in its visualization, as well as in its aurally and emotionally manipulative aspects. My own childhood memories are still clear, all the more so since this was my first "moving picture." My aunt Val took me and my younger sister Janet to a downtown theater in Detroit in 1944; in my memory Snow White is still scrubbing the palace steps and singing sweetly about her dream-prince; then she is dashing in terror through the dark forest to escape from her stepmother; and at last she finds the dwarfs' house with its wonderful child-sized furniture and exquisite background details. Even sharper in my mind is the dramatic transformation of the handsome queen to a hideous hag, one of the Disneys' stunning elaborations on the Grimm tale. At this point Janet's four-year-old voice still echoes in my ears as she yells "I want to go home!" But we remained to the melodramatic end.

Many years later I found myself in the small archives of Walt Disney Productions in Burbank, California, exploring file folders full of planning transcripts and preliminary sketches from the three years of production from 1934 to 1937.[9] It is now commonly known and proudly acknowledged by the Disney studio that the film was initially dubbed "Disney's Folly" even by some of those close to the Disney brothers. People simply could not believe that adults, who formed the large majority of film audiences, would pay to see a long cartoon based on a children's fairy tale. But because of the careful and explicitly detailed work that went into all aspects of the film, it became an overnight success that is re-released every few years.

The very first transcript I explored was a one-page outline dated October 22, 1934, that was simply a list of suggestions for characterizations. Snow White was to resemble actress Janet Gaynor, while Douglas Fairbanks was suggested as the model for the prince. Interestingly the Queen had no living models, but was to be a "mixture of Lady Macbeth and the Big Bad Wolf." She is finally developed as "a very majestic, cold, tiger-lady type."[10] The individualized dwarfs were also a challenge to the film-makers, who swung between extremes of buffoonery and sentimentality, eventually arriving at a compromise. By the end of the first year of planning all the major characterizations were well established, and the seven dwarfs had become central characters.

The only significant changes between 1934 and 1937 were with important secondary characters like the queen's mirror, her huntsman, and the prince.

The mirror and the huntsman were shifted from unwilling complicity in the queen's evil plots to acquiescent conspiracy with her. The former attributes were finally chosen. The prince was even more intriguing in his various manifestations. Initially Walt Disney suggested a key role for him and his horse, who were to be imprisoned in the queen's dungeon and rescued by birds and animals. These sequences eventually disappeared from organizational sessions, only to resurface two decades later in the Disney version of "Sleeping Beauty."

The final film of *Snow White and the Seven Dwarfs* closely follows the general pattern of the Grimm tale, despite the various changes motivated by visualization. For example, two significant scenes featuring the queen were modified for increased visual impact: the transformation from a beauty to a hag (in the Grimm tale she merely disguises herself as a peasant) and her fatal plunge over the cliff (instead of dancing to her death in heated iron shoes). These modifications would not exclude the filmed tale from Jones's list of Snow White texts described earlier.

The years of preparatory conferences contributed a number of alternate texts for the filmed rendition of "Snow White," each a very faint echo of the variability found in oral tradition. And while an actual audience did not contribute to these preparations, the film was undoubtedly successful because the Disneys had come to know their potential audience from past animated successes. Herbert Gans reminds us that such a projected, ideal audience plays an important though indirect role in such variability. "Every creator is engaged to some extent in a process of communication between himself and his audience, that is, he is creating *something* for *somebody*. This somebody may be the creator himself, other people, or even a nonexistent stereotype, but it becomes an image of an audience which the creator develops as part of every creative process" (317).

But of course film viewers see only the final "text" agreed upon by the Disneys and their co-workers; they do not experience textural variability. Like the Grimms' tale, the Disneys' film has no serious challengers to its status as the authoritative film version of the story. (An intriguing but dated parody titled "Coal Black and the Seben Dwarfs" is known only to film historians.)[11]

In summary, the Disney film isolates creators and receivers and offers them even less possibility of interaction since it furnishes sights, sounds, and motivations. The filmed text thus provides the narrowest bridge of all, with the most closed text and context. There is only one *Snow White and the Seven Dwarfs*.

As we have seen, the conceptual bridge of creative communication narrows progressively from oral to printed to filmed versions of "Snow White." The openness of text and texture also becomes more confined. Yet even the film, the most rigid and manipulative interpretation of "Snow White," does not prevent viewers from interacting in one way or another. The traffic is always two-way, even when the creative and receptive streams are separate. Because readers and viewers do indeed respond, the neatly-drawn lines between the three media considered above lose the sharp definition delineated here.

My son, like me, was five years old when he saw *Snow White and the Seven Dwarfs* while we were visiting Madrid, Spain, in April of 1976. He understood not a word of the Spanish dialogue, nor was he familiar with the story in any form, yet he followed the action with complete accuracy due to Disney's explicit visualization. He was disturbed by the wicked queen's death, however, and insisted that we sit through the story again hoping (though as an already-experienced movie-goer he knew it was futile) that the story would end differently. It did not, of course, so we had to find a printed text of "that story." The best we could do in Madrid was a simplified picture book with no clear treatment of the queen.

When we returned home I found and read him the Grimm tale, but this was no more satisfactory. I was then asked to tell him the story in my own words, which I did for the next several nights. Finally he informed me that when I told "that story" I was to have the queen fall asleep for one hundred years and then "wake up a nice lady."

By working through all three media and their possibilities he created his own version of the story. He was responding not only to the explicit and implicit content of the story, but also to the differing means in which this content was expressed through film, books, and narration. He created his own multi-textual and multi-textural tale by experiencing it through a variety of contexts. His text is worthy of the same consideration as those we have surveyed here.

If the medium is the message, the reaction to that message is still in the minds of individual receivers. (In fact, McCluhan himself seemed far less interested in active responses of viewers, regarding them in the main as placid consumers of any media expression.) As we have seen, each of the means of textual formulation has inherent possibilities and limitations for inviting creative participation. The oral tale, and particularly a *Märchen* like "Snow White," has the greatest potential for attracting such a response, not only because of its emergent quality and the immediacy of its continual recreation, but also because of its abstract nature. As with other abstract forms of art, the *Märchen* implies its message rather than explicitly revealing it. Max Lüthi speaks eloquently about this "open text" aspect of traditional oral tales. "Any attempt at a detailed description gives rise to the feeling that only a fraction of all that could be said has in fact been told. A detailed description lures us into the infinite and shows us the elusive depth of things. Mere naming, on the other hand, automatically transforms things into simple, motionless images. The world is captured in a word; there is no tentative amplification that would make us feel that something has been left out" (*European Folktale* 25).

For the *Märchen,* more is less. Lüthi reproaches the Grimms for the literary embellishments that pushed them away from the genuine, unselfconscious folk tradition. "They speak of the red eyes and wagging head of the witch and of her long bespectacled nose (Grimm, Nos. 15, 69, 193). Genuine folktales speak only of an 'ugly old hag,' an 'old witch,' an 'evil witch,' or simply an 'old woman'" (25–26).

The more detail put in by a creator, the less abstract and open the story. The Disney film, of course, is even more elaborately representational than was the Grimm tale. Yet, as my son has illustrated, the power of the *Märchen* can still be felt even in an elaborate and explicit movie like *Snow White and the Seven Dwarfs.*

When I began formulating this paper, the content of the story of "Snow White" as interpreted by the Grimms and Disneys was central to my thinking. As I tried to understand more fully how their respective interpretations came into being, the critical impact of the particular medium of presentation became increasingly obvious. Exploring the process of translating "Snow White" from oral to print to film allows us to see the dynamics of human creativity from a wider perspective than that inspired by content analysis alone.

It is not useful to think of Grimm and Disney versions in terms of faithfulness to any particular sources. More valuable, and considerably more interesting, is a broad conception of human expressive creativity. Both filmed and printed versions of "Snow White" take on their specific characters as influenced by the interplay of text, texture and context, and by the dynamics of medium and message.

Folklore scholar Linda Dégh reminds us of Lüthi's observation that *Märchen* have survived exploitations and intrusions of all kinds (including those of the Grimms and Disneys) without losing the powerful essence of the ancient oral tales that inspired them. "The common knowledge of the tales is so profound, so deeply ingrained, that, even without the story being told in full, a reference or casual hint is enough to communicate the meaning of the essential message of the tale" (Dégh, "Grimms' *Household Tales*" 102). She suggests that even an amusing television commercial in which the jealous queen consults her mirror to see the effects of her new beauty soap can call back the powerful death/rebirth principle of the whole of "Snow White" (102). She further develops the relation of *Märchen* and advertising in "The Magic Tale and Its Magic," especially on pages 66–68. Thus, in her opinion, any "text" of "Snow White," whether full or partial, serious or humorous, contributes to the continued life of this seemingly simple story.

Certainly the context in which "Snow White" is created affects the texture of its content in oral, printed, and filmed "texts." Still, neither the medium nor the content can fully define the message of "Snow White" for any active receiver. Each new context simply adds another text for consideration. And this, of course, includes the medium of the academic essay.[12]

II

Fairy Tales and Storytelling

6

Oral Narration in Contemporary
North America

(1986)

This was my first scholarly attempt to find patterns in the still-new art of professional story performances, or "platform performances," as they came to be called. At this time I was still immersed in women and fairy tales, and in fact, this talk was given at the same Princeton conference as "Feminist Approaches," chapter 4 here, and it also appeared in Bottigheimer's anthology, *Fairy Tales and Society*. Because it was my first attempt, it had all the feeling of new exploration, both the enthusiasm and the hesitations, and most particularly the struggle to find terminology that made folkloric sense in comparing traditional oral narrators with "platform performance" storytellers. As always, when we begin to follow new paths, we try to set out signposts for those who might follow, and that was what I had in mind here. I set up three categories that include all tellers in the continuum from traditional oral narration to recitations from printed texts, focusing on those who included folktales or fairy tales in their repertoires. That is, I disregarded those who preferred original compositions, personal anecdotes, or jokes.

I used as my touchstone three scholars who made profound contributions to narrative scholarship in general, and to mine in particular: Max Lüthi, whose text-based studies opened fairy tales to new interpretation; Albert Lord, whose collaboration with Milman Parry in Yugoslavia produced a deep study of the oral process of composition; and Linda Dégh, whose work with

Hungarian narrators brought new understanding to both personal and social aspects of actual storytelling. My challenge here was to see how their insights might apply to tellers who are far removed from actual oral tradition, composition, and social contact. When this article was written in 1986, there were still enough "platform performers" using fairy tales that such connections could be made. In the two decades since, more and more performers have come to rely on personal stories, original compositions, and anecdotes, which would have made this article much more difficult to write.

Also, when I began my work in contemporary storytelling, only Joseph Sobol and Charlotte Ross were beginning to devote scholarly attention to the "storytelling revival," as it was already called in the 1970s. Today there are masters' theses and dissertations, countless academic articles, and a new journal devoted entirely to the scholarly study of storytelling—*Storytelling, Self, Society: An Interdisciplinary Journal of Storytelling Studies.* Even so, many of the performers I mention here are still performing, and at least occasionally they still use traditional tales in their repertoires. While we may be past the golden age of the storytelling revival, as with the folksong revival before it, there is still much to be explored.

Fairy tales, known to scholars as *Märchen,* most often mean printed texts in books, for some scholars and most general readers. Folklorists are aware that behind each printed text are countless unrecorded tales by innumerable traditional oral artists, with no single telling capturing the full potential of any given story. Non-folklorists, however, place far too much weight on a single text, or at best a bare handful of versions and variants, without giving much, if any, attention to the dynamics of oral contexts. Traditional oral tales are meant to be heard, not read, and they exist in very specific geographical, historical, and cultural settings. No traditional tale can be fully comprehended without at least some understanding of its vitality in these settings.

In past decades, folklorists have examined traditional tales and tellers within specific tale-telling societies, and have contributed greatly to our understanding of narrative traditions. However, scholarly attention up to now has focused almost entirely on traditional tales, tellers, and listeners in oral settings. It is my intent here to expand the folkloric prospective to include what has been described popularly as "the storytelling revival," a phenomenon that arose in the 1970s. To provide context for this "revival," I will briefly examine traditional narration in the Anglo-American context as it continues to exist in rural areas of North America, as well the nontraditional urban storytelling that preceded and continues to exist along with revivalist storytelling at festivals and other organized storytelling events. This has been largely unexplored territory even into the 1990s, and as a former geographer I look upon my work here as preliminary map work on a new coastline. My hope is that other scholars, folklorists and nonfolklorists alike, will see the value in including contemporary storytelling in their *Märchen* (fairy tale, wondertale) scholarship.

I will concentrate here on the process of narration rather than on the *Märchen* as a unique genre, but I emphasize that these stories continue to exist alongside other narrative forms favored by traditional and nontraditional tellers alike. I have been constantly surprised at the resistance I have encountered from students, listeners, and colleagues when I have insisted that *Märchen* are still very much alive beyond the printed page. I contend that anyone who studies this genre with serious intent should at least be aware of its continuing oral vitality within known geographical and historical settings today, including contemporary performance contexts in organized storytelling events. I aim to provide a useful framework for anyone exploring the narration of wondertales today.

To clarify the literary and verbal artistry of traditional tales and tellers, I will briefly examine four folkloric studies that offer complementary approaches. The first of these is Max Lüthi's literary and philosophical work, *The European Folktale: Form and Nature,* which explores the traditional *Märchen* as a unique form of human expression. Lüthi challenges folklorists by insisting that the full power of the *Märchen* lies in the text itself, without reference to either individual narrators or specific storytelling communities:

> Although in many ways, like everything human, the folktale is to be interpreted historically, I have preferred to search for its lasting truths. Today more than ever I am convinced that, despite increased interest in the functions of tales and in what has been called folktale biology, the tales themselves merit the greatest attention, just as always. Even though much is clarified by their context, the texts themselves take on an ever new life with the passage of time. They speak to all kinds of people and to widely separated generations; they speak in terms that sometimes differ and yet in many ways remain the same. Only a small part of the secret and the fascination of folktales can be grasped

by research into the present-day context of their performance in days past. The secret of the folktale resides essentially in its message, structure and style. (Luthi, *European* xv)

Linda Dégh's study of Hungarian peasant narrators presents traditional tales in their oral and social contexts (*Hungarian*) and implicitly challenges Lüthi's text-based approach. In an article on her contextual approach, termed, as Lüthi mentioned above, "the biology of storytelling," Dégh insists on the necessity of looking at tales as they actually live for the people who tell and listen. She defines her terms precisely: "'Biology' indicates a significant switch in scholarship, from text to context. The term signals a change in concentration from the static view of artificially constructed and isolated oral narrative sequences, to the dynamics of telling and transmitting stories from person to person and from people to people, though means of direct contact, interaction, and resulting processes responsible for the formations and continual recreation of narratives" ("Biology" 1).

Another classic study of oral material in context, Albert Lord's *The Singer of Tales,* explores the ways in which traditional epic poems are learned, practiced, performed, and received. Based on Yugoslav heroic epics, his observations are nonetheless relevant to other narrative forms, particularly the complex *Märchen*. Like Dégh, Lord concentrates on the actual existence of oral narratives in specific communities at a definite time in history. Like Lüthi, he is interested in the artistic and historic merits of the texts themselves. He is also aware of the misunderstandings that literate societies impose on oral creativity:

A culture based on the printed book, which has prevailed from the Renaissance until lately, has bequeathed to us—along with its immeasurable riches—snobberies which ought to be cast aside. We ought to take a fresh look at tradition, considered not as the inert acceptance of a fossilized corpus of themes and conventions, but as an organic habit of re-creating what has been received and is handed on. It may be that we ought to re-examine the concept of originality, which is relatively modern as a shibboleth of criticism; there may be other and better ways of being original than the concern for the writer's own individuality which characterizes so much of our self-conscious fiction. (Lord i)

Taken together, these three folkloric approaches are all indispensable to a full understanding of traditional narrative forms as artistic, social, and personal expression. A fourth and more recent work, Richard Bauman's *Verbal Art as Performance,* is even more immediately relevant to the subject of oral narration. He emphasizes the necessity of viewing verbal arts in actual performance and in its broad social contexts in which artists and listeners interact. He defines performance flexibly enough to cover the various aspects of verbal creation addressed here, and I will refer to his work throughout this writing. "Fundamentally, performance as a mode of spoken verbal communication consists in the assumption of responsibility to an audience for a display of communicative competence. This competence rests on the knowledge and ability to speak in socially appropriate ways" (*Verbal* 11).

While in the broad sense his definition could also be applied to nontraditional arts like drama or opera, for example, he expands on the essential quality of verbal material as ever-changing rather than static, as "emergent" rather than scripted: "The emergent quality of performance resides in the interplay between communicative resources, individual competence, and the goals of participants, within the context of particular situations. We consider as resources all those aspects of the communication system available to the members of a community for the conduct of the performance" (*Verbal* 38).

Bauman's theoretical statements include actual texts and textual analyses by folklorists and anthropologists working in a variety of world cultures. By implication, then, he brings together the considerations expressed by Lüthi, Dégh, and Lord. While all of these studies should be recognizable to folk narrative scholars, they are generally not so familiar—if known at all—to those who focus on texts alone (for example, those engaged in strictly literary or psychological studies). For example, Bruno Bettelheim in his popular psychological study, *The Uses of Enchantment,* offers occasional lip-service to tale-variants in oral tradition and to the importance of hearing and not just reading stories, yet he demonstrates no convincing comprehension of the emergent nature of oral creativity.

On the other hand, North American folklorists writing in the 1980s, in devoting their attention to traditional oral narratives alone, have failed to consider the emergent potential of nontraditional storytelling as it exists today in schools and libraries, and at storytelling concerts and festivals. European scholars have been somewhat more attentive.[1]

Oral narration of both traditional and nontraditional stories is carried by tellers with "communicative competence" in three broad public contexts in North America.[2] These contexts include traditional tellers in rural areas of the United States and Canada; trained nontraditional tellers in school classrooms and libraries; professionally trained tellers at storytelling concerts, festivals, and other organized storytelling events. Even if this were a book-length exploration I could barely even scratch the surface of the ocean of story awash in the northern part of this single continent, given the dizzying variety of multi-ethnic and multi-racial possibilities (beginning, of course, with Native American sacred narratives told for thousands of years before European settlement). But for the limited purposes of establishing a basic model, I must limit my remarks largely to those of Anglo-American background. Even here, the diversity of tales, tellers, and traditions is magnificent.

Within the three contexts above, I explore tellers within three broad categories: traditional tellers, whose stories begin with European colonization and continue today; nontraditional tellers whose work in schools and libraries begins to blossom in the 1870s; and neotraditional tellers who brought storytelling to wider audiences from the late 1960s. My term *neotraditional* is deliberately paradoxical, highlighting the fact that many of these contemporary tellers, despite their recent emergence, combine old and new, traditional and nontraditional, in challenging ways.

Within each of these contexts and categories, storytellers learn and perform their tales differently, and of course the listeners receive them differently. I am more interested in the connections than in the differences, and hope to show how both connections and differences interweave in organized storytelling in North America today. I keep in mind the insightful comments of Lüthi, Dégh, Lord, and Bauman as I begin my explorations.

TRADITIONAL ORAL NARRATION

Folklore scholarship reveals that oral tales are the products of chains of individual narrators, most of them unnamed but still "present" in the stories. In the sense that each verbal artist contributes to any single tale, this body of literature can be regarded as a communally created product. We should remember, though, that this communal creativity is not super-organic, not some mystical concept suspended above human culture and individual personality. Creativity can only come into being when actual people tell actual tales. The first people on this continent were Native Americans, for whom narration was and is often a sacred expression. Countless other ethnic and racial groups continue to the active recreation of their communal treasuries of oral tales, and much of this has been and continues to be put down in print. As I have already said, it is my regret that I can only focus on Anglo-American material here, as it continues to exist in traditional, nontraditional, and neotraditional contexts in Canada and the United States.

Much popular and scholarly attention has centered on tale narration in the southern mountains of the United States. In two compilations of reworked tales by Richard Chase, for example, we meet storytellers whose tales can be traced to ancestors alive in the 1700s (*Jack* and *Grandfather*). The descendants of one such family, Ray Hicks, Stanley Hicks, and Hattie Presnell, have all performed at an annual southern festival that mixes tellers from all three contexts.

Other collections from the American south are less known than those of Chase, but equally rich in oral materials.[3] (There is also a major compilation of British material (Briggs), two modest collections of Anglo-Canadian tales (Fauset and Spray), and a small but significant contribution from New England (Gardner). Some but not all of these provide backgrounds that go beyond tale texts—names and descriptions of narrators, geographic and cultural contexts, and comments on the stories. These are all a rich source of oral material for anyone who wants to know more about oral folktales.

Within tale-telling communities whose oral traditions are still extant, tellers learn tales in the same way as they learn their language, as part of a holistic complex of cultural expression in a specific time and place. Tale texts are not isolated from daily life, nor are they self-consciously memorized and formally performed (that is, not as a "stage" production). Instead, they are gradually learned and absorbed through watching, listening, and imitating within the family, and then for wider audiences in the community. Traditional tellers, with the opportunity of hearing a variety of tellers and tales over long periods of time, develop a flexible concept of verbal creativity that is quite different from our literary perceptions of a story as a fixed text. They also learn, by observing many narrative styles and techniques in differing performance contexts, to find a balance between the traditional limitations of the tales and their own individuality in understanding and reinterpreting them. As Parry and Lord have emphasized in their work on Yugoslav epic poetry, such creativity is never static, and is capable of recreating not only old stories but also new ones based on traditional models.[4] It is precisely this kind of flexibility that allowed traditional European and British tales to find fresh roots in the New World.

Unlike other cultures (including Native American) where tale-telling was often limited to specific times of day or seasons of the year, much of Anglo-American storytelling could ideally take place at any time or place or situation that was socially acceptable, and for any length of time. Tellers and listeners tacitly determined what, for the moment, was socially appropriate. The precise wording and length of any given tale was in a constant state of emergence through performances in widely varied contexts. In larger public settings male narrators usually predominated, but within the intimate family or a small gathering of friends, women were active narrators.[5] An immediate example is the Hicks family mentioned earlier, who have all performed at the annual Jonesborough festival in Tennessee. While Ray and Stanley Hicks have performed regularly, Hattie Presnell has only appeared occasionally. Women tend to be seen, and to see themselves, as preservers rather than as creators of expressive forms, and thus they assume the role of passing on material to others, notably to children, rather than taking on the role of public performer.[6]

In summary, oral traditional narrators learn and perform their tales as part of a wider cultural milieu, and their tales are regarded as important artistic and cultural expressions. The tales are passed on both horizontally (intragenerationally within peer groups) and vertically (intergenerationally within family groups and the society at large), with men performing primarily in public for adults and women performing in private largely for children and close associates.

NONTRADITIONAL STORYTELLING

With the rise of liberal and universal education in the late 1800s storytelling came to be regarded as an important pedagogic tool. A lengthy study by Richard Alvey details the development of storytelling in schools, libraries, churches, and on playgrounds from the 1870s to the 1970s. Initially inspired by the innovative kindergarten programs modeled on the concepts of Friedrich Froebel, storytelling spread quickly into libraries and other child-centered institutions as a more flexible method of teaching. Classes in storytelling methods became part of educational and library school training. At one of its developmental peaks in the early part of the twentieth century, storytelling was even extolled by some as the primary means of education, along with other aspects of "folk" culture. A statement from the National Storytellers' League, founded by and for teachers in 1903, makes a strong statement along these lines: "We believe folk-culture is better than book-culture. By folk-culture we mean a rich social life in the home—folksongs, games, stories and the folk-dance; one touch of folk-lore would make the whole civilized world kin" (as cited in Alvey 36).

This sentimental misconception of "folk-culture" inspired the League to encourage storytelling among teachers at every level of public education. As the popularity of storytelling increased, however, so did the controversies over its proper functions. Some insisted that it was a wasted activity unless it offered only tales with clear pedagogic value, while others felt that stories and storytelling were valuable in and of themselves, and should not be altered to suit narrow interests.[7]

Librarians, too, were increasingly involved in storytelling and in debates over its value as either a means of leading children to books or as "art for art's sake." Librarians did not form a separate storytelling organization as had the teachers, but their national organization, The American Library Association (founded in 1876) and its publications firmly supported storytelling training and activities.

In addition to concerns about the uses of enchantment, teachers and librarians debated standards for proper storytelling: What could be considered "good" style and how were storytellers to be trained? Many books on these topics appeared, and various methods of training aspiring storytellers were proposed and tried out. Despite an abundance of organized storytelling on this continent, little agreement has ever been reached on either the value of storytelling, or on acceptable methods of training or standards for judging performance. The debate continues in contemporary storytelling magazines and newsletters across North America; these issues continue to affect the many ways in which stories are told today in organized settings. To complicate matters, storytelling courses are no longer a routine part of either library or teacher training programs today.

Contemporary storytellers who work largely in school and library settings, lacking the natural storytelling community of traditional narrators, must find their own methods of learning and performing stories, not to mention finding the stories themselves. Many attend workshops and courses that can last anywhere from a few hours to several weeks. Tellers typically perform individually in a classroom or in a library children's section, often to audiences of a dozen or more children. If adults are present they are there to accompany younger children, for whom the stories are aimed. In contrast to traditional communities, here the tellers are most often women, and this has been true since the earliest days of organized storytelling, as it was women who were the teachers and librarians.

Also in contrast to traditional narration, the school classroom and the library "story hour" restrict tellers both in physical setting and in length of performance. Most events last an hour at most, and the times are carefully scheduled in advance. The audience, too, is chosen in advance, and is supervised by teachers or librarians who often enforce "proper" behavior. Modern tellers, then, have far less flexibility and less possibility for spontaneity, since their performances are more formal. Also, the public at large no longer regards stories and storytelling as a significant literary expression. The *Märchen* in particular has lost footing, and at best is seen as child's play—or at worst as inappropriate even for young ears.[8] Thus these storytellers cannot rely on a knowledgeable audience of peers to judge their communicative competency. Often tales are *not told* at all but are read from books or recited from memory, with none of what Bauman calls "emergent quality." Nontraditional storytelling often resembles cooking from a recipe rather than recreating dishes learned from observing other cooks.

Also significant is the fact that nontraditional tellers, even those who proudly call themselves "traditional" because they favor folktales, are rarely aware of the dynamics of traditional oral narration, beyond sentimental notions of quaint old folks sitting beside a glowing fire and spinning out stories for rapt listeners.

In summary, nontraditional storytelling is no longer regarded as an important artistic expression for and by the public at large. It has been consciously learned rather than taken in as part of a cultural whole, and is offered in the restricted milieu of schools, libraries, and other child-centered contexts. Audiences are often larger, but usually composed of children. Women, who have predominated as teachers and librarians, have most often been the tellers. The dissemination of tales has been mainly from printed texts, and has been largely individual rather than either horizontal or vertical, since listeners have not been expected to pass on tales to others. In other words, there is no fully functioning oral tradition in this nontraditional context. Yet, despite their distance from actual oral telling, nontraditionalists have kept orally told tales alive for contemporary audiences, and thus provided a firm base for the development of neotraditional storytelling.

NEOTRADITIONAL TALE-TELLING

The seemingly spontaneous appearance of a more dynamic style of story-telling in the late 1960s and early 1970s is traceable to nontraditional story-telling. Many of the first performers were teachers or librarians who had given up their stable jobs for the risky life of free-lance performing. Tale-telling be-gan to move closer to oral traditional models as more tellers traveled the festi-val circuit, learning tales and techniques from other performers. Some of the other festival participants arose from actual oral traditional backgrounds, and their affect on neotraditional telling was felt as well. Folk-music festivals pro-vided a ready-made context for storytelling at first, but as this art form became better known, storytelling festivals began to appear. The two major festivals (Jonesborough, Tennessee, in 1973 and Toronto, Ontario, in 1979) spawned others across the continent. Adult audiences were attracted to old tales, and new tales formed on old models.

Since this phenomenon had not been carefully studied at its inception, its precise origins can only be surmised. Certainly the rich soil of the counter-cul-tural movement and the many folk-music festivals nourished a rich variety of revived craft and art forms, including storytelling. However nostalgic such re-vivals might have been initially, many now became firmly established as artis-tic expressions. The structure of concert stages and folk festivals provided models for storytelling events, which encouraged more performers to take the stage. One teller describes his beginnings as a storyteller in Berkeley:

> I was too old to be mistaken for a "Hippie," but as a "Beat" poet who identified with the new movement I was accepted by that generation ["Hip-pies"] and moved easily within it. Pete Seeger and Joan Baez were, and still are, very important to me, and folk music festivals were deeply moving. The performance skills and personal warmth of Pete and Joan, among others, won me over. That's when I began storytelling. I'm not a singer, so I started telling stories, and that filled a vacuum I so keenly felt in what I was doing at the time. (Harrell, 1984 letter)

As storytelling developed as an expressive art, more tellers began to experiment with a variety of creative oral styles, using many narrative models. Some, following the already-established model of the stand-up comedian, favored brief humorous anecdotes loosely strung together as purported personal experience stories. Others, often from theatrical backgrounds, developed entire routines in which stories were embedded. Increasingly, tellers of all sorts turned to the *Märchen* as a challenging medium for their messages. Such tellers viewed their performances as a deeper form of expressive art beyond the merely amusing. One well known teller, former priest and social activist Ken Feit, told storyteller and singer/musician David Holt that he saw his storytelling as a balance between entertainment and enlightenment: "I think stories should always be entertaining. It's the basic responsibility of the storyteller. But I think the kinds of stories that I like are stories that disturb, too, and raise questions" (Holt 3).[9]

Other tellers spoke of involving, provoking, and challenging listeners, of engaging them more fully in the creative process. Some favored traditional *Märchen*, folktales, and sacred tales of all sorts and from varied cultural traditions. Others created their own tales of serious fantasy. Even the most individualistic of these performers, however, emphasized originality far less than did literary authors. Ken Feit, when interviewed by David Holt, for example commented: "I call myself a storymaker as well as a storyteller. So almost all the stories I tell never existed before, until I created them inside of me. That's true in one sense, but there's also a sense that they probably pre-existed in some form I wasn't aware of—I just happened to be a vessel for that form and it became me" (2).

Such tellers bridged the gap between oral and written composition, using both printed and oral sources for their tales and composing their own versions in writing before performing them orally—not reciting them as fixed texts. American author Jane Yolen carefully shaped her fantasy stories in writing and only performed them orally when they were completed. She emphasized that she told them, rather than reading or reciting them (Yolen).

Others did the opposite, trying them out orally for live audiences before composing a written text. For example, Canadian children's author Robert Munsch composed his stories spontaneously during school performances in which children took part and made suggestions. "It may take me as long as three years of telling to get a story ready for print," he told a radio interviewer.

The connection between individual teller and specific tale remained philosophical and psychological rather than the social and cultural connections in oral tradition, since individual tellers consciously chose what stories to learn and tell before they told them publicly. Also, the emphasis was on a more dramatic performance that separated teller and listeners more forcefully than in traditional oral contexts. Thus the teller as an individualistic artist often became more important than the story he or she was telling. Concerts and festivals directed at adult audiences encouraged further development of storytelling as a theatrical event that was more familiar to audiences accustomed to mass entertainment.

Storytelling settings for festival and concert performances are even more circumscribed than those of school and library events. Not only are the stories told in specific places at very specific, pre-announced times, but they are often told from a raised stage with microphones, special lighting, and occasionally even stage settings and props. Audiences can range in size from fifty to more than a hundred, and in rare cases even into the thousands. Also, in stage-centered storytelling, more than one teller often shares the allotted time, often limited to ten or twenty minutes in duration. The more theatrical the event, the farther the distance between tellers and listeners. Finally, the theatrical nature of neotraditional performance is stimulated by the increase of seminars and workshops devoted to the self-conscious development of individual style and technique.

In a narrow sense, a virtual storytelling community of tellers and listeners has emerged in many urban areas. The establishment of an official American storytelling center in Jonesborough, Tennessee, has encouraged the emergence of local communities throughout the United States. The Storytellers School of Toronto, while not an official center in the same way, has had a similar effect on Canadian storytelling communities. However, because the Jonesborough festival is set in a rural, mountainous area in which traditional arts and crafts still existed, the organizers were able to regularly feature traditional narrators like the Hicks family mentioned earlier, along with nontraditional and neotraditional performers. Even so, the storytelling community here and elsewhere is only temporary.

It is impossible to say how long-lived these artificial communities might be, since they depend on conscious organization and are thus far less stable than societally-based traditional communities. Storytelling communities arise from a very small sub-section of their wider communities, and exist during regular meetings and perhaps occasional concerts and festivals. They can disappear quickly if people lose interest, either as tellers, listeners, or organizers. Also, tale-dissemination tends to be horizontal rather than vertical: certain tales and performance styles are periodically in fashion for a while, and then are replaced by other popular tales and styles as tellers are influenced by others performing in concerts and at festivals.

It is certainly clear that neotraditional performers who have arisen since the early 1970s vary widely in performance styles, story choices, and narrative styles. For the first few years the *Märchen*, both traditional and newly created, retained a central position in neotraditional performances. Gradually, however, more and more tellers turned away from traditional tales and focused on personal anecdotes, life experience stories, and original creations. Still, fairy tales continued to be told by many performers.

With the re-evaluation of the *Märchen* as material for adult entertainment, men re-entered the scene as narrators. This did not mean that women stepped back. They continued to retain their centuries-old position as storytellers, and held their own on concert stages with the men. In Canada and the United States in recent times, both women and men have been equally well represented at large public gatherings. For example, I surveyed the 1982 festival program while attending the 10th anniversary of the National Storytelling Festival in Jonesborough, Tennessee, where 22 women and 26 men took part as performers. Of the ten performers identified as coming from traditional backgrounds, however, only three were women, reflecting the male-dominated pattern typical public performances in such communities.[10]

As I noted earlier, neotraditional telling blends the old with the new, both in content and in style: an experienced performer may mix, blend, and bring together the flexibility of orally told traditional tales with the formality of consciously created original material. Also, the understated performance style of both traditional and nontraditional tellers might affect the more theatrical style neotraditional performers. At any given festival you might find tellers from all three of these storytelling classifications. You might also, very occasionally, see a single narrator who has passed through all three categories in her or his own personal history, beginning in traditional oral culture, being invited into library and school performances and then into festival settings, and eventually moving beyond her or his own stories and traditions into original composed material, some of which might even be produced in print. This was the case with Beech Mountain narrator Ray Hicks, who brought his traditional folk-tales to the festival stage at Jonesbourgh, and gradually shifted his repertoire to personal anecdotes, told with more animation.

As a folklorist with a deep curiosity about oral creativity, I was intrigued about all forms of oral telling that I experienced at contemporary storytelling events. It seemed to me that if verbal creativity was at the heart of much folklore investigation, these new forms of expression deserved more scholarly attention.

In summary, neotraditional tale-telling has regained some of the significance of oral expression as a viable art form for adults as well as for children. Both women and men have become equally recognized as performers in concerts and festivals, and also as workshop leaders. In neotraditional telling, stories are learned from books and other printed sources and also from other tellers during storytelling events. Because of the open nature of concerts and festivals, tales can be spread horizontally, with peers and listeners and fellow narrators, and vertically, within generations of a family, listening and later retelling the stories they heard. Also, the new contexts of public performance have brought together performers from all three of the categories I describe here. Thus the on-going interaction between traditional, nontraditional and neotraditional artists continues to blur the boundaries between them.

Contemporary tale-telling in North America is a complex phenomenon. Let us examine three narrators whose verbal artistry illustrates both the differences and the connections between the three broad categories discussed here: Donald Davis grew up in a tale-telling family in North Carolina, Laura Simms had been a librarian, and Jay O'Callahan was struggling to be an author. Thus we will be able to see how traditional, nontraditional, and neotraditional storytelling comes to life through these tellers. My comments on these performers are based on conversations with them in 1982–83, and on material by and about them in two publications: *Yarnspinner* and *National Storytelling Journal*.

Donald Davis emerged from a traditional storytelling background. His family had lived in Haywood County, North Carolina, since the late 1700s, and kept alive a rich and varied body of stories. Davis's primary narrative models were his grandmother, who told wondertales, and his uncle, who preferred humorous stories of various sorts. Davis did not set them apart in his mind as "storytellers," however, nor did he think of storytelling as a special activity but as an almost-daily event: "On days like that, storytelling was going on, but we didn't know it. There was no formal time set aside as "storytime," or any real separation of story from the total fabric of conversation. Story was the language of normal communication and the natural result of talking, much as going somewhere is the result of walking" (Stone, "To Ease" 3).

His casual view of tales and tale-telling almost caused their demise in his own life, since he took them for granted at home, but later rejected them when he began university studies. When he was introduced to the stories of Chaucer and Shakespeare, however, he began to re-examine his narrative heritage and to retell some of the stories he remembered to his classmates. "I recognized some of my stories there [in Chaucer and Shakespeare], and I also recognized that mine were better." He did not explain why he found his stories better, however.

Davis had never thought of tale-telling as a special activity for children, since his entire family was engaged in telling and listening: "In the storytelling of my childhood there was no distinction between stories for children and stories for adults. A story was told because it was to be told, not to entertain or to hold an audience. As we grew up we absorbed stories so often that the deeper and deeper levels of meaning emerged as we heard the same stories at a different age" (Stone, "To Ease" 5).

As a minister in Charlotte, North Carolina, Davis continued to perform his stories and to teach storytelling, though he did not regard himself as a "professional" storyteller: "People are always asking me when I am going to become a 'full time' storyteller. I guess I've been a full time storyteller all my life, but I just can't see myself making storytelling the end of what I do rather than the means by which I am who I am. Storytelling is not what I do for a living, but instead it is how I do all that I do while I am living" (Stone, "To Ease" 4–5).[11]

For Davis, storytelling was no more separate from his life than was his everyday language. In contrast, Laura Simms began as a library storyteller in the eastern United States, learning exotic tales from books and consciously performing them for children. Without oral models to draw on for either tales or narrative techniques, Simms had to develop her own ways of finding, learning, and performing stories. For her, research and conscious rehearsals were critical in preparing a story for performance. As an experienced teller, Simms was ready to develop her art beyond the library "story hour," and became a major performer in less than a decade. Instead of children, adults became her most frequent listeners. She founded a storytelling center in Oneonta, New York, and has developed an annual week-long storytelling residency for formally teaching her narrative techniques.

Because her connections with stories, unlike those of Donald Davis, were of necessity formal and self-conscious, Simms's relationships with her tales were more philosophical and personal rather than cultural and familial, and thus she often expressed herself more abstractly: "Storytelling is the direct and shared communication of something true about being alive. It is not only the story, but a combination of a living storyteller, situation, sound, and rhythm of voice, silence, gesture, facial expressions, and responses of listeners that makes it potent" ("Storytelling, Children, and Imagination" 2). As we can see here, her own performance experiences taught her what Davis learned by observing others as he grew up. But unlike him, Simms's library training motivated her to view storytelling as a specialized form of literature. Thus she considered herself a full-time professional storyteller carrying on an ancient art: "We have lost touch with the time when an entire village hung on a story; when every aspect of life was presented, questioned, and given meaning by story, music, dance, art, architecture and metaphor. But we still possess that common bond of existence whose continuous story we share with everyone. This is the source and power of the revival of storytelling today" (Simms, *National Storytelling Journal* 8). In her own way Simms came to understand that story and society are intimately connected, yesterday and today, and that the teller has a legacy that should be honored.

Yet another perspective is offered by Jay O'Callahan, an east coast writer who was drawn into storytelling more by chance than by design. As a neotraditional teller, in the terms I use here, he came to use and perform some of his own stories. He was a writer by profession but "a storyteller at heart," he claimed, and he found a new voice in combining these two arts: "In four years as a writer I earned $40, but I developed a hobby of entertaining children at a library by telling stories. One day a group offered me several hundred dollars to do the same thing, and soon after that the school system of Brookline [Massachusetts] paid me $2500 to tell stories to the upper grades and in the high school. It never occurred to me that I could be a professional storyteller, but suddenly I had become one." O'Callahan added another dimension to the term "professional" by measuring what he was paid in different situations, taking the category of neotraditional a further step away from oral tradition.

Like Simms, O'Callahan did not grow up in the traditional context described by Davis, and thus came to his understanding about stories and storytelling through his own experiences as a writer and as a live performer. He described storytelling as "the liveliest, most probing art in America—touching on drama, dance, healing, history, mime, music, poetry, politics—and all with a powerful intimacy" (O'Callahan). While he often performed his own written compositions, he also used folktales from around the world as he was drawn further out of his local milieu and into the festival circuit.

O'Callahan has performed nationally and internationally for large audiences of adults, and has also offered workshops of various lengths across the continent. Still, he did not lose sight of the storyteller's advantage of immediacy and intimacy. He expressed in the stories he performed and in the workshops he offered. He usually began working in his own local community of tellers in the Boston area; within this vibrant community he rehearsed his stories orally and tried out his workshop ideas. The potential impersonality of urban existence made him acutely aware of the importance of storytelling as an art form capable of touching modern audiences in the ways that listeners have always been touched by hearing a well-told tale: "Nothing has a chance to touch us very deeply these days. We need an opportunity to get away from other people's images and finally learn what is inside us" (O'Callahan).

As O'Callahan's reputation as a storyteller spread he came to use more of his own compositions, but he never abandoned the traditional folktales, including the *Märchen*. Perhaps because he went from the fixed text of writing into the flexibility of oral telling, he developed a sense of the creative possibilities of interactions with a participating audience. Thus his stories remained flexible and emergent, using Bauman's terms.

The fundamental difference between traditional narrators and non- and neo-traditional performers is the relationship between teller and community. To return to Bauman's definition of performance, all tellers discussed here assume "responsibility to an audience for a display of communicative competence" each time they perform. However, the "ability to speak in socially appropriate ways"—that is, to understand and immediately respond to one's live audience—is perceived differently by tellers and listeners in all three categories described here. In a traditional setting with a smaller and more familiar audience, where stories can arise spontaneously according to the situation, the teller can more easily determine what is socially appropriate simply by know-ing the listeners and by judging their immediate responses. In the more re-strictive and less spontaneous settings of classroom, library, and concert/festi-val stage, tellers usually present a predetermined program that offers little direct interaction with listeners. The fact that general audiences do not, in fact, form a full storytelling community, and thus are usually not personally known to the tellers, further encourages them to perform more formally rather than to be more spontaneous during storytelling events.

In general, traditional and nontraditional tellers are at opposite ends of a continuum in the relationship between teller and community. Between them are the neotraditionalists, who attempt to respond to their audiences in so-cially appropriate ways; many such tellers encourage direct interaction, trying to create an interplay between themselves and their listeners and thus to achieve some level of emergent quality. Those who reject dramatic models of mass entertainment in favor of developing this emergent quality can some-times overcome the lack of a stable storytelling community and emerge as full oral performers. As California teller Ruth Stotter wrote me in response to reading a draft of this article: "Another thought triggered by your paper was a reappraisal of what happened at my Bookseller Cafe evenings. The same peo-ple (basically) attended twice a month for 3½ years, most singles a few couples, a few families. They would stay and talk afterward, almost as if sharing the sto-ries and the time created a bond. There was a sense of community. Whenever I do regular storytelling programs like this it is an entirely different experience than a one-time performance for entertainment." Thus even an urban audi-ence can become at least a temporary "community" in the sense of being con-nected with the tellers, as was true for Jay O'Callahan in Boston.

Donald Davis, as a traditional teller who adapted to neotraditional con-texts, suggested the courtroom as an alternative to the theatrical stage as a per-formance model: "As a storyteller I do not work with a behaving audience but with an unpredictable jury. If it is clear the jury is not following my argument, I must respond to their challenge with a new approach. The evidence, the facts (the real story) don't change; by my approach, my presentation, my clothing of the facts (the words) must be retailored to suit this jury" ("Inside the Oral Medium" 7). Davis's words illustrate the dynamic tensions between traditional stability ("the real story") and innovation (his adaptations to "this jury") that is at the heart of oral storytelling.

Part of a storyteller's task is to educate an audience as well as themselves. Most audiences and most revivalist tellers, both nontraditional and neotraditional, have little or no connection with actual oral composition as it exists in traditional communities; their milieu is the printed page as a story source, and the stage as the formal setting for storytelling events. However, with increased contacts between traditional and revivalist tellers at contemporary festivals, concerts and workshops, storytelling as a fuller oral expression is coming into bloom. The relationship between written and oral literature has always been synchronic rather than diachronic, that is, there has always been an exchange between written and oral materials from both directions, oral to written and written to oral. This increasing synchronicity is illustrated by the three tellers above, Davis, Simms and O'Callahan.

Revivalist tellers have begun to free themselves from the printed page and the scripted dramatic performance by learning from other tellers. There is, however, misguided sentimentality about oral tradition, a sentimentality that is found in the works of the Grimm brothers themselves with their vague but compelling images of elderly narrators spinning out stories beside a glowing fireplace. Some modern tellers, building on this image, even call themselves "traditional storytellers" simply because they tell folktales. They see themselves as inheritors of the ancient tradition of storytelling, failing to comprehend the absence of actual diachronic (historical) relations between traditional and revivalist narration. Writer and storyteller John Harrell warned against such a nostalgic view of modern storytelling: "As literate persons, raised in a literate society, there is no way we can carry on oral tradition. We never belonged to it in the first place, and we cannot re-enter it like an astronaut coming back into earth's gravitational field" (63).

I am intrigued by the willingness of many contemporary performers to sincerely understand and review their position as inheritors of an ancient form of human expression. Neotraditional performers in particular often try to maintain a tenuous position between the full oral creativity of traditional narration and the literate tradition to which they belong and in which they receive and practice their art. Many insist that their art, despite their own literate backgrounds, is a truly oral accomplishment. Ruth Stotter, mentioned earlier, observes, for example: "The tradition has changed. Folklore is, by definition, dynamic. I feel I am a teller in the oral *tradition*. I feel comfortable calling myself a storyteller in the oral tradition because part of that tradition is people sitting down and listening to new and old tales. It is not the material alone that makes the tradition, it is the experience."

Many folklorists might insist that such narrators are not "in the oral tradition" no matter how they might view themselves, since they are not historically or culturally connected with a long-standing narrative community. I find it more useful to admit that while the revivalist tellers might not be the legitimate heirs of a full oral tradition, they are its stepchildren who demand recognition in their own right. Every *Märchen* reader will recognize the powerful claims of the neglected stepchild. I have no intention of claiming that revivalist storytellers fully parallel or succeed or even replace traditional narrators. They learn, present, and view their stories differently, and their connections with their audiences are not at all the same as in oral tradition. They do, however, function as verbal artists in rich and varied ways. In contemporary settings we can experience artists from all backgrounds and see how they diverge and converge: some, like Donald Davis, draw their folktales from a vibrant oral tradition—and at the same time tell their own original stories; others, like Laura Simms, bring vibrant new oral life to traditional tales from printed sources; still others, like Jay O'Callahan, create new stories on old models. All of them, and their many and varied contemporaries, offer us new perspectives on folktales in general and *Märchen* in particular as verbal artistry, as an expression of the people who tell and the people who listen.

Revivalist tellers provide us with the timeless artistry of the wondertale as examined by Max Lüthi, as well as with the more immediate social and artistic connections as suggested by Albert Lord, Linda Dégh and Richard Bauman. Through all the diversity and divisiveness of oral narration in contemporary North America, the *Märchen* continues its emergent quality in many contemporary performances.

7

Once Upon a Time Today

GRIMM TALES FOR CONTEMPORARY
PERFORMERS (1993)

This article on professional storytellers was another turning point. I had already written a few pieces for the nonacademic *National Storytelling Journal,* published by NAAPS in Jonesborough, Tennessee (e.g., "I Never Told," "To Ease the Heart"), but this particular writing was my first attempt to consider several nontraditional tellers and their processes of story formation for an academic publication. This chapter appeared initially in an anthology, *The Reception of the Grimms' Fairy Tales* (ed. Haase), and continued my earlier work on fairy tales. This time, however, these were presented from the point of view of the tellers, particularly those who self-consciously developed their own art of storytelling since they had not grown up in an oral tradition. As a folklorist, I was curious to see if I could continue to apply what I had learned about oral traditions and processes to this modern performing art.

Through questionnaires mailed to a variety of tellers across North America, I asked if they included Grimm tales in their repertoires, and, if so, how they treated these stories in contrast to others they told. In responding, they commented thoughtfully about their own work and about contemporary storytelling in general, and emphasized how significant it was for them to contribute to keeping this oral art alive. Many admitted that they did not favor the Grimm tales at all since these stories were too well known, but some acknowledged that they still told a few that were important to them personally, especially the more obscure tales. In addition to comments by the tellers, I included a list of the specific Grimm tales mentioned.

———

From the 1980s on, I have been first an observer of and then a participant in the so-called storytelling revival that has sprung up with apparent spontaneity in both Europe and North America. As an observing folklorist I have become fascinated with the folktale as part of an oral literature created thousands of years before writing was dimly conceived of as another way for human beings to speak to one another. Most folklorists examine folktales in the natural environment of an orally creative community, often one in which writing is still absent or at least weak as an artistic expression. My folkloristic interest has been drawn to urban professional tellers with no experience of any fully oral community.

I found that many urban storytellers I have heard in performance and in conversation have developed an understanding of the creative dynamics of composition. They do not merely repeat tales, they recreate them at each performance. It is possible for a narrative scholar to examine the correlations between texture, text, and context. Folk narrative research has been interested in discovering such correlations in traditional oral communities in which individual tellers are often too immersed in their art to answer the endless questions academics are capable of asking. Articulate urban performers are equally absorbed in their art, but since they have had to learn it consciously rather than absorbing it as part of an entire culture, they retain a self-consciousness that responds to detailed academic queries. Not surprisingly, storytellers love to talk.

As a folklorist I have been able to question a number of urban tellers about their understanding of the oral process in which they are involved. Most particularly I have wanted to find out the fate of the powerful *Märchen,* which has risen out of the long enchantment of "neverland" for many urban tellers. The folklorist in me asks how this sophisticated metaphoric genre manifests itself on the lips of those who know it only from childhood books—notably from the many translations of Grimm tales.

My view as a full participant in the storytelling revival as a performer is bound to be different. It is of direct personal interest to me that the *Märchen* seems to have returned to a full existence with adult audiences, who respond positively to the transformational and cathartic powers of this sort of narrative. Sweep away all the nostalgic trifles written today about quaint old peasants whiling away the hours before a comfortable fire—which is the sentimental view of traditional narration held by too many modern performers—and you will still find many tellers who understand that old stories do retain an ancient and uncompromising power.

The two streams of this essay flow along in their own channels and occasionally intersect: the first stream is my folkloric search for the place of traditional fairy tales in modern repertoires, and I use the Grimm collection as a model since it is still central in North American childhood reading [when this was written in 1993]. The other stream, which insists on continually flooding its banks here, is my storyteller's quest for the elusive muses of narrative artistry. I wonder if it is still possible to *tell* such stories effectively, particularly old and seemingly outdated ones, that carry the same expressive weight as good written stories, especially in an age where written literature is supreme.

Let me begin with the Grimm tales, because, as I have said, these are still the archetype and the stereotype of the fairy tale for many North American readers and listeners.

When I was conducting my dissertation research in the early 1970s one woman, Rita Romsa-Ross, reported that she assumed that the Grimm tales she read in English were English folktales. Her Mennonite mother had told her German stories *in* German (Stone, "Romantic Heroines" 314.) I was surprised to find this was true of most of the adults and children I interviewed at that time; they did not think of the Grimm tales as Germanic, but rather as "world" folk tales that belonged to everyone.

Despite the continuing popularity of this collection and its perceived position as a world treasury, I have heard very few Grimm tales told by professional storytellers. Since the tales had been so central to the dozens of people I had questioned in the 1970s I wondered if these tellers were deliberately avoiding them, or if the Grimm collection had lost its hold on North American readers. In order to find out I selected a number of professional urban performers across North America, all but one of whom I had heard in actual performance at storytelling festivals in New England, Tennessee, and California, as well as at smaller and more informal sessions.

I sent out a questionnaire to 25 tellers and received 17 responses.[1] The questions I asked were meant not only to discover the place of the Grimm tales in their repertoires, but also to uncover their understanding of the complexities of oral composition. I chose tellers who favored traditional stories and who treated them as serious literature rather than as something to parody. One teller said specifically: "I prefer not to 'fracture' fairy tales to make them more palatable to contemporary values" (Rubright). This is important to note, since some contemporary performers do "fracture" such tales, performing well-known tales ("Cinderella," "The Frog Prince," and "Hansel and Gretel" are favorite choices) as satires or parodies that proceed more from stereotypes of fairy tales as "happily ever after stories" rather than from any profound understanding of the *Märchen* genre.

The seventeen urban tellers who responded (often in depth) to my queries revealed that although the Grimm collection was certainly familiar to them, most chose to draw from less familiar material. Yet the few Grimm tales they included in their repertoires were carefully chosen for specific reasons and for particular listeners.

In order to allow these tellers to speak their own words as much as possible within the limits of this brief essay I will structure my first section in three parts, arranged according to the three basic questions I asked. The first of these was: "What part (if any) have the Grimm tales played in your tellings, both past and present?" Most responded that as children they had read the Grimms avidly and later found them to be important models for oral narration. For example, Barbara Reed, from Connecticut, says: "I consider these tales at the heart of folk fairy tales, and folktales at the heart of storytelling. Some I have told so long I don't remember when or where I first met them."

Another professional performer, Lynn Rubright of St. Louis, describes her early experience in strikingly similar words when she recalls not only the tales themselves but the human context in which these were told: "Grimm tales played an enormous role in developing my love of story as a child. My grandmother used to tell me Red Riding Hood, Jack and the Beanstalk [*not* Grimm] and Hansel and Gretel while I was nestled next to her warm body under the featherbed in the back bedroom during nap time when I was about four years old. It wasn't until years later that I recalled the warm and loving environment in which I was introduced to the Grimms' tales."

Elizabeth Ellis is a southern teller with knowledge of traditional Appalachian tales as well as childhood familiarity with the Grimm collection. She identified several Kentucky tales as being local variants of recognizable

Grimm tales: "I tell some Grimm-based fairytales. I grew up hearing Appalachian Mountain versions of some of those stories. I still tell some of them. I've messed with some of them, but others I tell pretty much the way I heard them."

Another woman, Ruthilde Kronberg, of German descent, found the Grimm tales even more central in her childhood: "As a child in Nazi Germany I used to get in trouble because I didn't do my homework. I read fairy tales instead. I think they saved my sanity because they taught me that the evil which was taking place around me would burn itself out. Which it did."

Not all contemporary tellers retained the Grimms as part of their active repertoire, however. Washington State storyteller Cathryn Wellner comments: "Though I do not tell tales from the Grimms, they have influenced me enormously. To call them favorite childhood tales is to ignore the fact that they were very nearly *the only folktales* I heard then. They taught me the pattern which still provides the frame on which I hang a tale: introduction, problem, development, denouement, conclusion. From them I learned that good triumphs over evil, that the weak can outwit the strong, that industriousness leads to success, that loyalty and honor are among the highest virtues."

It was interesting to me that the storytellers I questioned in 1987 gave the Grimm tales the same central place that they had for the children and adults I had questioned 15 years earlier as part of my dissertation research. The stories had *not* lost their popularity, as I speculated at the beginning of this essay. Quite the opposite. Respondents from both groups (1970s and 1980s) were able to name specific tales and accurate plot summaries.

Interestingly, those who were now storytellers listed a greater variety of tale titles (even when they were no longer telling Grimm tales) in response to my second question: "Can you describe any specific Grimm tales you've favored either now or in the past, and can you describe why these appealed to both you and to audiences?" Some mentioned only a few, others offered many titles. I quote Elizabeth Ellis in full because her response is both concise and detailed.

The June Apple Tree ("The Juniper Tree") I tell a lot. I love telling it because it helps people focus on those things in our culture that devour the lives of our children. Three Golden Shirts and a Finger Ring ("Seven Ravens") I enjoy telling, I guess because I have felt mute most of my life with my family. Don't Fall in My Beans ("The Lad Who Went Forth to Learn What Fear Is") is a perfect opening story—a scary/funny ghost tale. One of the most used tales in my repertoire. Beauty and Her Aunts ("The Three Spinners") never fails to get a laugh. Useful with adult audiences. Everyone appreciates a good scam. Jack and the Devil's Grandmother ("Devil with Three Golden Hairs") I used to tell, but not so much now. I really enjoy riddling stories. People seem to enjoy them a lot too. They bridge the gap between funny stories and seriously plotted tales. Mr. Fox ("The Robber Bridegroom") I tell a lot. I like its haunted quality. I also enjoy the spunky heroine.[2]

Barbara Reed names a dozen Grimm tales as part of her regular repertoire, commenting that she includes "all the old favorites, in B. Reed versions suited to the occasion."[3] She is one of the few tellers who incorporated "old favorites" instead of seeking out the lesser known tales.

The desire to find less commonly known tales was so strong that even a teller who favors the Grimms says, "I stay away from the ones popularized in this country such as 'Little Red Riding Hood,' 'Hansel and Gretel,' 'Cinderella,' 'Sleeping Beauty,' etc." Similarly Marvyne Jenoff, a Toronto writer and occasional storyteller, avoids certain stories precisely because they are well known. She says that the over-popularization of some stories "spurred me quite energetically in pursuit of unusual materials." A Winnipeg teacher and teller, Mary-Louise Chown-Quanbury, agrees that the Grimm collection is only one of many to select from: "There are so many stories to draw from that often I choose something else—eg. Nanabush, Anansi, Jack tales."

Cathryn Wellner was even more specific in her rejection of the more popularized Grimm tales: "Another of the problems in using Grimms' tales is that their adaptations and commercial uses have set up certain expectations for them. Children hearing 'Hansel and Gretel' or 'Rumpelstiltskin' have preformed images that skew the way in which they listen to the tales. I prefer to tell stories that do not set off an automatic reaction."

Of the 17 performers who responded to my questionnaire, only five identify Grimm tales as having a significant part in their usual repertoires. Only two, both German-born (Renate Schneider and Ruthilde Kronberg), build their repertoires around the Grimms. Schneider writes that "over the years I have told about 50 Grimm tales." She says that she includes both well known and obscure tales. Schneider indicates that twenty of the fifty tales she tells regularly are less commonly known stories from the Grimms, and many of the others are German tales from other sources: "Grimm tales play, of course, a big part in my repertory since I grew up with them and for me they represent and express the German countryside, where these particular versions were shaped. I tell only certain ones which to me give the special flavor of German philosophy and mood and myth." For the two German-born narrators who responded to my query, the Grimm tales are not just a collection of world tales but an intimate part of their cultural identity. As already noted, others regarded the Grimm texts in a more universal light.

Though she tells far fewer Grimm tales than Kronberg and Schneider, Elizabeth Ellis was as committed as they in expressing her reasons for regarding these tales as central: "I include the Grimm tales because they are rich and opulent sources of meaning. I can tell them over and over without tiring of them because there is always something there I never noticed before, always something powerfully parallel to my own life. I figure that must also be true of my listeners."

Barbara Reed named less than a dozen Grimm tales that she tells regularly, but still felt that these were central to her as a storyteller (as noted earlier): "I look back at the Random House/Pantheon edition [of Grimm tales], but I feel quite free and entitled to do my own versions of The Fisherman and His Wife, The Frog Prince, Snow White—fun to undo Disney—Cinderella when requested, Sleeping Beauty when I find a class of children so tired I want to put them to sleep. The Wolf and Seven Kids, Rumpelstiltskin, Rapunzel, Hansel and Gretel."

Maryland storyteller Susan Gordon wrote that she often did not know why a particular story appealed to her, but had learned that when a story (particularly the Grimm narratives) caught her attention, it usually had something deeply personal to offer her and would therefore have the potential of touching others as well. In speaking of two of her Grimm narratives, "The Juniper Tree" and "The Handless Maiden," she says in a lengthy letter: "The stories seem to be touching needs and areas of growth which I would not have named myself. [When I choose a story] my desire is to tell them a story that is, in some way, their story, which will provide them the opportunity to reflect on their own lives. In each of these instances the storytelling becomes very mutual, with the listeners not only helping you tell the story by their presence, but recreating the story and deepening it for both listeners and teller." Even though Gordon includes only the four tales ("The Handless Maiden," "The Juniper Tree," "The Boy Who Set Out to Study Fear," and "The Golden Goose") in her repertoire of "50 to 60," she insists that these are as important to her as any of her other narratives: "All of these stories make a whole for me, none is more important than the other." Like others, she notes the absence in her repertoire of the more popular titles, which she identifies as "the typical female stories, Snow White, Cinderella, Sleeping Beauty, etc."

When I compiled a full list of the stories named by these tellers I found a surprising variety of titles mentioned. I also noticed that while three of the more popular tales do still appear at the head of the list, they were far less prominent than was the case with those I interviewed in the 1970s. These titles are presented in order of frequency; responses are in parentheses, followed by Grimm (KHM) and Aarne-Thompson (AT) index numbers.

Tales Mentioned by Storytellers

Tales (no. of responses)	Grimm nos.	Aarne-Thompson nos.
Cinderella (5)	KHM 21	AT 510A
The Juniper Tree (4)	KHM 47	AT 720
Snow White (3)	KHM 53	AT 709
Hansel and Gretel (3)	KHM 15	AT 327A
Rapunzel (3)	KHM 12	AT 310
Rumpelstiltskin (3)	KHM 55	AT 500
King Thrushbeard (3)	KHM 52	AT 900
The Goosegirl (3)	KHM 89	AT 533
Wedding of Mrs. Fox (3)	KHM 38	AT 65
The White Snake (3)	KHM 17	AT 673
The Frog King (2)	KHM 1	AT 440
The Seven Ravens (2)	KHM 25	AT 451
Snow White and Rose Red (2)	KHM161	AT 426
The Robber Bridegroom (2)	KHM 40	AT 955
The Three Spinsters (2)	KHM 14	AT 501
Gifts of Little Folk (2)	KHM 182	AT 503
Maid Maleen (2)	KHM 198	AT 870
Rich Man and Poor Man (2)	KHM 87	AT 750A
Boy Who Went Forth . . . (2)	KHM 4	AT 326
Frau Holle (1)	KHM 24	AT 480
Brother and Sister (1)	KHM 11	AT 450
Jorinda and Joringel (1)	KHM 69	AT 405
Three Little Gnomes . . . (1)	KHM 13	AT 403B

continued

Tales Mentioned by Storytellers (*continued*)

Tales (no. of responses)	Grimm nos.	Aarne-Thompson nos.
The Three Feathers (1)	KHM 63	AT 402
The Water of Life (1)	KHM 97	AT 551
The Star Coins (1)	KHM 153	AT 779
The Singing Bone (1)	KHM 28	AT 780
The Twelve Brothers (1)	KHM 9	AT 451
The Two Brothers (1)	KHM 60	AT 567A
The Strange Musician (1)	KHM 8	AT 151
The Turnip (1)	KHM 146	AT 1960D
The Old Man and His Grandson (1)	KHM 78	AT 930B
Three Golden Hairs . . . (1)	KHM 29	AT 930
The Golden Goose (1)	KHM 64	AT 571
Maiden Without Hands (l)	KHM 31	AT 706
Bremen Town Musicians (1)	KHM 27	AT 130
Three Sons of Fortune (1)	KHM 70	AT 1650
The Queen Bee (1)	KHM 62	AT 554
Three Green Twigs (1)	KHM 206	AT 756A
Spindle, Shuttle, Needle (1)	KHM 188	AT 585
The Fisherman and His Wife (1)	KHM 19	AT 555
Brier Rose (1)	KHM 50	AT 410
Wolf and Seven Kids (1)	KHM 5	AT 123
The Tailor in Heaven (l)	KHM 35	AT 800
Frau Trude (1)	KHM 43	AT 334

As this list reveals, even "Cinderella" has only five tellers, and the other favored tales only two each. "Sleeping Beauty" was named by a single teller, and "Little Red Cap" does not appear at all except as a tale that is *avoided* because of its popularity (both Jenoff and Renate Schneider mention it negatively). Of the 46 titles mentioned, 40 are in the category of "romantic" or "magic" tales. Only four are animal tales (AT 65, 123, 130, 151) and two are humorous anecdotes (AT 1650 and 1960D). Interestingly the latter are named by male tellers. Theses titles reflect the exaggerated position that romantic "fairy tale" texts hold in most popular English translations that feature only 30–60 of the full Grimm collection.

Seven tellers maintained that the Grimm tales were not a regular part of their performing repertoire, six of these explaining that they preferred lesser known sources. Only one, Elizabeth Nash of Winnipeg, rejected the Grimms completely on the basis of their violence, though she did recall a few childhood favorites:

> I don't remember ever telling a Grimm story. That was not the result of a conscious decision. The brutality of some of the stories shakes me even now: the community that drove spikes into a barrel, forced an old lady into it and rolled it down the hill; the gang that heated iron shoes red hot, jammed them on an erring woman's feet and made her dance until she died. *This* child was distressed to tears by them on more than one occasion, and possibly that's why *this* adult has not told Grimm stories.

Interestingly she lists "Hansel and Gretel" and "Rumpelstiltskin" as former favorites, though both have violent resolutions. She also remarks that as a result of completing the questionnaire she decided she might try to tell "King Thrushbeard," a current favorite. (In fact she did try it at a small and informal Winnipeg storytelling group, Stone Soup Stories, in the winter of 1988. Her story was well received.)

John Harrell is another teller/author who has told very few Grimm tales; He names only "The Bremen Town Musicians" and "The Three Gifts of Fortune" ["The Three Sons of Fortune"]. In explaining why he tells these two he reveals his own understanding about the inherent power of old oral stories: "Bremen Town Musicians was a favorite tale of my wife's and when I would tell it to her, it always made her laugh heartily. It was good therapy. I [also] liked Three Gifts of Fortune because, like Bremen, it is so easy to tell." It is true that the Grimms have been justifiably recognized as editors of rather than as scientific collectors of authentic orally generated stories. Many of their reworked texts manage to express the not-so-simple simplicity Harrell mentions.

It is almost two centuries since the "Grimm Tales" were gathered together in another place and in another time and without a developed scholarly approach to authentic collecting, then translated into other languages and spread to other times and places. And still they have the potential to become vibrantly relevant to non-Germanic people like most of the tellers I have introduced thus far. All of these narrators had a clear idea of their reasons for telling tales orally, Grimm and otherwise, in response to my third and last question: "Why do you either include *or* exclude Grimm tales in your repertoire now." For example, Susan Gordon comments on her storytelling as a human expression that goes beyond theatrical diversion:

> When I entertain, it is my intent to just tell the story absolutely alive and let it do and be whatever it is supposed to be—funny, mysterious, scary, etc. That same thing holds true in any setting, but in therapeutic, educational and religious settings, the story is chosen with care to the occasion, with some knowledge of the people I'm telling it to. In those settings, often I have developed some ways to help us reflect on the story, think about it, and feel it more deeply, as well as providing a way for people to respond creatively.

Gordon seems to have developed a thorough understanding of this aspect of verbal artistry from her own experiences, despite her lack of contact with any specific oral tradition.

Several expressed this developed sense of narration as an emergent exchange between narrators and listeners brought together in storytelling events.[4] (John Harrell, for instance, highlights the difference between narrating and reading: "I prefer to tell tales rather than to read them because the communication is direct between me and the other person(s). With reading, the story is in the book. With telling, the story is part of me and I'm giving that part of me to you."

Toronto performer Marylyn Peringer also underlines the direct power of spoken rather than read or recited words: "I don't ever write out a text that I am learning. Writing freezes it, and then it freezes me. I just talk to myself when I'm alone—out loud, of course, getting through the story part by part until it sounds right."

For Jane Yolen, who both writes and tells stories, finding one's own "voice" is important: "I keep defining and then redefining what stories mean to me and how I can transmit that feeling (and those stories) in the best possible manner to others. When I listen to others tell, I realize that as good as they are, they are not me. I have to take the story again into my own mouth."

Each of the 17 tellers had their own firm ideas of what the oral process meant to them as recreated through their own words. California artist Ruth Stotter, for example, asserted that she found her personal connections while preparing and telling a story, and often was able to give her listeners a chance to discover and reveal their own: "At present I tell just a few stories from the Grimms—those that fascinate me by their symbolic interpretations and my psychological reverberations—giving me a chance to step back and ponder life. I often tell Grimm tales to adult audiences and we usually have a discussion afterward."

Many of the 17 considered their storytelling role as potentially transformational for the listeners as well as for the story. The words of Cathryn Wellner are most appropriate: "Though I avoid moralistic and didactic stories like some dread disease and squirm when I am forced to sit through one, I nevertheless perceive the storyteller's role as that of moral and spiritual bellwether in a secular society. The first task of the story is to entertain, for only entertaining stories will be heeded. But once the attention is focused we must ask ourselves, 'To what end?' I want my stories to be affirmations of hope, of belief in humanity's basic goodness."

At first glance these words seem to echo the sentiments expressed by Zipes in his introduction to his recent translation of the Grimm tales, when he says: "Today we have inherited their [the Grimm brothers] concerns and contradictions, and their tales still read like innovative strategies for survival. Most of all they provide hope that there is more to life than mastering the art of survival. Their 'once upon a time' keeps alive our utopian longing for a better world that can be created out of our dreams and actions" (*Complete Fairy Tales* xxvi).

Indeed these tellers would agree that the Grimm tales have offered them, as children if not still as adults, "innovative strategies for survival." But because story*telling* is most effectively done in the ethnographic present, the survival strategies are not utopian, not dreams of the future. These old stories still have the potential power they have always had to identify and address the most basic human concerns and contradictions as they manifest themselves today.

A more concrete example will bring this immediate aspect of told stories more clearly into focus. I use "The Juniper Tree," which was commented on by four of those who responded. This is one of the very few Grimm tales in which a victimized protagonist, in this case the boy murdered by his stepmother and devoured by his father, avenges himself directly rather than having the villain punished obliquely. Here the boy returns to life as a bird and rewards his loving sister and father by dropping down gifts, but punishes his mother by dropping a millstone on her. He then regains his human shape.

Each of the four expressed their own immediate reasons for finding this particular tale so compelling. Marylyn Peringer was moved by the simplicity of the story as told by a French performer: "I heard Bruno LaSalle tell it simply, movingly, and [he] sang the song of the bird as composed by one of the musicians in his storytelling troupe."

Marvyn Jenoff comments on the current popularity of the story with adult and mixed-age Toronto audiences as a result of two particularly influential tellers (Joan Bodger, who is a therapist and storyteller, and Alice Kane): "Both seem to feel that children need the violence in folktales to help them understand and articulate their own lives, which include at least the *awareness* of violence."

Elizabeth Ellis, too, says that she herself tells the story often in its Appalachian variant ("The June Apple Tree"). In fact she lists it first among the stories she identified as "Grimm" tales. As I quoted earlier, she says: "I love telling it because it helps people focus on those things in our culture that devour the lives of our children." Ellis's telling is close to the variant told by Kentucky narrator Uncle Blessing, who told it to Marie Campbell (*Tales from Cloud Walking*) in the 1930s.

Susan Gordon also tells this tale frequently, and she is considerably more expansive on her reasons for so doing: "Juniper Tree is a story which I told initially at a conference on the existence of evil. I had never told it before, but had developed the song for it. I planned to tell other stories, but the types of evil people were discussing—rape, batterings, sexual abuse, etc.—just seemed to call for that story. I talked to the fellow who hired me to tell, and he remembers the story as being as frightening as Stephen King is frightening, but offering hope." Gordon stresses that in telling it she follows the Grimm tale "with great beauty and faithfulness" while at the same time developing its immediate relevance, first by working through the characters and motivating forces for herself as she prepares the tale, and then through discussions with the audience.

> The trick of this story for me was allowing each character to stand out on their own. One of the best responses this story has received is when I told it to a long-term spiritual direction group I was leading and then had the listeners each take a character from the story and relive the story from that point of view, asking themselves what culpability each character had in the boy's death. It was an extraordinary process, in which each person was able to ad-

dress how they had contributed to the child's death and we began to see the step-mother as not just evil, but as incredibly isolated.

With Gordon and the other narrators "Juniper Tree" returns fully to life, ever emerging anew for each teller and for each audience. I too have experienced this emergent aspect while developing the Grimm tale "Frau Trude" (Grimm 43, AT 334). In this odd little tale a girl who is too curious encounters a witch who rewards her curiosity by turning her into a block of wood and throwing her on the fire. Interestingly, the story does not actually state that the girl was destroyed, which gave the tale a sense of incomplete resolution that left room for further creativity. I began playing with the idea of fire as an element of transformation, which brought the girl back to life in the form of a fiery bird. Through a succession of elemental transformations by Frau Trude the girl passes through the four elements of fire (as wood), air (as bird), water (as fish), and earth (as hare). After this she is challenged to free herself by telling one story that has never been heard before, and she goes out into the world to learn all the stories she can. When she returns a year and a day later to tell her stories she finds that Frau Trude has heard them all. Lacking any other, she begins in desperation to tell the story of her own adventures, and thus discovers that this is the unknown story that frees her.[5]

In June 1988 I was telling this story for an audience in Windsor, Ontario. I had just completed the girl's desperate words of her own story, "Once there was a girl who was too curious" and the audience began to applaud before I could reach the concluding lines, "and so she went free." I stopped in surprise, then realized that they had spontaneously discovered a more natural ending to my story, one that makes the tale circular by beginning and ending with the same words. This became my usual resolution from that time on.

Later that same year I told the story to a small audience gathered at the home of a friend in Quebec City, where I was visiting. Her daughter wondered why the girl had to go through all of the transformations. These seemed unnecessarily complex and puzzling to her. I recognized her instinctive recognition of the story's natural simplicity, and reduced the transformations to (fire/wood and air/bird), having her cross over water and earth to complete the cycle in her own shape.

Finally, in the spring of 1989 my story was retold to me (and the rest of the adult audience) by an 11-year-old boy who had heard it once from his mother.

They both insisted that they told it exactly as I had, but in his variant the girl remained in the shape of the bird until she had successfully told her story. It was immediately obvious to me that this was a more genuine and organic form for her, since she is more clearly in Frau Trude's power until her story is finally told.

Each of these transformations clarified the story by intuitively simplifying and rationalizing it. This delicate and vibrant balance between traditional stability and individual innovation is the very core of the creative process in oral composition. The narration of story is a perpetually emergent form of artistic expression; in the context of storytelling the texture of the story emerges as narrator and audience interact. Cathryn Wellner describes this exchange eloquently:

> The real work and the real joy come when I tell the partially formed story to an audience for the first time. I used to nearly work a story to death before testing it on an audience. Now I lay the framework and then begin telling it. There are a few things with which I am comfortable at that point: I know the story line, the nature of the characters, essential details, places in which I want to use a chant or a song, and something of the culture. The audience teaches me what the story is about, and each audience teaches me something slightly different. Through their reactions, I see where the story takes wings and where it is earthbound. Eventually, after many tellings, the story takes a shape which I tend to return to each time. It will always be fluid and unrepeatable. Sometimes an especially attuned audience will give me a moment of such clarity that I am stunned. The story becomes fresh and new.

The immediacy of the storytelling experience as described by Wellner and others quoted here emphasizes the fact that for them storytelling is not primarily a theatrical event confined by the convention of the fourth wall. Instead they address themselves candidly to the audience, and in some cases (particularly in more informal contexts) the audience responds with equal directness.

We have seen that the Grimm tales have lost their primacy in terms of quantity; most of the tellers do not feature many of the Grimm texts in their repertoires. However, the *variety* of titles mentioned is much greater than those recalled by the children and adults I interviewed in the early 1970s. Several tellers identified this collection as having provided a valuable model for an oral repertoire.

But why do urban performers bother with any traditional tales at all? In considering this question I have kept in mind the words of two narrative scholars, Max Lüthi and Linda Dégh, who in their own separate ways have devoted careful attention to the *Märchen* as a profound human expression.

While Dégh focuses on tales and tellers as they live in actual performance, Max Lüthi takes a more traditional literary view and examines tales in depth as artistic expressions that transcend tellers and times. In fact Lüthi becomes so deeply involved in describing traditional literature—notably the *Märchen*—that he himself becomes a storyteller who ponders the fate of traditional narratives that have served humankind for centuries. In a concluding chapter of *The European Folktale* he asks what new form of expression might equal the *Märchen* in offering a "new language of symbols," a modern expression that might "offer a playful overview of human existence." "In this future 'glass bead game,' science and art, fragmentary perception and comprehensive vision, and actuality and potentiality would come together as a unity, and the ancient contrast between folktale and legend would cease to exist" (*European Folktale* 106). His inspiration comes from Hermann Hesse's last novel, *The Glass Bead Game (Magister Ludi)*, in which the fictional narrator describes the twentieth century as a time of "gigantic consumption of empty whimsies," an age in which people have "struggled through a deluge of isolated cultural facts and fragments of knowledge robbed of all meaning" (Hesse 14). In response, a few creative thinkers have formulated a complex and meaningful form of play called The Glass Bead Game, "a new alphabet, a new language of symbols through which they [the players] could formulate and exchange their new intellectual experiences" (27).

In his interpretation of Hesse's inspired words Lüthi, a formalist, seems to assume that any "new language of symbols" would be expressed in a new literary form that would supersede old oral forms. I find Lüthi's optimism refreshing in his hope for a "new folktale" that will join poets and scientists in creative collaboration, but I think he has failed to give the told story its due as a continuing artistic expression.

Folklorist Dégh has always been interested in examining the endlessly creative methods that traditional narrators employ in weaving together tellers and tales and listeners. She has studied a glass bead game as it actually lives in our own world. And she has listened carefully and remembered thoughtfully. In a recent article on "The Snakeprince" (AT 425) she observes that the telling of *any* tale takes place in the ethnographic present, and that each tale has the possibility of making "the world of fantasy palpable by connecting it with the world of everyday reality" ("Snakeprince" 2). The urban tellers I questioned seem on the whole to be doing exactly this—performing in an ethnographic present, using old fantasies to speak to current realities without sacrificing the integrity of any traditional narratives they use. Dégh also emphasizes the deeply personal connection between tale and teller in words that are applicable to contemporary performance: "The told story also mirrors the narrator's specific conceptualization of the world and its affairs: his cultural and personal meanings. . . . The storyteller is never neutral but emotionally involved when featuring the personality of the cast" ("Snakeprince" 2).

It is clear from many the words of the tellers themselves that they are as personally involved in their stories as are good traditional narrators. But they are not self-indulgently so. Their interest is in breaking through the boundaries of the individual self, as well as breaking through the borders of the conventional fourth wall of the theatre. For them the told tale is the personal vehicle for this breakthrough and re-connection.

I often hear from my students that storytelling is a dead art, that the "fairy tale" in particular is frivolous and irrelevant. Not so. With many contemporary narrators these old stories take on new relevance, whether told fully, as with "The Juniper Tree" or "Frau Trude," or told more indirectly, as in the personal narratives of tellers like Wellner. Contemporary urban narration offers an impassioned challenge now, in *this* ethnographic present, and not in some utopian future. Wellner observes, for example: "There is a carelessness that runs through the industrialized western world. . . . If our only stories are those we read in the newspaper or watch on television or film, we can hardly be blamed for a sense of hopelessness. We need other stories, stories which celebrate life in all its complexity, stories that prod us to look at the world in fresh ways, stories that pose hard questions."

Wellner is one of many contemporary tellers for whom childhood contact with old oral tales, filtered through the printed medium, led to an understanding of a process of creation paralleling traditional oral composition. For such tellers the old *Märchen* (and other types of tales) have offered direct and indirect models for a personal, face-to-face artistic exchange that has the potential for simultaneously transforming tellers, tales, and listeners. In the immediate context of storytelling events old stories take on newly textured contours. The echoes of Grimm tales can still be heard in this new "glass bead game."

8

Social Identity in Organized
Storytelling

(1998)

A brief version of this essay was presented orally as a paper at the American Speech Communication Association in Atlanta, Georgia, in 1991 and later printed in *The Appleseed Quarterly*. I rewrote it at greater length for a festschrift in *Western Folklore* honoring Robert Georges for his pivotal work on storytelling events as forms of communication. I further developed it as a chapter in my book-length treatment of storytelling (*Burning Brightly*), and it was this version that I chose to include here. With Robert Georges's work on oral events in mind, I wanted to see how nontraditional performers actually came to call themselves storytellers. Narrators in oral traditions grow up with a "social identity," often from within their own family. Linda Dégh's long exploration of Hungarian narrators made it clear that the tellers themselves were clearly identified by their communities and had no need for self-identification. For nontraditional tellers the situation was more complex. I was curious to find out how they recognized their moments of identity, both self-proclaimed and socially recognized. Those I interviewed not only commented on their personal experiences, but on how they viewed the storytelling revival as a whole, and, of course, their place in it. For some, the moment of recognition was a dramatic "aha," while for others it was a gradual understanding that evolved as they gained experience. Like tellers in the full oral tradition, it was face-to-face contact in storytelling events that brought learning and recognition of who they were and what they were doing.

This was an exciting article to research and write, since it put me into contact with tellers in Canada and the United States who have a rich variety of backgrounds and interests. It spurred me to do further work on a topic that was fresh, new, and a bit daunting, since many folklorists still did not consider contemporary "platform storytelling" an apt subject for scholarly consideration. I wanted to see how far I could go with it.

Anyone present at an organized storytelling event would no doubt hear performers recount how they discovered when and why they had become storytellers. These narratives are not as simple as they might seem, since they involve on-going perceptions of emerging social identity by both tellers and listeners. Oral accounts on stage, along with written descriptions by tellers in directories and festival programs, reveal how tellers express their artistic and social decisions. How they describe themselves is often an indication of the performance style of the tellers, as well as their formative connections. For example, Ottawa teller Jan Andrews, who favors epics, writes: "I began telling stories as a result of organizing a program at Expo 86, hearing some of the great all-time tellers and marvelling at the depth and power of their work. A professional storyteller and children's writer, I prefer traditional material and have a particular interest in epics" (*1997/98 Canadian Storytelling Directory* 38). I have heard her present eloquent versions of long myths and epics in an effective low-key style, influenced by other tellers in the library-educational stream. Her self-descriptions in Toronto festival programs were similar in tone and style.

Toronto teller Dan Yashinsky's entries reveal a different approach to self-description. In many of the Toronto festival programs Dan focused on his primary position as the initiator of the 1001 Friday Nights of Storytelling and as one of the founders of the Storytellers School and its annual festival. For several years his entries were variations on this theme, emphasizing his contributions to the Toronto storytelling community. A reader would not guess from these entries that he was a stimulating performer with a dramatic style of presentation. His directory entry offers a striking contrast to his festival program descriptions; here his role as founder disappears and he reveals a different kind of energy: "Born to a crossroads heritage, I tell traditional stories from around the world. I call my approach "Scheherajazz"—a mix of wonder tales, personal memory, and of-the-moment stories" (*1997/98 Canadian Story-telling Directory* 46). Unlike Jan Andrews' description this entry does not re-late how Dan came to storytelling, but it does hint at his performance style by referring to both Scheherazade and to the legendary crossroads as a place of magical transformation.

Another contrast in the self-descriptions of these two tellers is that Jan An-drews emphasizes her connections with other tellers within her community, while Dan Yashinsky focuses on his own work as an original creator. Yet both are equally committed to, and identifiable by, their storytelling communities. The development of self-identity is a complex and exciting process, one that continues as long as a teller continues to perform. In this chapter I explore tellers at various stages of self-discovery as they struggle to find their place within specific storytelling communities and events.

Folklorist Robert Georges described storytelling events in a way that em-phasized their social and communicative aspects, whether events took place in traditional or in organized contexts; I find his inclusive statement to be an ef-fective position for examining organized storytelling. I stress this inclusiveness because many folklorists did not consider organized storytelling to be a proper subject for academic research. Robert Georges was one of the first folk-lorists to offer a path of investigation that opened the way for such an ap-proach. "There is nothing especially authentic or traditional about the mes-sages of storytelling events generated by the actions of the nonliterate or the preliterate, for storytelling events constitute one kind of communicative event within the continua of human communication and one kind of social experi-ence within the framework of social interrelationships among people, irre-spective of their relative social, educational, and economic statuses" (Georges 323).

Storytelling in all of its contexts is a dynamic experience in which partici-pants assume social identities as tellers and as listeners. In organized story-telling the social roles of tellers and listeners are often more rigidly defined than in casual "kitchen table" telling where conversation and stories flow back and forth. In contrast, as we have seen, platform tellers perform formally, often on a stage separating them from listeners, while audience members listen without interrupting. Both Jan Andrews and Dan Yashinsky, mentioned above, have become experienced tellers after some years of stage experience, but of course they began more modestly. This would be apparent if we had a series of self-descriptions over the years.

Organized events may take the form of hour-long concerts featuring a few tellers or festivals with dozens of performers, each of whom has found their own way to establishing a personal and social identity through direct experience in whatever venues and contexts they were able to find. That is, it is not enough to call oneself a teller; you have to convince others that this is so. The social and personal dynamic of organized storytelling is not unlike that of traditional narration in this case. Folklore scholar Robert Adams, who studied a Japanese woman who had developed as an active storyteller (although Adams uses a masculine pronoun here) observed that "in order for an individual to become identified in his community as storyteller, he must have sufficient opportunity to practice the craft, both in order to perfect his technique and to gain the recognition that only comes from wide exposure to an entire community" (355).[1] Adams underlined social identity as a dual process, a continually evolving perception that unfolded as narrators participated in events and evolved personal style and technique.

Self-definition is central to artistic development. In the case of organized storytelling, perhaps more than in traditional narration, there is often a confused sense of what it means to be called, or to call oneself, a storyteller. The term is vague enough to cover a multiplicity of performance arts: reciting memorized pieces or reading from books, relating personal anecdotes, satirizing and parodying folktales, doing one-person drama or stand-up comedy, or mime, dance, and puppetry. Obviously any teller's previous training will affect how they view themselves as performers, but as we saw earlier, the boundaries of professional identities are fluid. A teacher becomes an actor, an actor becomes a spiritual teller, a traditional narrator shifts from folktales to personal anecdotes (as master narrator Ray Hicks did in the course of his performances at public festivals).

I have been curious to learn what stages tellers mark as memorable in the process of their development from telling stories casually, as we all do, to taking on an identity as a storyteller. Not surprisingly, storytellers often communicate their formative experiences in narrative form, both orally and in writing. Joseph Sobol, who interviewed almost 100 American tellers, called these stories "vocational narratives" throughout his 1994 doctoral dissertation, "Jonesborough Days." Sobol's material is particularly rich in providing this kind of information in both breadth and depth. He cites numerous instances of formative identity stories—"And that's when I knew I was a storyteller"—for which I had largely anecdotal information. He claimed that experienced tellers have at least one and usually more stories that mark the stages of their conscious development as performers and that they regularly repeat these anecdotes as part of their performances.

I began to wonder how tellers define themselves after hearing formative stories told both on stage and informally at the first Jonesborough festival I attended in 1982. My formal quest, however, began in 1989 when I took part in a weekend retreat sponsored by the Storytellers School of Toronto. I noticed that one topic that kept arising spontaneously in conversation was the ways in which these people had come to recognize that they were storytellers in more than the casual sense of the word. I wanted to know how they had come to perceive and accept this social identity.

When I began to question participants at the 1989 retreat, I expected to hear variations on a typical statement I overheard many times at festivals and other events; these were usually delivered in a tone of awe and often concluded with the phrase, "and that's when I knew that *I* was a storyteller." The speakers often spoke the words as if they had had a conversion experience, which is appropriate phrasing for a movement described as a "revival." I continued to eavesdrop, fascinated with these assertions. Some of the tellers had been listeners at an event and said to themselves, "Well I could do that too" and consciously began to develop a new identity. Or they had been inspired by a teller and decided that they had been "called" to become a teller. Here are three brief examples quoted from Joseph Sobol's work, in the words of tellers who could name the moment when they assumed their identities:

"And at that moment I came to the notion of storytelling as my life-work." ("Jonesborough Days," 384)

"The most wonderful thing happened to me today: I have found out who I am! I'm a storyteller." (132)

"And that's when I knew. I just told people, 'I'm a storyteller.' And that's what I've been doing ever since. I've never turned my back on that. I haven't had a regular paying job with benefits since." (335–36)

Most of the responses I heard at the retreat, however, were not phrased in such a dramatic way. When I asked people there if there had been a particular moment when they recognized themselves as storytellers they did not make the pronouncements Sobol and I had were familiar with. Their "vocational narratives" were less focused on particular moments, more introspective. I guessed that the more intimate context of the retreat setting influenced the nature of their replies so I broadened the base by putting notices in storytelling newsletters in both Canada and the United States. All those who answered had already assumed their identities as tellers. Their responses, like those I had heard at the retreat, were retrospective rather than dramatic, looking back to the experiences they identified as formative moments. Some found these moments in childhood storytelling experiences and others recalled later periods of their development. All understood that they had been storytellers for some time and that their identity had evolved with their artistic (and life) experiences. Those who answered my published request by letter are cited by letter and date. Uncited material is from the oral and written responses gathered at the retreat. It will become clear from their replies that these particular tellers had undergone lengthy apprenticeships before becoming fully conscious of themselves as public performers.

Mary-Eileen McClear, from West Baden, Ontario, recalled taking her older sister's white mittens at age eight. She told her friends that her own mittens had turned from black to white because they were made of the fur of ermines, who turn white in winter. She saw with some surprise that she had become a storyteller in their eyes and explained: "I wasn't trying to impress them, or to lie. I remember thinking of it as a challenge: how much would they believe, how well could I convince them?"

Nan Brien remembered friends begging for stories when she was twelve. "They would chant, 'Nan! Tell us a story,'" and she complied. "At that time of my life, I knew that I was a big sister, a babysitter, a camper, and now best of all, a storyteller."

As a teenager Celia Lottridge decided on her own to entertain a group of children in wheelchairs at an afternoon party, but at this time she was already an experienced raconteur from having entertained her younger sister with stories when they were twelve and five, respectively: "I often told stories to her in the back seat of the car as we drove somewhere. I have no idea whether anyone else listened but Lucy certainly did."

Carol McGirr, a Toronto school librarian specializing in lengthy sagas and myths, told me an epic tale about discovering the essence of storytelling when she decided, at age six, to memorize *Peter Rabbit* so that she would still have the story even when she no longer had the book: "I'm sure the kids in the neighborhood were sick of Peter Rabbit. We'd be out in the yard playing ball and then we'd sit down to rest, and I'd start, 'Once upon a time there were four little Rabbits who lived with their mother under the roots of an old fir tree, and their names were Flopsy, Mopsy, Cottontail, and Peter.' And it would go on and on until I finished the whole story" (McGirr).

Childhood memories framed the later development of Mary-Eileen, Nan, Celia, and Carol, providing them with the first of many other moments of recognition as storytelling became part of their professional lives. In contrast, George Blake grew up surrounded by stories in Jamaica, but his early storytelling background did not at first come to mind when he emigrated to Canada. He says, "I never heard the term 'storyteller' when I was a boy in Jamaica, though I was exposed to hearing many stories from 'elders,' teachers, and my contemporaries." He could not understand why urban tellers were so concerned about calling themselves storytellers, until he experienced his own moment of recognition, as an adult in Canada: "Some weeks after I had told stories at my local public library (to an adult audience) a woman approached me in a store and asked, 'Aren't you the storyteller who was at the library?' That was when I received my identity as a storyteller."

Others reported similar responses that fostered their self-recognition. Lynn Williams was surprised at the effect her first story had when she told it as part of her job as interpreter at a historic house in London, Ontario: "I had learned a suitable version of the legend of the Blue Willow and told it at the next opportunity. The children were captivated and I was overwhelmed at the intensity of their attention to the story. I felt the power of storytelling as a teller and it was an inspiring sensation."

Several people could recall specific individuals who not only recognized what they were doing but named it. Canadian writer and performer Robert Munsch, for example, described an incident in 1979 in which he was entertaining two children in a car on the way to the airport. He reported the boy, Otis, saying, "You're a storyteller. You're a *fancy* storyteller." He had considered storytelling to be hobby but began to take it more seriously: "From that point on I decided that that's what I had become and that's what I was going to be" (Munsch, letter to the author). This was the kind of anecdote I had heard from various American tellers describing how the title "storyteller" had been conferred on them by a listener, often expressed in legend style.

Yet even after experiencing such an affirmation of the potency of directly related narratives, tellers still mentioned a sense of inadequacy once the actual storytelling event ended. Carol Howe was initially thrilled by her first performance but then expressed ambivalence: "Several people came up afterward to tell me how much the story meant to them—and for the rest of the evening I felt like a storyteller. The next day I knew only that I could tell stories." She added, "The response is crucial—you can't be a storyteller with no audience."

For Mary-Eileen McClear the immediacy of storytelling events influenced her sense of social identity: "It's not something I consciously think about or question until someone questions me and then I begin to wonder. Am I really a storyteller, am I fooling myself, cheating the people who come to hear a 'real' storyteller? The doubt can run riot until the next time I tell a story."

Paula Graham, a high school math and science teacher, said she had been using stories in class for years yet still felt uneasy calling herself a storyteller, though her listeners, in this case her high school students, saw her as one: "It's gradual. I'm becoming aware. I sometimes feel like a pretender to the title of storyteller. Even though the 'nature of the beast'—*homo narrans*—is to be a storyteller, I don't usually see myself as a one. But my students do."

Indeed, listeners play a role even when they are not at all aware of it. This is central in oral societies where narrating is still highly regarded and storytelling events still offer ample contexts for human creativity. In organized storytelling, however, the teller assumes (often by default) more responsibility than the community in developing a social identity because storytelling is not widely regarded as a performing art. This means that the opportunities for formal narration are limited and must be sought out or even created by the performers, who cannot simply wait for spontaneous storytelling events to occur. Even though more tellers and listeners now recognize storytelling as a performance art, self-recognition is still problematic. Social identity does not arise from the community as a whole as it does in a more traditional context. Instead, tellers develop their sense of vocation from their experiences in a series of storytelling events. They are led to self-definition by different groups of listeners who may not, in a meaningful sense of the word, form a community at all and who may be quite inexperienced about the aesthetics and the dynamics of oral performance.

As we have already seen, those who tell stories as part of their occupation are often confused about their possible identity as tellers. Alice Bur from Mississauga, Ontario, began to use storytelling to develop new teaching techniques; she was comfortable narrating in her own classroom, but ambivalent about regarding herself as a storyteller outside of it: "Sometimes I think I'll give up teaching and perhaps go into classrooms in a new capacity—as a storyteller! But then once again I come back to the reluctance I feel about moving in that direction. I don't want to be a storyteller/performer. I don't feel ready."

Her sense of not being prepared is a part of the challenge of developing a social identity. Since the community at large does not offer what Adams calls "sufficient opportunity to practice the craft," which is how storytelling is learned in traditional contexts, urban tellers must learn in other ways. They can take workshops and classes but this does not guarantee performance opportunities. Identity comes only from on-going direct experience, constant interaction between listeners and tellers. Despite statements to the contrary no one can confer the title of "storyteller" on anyone else, though such pronouncements may help tellers see themselves in a new light.

The growth of storytelling as a money-making profession has caused full-time tellers to rethink their social identities. As Mary-Eileen McClear put it earlier, she was worried that she was not, in fact, a "real" storyteller. I heard similar responses from other retreat participants who did not want to lose their initial exuberance for storytelling in order to become self-supporting professional performers.[2] Furthermore, some people who opportunistically describe themselves as professional storytellers in directories and publicity brochures may not have much experience in storytelling events at all. As Ruth Stotter, a performer who also heads a certificate program in storytelling, notes: "Anyone who takes a class or sometimes even a single workshop can declare themselves a storyteller and begin to charge for their service. How do we distinguish between amateurs and professionals then, especially since there are many misconceptions about what storytelling is and is not?"[3] This was not the case in the earlier history of the profession, when both library and educational professions offered training programs that prepared students for storytelling in a disciplined way.

While my formal interview sampling here is small, I have supplemented it with rich material found in other sources, especially the work of Joseph Sobol, past issues of the journal and newsletter published by the National Storytelling Association, performer directories and festival programs, and my own experiences with many tellers and listeners. Directories and programs portray tellers in a less ambivalent light than have the personal letters quoted above, since they are usually self-descriptions intended to publicize the performer. Thus dilemmas in the development of social identity seem to disappear in such writings. For example, we learn that Marylyn Peringer (featured in chapter 11 here), began her two-decade career as a teller gradually, through her teaching experiences and an interest in French: "[I am a] former high school English teacher, later studies in French language and literature, including a year in Paris, paved the way for my interest in French-Canadian folktales and legends which I now tell bilingually or all in French" (*1997/98 Canadian Storytelling Directory* 44). Her earlier experiences in teaching encouraged Marylyn to be sensitive to the educational aspects of stories.

In the same directory Toronto teller Bob Barton wrote that for him storytelling "grew out of my experiences as a classroom teacher (English/Dramatic Arts)" and adds that "now, as a full-time teller, I am still committed to supporting classroom teachers in their work with stories in the classroom" (*1997/98 Canadian Storytelling Directory* 39). He seems to down-play his background in drama here, though in fact it was central in his development as a storyteller.

Librarian and storyteller Alice Kane described her reluctant beginnings as a storyteller as part of her career: "This was not for me; I was shy, I stammered. Suddenly the time [of training] had passed, I had been to library school. I was a children's librarian. I had well defined duties, and one of them was to learn and tell stories" (63). Despite her resistance, Alice Kane gained experience (along with her colleagues), telling stories "with dry mouths and shaky knees." She became a mainstay of library storytelling in the Toronto area for many years, an inspiration to countless numbers of tellers and listeners.

For others, storytelling was a less predictable vocation. Canadian writer and teller Joan Buchanan described an experience similar to one reported by many of the tellers interviewed by Sobol, of being unexpectedly challenged to tell stories. Joan, who wrote, "I can remember distinctly the moment I became a storyteller," described going to an Australian storytelling event where the invited storyteller had not yet arrived and children were waiting. A friend said, "Joan, you're a writer, you can do some stories for the kids, can't you?" She did not hesitate long and later reported enthusiastically: "I found that I could do it. I was a storyteller!" (Buchanan).

Oklahoma teller Fran Stallings reported a similar challenge when early in her performing career she was invited by a teacher to tell the entire *Odyssey* over a span of several months. She already had a number of years of experience, "but those months with *The Odyssey* put me in touch with something more huge, more powerful, and older than any little story I had played with before. It was certainly not the first time I was called 'a storyteller.' Better perhaps to say that it was the first time the storyteller called to *me*" (Stallings). Joan and Fran were certainly not novices when they were "called," in this case literally, to take the floor, but these experiences did set them on a firmer path toward platform storytelling as a more regular activity.

Storytelling directories and festival programs are a key source of expressed identity, as we have seen above. In addition to providing descriptions most often written by the tellers themselves (even when this is expressed in third person), these entries allow us to observe the evolution of a teller's identity over time as they emphasize different aspect of their professional persona, and also the stability of that identity.[4] Here are Toronto festival program write-ups for Bob Barton, who has appeared at many of these annual festivals. In the first festival program (1979) he provided an expansive entry:

> Thanks to the early advice and guidance of Bill Moore, who was at that time Supervisor of Oral English for the Hamilton Board of Education, I learned how to involve children in stories in an active, oral way. A decade later as an English Consultant involved in assisting teachers with the teaching of dramatic arts, I discovered that story was one of the most valuable structures available to the teacher as a starting point for drama. Re-enacting a story was not the point so much as finding ways to approach the story which would help to deepen the children's understanding of the original story.

Bob was already an experienced teller when he composed this statement. We see in both presentations an emphasis on his role in "assisting teachers," such a strong theme that it is repeated almost two decades later in Bob's directory entry where he emphasizes that he is "still committed to supporting teachers in their work with stories in the classroom" (*1997/98 Canadian Storytelling Directory* 39). After his lengthy entry in the first festival program Bob becomes consistently succinct, identifying himself simply as "a teacher . . . of dramatic arts" (1981) and as "a founding member of the Storytellers School of

Toronto" (1985, 1987, and later programs). In 1988 we see a significant change as he begins to move more regularly beyond his local community after the publication of two books on storytelling and to "travel throughout Canada and the United States as a storyteller and language arts consultant," which is simply repeated in the next program write-up in 1990. By 1991 he is on the Board of Directors of NAPPS (renamed National Storytelling Association, NSA) and is traveling so frequently that he is not in Toronto for the festival. By 1995 he describes himself as traveling "widely to offer workshops and tell literary and traditional stories" and as "the author of children's books and books on storytelling." This festival featured Bob and other authors at a Storytelling Festival book-launch, underlining his growing identity as an author. In the 1997 program, Bob comes full circle, dropping his wide travels but not his books: "Bob Barton has been performing in festivals and schools since 1979. He is also the author of several books for children and adults."

It is not surprising that we see no dramatic changes in his write-ups for two reasons: Bob was already an experienced teller for more than two decades, and he is also by nature as succinct in his writing style as he is expansive in his oral style (which reflects his background in dramatic arts). We could expect to see more fluctuation in the self-description of a teller who was just beginning, trying to find new ways of expressing their developing identity as it evolved over the years.

Not all experienced tellers settle into such a comfortable sense of identity, however. For example, here are entries for Joan Bodger, written over a period of years in Toronto festival programs:

> For more than thirty years I have been telling stories professionally. In the 1960s I started telling stories on street corners in New York, and in the same period began using stories in a therapeutic setting. Nowadays I use stories in my Gestalt practice (mostly with adults). In my other, secret life I accept straight storytelling gigs all over North America. (1979)

> Author of "Clever-Lazy, The Girl Who Invented Herself"; she [Joan] weaves folklore into her life and writing. (1981)

> Joan comes from the kind of family that would make a story out of a shopping list. Founding member of the Storytellers School. (1985)

Joan Bodger "turned professional" in 1948. Ten years ago she helped create the Festival and The Storytellers School of Toronto. She has told stories in Australia, Japan, Jordan, and the British Isles and the U.S. (1988, 1989, and 1991)

Joan Bodger has been a storyteller for almost fifty years. She is writing a book about the life she has lived and the stories she has told, how they interact. (1995)

Joan emphasizes a different aspect of her storytelling persona with every entry, except for three years when she repeats the same write-up with minor changes (she adds "and the U.S." to her storytelling travels as an afterthought, since she had certainly done a lot of workshops and performances there before 1989). In 1979 she is a street performer and a therapist, in 1981 an author, in 1985 a member of a creative family and a founding member of the Storytellers School, in 1988–91 she is a pioneer and a traveler, and in 1995 she is summing up her life. Of all the entries I have read, Joan Bodger's comes closest to narrating the life of the teller in short bursts of prose, each one revealing a different place on her map of experience.

I noted earlier that these moments of recognition are often told as narratives that recount experiences from specific storytelling events. These "vocational narratives," as Sobol called them, frequently enter tellers' repertoires as preambles to their performances, then spread as legendary narratives to other tellers. Sometimes these accounts may even be associated with traditional stories, making them stories within stories within stories. Canadian teller Ted Stone wrote to me about a woman for whom the fable of "The Grasshopper and the Ant" was a formative metaphor: "She would remember that story and then would be afraid to try because she didn't want to starve like grasshopper. One day she admitted this to a friend, who said "But Cynthia, that story was told by an ant." So she became a storyteller, and made a rather nice story out of how she became one" (Stone, Letter to the author).

The grasshopper, not unlike free-lance storytellers, is in danger of starving because he does not behave like a practical ant. Many performers mentioned here are understandably hesitant, even after some years of experience in storytelling events, because storytelling is an uncertain profession that does not guarantee a steady income (or a safe cache of winter food). One such teller observes that "very few of us in this evolving role of storyteller are paid enough money to live on, which makes issues of financial reimbursement even more complex—and brings us back to the confusing modern role of storyteller" (Birch and Heckler 34).

Such ambivalence about assuming a social identity as a teller is rarely found among those growing up in an oral milieu, where narrating is a more natural occurrence, both casually and formally. Here money was not usually a primary motivation, even when collectors offered to pay for what they took away. In a society such as ours, however, formal storytelling is less spontaneous and less recognized as an art than in traditional oral milieus, opportunities for telling stories professionally often have to be sought out, and formal training is less developed than for other arts. It is not surprising that many feel unsure of their social identity as tellers.

Yet despite the problems and challenges, or maybe even because of them, the number of people who identify themselves as tellers continues to rise steadily. Alice Kane, who began as a shy library storyteller but who became a skilled performer in a few decades, commented on this continuing vitality: "In a day of highly efficient communication such as the world has ever known before, storytelling remains the most effective form of communication. Through storytelling strangers can converse. Even the shyest and most reticent can speak from the heart, and the listener, even the silent listener, responds completely—and no two in exactly the same way" (68).

The ever-emergent quality of face-to-face experiences is a powerful characteristic of actual storytelling events. Within the social and artistic context of these events tellers begin to establish and develop their identities. In a positive light, the hesitancy of tellers cited here reflects the on-going evolution of storytelling as a developing profession, with constantly changing means of establishing standards and limits. In the following chapters, we will meet several tellers whose individual identities and storytelling preferences have unfolded over years of experience in one or the other of the four major streams and within a recognizable storytelling community.

9

Burning Brightly

NEW LIGHT FROM AN OLD TALE (1993)

Here I begin to explore my own development as a teller, focusing on a story that I read first in the early 1970s when doing library research on my dissertation. At that time, of course, I had no inkling that I might ever tell anyone the distressing story of "Frau Trude," whose cruel punishment of a girl for her curiosity enraged me. In discussing the story as it developed through oral performances, I provided a brief history of my writing in the previous sixteen years, playing on the heroine's inability to recognize her own story. This allowed me to ask, "How often do we deny our own creativity while extolling that of others, or claim our own lives are not very interesting in comparison with those of others?" I allowed the girl in my revised version to answer this question for herself when she finally discovered her own life-saving story. This chapter appeared first in Joan Radner's anthology *Feminist Messages* (1993).

In exploring a single story and how it came to life, the challenge was to see if I could balance the subjective and objective in ways that would be meaningful to others. One of these balances was a consideration of then-current views in feminist folktale scholarship, a topic I would return to in later articles as feminist positions continued to evolve. The use of this particular text, "The Curious Girl," whose heroine survives Frau Trude's fire, inspired me to end with a question that would be relevant to any academic writing, not just my own: "Is it possible to ignite oneself without being consumed?"

———

In an old Grimm tale, a girl is warned by her parents not to visit a witch who lives in a strange house in the center of the forest; she disobeys them, seeks out the crone in the heart of darkness, and is turned into a log for her efforts. This short tale that I came upon while doing research for my doctoral dissertation has become an unexpected focus for my work as a folklorist as well as a performing storyteller.

Looking at what I have written over the past sixteen years, I see that my academic creations have expressed a microcosmic view of the world I see as a whole, a world in which human beings are endlessly curious and creative and imaginative even against all odds. But how often do we deny our own creativity while extolling that of others, or claim our own lives are not very interesting in comparison with those of others? The girl in the story thinks it is the crone who is interesting and curious, and thus she denies the value of her own story, with unhappy results.

I write about this story because I sense that the metaphor it offers might be of use, since it deals with the dangers and rewards of the deep and abiding curiosity that has led us to the varied places we now occupy in our own lives. Our inquisitiveness has led us into dangers, guided us to trees of knowledge where we have met our serpents, carried us to witches ready to challenge and respond. Transformation is inevitable.

It is transformation that I speak of here, not only that of the curious girl but also the transformation of myself as an academic writer and a storyteller, with the hope that others might recognize some parts of their own stories as well.

One of my own pleasantly impossible tasks has been an exploration of how and why stories come into being. Though I did not know it at the time, this task was hidden in my very first academic explorations of folktale heroines, begun in the early 1970s and developed throughout the 1980s. Initially, I was interested in finding out how heroines were portrayed in both traditional and popularized tales and, more specifically, how these portrayals were received by contemporary readers and listeners. During a series of interviews, I discovered that girls and women remembered the fairy tales they had read as children, while boys and men generally did not (though a few did recall reading many of the same stories). Transcripts of these interviews, with individuals from ages eleven to sixty-eight and with small groups of three to five girls from ages eleven to seventeen, are in Appendix X of my dissertation ("Romantic Heroines").

My interest in stories continued to grow over the next few years, but it began to take unexpected turns. I found it was not enough to examine folktales and to question others about them; I had to tell them as well—first as part of my lectures, where a summary of a tale was merely an illustration of a point I made, but then as a separate thing, as a "performance" in which tales were told merely for the sake of telling them. As I took part in professional storytelling events and observed other tellers, I was able to see firsthand and over an extended time how tellers, tales, and listeners interact in the living process of verbal artistry. Of course my curiosity was expressed in writing, because that is how I learned to tell academic stories.

Personal curiosity is not enough, though. Helpers are needed all along the way. It is simply not true, as we have been taught, that we stand on our own two feet armed and ready to move through our lives as if we were in constant battle with opposing forces. The girl in the story does set out on her own, but her transformation depends on meeting the woman who will test and challenge her. I cannot fail to mention, then, that all of my curiosity would be empty without the patient attentions of Linda Dégh, whose own deep curiosity about the hows and whys of people and the tales they tell has inspired her to write widely about folktales as serious forms of literary expression. In a recent article she comments on storytelling in modern society, noting that "It is society which maintains the need for stories and provides occasions for telling them," and wonders what it is in our contemporary urban existence that continues to draw us to old stories ("The Variant" 169).

I, too, wonder what holds the attention of four hundred junior high school students and their teachers sitting for forty-five minutes in a school gymnasium listening to an old tale about a crone and a girl who is too curious. I have no clear answers, but the quest for them has led me on.

The words I offer here are my first attempt to express in print what I have learned as a scholar of tales as well as a teller of tales. I describe the evolution of one particular story, "Frau Trude" or "Mistress Trudy" (AT 334, Grimm 43), from its beginning as the single text I read in 1973 to its most recent telling as of the writing of this essay. It may sound like a simple task to report how "Frau Trude" became "The Curious Girl," but is has been the most difficult writing I have done yet, since I have had to be both the academic and the performer, both the curious girl and the crone. As a folklorist, I ask myself how and why the story was learned and told and how it developed in the oral context. As a storyteller, I ask myself how the various performances shaped the tale as it was told and retold to listeners who consciously and unconsciously influenced the movement of the story.

Coming to terms with Frau Trude was a different challenge from what I was used to meeting in my academic writing: her story demanded unraveling its patterns of significance from the inside out instead of interpreting from the outside in. Like the girl in the second text of the tale, I had to discover the unknown story. So you will be able to follow what I am saying more fluidly, I print both texts in full here, one as I read it in a translation of the Grimm tales and the other a single written text of my oral variant developed over a few years of performance.[1]

My task is to describe how the first text evolved into the second; to discuss the impact of my own interpretations and of audience responses and influences; and to examine the metaphoric relationship to actual everyday life on a small scale. And I intend to have fun while doing so.

I first met Frau Trude while reading traditional tales as part of my dissertation research. I spent three years sitting on those tiny little chairs in the children's section of dozens of libraries, reading through the folktale collections. When I met Frau Trude, she did not offer pleasant company. Her story enraged me because it seemed to be viciously and precisely aimed right at me. I was that overly curious and disobedient girl, and I did not like the fact that she was eventually overwhelmed and destroyed by the witch. It was an ugly story, but it was part of what I was studying. I cited it, put it into my dissertation statistics, and classified it according to the neat four-part scheme I used for describing folktale heroines. After that, I occasionally used it as a negative example when I was conducting interviews, but I did not find it useful in any other way. I never would have judged it suitable for performances.

But Frau Trude did not wish to be forgotten. Her story returned most unexpectedly, ten years after I had first read it, when I was trying to resolve another story that I had been working on. I carefully reread "Mistress Trudy" to see if I had missed something. Here is the text as I found it in 1973 and reread it again in the same book ten years later, the whole story told in two brief paragraphs.[2]

MISTRESS TRUDY

Once upon a time there was a girl who was stubborn and inquisitive, and whenever her parents told her to do something, she'd never obey. How could she get along well? One day she said to her parents, "I've heard so much about Mistress Trudy; I'll call on her sometime. People say that her house looks queer and that there are many strange things in it. I've become quite curious." The parents strictly forbade her going there and said, "Mistress Trudy is a wicked woman, given to evil doings, and if you go there, we'll disown you."

The girl paid no attention, however, to her parents' orders and went to Mistress Trudy's just the same. When she got there, Mistress Trudy asked her, "Why are you so pale?" "Oh," she answered, shaking all over, "I'm so frightened at what I've seen." "What have you seen?" "I saw a black man on your stairs." "That was a charcoal burner." "Then I saw a green man." "That was a huntsman." "Then I saw a blood-red man." "That was a butcher." "Oh, Mistress Trudy, I shuddered; I looked through the window and I didn't see you but I did see the devil with his fiery head." "Is that so!" she said. "Then you saw the witch in her proper garb. I've been waiting for you for a long time now and have longed for you. Now you shall furnish me with light." Thereupon she transformed the girl into a log and threw it into the fire, and when it was all aglow, she sat down beside it and, warming herself at it, said, "That really does give a bright light."

Not surprisingly, this unpromising story did not become part of my repertoire when I began to perform folktales in the mid-1970s. However, a few years ago when I was playing around with a story of my own composition about a girl lost in a forest, it had refused to resolve itself. "Frau Trude" returned unexpectedly to mind. I turned aside this intrusion, but the story would not go away. As stubborn as the curious girl, I resisted until curiosity nudged me into rereading the Grimm text to see if there was some hidden potential I had missed. At first I found nothing, but I decided to try retelling it as close to the Grimm text as possible to free whatever had caught my unwitting attention. Only after several tellings did I sense something in the girl's transformation by fire that had been missed in that first reading: The girl gave a bright light when she was thrown into the fire. I also heard Mistress Trudy's words with new ears: "I've been waiting for you for a long time now and have longed for you."

With these equivocal words, the story began to develop new configurations, and after five years of retelling, it transformed itself into something quite different from the cautionary tale I had first read.

The story was on its new path, it continued to flow, with the theme of transformation rather than destruction as its central motivation. Frau Trude lost none of her properly menacing cronishness; she continued to be as threatening as she was in the Grimm text, but she was also willing to accept and reward the girl's curiosity and persistence instead of simply annihilating her for improper behavior.

Here is the text of my retelling as of June 18, 1990. This is a written recreation composed specifically for this essay. I have told the tale often enough that this is an accurate artistic recreation, if not an objective scientific rendering. It will serve our purposes in this form. This one text is representative of the many that have moved the story toward its present shape, one that has been relatively stable for the last two years. It remains, in my own mind, multitextual.

THE CURIOUS GIRL

Once there was a girl who was stubborn and curious, and always disobedient to her parents. Whenever they told her to do one thing, she'd do another. Now how could a girl like that not get into trouble? And she did.

One day she said to her parents, "I think I'll visit Frau Trude one day. They say she lives in an interesting house full of strange things, and I'm ever so curious to see her."

Her parents protested. They said, "Frau Trude is a godless woman who does evil things, and if you go there you will be our child no longer!"

But she did not listen. Without telling her parents, she set off through the woods one day. Soon she crossed a small stream, and when she stepped onto the other shore the woods around her seemed darker and more dismal.

As she walked along she suddenly heard a sound like thunder coming from behind her and she turned to look—and saw a dark rider on a dark horse who came roaring toward her.

She leapt aside.

When they had passed, deep darkness fell all around her and she could no longer see her way. But she continued on, following the path beneath her feet.

Soon after she heard a raging sound behind her and turned again and saw a glowing red rider on a red horse speeding toward her and she leapt aside. When they had passed the sky above became blood red.

Now she was frightened, but she continued on her way.

After some time she heard a deafening sound behind her and turned again, this time to see a brilliant white rider on a white horse flashing toward her. She threw herself out of their path. When they had passed by, bright light shone all around her and she found herself in a clearing at the very heart of the dark forest.

And there indeed was a strange house, and around it was a fence made of human bones. The curious girl was terrified, but she crept up to the house and looked in the window. There she saw the figure of a woman, all in flames but not consumed.

The girl heard a voice call her name and then bid her to enter. She stepped up to the door and slowly entered.

When she was inside she saw only an old woman sitting beside the fireplace. This was Frau Trude, who spoke to her politely:

"Why are you so pale and shaking, my dear?" she asked.

"Because I've seen many strange things!"

"Oh? What have you seen?"

"As I was walking I saw a dark rider on a dark horse."

"That was only my Dark Night."

"Then I saw a red rider on a red horse."

"That was my Red Morning."

"But then there was a white rider on a white horse."

"Yes, that was my Bright Day. And what else did you see, my dear?"

"Oh, then I looked in your window, Frau Trude, but I didn't see you at all— I saw a woman all in flames."

"Did you, now! Then you have seen the witch in her true form. I have been waiting and watching for you and longing for you. You will burn brightly for me."

And so saying, Frau Trude turned the girl into a log and threw the log on her fire. As the fire blazed up she sat down next to it to warm herself and said, "Indeed, it does burn brightly."

Suddenly a shower of sparks flew out of the fire and into the air. Frau Trude leapt up, and changed the sparks into a fiery bird, and then she caught the bird.

"Clever girl! But you'll never get away from me! You will remain a bird, my servant for all eternity—unless you can fulfill my bargain: If you can tell me one story that I've never heard before, I'll let you go. If you cannot, you will be in my power forever."

"That's not fair," replied the girl who was now a bird. "You know many more stories than I do."

"That is true," said the old woman. "So I'll give you all the time you need to learn more. Return to me when you're ready. I will be waiting for you."

The girl flew away in the shape of a bird. She thought of all the languages she could speak now, knowing that the birds understand the speech of all living things. And so she began to wander in the world, flying everywhere.

She went to the east and to the west, north and south, and everywhere she learned more stories. She spoke to the trees and all green growing things, to the birds and all others who could fly, and to all creatures who could creep, walk, leap, or swim. And she wandered in villages and towns and cities, learning stories from everyone who lived there.

A long time had passed and the girl had become a woman, still wandering in the shape of a bird.

One day Frau Trude heard a strange song outside her house in the heart of the dark forest. She went out to see, and found a fiery bird singing from the tree nearest her window.

"Ah, it's you," she said. I've been waiting. Have you brought me a story?"

"Yes, I'm ready now," the woman who was a bird said boldly. "I have all the stories in the world to tell you!"

"Good," Frau Trude answered. "I haven't heard a fine tale for a long time. Begin."

And so she told Frau Trude all the stories she'd learned from all of creation. Some were short and some long, some were plain and others fancy, but they all carried the truth in them.

When she finished, Frau Trude gazed at her warmly and exclaimed, "Excellent stories, and well told too. But I knew every one of them long before you were born!"

The woman who was a bird stood speechless. She had no more stories. But when she opened her mouth to cry out, words came out on their own, first one at a time and then running together like a small river:

"Once there was a girl who was stubborn and curious, and always disobedient to her parents. Whenever they told her to do one thing she'd do another . . ."

On the surface of the text alone, the two stories seem quite the opposite in their resolution. "Frau Trude" is a stark cautionary tale that warns of the dangers of disobedience and curiosity for girls, but "The Curious Girl" rewards these same risks. Not only does the girl survive and mature, but she becomes empowered as well. How could these two stories be related in meaning at all? There must have been something I was missing.[3]

I reread the story as I had first encountered it to check on the wording and to see its relative situation in the Grimm collection. The surrounding stories are similar and might have colored my initial reading. "Mistress Trudy" is placed between "The Godfather" and "Godfather Death." Their similarities were as fascinating to me as if they had been musical variations on a theme. In all three tales, the protagonists must confront an overwhelming force that threatens their existence.

In the first story, "The Godfather," a father sets out to find a godfather for his child and meets a stranger who gives him a bottle of magical water that cures death. For no particular reason, the man decides to visit the stranger and meets objects on the way up that he does not understand and that the godfather later lies about. When the man insists that he has seen the godfather through the keyhole, wearing horns, he is yelled at and runs away in fear.

This dissatisfying story is a badly garbled variant of "Godfather Death," which comes right after "Mistress Trudy." While "The Godfather" lacks clear motivation and certain resolution, "Godfather Death" is strong in each of these: a son is promised as a godchild to Death, who, when the child has become a man, gives him water that cures any illness. The godchild misuses the water twice: first, when he cures a poor man out of compassion and is warned by Death, and second, when he cures for more selfish reasons and is carried off by Death.

"Frau Trude," or "Mistress Trudy," presents yet another variation on the theme of supernatural relationships. The girl is not promised to anyone by her parents; in fact, they try to warn her against unholy alliances. She goes out of her own curiosity. She does not receive any magical objects either, which is appropriate given her more tenuous relationship: she's an intruder, not a godchild. In contrast to the first man, she knows what she is doing and is definitely more adventurous: "I think I'll go and see her one of these days," she tells her parents. The man in "The Godfather" simply muddles through with no plans. Frau Trude is also a much more formidable opponent than is the silly godfather, who lies about the objects on the stairs and who yells at the man, "Damn you, that's not true," but allows him to escape. Frau Trude's answers are deceptively more gentle and patient than his—and her quarry does not get away.

In the more forceful "Godfather Death," the deadly godfather, unlike Frau Trude, is initially a mentor who teaches his godchild how to cure illnesses. This motif revealed new possibilities for the crone in "Mistress Trudy." It is another negative example of what happens when one challenges the mentor before one is ready to do so. The silly man in the first story gets away because the godfather is even sillier. The other two are not so lucky. They both meet death in the form of fire because of their arrogant disobedience. She is turned into a log and thrown on the fire, while he is taken to a dark cave where he watches as his candle of life is extinguished.

In this trio of stories, all three of the characters are disobedient, but the first is so incompetent that he does not even know where he is going or why, while the last one is too calculating and ambitious. By contrast, the girl is self-motivated but not greedy, and she does not run away. Nor does she have her flame extinguished. Quite the opposite—the fire blazes up.

What caught my unconscious attention was the fiery nature of this girl. Unlike the two men, she single-mindedly seeks out her antagonist against the advice of her cautious parents. She is disobedient, and she is looking for trouble. But then other folktale heroines are also disobedient. Snow White cannot resist her witch either, nor does Sleeping Beauty evade the spindle. Cinderella sneaks off to the ball three times and returns home, where she lies cleverly to protect herself. It is not difficult to find all sorts of heroines who are disobedient; therefore, I reasoned, it must be this girl's particular form of defiance that dooms her in the Grimm text, since disobedience is so widespread. She is, after all, stubbornly set on visiting "a godless woman who does evil things"—a crone, a witch, a hag, an old woman who is too intriguing to miss.

I remember that the "witch" in our neighborhood lived right across the street. She wore strange clothing and kept a "jungle" (she called it a garden) in her yard that she watered at dawn and at midnight (or so my sister and I believed). My mother told us to leave her alone. Once we sneaked into her "garden" when she was away to see if there were any curious things there, but we escaped safely before she returned and so avoided being turned into logs. We never went there on Halloween, not did any of our friends. I have since discovered that most of my students have had at least one witch in their neighborhood. Most of us have. One year a student went back to interview the kids on the block where she had grown up and discovered that their witch was her own mother! These women were fascinating, even if they were pitiful. They excited my curiosity when I fell into the field of folklore. Witches have never been like anyone else we know. They might even live "in an interesting house full of strange things," as did the woman across the street from me. Frau Trude lives.

One reason she lives is to warn that curiosity is just as dangerous as our mothers tried to tell us. If we take her warning as a challenge, we might learn something. Maybe.

It is easy to be distracted by the negative "noise" about the dangers of curiosity in "Mistress Trudy" and to read it as the cautionary tale it was meant to be. What came through to me between the lines was something else, though. Even when my conscious mind furiously rejected the apparent destruction of the curious girl, something of her determined inquisitiveness remained in my mind for several years. Certainly, it was related to my own mulish insistence on disobeying my mother whenever she said (with some frequency) "Girls don't do that," whatever "that" happened to be at the moment. (I note that my mother's memories of my childhood are quite different—and perhaps more objective—than mine, if such things can be measured. She recalled encouraging me to be adventurous rather than hindering me. I never told her that in my childhood I had "made" her the witch in my dreams, though I now think she might have smiled.) The still-angry child in me recognized the girl in the story who did not allow her parents to subdue her curiosity, even though they threatened her with abandonment.

But she, unlike me, did not sneak into the witch's domain unseen. She arrived at Frau Trude's strange house in broad daylight after a harrowing night journey, pale and shaking but still able to open the door, enter, and respond to Frau Trude's questions. Frau Trude's ironic words, "I've been waiting for you a long time now and have longed for you," herald her violent transformation by fire. She is told she will burn brightly, and indeed she does. That caught my attention.

In fact, it was the girl's transformation into a block of wood that sparked my interest when I reread the tale. I was able to see her test by fire as an elemental encounter, and once my mind was open to this more positive possibility, the other elements began to present themselves as I began to reexperience the story and eventually to try retelling it. As the story evolved, the curious girl passed through fire as a log and then a shower of sparks, through air as a bird, through earth as a wild hare, and through water as a fish. Through these metamorphoses, she experienced the sacrifice of her ego-self, which in the end gave her even greater power—freedom over herself as a fuller human being. In finding the unknown story—her own—she connects herself with all of the other stories she has brought back for Frau Trude, her teacher.

In this new light, the Grimm tale seemed to me not so much disagreeable as unfinished, open-ended. Story-tellers usually understand the open-ended nature of traditional tales as well as folklorists do, because such flexibility keeps any individual story alive by giving the teller enough room between the lines to convert old into new.

The conversion of the story did not happen all at once. Frau Trude was not an easy woman to live with, and I did not want to risk her ire by mistelling her story. I was very cautious when I related it publicly for the first time, opening with the Grimm text word-for-word (it was short enough for me to memorize easily) and then re-forming the story into my version of "Curious Girl." My intention was to emphasize the negative contrast of the two stories, one which I viewed as "bad" and the other as "good." I continued to recount the stories in this way to many different audiences, listening for their responses. Gradually the story began to change.

It was (and still is) a surprise to me that my senses of the two seemingly opposite tales started to grow toward each other, until they became two sides of a coin rather than two separate coins. Variations on a theme. Eventually, they united into a single text, so that the beginning of "Curious Girl" came to be phrased in words echoing from "Frau Trude." In this form the story of "Curious Girl" continues to unfold.

What continued to push the story into new growth was my own curiosity. I wanted to know what happened to the girl after she was thrown into the fire. How did she survive, and why? I knew there was something about to happen next, but I did not know what it would be. Every time I told "The Curious Girl," I learned at least one thing that I had not noticed before, and each thing that I learned gave its energy to my next telling. In this way, the story grew on its own, and it became easier and easier to tell as I myself became more willing to enter through Frau Trude's door.

When I first began using the story in Winnipeg schools, the girl went through various transformations that represented the four elemental forces of fire, water, air, and earth. This got to be very elaborate. After her fiery rebirth, she took to the air as a bird, became a fish, and then a rabbit burrowing into warm earth. She was finally caught by Frau Trude who offered to give her own shape back if she could tell a story that Frau Trude had never heard. This challenge has become the center of the story for me, and for many listeners as well, and, through months of retellings, gradually provided me with a clear focus that burned away extraneous material.

Four audiences in particular had a direct impact on the unfolding of the story, and I will describe them in some detail.

The first experience happened in Winnipeg, when I heard my own story told back to me by a nine-year-old boy, David Quanbury, at the bi-monthly gathering of Stone Soup Stories. At this time "The Curious Girl" was just evolving, and I had told it only once at this gathering sometime earlier in the year. A dozen of us were sitting around casually sharing stories of all sorts when David asked if he could tell one. He had heard "The Curious Girl" told by both me and by his mother, Mary Louise Chown-Quanbury, and wanted to share it. In my tellings, the girl-as-bird had been given her own shape back right away, so that she could go into the world and learn more stories. David "forgot" that, and simply had her remain as a bird until she told her final story. This simple alteration was much more powerful in motivation, and so spontaneous that both he and his mother were certain that I had always told the story that way. I decided that they were on to something important, and began to make sure that the girl was still in her bird form at the conclusion, though she had begun to go through other transformations while gathering stories.

Here is the second experience. I spent a week in September of 1987 visiting my friend Vivian LaBrie and her nine-year-old daughter in Quebec City. One night she invited her neighbors and their children for a candle-lit evening of storytelling in which everyone contributed. When I told "Curious Girl," Vivian's daughter asked her mother in French, which was then translated for me, "Why does that girl have to turn into all those animals?" As I pondered her question, it became clear to me that the four elemental transformations were indeed unwieldy and unnecessary. It seemed that I had become an elemental fundamentalist, telling myself to "get all four of the elements in or this won't work."

I stopped telling "Curious Girl" for a while and let my imaginary bird fly free. For several weeks I pondered the child's question, and heard what was between the words—"Why do you adults make your lives so complicated?" Eventually I came to understand that the elemental forces did not need to be expressed so explicitly. I began to try out other combinations, until only the fiery sparks and the bird remained explicit. Water and earth were implied when she had first stepped over the stream and entered the bewitched forest. The story had begun to simplify itself, to become more lucid and transparent. I was ready to begin telling it again.

The third experience came in May of 1988. I was attending the annual meeting of the Folklore Studies Association of Canada in Windsor, Ontario. One evening I was invited to participate in an evening concert sponsored by the Old Sandwich Song Circle, for an audience of adults. I stood in front of fifty or so strangers who were accustomed to hearing songs and occasional stories, all sitting around the room in metal folding chairs that clanked when anyone shifted. They had already spent an hour listening to folk music, and I decided to risk telling "The Curious Girl" again to see what might happen. As I aimed the story at those particular listeners that night, a few new phrases found their way into the story, but the most memorable transformation came at the end. As the bird finished her own story, the one that had never yet been heard, I started to pronounce Frau Trude's words that freed her. Before I could speak Frau Trude's disenchantment, the audience began to applaud spontaneously—as soon as the bird-as-girl finished her story. I stopped there, of course, feeling that I had not finished. At first I was perplexed, wondering if they were anxious to end the evening after so much singing. But then I understood that they had instinctively found the natural ending to the story. I saw the open-ended potential of the conclusion, and its circular movement that begins and ends with the same words—"Once there was a girl who was too curious . . ." These have been the concluding words ever since, bringing readers/listeners more directly into the act of creation by leaving the final resolution in their hands (and minds). The creative ambivalence matches that of the Grimm text, which ends with the girl being thrown into the fire as a log, ready for new birth.

In October of 1988 I had the final formative experience when I told the story as part of my presentation on a panel titled "Women and Power," at the annual meeting of the American Folklore Society. My function on the panel was to provide a metaphorical example of what we had all been discussing, and "The Curious Girl" seemed an ideal choice since both the girl and the crone revealed their complementary powers. Five of us sat at the front table making our presentations to an audience largely composed of women. They were alert and thoughtful. Since I was the last presenter, the discussion that followed began with a variety of responses to the story itself, and to its connections with the other presentations. Many centered their remarks on the girl's belated recognition of her own life story, a topic that was relevant to other panel members as well. Participants also acknowledged that telling one's own story is only the beginning, and that true freedom (transformation) comes only when one's own stories connect with all others. It was also suggested that any who fail to go beyond the ego-identity of their own story would remain in service to the inner crone (Jung's "shadow" archetype) instead of growing into equality with her.

The contributions of this particular audience deepened my own implicit perception of the story rather than bringing about any explicit changes. For example, we talked about the story as an academic metaphor; as academics we have been trained to look into a "window" and describe what we see there, or what we think we see there. Often our academic vision is as limited as that of the girl. What she thinks she sees there is only one aspect of what is there potentially, in this case a woman surrounded by flames but not consumed by them. This image has strengthened itself in my mind as a result of telling the story to this particular audience, who encouraged women to become that powerful woman in the midst of the transformative flames.

This story has grown as I have told it over the years, in response to the various audiences and also related to my own changing context and ripening perspectives as I have aged. I am the mother of a very curious daughter, Rachel, and I understand more fully how mothers have every right to fear for the safety of their adventurous daughters—and even to threaten them with all sorts of frightening things out of love, however misguided. This understanding softens the mother's warning for me; she cautions her daughter about dangerous curiosity, but no longer threatens her with abandonment.

I also know fully well that one cannot be a mother without also being a witch at times, as I know from being both daughter and mother and crone. The mother's warning *and* Frau Trude's challenges contribute to the girl's transformations. What was, to me, implicit in the Grimm cautionary tale comes into full bloom in the reconstructed story. The "good" and "bad" mothers become one, both protecting *and* testing the girl who wants to find out about the world and her place in it.

I have also learned that change always brings trouble of one sort or another. It is very tempting for us as women to remember how we have been cautioned (and have internalized these cautions) to turn away from our challenges—our own unknown forests and all strange characters—as we meet them actually and metaphorically in our lives.

It is easier, too, to accept the dualistic perceptions we have been surrounded with, and to sort people into positive and negative, good and bad, light and dark. In this scenario, Frau Trude is indeed the "godless woman who does evil things," and the girl is indeed tragically disobedient. When I first began to tell "Mistress Trudy" and "Curious Girl" together, I kept these stories separate, splitting them into "bad" and "good" variants with the intention of contrasting them. As my own perceptions moved away from dualism, I found that I no longer needed to split the stories and tell each one on its own. They became one for me as I came to accept the girl's overly curious nature, and to see her ensuing treatment as both warning and challenge at the same time, and her punishment as transformation rather than defeat. In this way the girl's path to her own enlightenment burns brightly before her. Even in the Grimm tale, the potential for transformation glows in the conclusion of the story where the log is tossed on the fire and burns brightly, but is not consumed.

Thus it is *not* obvious that "Mistress Trudy" can be seen only as a cautionary tale. This perception came to me from telling the tale rather than thinking about it and judging it, and from listening to what others had to say in addition to struggling through my own analysis. I am not suggesting that analysis is not useful, but I found that it was only a small part of the evolution of this story. Thinking alone did not solve the mystery of the woman in flames who throws the girl into the fire. I had to experience this mystery much more directly in order to feel the fire in the story, to discover its transformative power. This story, more than any other I have told over the years, has taught me to risk losing my own metaphorical shape (in this case my "shape" as an academic) to find out what is beyond the forest and the fire. Yes, I am curious.

In the spring of 1990 I finished this essay yet again after many tries, and sent it off to Jo Radner for her editorial response. When I read the concluding words of her letter, they seemed to capture my intent so clearly that I include them here: "Tellers can go all over the world learning other people's stories and they can tell them well; but the story they *need* to tell (to themselves at least, if not the public) is the only one they have—their own. That is the base from which we really learn to understand the languages/lives of other creatures, the way we save our lives from the strangers who would consume us for their own purposes" (Radner).

While composing and reviewing this writing over a three-year period, I have sensed an unspoken, continuing dialogue between that curious girl and the crone as they tell and retell their stories to one another. Because it has been a dialogue rather than two monologues, the story of the story has grown in my own mind, and has deepened in performances. I have been drawn into the fire. Relevant parts of my own story exist just beneath the surface of the told tale, unspoken but understood. They have become part of the silent dialogue between girl and crone in ways that are illuminating rather than self-indulgent. Yes, a fine tightrope to walk.

This writing has frustrated me more than anything I had written before it. Not the least of my discomforts is that I understand the power of *telling* stories all too well, which has made it difficult to put the words down in print for an unknown and unseen audience. I sit here at my modern writing machine on a rainy night in June imagining the curious girl having to type out all of the stories she had learned and then sending them off to Frau Trude in the morning mail. If she had done that, mailing them instead of telling them to the crone face-to-face, she probably would have been compelled to become a bird again. That is a sobering thought.

On the positive side, my attempt to set down this story's story in print has compelled me to look at the tale from very different angles and to sketch the different shapes it has taken as it has moved along in different times and places. In doing so, I have become more aware of the essences of character and action and motivation that have moved *me* along: the dynamic union of negative and positive forces that bring about metamorphoses; the dangers and the ecstasies of deep curiosity; the punishments and rewards of freedom-seeking, of finding one's own path; the absolute necessity of listening carefully to the stories of others as well as the deep need to tell our own, as part of the ocean of stories. And I wonder: Is it possible to ignite oneself without being consumed?

10

Difficult Women in Folktales

TWO WOMEN, TWO STORIES (1997)

Having raised the topic of difficult challenges, I now began to explore difficult women as both characters in the tales and as tellers of the tales. With this writing I freed myself from ambivalence about the legitimacy of looking at platform storytelling. It was particularly appropriate for the anthology in which it appears, *Undisciplined Women,* edited by Pauline Greenhill and Diane Tye. I examined the work of a nontraditional teller who re-formed a Grimm tale by discussing it with her audiences, and a poet and sometime storyteller who recreated her own startling revision of "Snow White." To put them in perspective I drew on four papers presented at the International Society for Folk-Narrative Research held in Budapest, Hungary, in 1989. Each author used folkloric tools to explore narratives in way that I found meaningful for my work on contemporary platform performances.

This particular article was a good bridge between my earlier investigations on women in folktales and later writing on contemporary tellers of such tales. I was now fully engaged in interviewing tellers who used traditional tales, as I continued to follow the illusory path through the ubiquitous fairy tale forest.

As I child I had a guilty fascination with the undisciplined women in the folktale books I inevitably received at Christmas (or was it only one that seemed like many?). I secretly approved of their deliberate belligerence as elder sisters and as old-wife hags, but I also noted that justice prevailed. I wondered if it was possible to be an undisciplined woman without suffering the gruesome fates of Cinderella's stepsisters or the wicked women in "Hansel and Gretel" and "Snow White." Many years later, while interviewing girls and women for my doctoral dissertation, I found others who admitted to a similar fascination with "bad" characters. Their unexpected reactions compelled me to expand my notions of folktale women and to break away from my simplistic good woman/bad woman approach.

While I worked on my dissertation in the early 1970s, professional story-telling was in the full process of bursting into bloom as a performance art, after several decades of quiet activity in libraries and schools. My continuing interest in women and folktales eventually led me to a curiosity about this "new" telling of old tales, and I began a formal examination of the phenomenon. In previous articles I have described these professional tellers in general (chapters 6 and 8), surveyed stories favored by a sampling of tellers in North America (chapter 7), and examined the Grimm tale of "Frau Trude" in detail as it developed through several years of oral performance (chapter 9).

I have also been motivated by others who have studied individual artists and their personal connections with their stories, most notably the Russian scholar Mark Azadovskii (*A Siberian Tale Teller*). Although I am not suggesting that urban professional performers are part of "pure" oral tradition of the sort usually investigated by folklorists, I see that a parallel tradition has come into being through the popularization of folktales over the past few centuries. While the current storytelling revival is popularly believed to have begun in the twentieth century, it actually begins with publication of a handful of stories based on folktales, rewritten by Charles Perrault in the late 1600s.[1] Fairy tales leapt into prominence with the editions of the Grimm brothers little more than a century later.[2]

These two collections were widely translated, spreading the tales far beyond their original times and places, and were taken even further by Walt Disney Productions. *Snow White and the Seven Dwarfs* was based on the Grimm tale, while *Cinderella, Sleeping Beauty,* and *Beauty and the Beast* were reworked from Perrault's collection. The Disney versions have played a most significant role in the popularization of stories that were already well known, further reworking the stories that had already been reinterpreted by Perrault and by the Grimms.

Contemporary storytellers in North America have continued the reworking of popularized folk and fairy tales in both oral and written forms, as we will see here. When I surveyed tellers who favored traditional sources (notably Perrault, Grimm, and Andrew Lang), two of those who responded offered examples of their work inspired by Grimm tales. I was excited to see that each featured decidedly undisciplined women—the unnaturally cruel stepmothers in "Snow White" and "The Juniper Tree." Each transformed their stories in very different ways.

Marvyne Jenoff is a Toronto poet and storymaker whose transformed queen in "Snow White: A Reflection" shifted between oral and written composition in the few years that she struggled with it. It had remained unpublished until now, as she continued work on her own collection of reworked fables and folktales, finding them a challenging contrast to her more autobiographical poetry and prose. I have heard her tell some of the dark Grimm tales at various annual storytelling festivals in Toronto in the 1980s, and have read some of her original compositions based on tales and fables. It is a pleasure to present her "Snow White: A Reflection" here.

Susan Gordon is a folklorist, oral performer, and workshop leader situated in rural Maryland. She devoted several years to a handful of traditional tales, including "The Handless Maiden" and "The Juniper Tree."

Jenoff and Gordon use different means to accomplish similar objectives: Jenoff reinterprets the text through her own direct interaction with the story; Gordon does so indirectly, through subtle changes in tone and emphasis and also by drawing out the listeners and engaging them after the stories are told. Thus we will see that Jenoff completely remotivates the wicked queen in "Snow White," while Gordon stays close to the Grimm text but finds extra-narrative ways of challenging stereotypes in "The Juniper Tree."

My interest in their reinterpretations resulted in this writing, initially presented in briefer form at the International Society for Folk-Narrative Research in Budapest, Hungary, in 1989. The conference topic, "Storytelling in Contemporary Society," inspired presentations on a wide sampling of genres, from traditional oral tales to urban legends, jokes, and family stories. Four in particular were directly relevant to my interests in the conscious artistic reworking of folktales, and have influenced this writing; I will describe these four briefly.

The first, by Giovanni Bronzini, reflected on the communication of folktales in the new millennium. He believed that folktales would continue to be an important expressive art, due largely to their archetypal nature which allows them to function "as a catalogue of the destinies a man or woman might have" (Bronzini 5). However, he observed that the continuing fragmentation of everyday life, along with increasing literacy, would favor writing and electronic reproductions over oral narration as the medium of creation. We can see how his observations apply to Jenoff's and Gordon's artistic efforts, especially in the sense of archetypal energy. These two tellers, and others, offer a challenge to Bronzini's suggestion that oral performance will gradually decrease in artistic importance. Even Jenoff, whose rethinking of "Snow White" is accomplished mainly through writing and rewriting, has experimented with telling this and other traditionally inspired stories of her own. Gordon continues to use both performance and verbal interchanges with listeners to extend her artistic efforts. More important, they are not simply reproducing traditional material, but are demonstrating how old tales in new forms still have the potential to express the deeper values of human existence—and furthermore to confront these values and not only to mirror them.

Both Jenoff and Gordon offer challenges to the assumption that oral performance will cease to be important. Even Jenoff, whose rethinking of "Snow White" is here accomplished through rewriting, has experimented with retelling this and other traditional tales. Gordon, in contrast, relies almost entirely on oral performance of her stories.

A second conference paper focused directly on the oral nature of modern professional performances—in this case, the "revival" of storytelling in France since the late 1960s (Gorog-Karady, "New Professional"). Veronika Gorog-Karady noted that many urban tellers in France, who rely primarily on printed sources, reinterpret the tales to suit new contexts. To achieve relevance for their listeners, some employ theatrical models that take them away from the "original" story as they learned it, while others remain close but bring new life to their stories by other means. But no matter what means tellers used, Gorog-Karady regarded their artistic efforts as a renewal of "one of the most democratic forms of aesthetic awareness" (3) and noted that tellers and listeners alike take part in an "intimate complicity" that goes beyond the more usual dichotomy of performer/audience. In interactive performances, a story's significance lies beyond the words of the spoken text. We see this clearly in Gordon's work, as she negotiates with her listeners each time she retells "The Juniper Tree"; their spontaneous responses expand the sense of the story even though her spoken text may not change significantly from one telling to the next.

Many contemporary storytellers have developed a sense of composition that, at its best, parallels the creativity of narrators in traditional oral communities. Gorog-Karady's observations on Parisian performers is easily applicable to Jenoff and Gordon: "The appearance and relative success of a new story-teller undeniably constitutes a return to an expressive form which had lost, for a greater or lesser length of time, all pertinence among the common symbolic products of contemporary society. This revival is obvious even if today's listeners no longer hold the same relationship to folktales as the peasants of yore" (1–2). The "common symbolic products of contemporary society" here are the abusive mothers who violate the basic trust of motherhood by threatening their own children. The unpleasantly relevant tale of childhood abuse is retold daily in mass media accounts and personal revelations, most of which are, thankfully, far less extreme than those Jenoff and Gordon use to connect their old stories with present realities.

A third presentation at the international conference challenged the narrow notions of storytelling as an old traditional art. Vilmos Voigt's presentation in Budapest placed the seventeenth-century stories of Charles Perrault and the nineteenth-century tales of the Grimms firmly in the "modern age," and emphasized the history of literary exchanges between oral and written materials ("Modern Storytelling"). He noted that popular folktales had survived not only in printed collections and electronic reproduction, but also in parodies, satires, jokes, and commericial advertisements. Seen in this light, the stories of Jenoff and Gordon can be regarded as a legitimate part of a long literary tradition, one in which "folk" tales continue to evolve in form and meaning as methods of artistic communication.

Considerations of "folk" and "non-folk" and oral versus written expressions did not concern Donald Ward at all. Instead, he emphasized the broader concept of *homo narrans;* human beings evolving as natural story makers were and are, in Ward's opinion, capable of reflecting on reality and transforming it through personal interpretations of stories. He observed that active story making begins with what he called "idionarration," an informal process that occurs when we are alone with our own thoughts: "These moments of solitary reflection are, I suggest, a vital element in the processes that ultimately lead to social change. It is in these moments that narrative structures that later enter into the dynamic between the individual and his [or her] society have their genesis" (Ward 6). Ward cited personal stories told to one of his graduate students by abused and homeless women who reworked their lives by rethinking their own stories. I suggest that both Jenoff and Gordon, each in her own way, clearly and spontaneously used the idionarrating process in forming their stories; in these stories they have expressed their private reflections that were developed in solitude and later presented in public. Each woman was conscious of the potential impact of these "idionarrated" stories of two very undisciplined women from the fairy tale world.

MARVYNE JENOFF

Jenoff was already a published poet when she began to take an interest in telling stories. In preparing to work on the story of "Snow White" for reworking, she searched through all translated English versions she could find, including an early Grimm text featuring the natural mother as the villainess and the father as the rescuer. She deliberately chose to use this early text because it was so completely different from the well-known version—which had been further changed and popularized by Disney.

In this early text, the mother wishes for a lovely child, but later regrets this as Snow White matures into a beautiful young woman who becomes a rival, in the mother's eyes. She herself takes the girl out to the woods to pick flowers, and then abandons her there. The frightened girl finds her way to the house of the dwarfs, not the kindly beings of the Disney film but still willing to be helpful. When her mother discovers her there after consulting the magic mirror, she uses the familiar motifs of the poisoned comb, strangling bodice, and fatal apple to destroy her daughter. In this version it is the girl's father, not the prince, who finds and removes her coffin, taking it back to his palace. There he orders his royal physicians to revive her by tying her arms and legs to ropes connected to the four corners of the room. It is only after she is revived that the prince fortuitously appears to claim her, and the story proceeds (as in later editions) with the cruel queen attending the wedding and dancing to her death in red-hot iron shoes (David and David 303–15).

Jenoff found this odd story to her liking and used it as the model for her retelling. The first of two manuscripts she sent me began with the mother's dream: "One winter morning the Queen had a dream. She dreamed of the steel city she could see through her window, of colours, of birds, of searching through endless summer. And in the dream there was a child, her daughter, with the strange name of Snow White. Waking, radiant, the queen told it all to the king."

Jenoff continued her subtle transformation of the texts by giving the father a more overbearing role. He bans all mirrors, and then all seasons, to keep his wife and child young when he abandons them to go off to war. Without the mirror the motif of vanity does not develop; the queen does not become jealous of her maturing daughter, and thus they develop a loving relationship rather than deadly enmity.

Snow White's innocent curiosity about the world, encouraged by her mother, eventually draws her away from home and into the Steel City that replaces the fairy tale forest. The girl is found by the dwarfs, misguided urbanites who turn her into a starving fashion model. Her mother searches incessantly and finally rescues her from the opportunistic dwarfs, who are only interested in image and facade. Snow White is returned to her home, where her mother gradually reintroduces her to a more natural life in which birds sing, the seasons pass, and love between human beings can develop naturally.

Marvyne Jenoff sent me two unpublished versions of her text. The first, done in 1989, had been put aside because she could not find a satisfactory resolution. After reading an early draft of my article, she was inspired to work on it further. In both versions she reunited mother and daughter, and eventually the prince. The 1989 text is noticeably longer, filled with lengthy poetic descriptions. The later text, included here, presents a more focused story laced with occasional humor. (Her full text is included at the end of this chapter).

Jenoff's involvement with the story is with the mother, who becomes the central character in this text. The shift of focus from daughter to mother fundamentally alters the balance of the story; if the mother's character is positive, the threatening forces must be found elsewhere—in this case, the overbearing father and the opportunistic dwarfs. However, these antagonists are not portrayed as evil figures, or even as consciously destructive. Evil is expressed through the anonymous Steel City and its inhuman technology that creates the pretentious world of fashion modeling, and also the helicopters that carry men off to war.

Jenoff's identification with the characters gives this text its vibrancy. Each character is carefully considered in what Donald Ward would no doubt call "idionarration." This is implied in her own description of how stories develop for her: "In any story (I am "doing" Snow White and Cinderella) I have to consider all the characters and their relations to one another and what happens, and I'm bound firmly and complicatedly to the text" (1989 Letter to the author). Her emphasis on character rather than on action or motivation underscores the message she wishes to express in her text: that sinister forces unfold when we forget our personal connections to other living things and to the natural world.

Narrative scholars have examined the personal and psychological relationships between tale tellers and their story characters. Linda Dégh, for example, stresses such personal association as central in traditional narration: "The narrator weaves his own person into the tale, he imparts his own point of view when he tells the tale. His own fate is involved in the situations of the tale; he identifies himself with the tale action; and he interprets all the life expressions of his people" (*Folktales* 182).

Jenoff's approach takes this well-known tale in very different directions that reconstruct the story without a loss of its vitality. By re-figuring the evil mother or stepmother as helper rather than destroyer, Jenoff offers a transformed text that speaks specifically to those for whom "steel cities" are not only dehumanizing but dangerous. More specifically, she challenges the woman-against-woman conflict found in so many popular fairy tales—daughters threatened by mothers/stepmothers or elder sisters or "bad" fairies, not to mention false brides who try to replace them. In this way, Jenoff moves in deliberately in undisciplined directions, focusing on relationships between women that lead to freedom rather than competition and control.

SUSAN GORDON

I first heard Susan Gordon in 1982, at a week-long storytelling residency where she was working on "The Maiden without Hands." This Grimm tale, along with "Dummling" and "The Juniper Tree," has been a central story in Gordon's workshops and performances over the years. Her version of the tale that she calls "The Handless Maiden" deals with violence against a woman, while "Juniper Tree" centers on violence by a woman. Because she writes about "Maiden" so eloquently elsewhere ("Powers"), I will not treat it here. Still, her comments are often relevant. I cite these from two letters and a cassette tape she sent me in 1989. As an example, her reasons for choosing to work on "Juniper Tree" apply to "Maiden" as well: "I initially came to the story seeing it as a depiction of great depravity and evil, which it is. But I think that the process [of storytelling] is one of balance, that guilt and self-hate alone will not allow one to really achieve personhood" (Gordon, May letter).

The story of "great depravity and evil" begins gently, with the familiar motif of parents longing for a child. As in "Snow White," the mother injures her finger, sees blood on the snow, and wishes for a child as red as blood and as white as snow. A son is soon born, the mother dies, and the man finds a new wife with her own child. Motivated by jealousy, she kills the boy and puts the blame on her own innocent daughter, whom Gordon names Anne Marie, then cooks the boy in a stew and serves this to her unwitting husband when her returns home, claiming that the boy has gone to visit a relative. After the grisly meal, eaten only by the father, the grieving Anne Marie carefully gathers the bones and plants them under a juniper tree, from which the boy reappears as a vengeful bird who rewards his father and sister with gifts but kills the stepmother by dropping a mill wheel on her. He then regains his human form.[3] (A full text of Gordon's story is included at the end of this chapter).

Unlike Jenoff, Gordon holds so closely to the Grimm text that she even reproduces the sounds she describes: the chest closing on the boy's head, the turning mill wheel, the twenty millers cutting a new wheel, and most importantly, the singing bird. Her own "idionarrative" touches come in her wording and interpretations. She makes no significant alterations in plot or character, and she offers no shifts of viewpoint.

Like Jenoff, Gordon's attention is caught by the negative mother portrayed in the story, but instead of transforming this mother into a nurturing woman, as did Jenoff, Gordon tries instead to illuminate how all four of the characters are ambivalent enough to allow for at least some interpretation. She subtly emphasizes how the story and each of its characters are caught in a struggle with evil in ways relevant to her modern listeners: "Maybe a real confrontation with this story pulls a person up short and makes them realize the level of human depravity, but I think the real integration of the evil aspects in us only takes place over time" (May letter).

Because she remains so close to the text, Gordon finds it problematic in terms of contemporary expression. In particular she has come to find some of the most gruesome parts of the story almost ridiculous. As she comments in the same letter: "I must say that when I went to tell the story for you on tape, parts of it did seem harder to tell without laughing, basically the parts that are the most horrifying, like the cutting off of the boy's head, the setting of his head on his body, and its knocking off by his sister. While I know full well the horror of them, they seemed almost ludicrous and slapstick" (January letter).

Gordon does not merely recite the story, but manages instead to subtly extend it through her creative involvement, while still remaining faithful to the Grimm text. She narrates it in her own words rather than reciting it by rote from the printed text, which gives her the opportunity to suggest delicate shadings of character in her own words and intonations. She also emphasizes the song with which the bird serenades the other story characters, giving this grisly tale a more lyrical tone. Most important, she engages the audience directly by asking them to reflect on their own interpretations of its meaning.

Precisely because her telling is so faithful to the Grimm text, even the smallest deviations from it are significant. The sister is even more pathetic in her continual weeping for her murdered brother, but also in her innocent exuberance when she receives the red shoes dropped by the bird. The father's insensitivity is expressed by his brusque demands for his dinner and his sharp words expressing his greed in keeping it all to himself: "All of this is for *me*. None of you may have any of this." In the Grimm text his words are softer and more ironic when he says, "Give me some more! I'm not going to share this with you. Somehow I feel as if it were all mine" (Zipes, *Complete Fairy Tales* 89).

The stepmother, too, is portrayed somewhat more tragically. She alone understands the true meaning of the bird's song and goes out to meet her fate, saying mournfully (in Gordon's voice): "Then I will go out and see what the bird has for me." Gordon makes her own compassionate identification more explicit when she states how she came to understand the story as "unrelentingly patriarchal," in her words; "both in its depiction of the woman as solely responsible and in the solution to kill [only] her" (May letter). That is, she feels that the Grimm text fails to implicate the father in the tragedy. Because she makes only limited modifications to the Grimm text, these might easily go unnoticed without her additional comments, particularly her emphasis that each of the characters is responsible for the outcome: "It was when I finally had her [the mother] and didn't diminish her, just let her be who she was, that I then began to—the story began to—de-focus off of just her and began to move to look at the other characters. A very simple thing to notice is, *where is the father?*" (May letter).

Gordon finds her own storytelling voice in the bird's song, which had to be exactly right before she could tell the story; "I worked for a long time trying to learn the song, which I felt was so important to the story" (May letter). Since the bird is the teller of the boy's tale, Gordon, as singer of the bird's song, is bound by her identification to the son rather than the stepmother. The bird unrelentingly punishes the murderous stepmother but rewards the devouring father, which makes it all the more difficult for Gordon to resolve her own doubts in retelling the story.

She solves this in part by dividing her audiences into small groups and asking them to retell the story from other points of view. They are asked to portray the mother as sympathetically as they can, and to reconsider the daughter and father as accomplices in the crime rather than as innocent bystanders. Her performances are for very specific audiences, often those who are either victims or perpetrators of abuse, and whose interests she is aware of in advance. Audience context thus has a more direct effect on the increased understanding of the story as it comes back to her from their responses: "In therapeutic, educational, and religious settings the story is chosen with care to the occasion, with some knowledge of the people I'm telling it to and the desire to tell them a story that is, in some way, their story, which will provide them the opportunity to reflect on their own lives" (January letter). She modestly feels that it is such audience responses, rather than her own retellings that have helped to encourage a more compassionate perception of the extremely undisciplined woman in this story, encouraging listeners to interact directly with the story through their own experiences. In this way the story reverberates from teller to listeners and back again without interfering with the text of the tale.

Stories like "Snow White" and "The Juniper Tree" retain a great deal of transformative power for tellers and for listeners because they function literally and figuratively at the same time. This is certainly the case for many of those who hear Gordon's stories and can then reflect on their own difficult childhoods. When real violence is treated at a distance in a seemingly unrealistic folktale, both teller and listeners can create their own space for making personal connections. Such stories can also function as an emotional release from the adult stresses of ordinary day-to-day parenting, or from childhood fears of abandonment. I say this as a child who fantasized that my own parents were, secretly, mean steparents, and as a mother myself who had fearful dreams of losing my two children in natural disasters.

Jenoff and Gordon have consciously chosen old stories with the intention of finding new meaning for them, seeing in them "a catalogue of the destinies a man or a woman might have" mentioned earlier (Bronzini 5). Both women were led through their stories by very personal "idionarration," as discussed earlier by Donald Ward, rather than by intellectual explications. In their differing ways, they have tried to reconstruct old/new stories for today, allowing the tales to function as both reflections of lived reality and as a means of transforming it.

In selecting stories that center on the figure of powerful women who (in the Grimm texts) seem incapable of using their strength for creative purposes, these tellers are very aware of their own involvement with their stories, and with the transformative potential of traditional tales in contemporary life, they find some hope for their protagonists/antagonists. Gorog-Karady's comments on Parisian performers are entirely relevant here: "Above all, the folktale deals with a different world, an 'otherness' which is controlled by a different logic than that of the real social world. This logic can easily transgress the rules of 'alienating' reality. . . . A new, intimate, even participatory relationship develops between creators and their audiences that calls out to an imaginary world which adults generally repress in dreams, games, the unconscious" (4). Her comments on urban performers parallel those of Dégh, who stresses that for traditional narrators "the told story also mirrors the narrator's specific conceptualization of the world and its affairs: his cultural and personal meanings" ("How Storytellers Interpret" 48). By finding their personal and cultural voices in these stories that are, in essence, transformational, Gordon and Jenoff strive for potential metamorphosis of the internal world for themselves, their characters, and their listeners.

For Jenoff and Gordon, the "cultural and personal meanings" center on older, powerful women who fail to use their strength more positively. The tellers' "idionarrative" comments in personal letters to me revealed that they were aware of their involvement, and of the transformative potential of traditional tales in contemporary life. Gordon, for example, uses her storytelling in general, not only in this particular text, to encourage listeners to tell their own difficult stories and to reflect on their own lives. She concludes her article on another Grimm tale, "The Maiden without Hands," by saying, "I hope that you will hold 'The Maiden' against the fabric of your experience, as I held the Grimms' tale against mine, and note where the story informs your life, and where your life informs the story, and create it anew" ("Powers" 285).

In their personal struggles with these stories, holding them against the fabric of their own experiences, Jenoff and Gordon attempt to transform stereotype to archetype. It is in this way that traditional tales are kept alive and made accessible to a world of new possibilities.

SNOW WHITE: A REFLECTION

(Marvyne Jenoff, 1993, reprinted from the *second of two manuscripts Jenoff sent*.)

The King and Queen were sad because they had no child. The King was annoyed because the Queen's beauty was marred by her sadness.

One winter morning the Queen was embroidering the scene outside her window. The King was looking beyond her at the Steel City in the distance. Their sad eyes met, and the Queen pricked her finger.

That night the Queen dreamed of colors, her own red blood against the black window frame. She was dreaming of a daughter, named Snow White for the winter snow. She was searching for her daughter, birds searching with her, through an endless summer. Waking, the Queen told it all to the King.

The King thought a daughter would be a good start. From that time on he was always at the Queen's elbow as she embroidered garments for the child growing inside her. In time the child was born. Everyone was prepared to love her. Their love was reflected in her face, and they saw her as beautiful.

When Snow White was still a child the King went reluctantly to war. He ordered the soldiers to start out on foot and then prepared his helicopter. On the eve of his departure he had a dream that made him sit up. He was searching for his wife and child but kept finding only a harsh woman who spoke in rhymes to her evil-looking mirror. To prevent this dream from becoming prophetic, he issued an edict banning all mirrors from the kingdom, in deference to the seriousness of war. To foil the rest of the dream, and to keep his wife and child waiting for him exactly as they were, he banned the years as well as the seasons, so that no one would die or age or even grow. No sooner was the edict signed than the earth seemed to shudder to a stop on its path, seemed to spin out of control through dark, light, dark, light—then settled in a succession of long summer days.

With no mirrors the Queen looked at her child for confirmation of her own beauty. But she soon realized that in her husband's absence she no longer had to

be preoccupied with her appearance. She did as she pleased. She involved herself in every detail of caring for her child. She bathed her and dressed her,
taught her to spin, weave, embroider, and read. They made up games and
rhymes. And when the Queen realized that through her husband's edict, no
harm would come to her complexion, they spent their time outdoors. Snow
White loved the mingled summer fragrances. She ran after the birds, imitating
their calls. She learned to love every detail of her mother through the endless
summer.

At the same time Snow White was curious about what lay outside the castle.
The gate was often unattended now with the men at war. One day as Snow
White was looking through the gate she saw a small, oddly shaped man, a
dwarf, walking along, swinging his arms and singing to himself. Snow White
hardly remembered men. She wriggled out between the bars of the gate. Imitating his jaunty walk, as children do, she followed him into the Steel City. When
she saw that she had lost her way she stopped him and asked for help.

The dwarf had no idea what to do with a young girl in an ermine robe and
a diamond tiara alone in the city. He took her back to the penthouse where he
lived with his six brothers. It was easier to think with the seven of them together.

At first the dwarfs were shy. But Snow White described her life in the castle,
and told them how she happened to wander off and how much she missed her
mother. The dwarfs were charmed to a man, and determined to help her. Being
sophisticated city dwarfs they would do better than return her to her archaic existence. They would show her the modern world, the better world. Not being
quite part of this world in the way that they wished, they were very aware of
trends.

This was a time when women, with only each other to look at, dressed as
wildly as they wished. But in order to admire themselves, they had to catch their
reflections in windowpanes when the sun was at just the right angle. There were
no mirrors in the Steel City either. Some became fashion models to see themselves in magazines and on television. The dwarfs decided, then, to turn Snow
White into a fashion model with the advantage of a young start. All seven of
them went out to arrange modeling assignments for her. They left her in the
penthouse and forbade her to let anyone in. They didn't want her to wrinkle her
skin by smiling or speaking to anyone.

Snow White appreciated their kindness. To please them she did nothing but
gaze at her own image on commercials and in photos they had pinned up on the
walls. Birds came to teach her: the owl, the dove, the dodo, the raven, and the

Canada goose. But Snow White was absorbed in her task and didn't see them. The birds couldn't even make themselves heard through the sealed double glass of the penthouse windows. Thus, still and silent, Snow White spent her days. But at night her dreams were filled with birds with frantic messages, and her mother dancing with supplicating motions. "Come home, my child," she seemed to say. "Come home."

One day as the Queen was out looking for her daughter, she noticed some birds on the ground, pacing around a magazine. On the colorful cover was a picture of Snow White, older and thinner and smiling in an unfamiliar way. A breeze tore the cover loose and carried it into the city. The Queen followed its fluttering path through the streets to the right building. As the cover flew high upward and disappeared, she entered the building and found Snow White, more or less safe, in the penthouse.

The Queen had brought a sash which she had woven herself of silk and cotton in the colors of the fields. When she wrapped the sash around her daughter's waist, Snow White fell into a swoon of pleasure. As a model she was accustomed to wearing vinyl, hard leather, or even metal, and she couldn't remember ever feeling anything as soft as her mother's sash that touched her so gently. The Queen sat next to Snow White and held her hand, and said she would take her daughter home, at last. But Snow White told her about the seven dwarfs and their plans for her. The Queen was pleased she had made some headway. Before the dwarfs could find her there, she hurried back to the castle.

Later, when the dwarfs revived Snow White, she was so sparkling and wistful that they had to warn her very sternly not to let anyone in at all. Snow White wanted to obey, though she couldn't help but wish her mother were beside her. Sealed in the fluorescent room at night, there was the feel of grass in her hands and the scent of her own skin in the sun. During the day she began to dance a little when the dwarfs were away.

The Queen soon returned with a wooden comb she had carved herself. Snow White's hair had been bleached, colored, permed and then straightened, but had never been combed with wood, and never so gently. Snow White once again fell into a swoon. The Queen, sensing the seven pairs of footsteps coming closer, left Snow White once more and retreated to the castle. This was the second time she had failed to rescue Snow White, and she was uneasy.

This time when the dwarfs revived Snow White she was animated, and her simplest movements held them fascinated. They repeated their warning more strongly. Angrily. For each of them fervently, secretly, recalled his mirror-image and hoped, to a man, to find out what husbands did and marry Snow White himself. Why would she want a visitor? Did they not provide well for her? Were they not fine fellows, the best of company? Snow White determined to obey. In her sleep there were the dwarfs, much larger, arms folded as if to block her dreams that nevertheless got through. In the day she danced, and thought of summer flowers.

Next, the Queen brought an apple, which she had picked herself on the castle grounds. At first Snow White couldn't remember what an apple was for—her working diet was bland liquids. At her mother's urging she bit into the apple, and at the unaccustomed tartness of the first taste she fell again into a swoon. The Queen, afraid of the dwarfs, retreated once again without rescuing Snow White. This time the dwarfs could do nothing for her. This was the third time, and they knew the power of the number three. They laid her out on her bed in what they hoped was a comfortable position.

Snow White neither woke nor stirred in her sleep. But as loyal supporter of the King's edict banning change, they never once believed that she could be dead. They dreamed the sky was a great mirror seeking beauty. And so they built a coffin-like structure out of a special kind of glass to display and protect her at the same time. Gently they arranged Snow White inside it and carried her up to the penthouse roof. Each thought to himself that it was just as well for this to happen now, for the trend was that women were getting bored with modeling. They no longer had to think about keeping their figures, and without exercise they became despondent. They wanted change, they wanted seasons, even years. And they wanted their men home.

Motionless in the coffin Snow White craved her mother's gifts, her embrace, her fragrance. She dreamed of the dwarfs chasing birds. She dreamed of her father in his royal helicopter with people bowing to it. Once more birds came to teach her: the owl, the dove, the dodo, the raven, and the Canada goose. But the dwarfs had designed the glass for their own purposes, and once again the birds couldn't reach her. The dwarfs brought their TV up to the roof to watch her, and there they were, all on the roof of the penthouse, when the King returned from war.

From the helicopter the King caught sight of Snow White looking exactly as he remembered her. He congratulated himself on his foresight. His immediate concern was to cure her and take her home to the Queen, where he would restore the life he had left. Scattering the birds and the dwarfs, he brought the helicopter down on the penthouse roof.

The King had once traveled with poets, then with philosophers, then with jesters. With him now in the helicopter were physicians, who were happy to have a change of scene after the sights of war. They were very interested in curing Snow White and finding out what she would say after her near-death experience. She was one of the rare people who had experienced both the ancient world of the castle and the modern world of the Steel City. When they arrived home they removed her from the coffin and laid her down on a bed in a special room in the castle. They researched modern cures, but then hers was no modern affliction. They researched ancient cures, and finally agreed on the one where string was wound around the afflicted person and fastened to the four corners of the room. It took them forever to find enough string, the kind that had been used to tie packages, because no one saved string anymore. The King, fancying himself a scientist, joined the physicians in their search. The kingdom might have had to wait forever for the return of seasons if not for the innocent intervention of the Queen.

The Queen was happy to have her daughter back, and every day she bathed her and rubbed scented lotions into her skin. She dressed her in different kinds of cloth so the variety of sensations would tempt her to wake. Snow White stirred with pleasure. She sat up, then walked a little. As her energy came back she remembered fields. Mother and daughter picked apples together, and Snow White ate them, apples of every color. When her throat was opened again she began to speak, and to sing. They read from ancient books they found in the castle. They spun, wove, and embroidered. During these full and endless days the birds were at last able to reach Snow White and to teach her what they knew. The owl taught of wisdom and folly. The dove spoke of peace and war and the dodo of pride and humility. The raven told stories, and the Canada goose told of recovery from being an endangered species.

Then the Queen, defying the King's ban on seasons, decided to teach her daughter one last thing. She taught her how to prick her finger. At that moment there was a great shudder beneath them as the earth spun forward on its path, sped on by the pent-up years, the seasons hot and cold as they flashed past. Snow White, dizzy with unfamiliar motion, soothed her bleeding finger in her mouth. She grew taller, became a woman. Love for her mother, the lessons of the birds, all she knew, surged through her changing body.

The Queen gazed at this woman, her daughter. Beyond her, through the open window, she saw the Prince, black hair, red lips. The last part of the

Queen's long-ago dream was falling into place. She embraced her daughter and discreetly left the room.

The Prince had been searching ever since he could remember. Not finding her in the Steel City he searched further, and finally reached the far side of the castle. There he felt the ground shudder and the earth begin to turn. At least he would experience the seasons that he had heard about. Exhilarated by the motion, he was drawn to the castle window. Snow White waited.

Being a Prince he had been exposed to only the finest of popular culture, and thus had never seen a woman as old as himself. As he looked in the window he recognized at once what had been missing from his life. You must be Snow White, he said. She agreed. He reached up to touch her hair. The faint smell of blood was in the air, and the chill of winter. What new worlds were these, inviting him?

He touched her hair again, and she touched his. And, as everyone knows, they began to live happily ever after.

THE JUNIPER TREE

(Susan Gordon, 1989; *Text transcribed from unedited tape sent by Gordon.*)

There was once a wealthy merchant who was married to a woman who was kind and good and they had everything they desired, except for the thing they desired most—and that was a child. And although the woman prayed and prayed for one, still they did not get one. And one day in the winter she was standing out in her yard beneath the juniper tree and she was peeling an apple when the knife slipped and it cut her finger. And three drops of her blood fell upon the ground. And she thought,

"If only I had a child as red as that blood and as white as that snow."

And suddenly she felt as if it might come true, and she went into the house.

A month passed and the snow was gone; two months and everything was green; three months and the buds began to come out on the trees; four months and the flowers were in bloom and trees were dense and tangled and thick and birds sang among them; five months and the blossoms on the trees fell and the air was so sweet that when the woman stood beneath the juniper tree it was as if her heart leaped within her, and so she fell on the ground and gave thanks; six months and the fruit on the trees grew round and heavy—and the woman grew very still; seven months and the fruit grew ripe and the woman ate the juniper berries greedily; eight months and the woman was so sick that she thought she would die, and she begged her husband to bury her beneath the juniper tree; nine months and she gave birth to a child who was as white as the snow and as red as the blood. She held him in her arms, she looked at him, and then she died. Her husband wept bitterly, and buried her beneath the juniper tree.

Time passed and still he wept, and more time and still he wept, and more time, and he ceased crying, and more time and he took for himself a second wife. Now, by this woman he had a child, a daughter—but his son was as white as snow and as red as blood, and every time his new wife would look at him it would cut her to the heart, for she desired all of the merchant's wealth for her daughter. And so it seemed to her that the boy was always underfoot and it was as if the Evil One spoke in her ear, and she began to pinch him here and push him there and pummel him, so that the boy was always bruised and in a fright and he had no safe place to hide.

One day, when the boy was at school, Ann Marie followed her mother up into her mother's bedroom, and there her mother had a chest filled with apples. And Ann Marie said,

"Mother, may I have an apple?"

And her mother said, "Why yes."

And she bent over and reached for a red, ripe apple and handed it to her daughter. And as she did so, Ann Marie said,

"And my brother—can he have one too?"

That angered the woman, and she said,

"He can have one when he comes home from school."

And then she turned, and she looked out the window and she saw the boy coming. It was as if the Evil One spoke to her and she snatched the apple out of her daughter's hand and she flung it down into the chest and said,

"You can have an apple after your brother's had his!"

Ann Marie went downstairs, and when the little boy came up the stepmother said to him in a loud voice,

"WOULD YOU LIKE AN APPLE?"

And the boy looked at her and he said,

"Oh mother, you look so wild today, strange and wild."

And the Evil One made her speak to him kindly:

"Wouldn't you like an apple?"

And she lured him on, and he said,

"Yes mother, I would like an apple."

She lifted the lid on the great chest: "Take one," she said. And the boy bent in to get an apple—and the mother brought the lid down CRUNCH! on his head. His head flew off and rolled among the apples.

Then the mother said to herself, "What have I done! How can I get out of this!"

And then she sat the boy's body upon the chair, and she reached in and took out his head and put it upon his neck. She took a silken cloth from her drawer and wrapped it round and round his neck. She set the chair by the door and put the apple in his hand.

Then she went downstairs and was boiling a great pot of water, when Ann Marie came in and said, "My brother's sitting in the chair so still and white. He has an apple in his hand but when I asked him for a bite he would not speak to me."

And her mother said, "Go back up and ask him for the apple. And if he still will not speak to you, box him in his ear."

So Ann Marie went back to her brother and said, "Give me a bite of that apple."

But he did not speak to her, so she slapped him—and his head fell off his shoulders and rolled across the floor.

"Mama! Mama! Mama!" Ann Marie came running into the kitchen— "Mama, I hit him and his head . . . MAMA! MAMA!"

And her mother turned and looked, and said, "Ann Marie! What have you done, you foolish girl! Well there's nothing to be done for it now, except to hide it."

And she went and picked up the boy's body and laid it upon the table, and gathered up his head and placed it there as well. She took a knife from the drawer in the table and began to hack his body up and throw the pieces in the kettle to boil. Ann Marie stood by the pot and cried and cried and cried, until the water needed no salt.

Late in the afternoon when the father came home from work, he walked in and he said, "I'm hungry, I'm ready for dinner."

And his wife said, "I have a fine stew cooked for you."

And Ann Marie cried and cried and cried—and the father said, "Where is my son?"

And the wife said, "His uncle came for him—your first wife's brother—and he's taken him down to his place to live for a while."

*"But how strange," said the father, "for him to go and not to say good bye to
me."*

*"Oh he'll be back," said the mother. "They'll take good care of him. He'll only
be gone six weeks." And Ann Marie cried and cried and cried. The father said,*

*"Still, how strange that he would say nothing. Well never mind. I'm hun-
gry. Give me my dinner."*

*And his wife dished up the dark black stew that was his son, and the man be-
gan to eat—and he ate and he ate and he ate. And he said,*

"All of this is for me. None of you may have any of this."

*And so he ate all of the stew—until it was gone. He chewed on the bones and
then flung them beneath the table.*

Ann Marie cried and cried, and he said to her,

"Your brother will be home soon. You'll see—it will be all right."

*Ann Marie bent beneath the table and she gathered up all the bones of her
brother, wrapped them in a silk cloth, and took them outside and laid them beneath the juniper tree. And when she laid them in the grass, suddenly the tree
began to move. The branches went back and forth like hands that are clapping
when they are happy. And a mist rose out of the tree, and from the center of the
mist flew a great golden bird, singing. Ann Marie looked down at the base of the
tree and she saw the bones of her brother were gone, and suddenly she felt
happy—as if he had come back to life. And she went into the house and ate her
supper.*

*The bird flew down into the village and sat upon the roof of a goldsmith's
house, and sang out:*

My mother she killed me,

My father he ate me,

And my sister, Ann Marie

Laid my bones at the juniper tree.

Ohhhhhhhh, What a beautiful bird am I.

*The goldsmith came running out of the house so fast that he left one of his
slippers behind, and he stood out in the street, a slipper on one foot but barefoot
on the other, and a chain—a golden chain—in one hand and his working tools
in the other. And he said,*

"Oh bird, that was wonderful. Sing it again."

But the bird said,

"Oh no, a second time I do not sing for free. Give me a gift."

And the goldsmith flung the golden chain up to the bird and said,

"There. Sing it again."

And the bird caught the chain in his right claw and began to sing his song.

And then he flew away, down to the cobbler's house, and again he sang out:

(sung slowly) My mother she butchered me,

My father he ate me,

My little sister Ann Marie

She gathered up the bones of me,

And tied them in a silken cloth,

And laid them under the juniper tree.

Ohhhhhhhhh, What a beautiful bird am I.

The cobbler came running out of the house and said,

"Oh bird, that was wonderful. Sing it again."

And the bird said,

"Oh no, a second time I do not sing for free."

And the cobbler called out his wife and his workers and his daughter and said,

"See, look—look at that beautiful bird. You should hear the song that he can sing."

Then he said to his daughter,

"Go upstairs and you'll find in the attic a pair of red leather shoes. Bring them out and give them to the bird."

And the daughter ran upstairs and she brought down the red leather shoes and she held them up into the air, and the bird flew down and took them in its left claw. And then he sang again.

My mother she butchered me,

My father he ate me,

My little sister Ann Marie

She gathered up the bones of me,

And tied them in a silken cloth,

And laid them under the juniper tree.

Ohhhhhhhhh, What a beautiful bird am I.

And then the bird flew on until he came to a linden tree beside a mill. And there, there were twenty millers hewing a millstone and the mill went "clickety clack, clickety clack, clickety clack, clickety clack." And the men chopped, chopped, chopped, chopped. And the bird sang out,

My mother she butchered me,

(And two of the millers stopped working.)

My father he ate me,

(And three more stopped.)

My little sister Ann Marie

(And several more stopped.)

She gathered up the bones of me,

(And there were only five millers still working.)

And tied them up in a silken cloth,

(And now there were only two.)

And laid them under the juniper tree.

(And now only one.)

Ohhhhhhhh, What a beautiful bird am I.

And the last miller lay down his tools and said,

"Oh bird, what a beautiful song. Sing that again."

And the bird said,

"The second time I do not sing for free. Give me the millstone."

And the miller said,

"It is not just mine to give. It belongs to all of us."

And he turned to the other millers and they all said,

"Oh yes, give him the millstone. Give him the millstone, and let him sing again."

And so he did. Then the bird flew down and put his neck beneath the millstone and flew back up into the tree with the millstone around his neck, red shoes in one claw and gold chain in the other—and then he flew away again—flew away towards his own home.

And then he perched on his roof and he sang out:

My mother she butchered me,

My father he ate me,

My little sister Ann Marie

She gathered up the bones of me,

And tied them up in a silken cloth,

And laid them under the juniper tree.

Ohhhhhhhh, What a beautiful bird am I.

And his father said,

"Ah, suddenly it feels like summer in the air, so warm and . . . somehow I feel like soon I'll see my son again."

DIFFICULT WOMEN IN FOLKTALES

And the mother said,

"No! No! It's cold out there, not warm. It feels like a great storm is coming!"

And the bird sang out:

My mother she butchered me,

My father he ate me,

My little sister Ann Marie

She gathered up the bones of me,

And tied them up in a silken cloth,

And laid them under the juniper tree.

Ohhhhhhhhh, What a beautiful bird am I.

And the father said,

"Oh what a wonderful song. Oh look, look at the bird out there, it's singing. I want to go out and see him."

His wife said,

"No! Don't go out there! I'm so afraid. My teeth are chattering and I'm so cold inside—but I'm burning up!"

And she ripped open her blouse. And the father said,

"I'm going out to see what the bird has for me."

And he stepped outside, and Ann Marie cried and cried, and the mother flung herself down full length on the floor and her cap fell from her head.

The father stepped out and the bird sang:

My mother she butchered me,

My father he ate me,

My little sister Anne Marie

She gathered up the bones of me,

And tied them up in a silken cloth,

And laid them under the juniper tree.

Ohhhhhhhhh, What a beautiful bird am I.

And he dropped down the gold chain and it fell around the father's neck. And the father came in and said,

"Look—look what the bird has given me. He's a wonderful bird. And the air outside—it smells like cinnamon. But the mother said,

"No! No! We're all going to die!"

And then she lay still as if she were dead herself.

And Ann Marie said,

"I'm going outside to see what the bird has for me."

And Ann Marie went out and the bird sang:

My mother she butchered me,
My father he ate me,
My little sister Anne Marie
She gathered up the bones of me,
And tied them up in a silken cloth,
And laid them under the juniper tree.
Ohhhhhhhhh, What a beautiful bird am I.

And he dropped down the red shoes, and Ann Marie caught them and put them on her feet and danced and danced and danced all around the yard. And then she came in and she said,

"Look—look what the bird has given me. I feel so happy."

The mother said, "No!" But then she said,

"I will go out and see what the bird has for me."

And the mother stood up, and walked outside.

Ohhhhhhhhh, What a beautiful bird am I, he sang.

And the bird dropped the millstone, and it crushed the stepmother. And there was smoke, and a splat of grease, and that was all.

The father and Ann Marie heard the sound and they came outside—and there they found the boy back again. And the boy took his father by one hand, his sister by the other, and they went inside and sat down and ate their supper.

[Susan concluded her story on the tape by commenting, "Well, that was a very rough telling of it!" Her abrupt ending is, almost word-for-word, from the Grimm text and not from Susan's interpretation.]

11

The Teller in the Tale

(1998)

Here is the fruition of my folkloric curiosity about the process of oral creativity in platform storytelling, as it actually came to life for two tellers in specific contexts. I was witness to the process of creativity, listening to the told stories as I taped them, and transcribing the texts fully so that readers could later make their own connections between teller and tale. The two tellers offer contrasting experiences: Stewart Cameron was aware of the various ways in which his son affected the development of the fictional "Jack" character in his tale, discovering as he told the story over the years how other people he knew wandered in and out of it as well—including, to his surprise, finding himself in the father/king. In contrast, Marylyn Peringer did not at first see how outside influences had woven themselves into her tale of thwarted fate, but when she told it to me privately, familiar people and objects became more apparent to her.

In this piece, written originally for my book *Burning Brightly* (141–76), I discussed how both conscious and unconscious innovations made each story

An earlier version of this chapter, focusing on Stewart Cameron, appeared as "Jack in Toronto" (McCarthy 250–71), and was used with the permission of the University of North Carolina Press. I am grateful to William McCarthy and William Ellis for editorial suggestions.

a living experience for these tellers, and of course for all their listeners over the years. Stewart and Marylyn were intrigued to ponder with me what they experienced in their own stories, and in doing so revealed the oral process more fully.

In terms of my own development, writing this essay gave me a firm sense of the value of applying folkloric tools and perspectives to modern performers, those who actually participate in an oral process and not a scripted performance or a recitation of a book-story. It was exciting to see how each, in their individual way, was ardently committed to stories and listeners, and to the whole complex process of creating with spoken words at a time when storytelling was thought by many—including my university students—to be a dying art.

It is widely understood that fictional characters are often patterned, wholly or in part, on actual people. Features, forms, voices, motivations, and the general demeanor of familiar acquaintances find their way into imaginative stories. The preferences and judgments of authors also guide their stories. This is no less so for folktales than for any other kind of story. It is no secret that fact and fancy are not as distant in the expressive arts as we think them to be in ordinary life. How does the process of actualizing fiction come about? I was curious to discover if this was a conscious decision or a spontaneous act. I wondered, too, how these choices might contribute to or detract from the effectiveness of a story, for the listeners and for the narrators.

I addressed these points through the responses of two Toronto area performers, Stewart Cameron and Marylyn Peringer, familiar to me as tellers and as colleagues. Over a period of several years we shared information in open-ended interviews and through casual conversations and letters. I had also observed them in a number of storytelling events, private and public. In order to keep their remarks closer to this creative context, our interviews took place around the telling of a story of their choice. Each approached the act of creation in different ways and with different degrees of consciousness. Stewart Cameron was aware that he was modeling Jack in "The Three Feathers" on his own son, but until I began to ask how and why, he had not realized how intricate and continuous this process had become. Marylyn Peringer was surprised to discover how familiar people and objects had come into her stories unexpectedly, and how much they enriched the stories for her. From the perspective gained in the interview context, both were able to comment on the subtle ways that their stories reflected their concerns about their own lives and convictions.

A formal interview has the advantage of placing a story in a different perspective for the teller by taking it out of the more natural context of the storytelling event, the platform performance. In the midst of repeated tellings in different contexts a story takes on a life of its own, but when a narrator is asked to consider an episode, motif, or character out of the performance context they must stop the story in midstream in their minds in order to sense what is happening as they tell it. In this way they might detect how the familiar waking world has suggested an intuitive interpretation that they are not aware of—or not fully so. They see for themselves how they awaken a printed story by breathing their own lives into it.

The interchange of reality and fantasy is not surprising to narrative scholars, who have long recognized folktales and wondertales as significant literary expressions. Many of them have concentrated on oral material developed over generations in European communities and further evolved in North American materials.[1] When traditional narration arises from the overall social fabric of a community even the most fantastic story is alive with local characters, settings, motivations, and other narrative attributes that reverberate for tellers and listeners. A story figure might have the face or disposition of a neighbor, a situation might arise from the teller's own experience, a house in the forest might be a familiar home. As we saw in the introduction, narrators who grow up listening to *Märchen*, legends, and other stories of a community learn them in the context of personal associations that join the common reality of everyday life to the very uncommon reality of the stories in which trees speak and ants can help a heroine or hero succeed. This story-world that exists between what we call fantasy and reality has intrigued many who have explored wondertales. The observations of Linda Dégh (*Narratives in Society,* particularly 93–151), Max Lüthi (*Once Upon a Time* and *The European Folktale*) and Lütz Rohrich (*Folktales and Reality*) are invaluable in understanding this betwixt and between world of reality/unreality. Dégh explores actual tellers of tales, Lüthi focuses on the stories and their deep magic, and Rohrich comments on the abiding connections between the fantasy of tales and the waking world of reality.

For tellers of these tales it is a challenge to find their own feet as they balance between seemingly separate realities that are, in wondertales, one world. Their artistic innovation develops as they become increasingly experienced in drawing together their own real and fictional worlds. It is not only that the tales live in tellers' minds, but that tellers live within the stories—not literally as participants but as temporary visitors, walking along with their protagonists, as we will see in the stories and comments of Marylyn Peringer and Stewart Cameron. Out of curiosity I casually questioned tellers and listeners about their own place in a story; those who were able to imagine themselves actually inside found that they were moving just behind the protagonists and often a little to the left so they could see where they were going. Some could even estimate the distance, usually from one to three feet. One teller suggested that this distance might even indicate how close she actually felt to a particular character.

For many tellers in traditional and in organized storytelling, the story as they learned it from a person or a book is sufficient as a place to begin; they have only to remember the sequence of events and characters, the necessary repetitions, the opening and concluding phrases, and they can build their own story. But for some this becomes too rigid, too restraining. Folklorist Linda Dégh considered the issue of how traditional narrators with more than ordinary talent retained the storyline yet managed to rise above it to fashion an artistic composition; she affirmed what we will see in the case of Stewart Cameron and Marylyn Peringer—that creativity occurs in the skillful embroidery of detail. Dégh observed that this kind of elaboration was quite the opposite of the brief narratives (jokes and anecdotes, for example) so popular in our contemporary lives; in these kinds of stories detail is deliberately left out in order to put the weight of the story on the punch line. "In contrast," she stated, "the good narrator of magic tales must prove his art within the framework of the tale by including his own thoughts and weaving his personal opinions into the tale" (*Folktales and Society* 224). And, I add, thinking of Marylyn, *her* thoughts and opinions.

In addition to elaborating on details and expressing their own viewpoints, tellers also deepen a story by connecting it to their own everyday lives. This might be true of only some parts of a tale, as when North Carolina narrator Ray Hicks identifies himself with the Jack character in his tales (Sobol, "Jack in the

Raw"; Oxford, "They Call Him Lucky Jack"). Personal preferences of individual narrators are essential in understanding the dynamics of creativity. Lütz Rohrich is eloquent in his comments on the relations of tellers and their tales in his detailed study, *Folktales and Reality:* "Psychological analysis of narrators reveal that informants always prefer certain themes and rarely go beyond the bounds of their personality. Although tradition provides the materials for the plot, the folktale nonetheless allows for individual differentiation" (204). This is no less true in organized storytelling, where we find the artistry of "individual differentiation" manifesting as the skillful interweaving of communal and personal interests. However, narrators in oral tradition feel a strong commitment to a community of tellers, as we will see in the case of Joe Neil MacNeil.

Platform performers are freer to develop their storytelling repertoire and style in isolation if they choose. They can simply claim a story, lift it free from any relevant cultural context, and rework it as their own without reference to its traditional associations. This is all the easier because many popular folktale collections provide no context beyond a generalized source. A teller might mention the country of origin, but there is often no contextual information that expands the story and offers possibilities for interpretation. Rarely if ever are the original tale-tellers identified. Such stories are often regarded as "public domain" material, free to be used and manipulated as a teller sees fit. Some tellers respond by simply reciting the story as they learned it, adding nothing at all from their own experience; others go to the other extreme, modernizing and personalizing tales extensively, deconstructing the old and recreating "modern" (or "postmodern") tales in an entirely new context.

Between these two ends of the creative continuum there are tellers who respond by doing their own comparative research by trying to understand how stories arose from living narrators in a specific time and place. Marylyn and Stewart each found their own ways of seeking this kind of connection with the stories they tell here. I wanted to discover how they faced the challenges of modern audiences, how they found ways of bringing stories to life from printed texts without transforming them into postmodern literary stories. Their methods and motivations were different, but both had similar views of folktales as enigmatic metaphors for modern life, and for adults, not only for children.

Also, by identifying themselves directly and indirectly with their stories and story characters instead of taking a more objective, critical outsider's stance, they parallel the traditional narrators described by Linda Dégh: "The personal text not only shows the narrator's ability in formulating a story from available plot episodes, but also his or her way of making the world of fantasy palpable by connecting it with the world of everyday reality: the told story also mirrors the narrator's specific conceptualization of the world and its affairs: his cultural and personal meanings" ("How Storytellers Interpret" 48). We will see how these observations come to life in the two texts included here, and in the tellers' comments on their own stories. (Full texts are included at the end of this chapter).

Marylyn Peringer and Stewart Cameron were active in the widespread Toronto area storytelling community for a number of years. Like many others I met they were aware of their personal preferences for certain kinds of tales as well as the place of the tales within particular oral traditions. Many of Stewart's songs and stories were of Scottish origin, whereas Marylyn had found that French tales and legends drew her strongly. Each sought out other variant texts of a story when they could find them, both in print and in oral tellings. Marylyn did further research in order to gain a fuller sense of social and historic contexts as well as aesthetic possibilities. They were also attentive to ways in which the tales reverberated from their own past and present lives and back again, as the stories developed through performances.

I met both Stewart and Marylyn during the 1985 Toronto festival, the first of several I attended. A few years later I asked if they would take part in individual interviews centered around the retelling of a favorite story, and if they would discuss how it reflected their experiences as performers. Both agreed enthusiastically. The story Stewart told, "Jack and the Three Feathers," was one I had heard at my very first festival, though I did not know then that it was a particular favorite of his because Jack had gradually taken on the character of his son Duncan. The interview and the narration of "The Three Feathers" took place in 1988; we exchanged letters the next year, which allowed Stewart to reflect on this story in particular, and on his storytelling in general.

Ten years passed between the time I met Marylyn in Toronto and our long-overdue formal interview on a park bench in the Yukon in 1994, though we conversed at several festivals and corresponded regularly in between. Marylyn chose a French-Canadian tale, "The Horoscope," that reflected a number of facets of her life, among them her love of the French language and her Catholicism.

By looking at these two tellers and their story examples I hope to show how reality enters the realm of the wondertale. All quotations are from our interviews, unless otherwise noted.

MARYLYN PERINGER

In response to one of my questions about "The Horoscope," Marylyn said, with a hint of surprise, "Oh, the story is more than the story," meaning that she was aware that the basic storyline was only the framework for meaningful expression. I explore how she came to realize this after several years of telling the story.

Marylyn discovered "L'horoscope," an Acadian legend told by Benoit Benoit, in a collection by Luc Lacoursiere.[2] In it a farmer asks an astrologer to predict the fates of his three sons and is told that the oldest will be hanged at 21, so he decides to avert this by working his son to death. The son eventually leaves home, meets and befriends a mysterious stranger and they work together on various farms and then in a shipyard. Here he falls in love with and marries the owner's daughter; on their wedding day the horoscope prediction is revealed but the friend, actually a guardian angel, saves the young man from his fate.

After listening to Marylyn tell this story I asked her how her identity as a storyteller had evolved. Like many tellers I met, Marylyn's first public experience was accidental; she had decided to do her oral presentation in a French conversation class on the rich store of Quebecois lore and legends, not realizing how challenging this would be. As she described it, it was "the beginning of a whole long tale" that continues today after almost two decades of research and performances. Though her performing career has centered on bilingual tales, Marylyn is neither French nor Canadian; she grew up in New Jersey, the child of an English father and a Maltese mother. Her interest in French Canada that began in the conversation class blossomed as she told more and more stories from French-Canadian traditions.

Marylyn placed high value on precision, loyalty, and integrity in her life and in her stories. "I've always liked creating order," she said, and expressed this in her careful preparation and telling of stories. She felt that the detailed research she put into each tale "informs your telling, and makes it more authoritative and more confident." This was, she thought, of utmost importance for professional tellers who relied on printed stories; that is, to recreate at least some of the social and cultural context.

Marylyn recalled how she rehearsed the story of "The Horoscope" several years earlier, pacing back and forth in a dormitory in Moncton, New Brunswick, where she was preparing to give a storytelling workshop. She learned and told it in French for her Acadian audiences, but told it to me in English. As she practiced it aloud to herself she began "to smooth out the few inconsistencies in the original." She struggled with the scruples of changing a collected text, aware that a folklorist would say, "It has to be left that way, that's the way the story was told." She felt that there were "artistic decisions that I made in order to make the pattern clearer. I suppose that I felt that the pattern had to be as clear as some of the images in the story were to me." She carefully chose to make slight alterations that were appropriate for her as a performer rather than a researcher, responsibly aware of what she was doing and concerned about being faithful to the "the spirit of the story" rather than the exact word-for-word text. For example, she felt she needed a clearer motivation for the father trying to work his son to death, and thus had him overly concerned about family reputation (he would have been embarrassed to have his son hanged publicly). She increased the ties of friendship between the young man and the enigmatic stranger rather than emphasizing his mystery, as in the legend. She also portrayed the shipowner's daughter as livelier and more decisive, strengthening her presence in the story. She ended the story by describing the happy couple rather than focusing on the guardian angel as he disappeared. She was aware that these modest alterations, particularly in the conclusion, shifted the nature of the tale: "The ending I added, because in the original he just walked away and they never saw him again. He just walked away and that was all, and I wanted to put, I don't know, I thought it deserved a more fairy tale type ending—'And all the days of their lives . . .' a happy-ever-after type of ending which was related to their marriage in some way." This seemingly small change transforms the story from its original legendary form into a folktale, by emphasizing the happy union of the couple rather than the supernatural feats of the guardian angel.

In order to avoid arbitrary changes made simply for personal reasons, Marylyn began extensive research on French tales in the United States and Canada. She sought out comparative material from the Robarts Library at the University of Toronto, from publications of Laval University in Quebec, from back issues of *The Journal of American Folklore,* and from "all sorts of books and transcriptions of tapes, collections from here and there, folktales, fairy tales, lore, commentaries on the stories." She discovered variants of the story from Spain, Czechoslovakia, and Ireland, not to mention a version from India called "Savitri and Satyavan." Since much of her material came from scholarly collections rather than from popular books she understood that the story was indeed more than the story, as she put it; that outside the context of a functioning community the texts lost some of their significance and that she had to work to recontextualize them: "Most of the sources I got them from came from storytellers whose listeners were familiar with all the tales so not everything had to be explained. So of course I had to do so much preliminary work in just explaining the beliefs that had given rise to these particular stories."

Through her own research, Marylyn discovered that she needed to know more about the overall context of her stories from the viewpoint of their original tellers. In this way she was able to create a more relevant context for herself as well as for her listeners. She was interested to hear from our correspondence that this approach was favored by narrative scholars. I have mentioned Henry Glassie's work in Northern Ireland, and here his comments are most relevant: "Context is not in the eye of the beholder, but in the mind of the creator. Some of context is drawn in from the immediate situation, but more is drawn from memory. It is present, but invisible, inaudible. Contexts are mental associations woven around texts during performance to shape and complete them, to give them meaning" (33). This elusive contextualizing was what Marylyn tried to sense in her own search. In order to become a more effective creator herself she tried to see into the mind of the creators with whom her stories arose.

In the long process of seeking out and preparing narratives from French-Canadian sources Marylyn developed a sense of comparative research that is one of the invaluable tools of a folklorist. She was especially excited to find the version of "The Horoscope" from India, "Savitri and Satyavan" mentioned earlier. In this story a young woman falls in love with and marries a man even though she knows that he is fated to die on their first anniversary; she manages to trick Yama, god of death, into three promises that can only be kept if the husband lives. Marylyn said with wonder, "It's the same story! How did that story get half way across the world into some little French-Canadian fishing village in New Brunswick?" She occasionally told both together without commentary, allowing them to echo from one to another. This curiosity led her to appreciate comparative work on folktales, and in particular the value of indexes that listed the titles of variant texts, and of the motifs within stories.[3] Any teller using these invaluable tools could find comparable stories and story motifs from a broad range of cultural areas.

One of the aspects of both texts that attracted Marylyn was the central place held by promises that were made and kept. In "The Horoscope" the astrologer promises that the son will be hanged on his 21st birthday, but he is saved because he promises his mother that he will pray to his guardian angel—who eventually saves his life; the son is faithful in his promises to his mysterious friend, to the shipyard owner for whom he toils, and to the owner's daughter whom he pledges to marry. In the Indian variant the daughter extracts promises as well as keeping them: she compels her father to promise that she can choose her own husband, promises a young man's parents that she will protect him, and later tricks Yama into promises that save her husband's life. Marylyn remembered another story that hinged on promises, a Quebecois legend in which the corpse of a murder is insulted by a young man and returns to life to avenge himself; the young man is saved by promising to have the corpse properly buried and to show respect for the dead—and he keeps his promises. None of these stories contain the deliberate disobedience and cunning capriciousness that we will see in Stewart's story of Jack.

The motif of faithfulness was one of the ways that Marylyn connected her stories to the world of experience, observing that such stories offer hope for "things coming around right" when we maintain our integrity. "I always try to keep my promises, and I'm so grateful when I find that reinforced in a story." It is not the rigidity of morals she found compelling but the fact that the characters demonstrated "so much love, so much faithfulness."

She also expressed an interest in stories featuring angels and devils, at least in part because such stories stress the constant human struggle with good and evil. These figures are particularly favored in French-Canadian tales of all sorts, humorous folktales, legends, and wondertales. Thus it is not unusual that the guardian angel in "The Horoscope" takes the place of the fairy godmother or other typical folktale helpers. She commented that this was particularly true for French-Canadian [Catholic] legends; "you know, they give the devil so much time, so I can see them putting an angel in for a little bit more equal time for the other direction."

Marylyn found that as she told this story (and others) it gradually began to express aspects of her own life—people she knew, objects she was familiar with, situations she had experienced. The shipowner's daughter came to resemble a lively young woman in her choir; the mahogany table at the wedding feast was her mother's table, which Marylyn had often polished as a child; the keeping of promises and of creating order were a daily part of her own life. She remarked that such personal content was usually known only to her, that she did not "always say all the things I know about a story," but felt that what she understood might carry over to listeners: "I think it [personal details] always exists in an invisible sort of way—and it certainly clarifies the pictures you get of things. You see more clearly, and the more clearly you see, the more clearly your audience can get their own images."

Marylyn was puzzled at first that she could not "see" the young man as clearly as other characters, and realized that this was because she was viewing the story from his point of view: "In so much of the story I am him, I see everything through his eyes, and that's why I don't see him—and I have no wish to look in a mirror and see what I look like!" In other words, it is not personal ego that dominates the character but quite the reverse; Marylyn finds herself taken into the story instead of consciously placing herself there by identifying with the young man. She does not become the character, she moves through the story as if she were accompanying him even more closely than his guardian angel.

She realized as she was telling "The Horoscope" this time, to me, that it had grown so personal that she could hardly tell it without tears. "I'm starting to cry more and more every time I tell that story, and I think it's because of the people I'm telling it to. They all become part of it." She recalled times and places she had told "The Horoscope" to her young son, Steven, while giving him a bath (she often practiced first with her family), watching his eyes grow wide with fear as the rope descended; to a married couple celebrating their anniversary and thinking back to how they met; to a roomful of parents at a workshop in Manitoba who were all in tears at the end of the story; and to a group of friends at the wedding reception of the young woman in her choir who was embodied in the shipowner's daughter. "They've all become part of the story," she said, as she explained the tears that came as she concluded the story with me.

Because the story had become so personal, Marylyn said that she did not tell it casually but always waited to "sense out the reaction of listeners" in order to guess how they might respond. When I asked what indications she looked for she replied that listeners might indicate readiness by the kind of attention they paid to the other stories she had told, whether they were sitting attentively or nonchalantly, if there was fidgeting or giggling, or if listeners were simply not in the mood for a serious story. She was careful for herself as well as for her listeners because the story was so important to her: "I'm not really sure, but it's a very powerful story, and I know that it moves me very much."

Marylyn felt very strongly that her research and contemplation, her artistic decisions, audience reactions, and memories of the listeners themselves, all helped bring a story to life. Marylyn insisted, as I said earlier, "Oh yes, the story is more than the story," and now we can see more fully what she meant by her enthusiastic statement. But while she understood the work she put into her stories, she also seemed to downplay these contributions with her concluding statement, "What more can I say? The stories say everything." The apparent contradiction is clarified by understanding that the story becomes enriched through her research, her personal connections, and the responses from both Marylyn and the many listeners who have heard it; these all become a natural part of the narrative so there is nothing more for Marylyn to add, except to try and trace a few of the threads of her weaving for an inquisitive folklorist.

STEWART CAMERON

Stewart began his telling of "The Three Feathers" with a familiar opening describing the family context: "Once upon a time in Scotland there was a king, and he had a very, very prosperous kingdom, and he had three healthy, strong princes, sons, to look after—and to look after him. Now he was getting on in years and his mind was bending towards just who he was going to leave this kingdom to."

Stewart used his own son as a living model for unworldly Jack but when he spoke these words in Toronto in 1988, he did not know that he would find his own mind "bending towards just who he was going to leave this kingdom to." Barely a year after he spoke these words he died of cancer, a great loss not only to his family but to storytellers throughout Canada.

Stewart, of Sudbury, Ontario, began his performing career as a singer who favored "the ballads with their long and complicated plots full of blood and mayhem" (1979 program, Toronto Festival of Storytelling). His fascination with "complicated plots" led him to traditional tales, which began to take a regular place in his repertoire in the 1980s when he became a regular contributor to the annual Toronto Festival of Storytelling and to many of their weekly

Friday night gatherings. Stewart did not come to ballad singing and story-telling from a traditional background in a rural community, though both he and his wife, Dianne, learned some of their songs and music from their respective "pan-Celtic" families. Dianne wrote to me the year after his death: "We were certainly exposed to people in our families and immediate neighborhood who could sing, relate anecdotal stories, or talk about family history. Stew played accordion and guitar as a child, and was very early involved in doing Scottish songs for his family gatherings" (1990 letter).

Unlike many other urban, non-traditional performers Stewart appeared most often with his family. Dianne was an experienced singer and son Duncan and daughter Moira were gradually brought into the act as they matured. Dan Yashinsky, one of the founding members of the Storytellers School, recalls Cameron's performances at the weekly Friday night gatherings: "There would be singing, funny stories, ghost stories. The audience would join in—and I'd leave feeling like I'd been to a party in a very warm, friendly living room" (*Appleseed Newsletter* 5).

These performances were closer to the more intimate oral traditional model than to the more usual theatrical model of many urban storytelling events, possibly because they grew naturally from the family setting. Daughter Moira Cameron remembered that storytelling was always important: "At home, storytelling came naturally to my father. Having two story-minded kids certainly gave him ample inspiration to learn and tell stories in the home environment. My father would tell me a story almost every night before bed. Often, because his stories were so long, he would have to tell them in several installments—one each night—until the story ended. 'The Three Feathers' was one of my favorites" (1990 letter).

Because storytelling and singing began at home, Stewart (and the Camerons as a family) developed a strong sense of performance as a communal exchange in which tellers and listeners were not separated by a "fourth wall," and also in which the individual performers functioned as part of the ensemble. Stewart was always aware that any single story or song was only one link in a complex chain of artistry. He never viewed "Jack and the Three Feathers" as his own story even when it became one of his favorites and took on unique features as a result of his frequent retellings. Still, this story came to be associated with him in the Toronto community.

I first heard Stewart tell "Jack and the Three Feathers" in 1985 at one of the Toronto festival "swap sessions," when he introduced it as his favorite tale.

The next year I had the chance to hear his story again, to ask him about how he had learned it and why he loved it so. He said he had first heard Jim Strickland tell the story at one of the regular Friday night events in Toronto, recorded that performance, and got permission from Strickland to retell the story: "The story when I first heard it [from Strickland] had an immediate appeal. I won't bother to analyze why—it just did. When I began telling it, it developed a life and purpose all its own" (1988 letter).

In 1988 I returned to Toronto and was able to tape Stewart's retelling of the story as it had evolved after several years of performances at home and in public. The annual Toronto Festival of Storytelling, with dozens of tellers and large crowds of avid listeners, was taking place all around us, but we managed to find a quiet room with no one else present. We shut the door hoping for complete privacy, but as I turned on the machine and Stewart began to speak, three boys (I would guess their ages as eight, ten, and eleven) came in noisily and sat down at a table near the door, across from where we were sitting. I tried to ignore their presence, hoping that they would realize we were taping a story and would quiet down, but Stewart acknowledged them with a nod and launched into his story. They went on with their own loud conversations, pretending not to listen but casting glances in our direction. Stewart turned occasionally and addressed parts of the story to them directly and they began acting out the roles of the three sons among themselves.

Thus instead of being a distraction, the presence of these three boys inspired Stewart to add details that I did not remember from his earlier telling, and to act out more of the story with broad gestures, facial expressions, and changes of voice. These elaborations made the story much lengthier than the one I had heard in 1985, and considerably richer. Also, he told the entire story with an engaging Scottish accent that I did not recall hearing in 1985.

About halfway through the story the door opened again and a man wandered in and sat quietly in the opposite corner, paying no obvious attention to what was going on. I was surprised to see that Stewart seemed, momentarily, to lose his concentration. The casual conversational tone and natural pace shifted into a more formal and elaborate style, which lengthened his tale even more. (In my memory the story as told in 1985 was not more than ten minutes long, but this telling took up the full side of a half-hour tape.) Stewart quickly recovered his balance, and when he finished the story he addressed his closing words to the three boys, who had stayed to the very end, each keeping in character within the story. He then turned to the man in the corner, who was, as it turned out, Jim Strickland himself. I understood why Stewart had become concerned with Jim's entry; telling a story in the presence of the one who "owns" it (in the teller's mind at least) is a daunting feat.

Stewart was aware of the effects of both the boys and Jim Strickland. He commented that the story "wasn't very tight," noting that he had not told it for a while. He admitted that Strickland's presence had affected his telling of the tale and seemed to feel that he had not "done as well" as usual. He did not discuss the three boys, though he had obviously enjoyed their presence and benefited from their participation.

The process of evolution is enlightening even when it is seen in the fleeting history of a single variant told by one person. Stewart, of course, was aware of the longer evolution of the story over the few years in which he told it. He was sensitive to the immediate effects of audience on performance and of his own response to the differing contexts of storytelling within his own family and in public performances. For example he described how the motif of Jack's "mucking about in the mud" came to take an increasingly central part in his telling because both he and his audiences found it compelling. (Strickland's variant has Jack "puttering about in the back garden.") "When I began telling it to my kids I found that it changed considerably [according] to my audience's response. My son Duncan was heavily into the wonders of mud at the time and spent many hours mucking around in our 'back garden.' I naturally enlarged the importance of this part of the story" (1988 letter).

Another memorable feature of the story is the convincing vitality of Jack and his opportunistic brothers, which also evolved as Stewart became more experienced: "The characters within the story gradually assumed their own peculiar personalities as I told the story. Jack becomes not so much a fool as an absent-minded child, too full of his own world and imagination to be overly concerned with the 'real world' around him. His brothers, on the other hand, are worldly wise and socially conscious. They do the right things, go to the right schools and generally excel at doing what princes are supposed to do" (1988 letter).

Stewart understood that such narrative developments were a natural part of the storytelling process and did not try to hold himself rigidly to Strickland's text, commenting in his letter that "other things have crept into my telling of the tale as well." His critical portrayals of the ambitious brothers and of the two somewhat pompous kings, human and frog, contrasts with his sympathetic portrayal of Jack, who simply refuses to play the worldly game available to him through his position as prince in a royal family. Stewart was also fond of the frog princess who allows Jack to continue his adventures in the mud even after they become king and queen. Indeed, Stewart emphasizes that even marriage and regal responsibilities do not squelch Jack's love of play. It was this conclusion that expressed his sense of the story most fully. He ended his letter to me by quoting it fully, and poetically. I quote it here exactly as he wrote it:

> The ending of my tale is different also. Jack ends up marrying the princess
>   and inheriting the kingdom, but:
> She is as wise as he is foolish,
> As industrious as he is lazy.
> And she is quite understanding
> When he slips away from his kingly duties
> And putters about in the back garden;
> For after all, considering her background,
> She knows just how much fun that can be

This written text can be compared to his closing words in the oral story. It is obviously a central feature of the story, not just a convenient way to end it.

Tellers of tales in all times and in all places have always faced the challenge of making their stories convincing for their audiences and for themselves without losing the integrity of the story. Stewart understood that the creative balance between teller and audience was by its nature a risky venture in which the teller's interpretations were destined to be acclaimed by some listeners and rejected by others. He noted, for example, that he was sometimes faulted for digressions and anachronisms, such as his elaborately detailed descriptions of Jack "mucking about in the mud" as well as playing with Lego, and for "side allusions to the [British] Royal Family" that were not always complimentary. He felt that his responsibility to his listeners was to create an immediately entertaining story without denying his own faith in the deeper realities of the tale: "This approach is a tricky business. I do not require my audience to believe in what I tell, but I make damn sure they know that I believe in it. My characters are real and the story I tell is important, no matter how far-fetched, fantastic, or ridiculous" (1988 letter).

In his desire to remain true to a story as well as to the audience, he struck a balance between stability (telling it as he heard it from Jim Strickland) and innovation (responding to his own aesthetic sense, his own life experiences, and the immediate performing context). He believed in the inner truth of the story but he did not demand this of his listeners: "Anachronisms abound in all my telling. Some consider this a fault. They say a storyteller should create a self-consistent world conducive to a willing suspension of disbelief. I don't even attempt to do that in many of my tales. I find that I can draw more people into a tale if I don't insist on 'suspension of disbelief' as a prerequisite" (1988 letter). Stewart was certainly willing to suspend disbelief, to see Jack as a convincing human being and not merely a character to be manipulated for theatrical effect.

Like the aging king in his story Stewart passed on a living legacy, not only to his family but to those who heard and remembered his stories. Stewart's modern Jack retains his place as an ordinary hero, adaptable to challenges and adversity and utterly lacking in worldly ambition even in modern urban life. Like Marylyn, Stewart brought life to this story by allowing it to develop from personal connections in his own life, sometimes aware, and sometimes not, that this was happening. Like Marylyn in "The Horoscope," Stewart found himself in his own story as it grew.

I began this chapter by asking how professional storytellers might "modernize" a wondertale without losing the balance between traditional stability and individual innovation. We have seen how Marylyn Peringer and Stewart Cameron were clearly conscious of their commitment to the stories as they first learned them, not because they were unwilling to make any changes but because they had a sense of connection with the wider tale-body from which individual texts arose. They developed the textures of their stories by reworking them for the different contexts in which they retold them again and again. In the continual telling of the tales their personal life experiences came naturally into the stories as reflected in characters, objects, and their own ethical views. They saw the reality of the stories, and this sense gave their performances a more compelling quality.

Lütz Rohrich, speaking of the nature of reality in folktales, noted that among traditional narrators it was the younger and less experienced tellers who considered folktales to be unrealistic; older narrators found them to offer ample range for expressing the realities of life as they knew them. As he noted: "Unique personal experiences can supply a narrator with a lifelong stock of motifs and give his or her narratives their unique stamp" (*Folktales and Reality* 202). We have seen how these two tellers skillfully drew on their wealth of personal experiences to bring old tales to full life in the modern world. By understanding and developing the full power of metaphor, they offered what Rohrich described as "a link between the present and an archaic, magical predecessor of our world-view," one that was not bound by time and place nor by politics and history (*Folktales and Reality* 4).

It is obvious that a teller learns from experience what is effective and what is not; but what also comes with experience is the many subtle ways in which one's own telling of a tale comes to reveal one's own life. The personalizing of the stories by both Marylyn and Stewart was not entirely a conscious process; as often as not this was discovered after the fact, sometimes only during our interviews and correspondence.

The two texts here cannot be regarded as typical of the full repertoires of these two experienced tellers, but since each was freely chosen, we might assume that these particular stories reflect strong individual preferences. Marylyn's choice revealed a partiality for protagonists who find themselves in impossible situations and must rely on help from an unexpected source. The young man in "The Horoscope" was a good-hearted and somewhat naive protagonist whose integrity and devotion are rewarded by a guardian angel. Marylyn's involvement in the Catholic church, as an active participant and as a choir member, provided her with inspiration for re-visioning characters, objects, and situations.

Stewart's sense of the reality of the story was very clear. He insisted more than once that his characters and his stories were genuine for him even if they might not be so for all of his listeners. Stewart was aware of his conscious artistic reworking, but he also understood that the elements of deepest verity for him (the characters of the old king and his youngest son) arose gradually and were as much intuitive as deliberate. Stewart did not opportunistically adjust the story to fit his family, but told it in such a way that his life experience had a place for expression.

I also note that a firm bond between these tellers and the supportive Toronto community is implicit in the unfolding of these stories within the dramatic context of events sponsored by the Storytellers School; both were regular contributors to the weekly Friday night events and the annual festival as well as other local events, and these particular stories are still associated with them. They have become the tellers in the tales because they allowed the tales to live within them, and this continues to be recognized and honored by members of the Toronto storytelling community.

THE HOROSCOPE (MARYLYN PERINGER, 1994)[4]

Marylyn told me this story as we sat on a park bench overlooking the Yukon River in Whitehorse, where we were performing at the annual storytelling festival in the Yukon. The taped story has intermittent background noises from children playing behind us, a dog barking, the siren of a police car across the river, and the constant wind that almost drowned out the story at some points. Marylyn interrupted herself at the beginning to ask if I wanted her to tell it in French or in English. We agreed on English with occasional French phrases in order to retain some of the flavor. I have used poetic indentation to indicate the two points in the story where Marylyn breaks into almost rhythmic chant when she is completely immersed in the story—so much so that her conscious use of French disappears at these points. The story as she tells is a variant of AT 934B, "Youth to Die on His Wedding Day." Marylyn takes her variant from Luc Lacoursiere's notes on the text, "Hero Avoids His Predicted Destiny."

———

Il était une fois, *Once upon a time there was a farmer, and he had three sons. One day, when these sons were almost completely grown up, he went to* un astrologue, *the astrologer, to have their horoscopes read. He gave* l'astrologue *their birth dates and the astrologer consulted his charts, he consulted the stars, and then he said, "Monsieur, I have the horoscope for your three sons:* le cadet, *your younger son, he's going to be a priest."*

"Oh, wonderful!" said the farmer.

"And your middle son, lui, il sera avocat, *he's going to be a lawyer."*

"Oh, marvellous, merveilleux!*" said the father.*

"But your third son, Monsieur, I don't like to tell you."

"Oh tell me, tell me!"

"Well. . . your eldest son, l'aîné, *he . . . well, when he's 21 years old, on the very date of his birthday, he is going to be hanged."*

"He's going to be hanged? My son? That's impossible. My eldest son, he's a good lad, he's never done anything wrong!"

"I'm sorry," said l'astrologue, *"but he's going to be hanged. That is his fate. It is written in the stars. There is nothing we can do."*

And so the farmer stumbled out of the house of the astrologer completely bouleversé, *shaken. What was he going to do? His eldest son, hanged, at 21! You see, the father had quite a bit of property, and he had made provisions that when he, the eldest son, was 21, he would come into that property. Now did it mean that the government who hanged him could take the property too? And the disgrace upon the family . . . oh, this could not happen, thought the farmer. This could not happen. The farmer's heart hardened. By the time he got home his mind was made up.* "My eldest son will not be hanged on his 21st birthday," he said. "He will not be hanged because he will already be dead, from too much work."

So the next morning at 5:00 the eldest son was pulled out of his bed, thrust out into the fields, given a list of tasks that would be too much for ten men to do, and told not to come back until they were all done. And so the poor eldest son travaillait, travaillait, travaillait, *worked on and on. He didn't stop to eat, he didn't stop to drink, he didn't stop to rest . . . he wanted to please his father and he was obedient, so on and on he worked, and he didn't get home until two o'clock in the morning. He stumbled in half dead with fatigue and his father was still up, and he said,* "Papa, pourquoi me punis-tu? *Why are you punishing me? What have I done?"*

"Oh, you haven't done anything," *said the father,* "I'm just checking, to make sure you deserve that inheritance you're going to get when you're 21." *And the next day, the very same thing;* à cinq heures du matin, envoyé aux champs pour travailler. *And once again he came in more dead than alive, and again he said,* "Papa, *what have I done, why are you punishing me?" And again his father said,* "Moi, je ne te punis pas, *but I'm not punishing you. I'm making sure you deserve that inheritance."*

And this went on for a week, and by the end of the week, well, the poor eldest son, he was nearly dead, and he knew that he certainly would die if he stayed. He decided that he would leave the farm, and he went to his father and said, "Papa, je quitte la ferme, *I'm going to leave the farm, I'm going to leave you. I'm going to go away, I'm going to go so far away that you'll never see me again. I can't stay here—I'll die if I stay here. But before I go, can't you please explain to me what this is all about?"*

And his father said, "Given that you're going away, alright, I'll tell you. You see, I went to see* un astrologue. *I wanted to have your horoscope read, you and your brothers. And* il m'a dit, *he told me,* 'le cadet, *the youngest, he's going to be a priest; and your older son, he's going to be a lawyer,* avocat.' *But you,* mon fils, *he told me that when you're 21, on the very date of your birthday, you're going to be hanged."* "Il a dit ça! Moi?" "Yes, Oui, voilà ce qu'il a dit—*yes, you, that's what he said.*

And for a long time the eldest son didn't say anything, and then at last he said, "Well, Papa, if that is the case, I will go so far away that when it happens, no one here will hear about it. Thus no shame will be visited upon my family. You can give my inheritance to my brothers." And away he went.

But before he left, he said goodbye to his mother, and she cried, because he was her favorite. She wept, and she said, "Mon fils, mon fils, *what's going to happen to you? You're going out into the world and I have no friends, no relations that I can ask to look after you. Look, you must promise me something. Wherever you go to find work, find the nearest church, go in, and say a prayer to your guardian angel,* ton ange gardien. *Because you know that each of us has an angel looking after us, and if you pray to your guardian angel, then I will know that someone is looking after you." So of course he promised his mother that he would do this, and then he left.*

Now the only kind of work he knew was farm work, so he got a job at a nearby farm, and when he finished there he went to another farm a bit farther away, and always a little farther. But he didn't forget the promise he'd made to his mother. Every time he changed locations, he found the nearest church, and he'd go in, get down on his knees, and say a prayer to his ange gardien. *And thus the summer passed, and it began to be fall, and the young man was walking along the road looking for another job. He passed a young man of his own age seated at the side of the road, and he [the seated man] said* "Bonjour, où vas-tu, *where are you going?"*

"Bonjour," *he answered, "I'm looking for a job."*

"Oh, moi aussi, *I'm looking for a job too. Let's go together."*

So they went together. They went together, and a farmer hired them for harvesting. Oh, about six weeks they were on that farm. A lot of work. They worked well together. They got to be good friends. Such good friends that when the farmer dismissed them because the harvest was over, they decided to stay together to get some more work. So they knocked at the door of another farm, but no, that farmer didn't need them. All the work was done. Who was going to hire someone in winter? At farm after farm the door was shut in their face.

So they decided they would stop looking for farm work and go to the city to see what work they could find, and they journeyed to a city that was on the sea coast. And there was a chantier, *a shipyard, with a sign outside that said "Men Wanted."*

"Oh," said the young man, "here they're building ships—I don't know how to do that." But his friend said, "Oh, don't worry, I have experience, I'll teach

you." So the young man knocked at the door and the owner opened, and said, "Yes?" And the young man answered, "Well, we're looking for work." And the owner said, avez-vous de l'expérience, *do you have experience?" And the young man said,* "Non, je n'en ai pas, mais mon ami, il en a, *I don't but my friend does, and he's going to teach me."*

"Well, I can really use some more help," said the owner, "so come on in and see what you can do."

The young man and his friend went in, and, oh, it was busy in that shipyard! There was a team of ten men working over here and a team of eight men working over there, and there were about fourteen men on another boat. But the owner took them to a place all by themselves, and there was a lot of wood there. So he said, "Start on the keel. Start on the keel—I'll let you two work all by yourselves and I'll see how good you are."

So the young man and his friend started all by themselves. And you know, that young man learned so well, and his friend taught him so well, that within three weeks they'd caught up to the other teams, even though there were so many more men in them and they'd had a head start. They caught up to them, and in another couple of weeks they'd finished the keel. Everyone was amazed at the quality of their work.

When it was finished, the young man's friend said, "You know what the next step is—the planking, le bordage, *why don't you go to the owner's house and see if you can get it [the wood for the planking]."* So the young man went to the owner's house, and he was just about to knock on the door when a window at the side of the front door opened wide, and the prettiest girl he'd ever seen, une jolie demoiselle, *said,*

"Bonjour, jeune homme, es-tu venu me rendre visite, *You've come to see me?"*

"Oh, mademoiselle," he said, "I wish I could, but I've come to talk to your father. It's business—I need the planking for the shipyard."

"Oh, well," she said, "I'll go and get him." And she left.

The father was very, very pleased at what they had done, and gave him le bordage, *the planking, and the young man got all of that material back to the shipyard, and he and his friend worked and worked for five more weeks and the planking was all in place. Then his friend said,* "All right, the next step is les mats, *the masts. Go and ask for the materials."*

So the young man went back to the house, looked up at the window, and sure enough, before he had a chance to knock at the door la fenêtre s'ouvra, *the window opened, and there she was, that beautiful girl. She said,*

"*Bonjour, jeune homme, this time have you come to see me?*"

"*Oh,*" he said, "*I would so love to, but it's business again. I, I have to get the materials for the masts.*"

"*Well,*" she said, "*I'll go and get Papa, but before I do, could I ask you a question? Es-tu marié ou célibataire? Are you married or single?*"

"*Oh, moi—je suis célibataire,* he said, "*I'm single.*"

"*Oh!* Quelle belle réponse! *That's good! Now I'll go and ask Papa.*"

The father came back, and was very pleased to find out what they had done, gave him the masts—or at least the materials for the masts—and the young man took them back to the shipyard, and he and his friend worked four weeks more and the masts were in place. Then his friend said,

"Le dernier étage, *the last step of all,* les voiles, *the sails. Go and ask.*"

Oh, the young man went off with a happy heart towards the house of the owner, and sure enough, la fenêtre, *the window was wide open and there she was again, that beautiful girl.*

"Bonjour, jeune homme."

"*Hello,* mademoiselle, *it's nice to see you again.*"

"*Ah, did you come to see me this time?*" she asked.

"*Oh,* mademoiselle,*" he said, "*I do wish I could, but I've got to get the sails, that's what I've come for.*"

"*Alright,*" she said, "je cherche Papa, *I'll go and find Papa. But before I do, can I ask you another question? Are you in love with anyone?*"

*He turned red—"*Je n'y ai jamais pensé, *I've never thought about it.*"

So she said, "I have, and it's you I love. Do you want to marry me? C'est toi que j'aime. Veux-tu m'épouser?*"

"*Ah oui, mademoselle, bien sûr, of course I do—oh, wait a moment. I'd better go ask my friend's advice first. I don't like to do anything without consulting him. We're a team, you know. Wait a minute, don't go away!" And he ran back to the shipyard.*

His friend said, "Alors, les voiles, *aren't you going to bring the sails?*"

"*Never mind the sails, this is more important! Guess what happened! The owner's daughter, she wants to marry me, what do you think?*"

"*I think that's a good idea,*" said his friend, "*She's a nice girl. You should marry her.*"

"*Oh, wait until I tell her!" And he went running back to the window, and he said, "*mon ami, il dit 'oui,' *my friend says 'yes'!*"

"*Wonderful,*" she said, "*but now, what date?*"

"*What date?*"

"*What date shall we be married?*" she said.

"*Oh—I'll ask my friend.*" So he ran back to the shipyard again.

"*Où* sont les voiles? *Where are the sails!*"

"*Oh, never mind that. She wanted to know what date we should be married.*"

"*Well,*" his friend said, "*I think we should get the boat finished first. So, if you got married . . . if we launched the boat in the morning, you could get married in the afternoon.*"

"*What a wonderful idea! I'll go and tell her.*"

So he left the shipyard and ran back to the window and called, "Après le lancement—*after the launching?*"

"*Yes,*" she said, "*after the launching. Now I'll go and get Papa.*"

So her father came to the door, and found that not only did the young man want material for the sails, but also the hand of his daughter in marriage. And he gave it, he gave it joyfully! For, you see, she was his only child, and in those long-ago days women weren't allowed to run businesses by themselves so he knew that whoever married her would end up managing the shipyard. He wanted her to marry someone who was intelligent and honest and hardworking, and the young man was all three—so he gave them his consent, and he gave him material for the sails.

The young man carried them back to the shipyard, and he and his friend worked putting those sails up, installing them, and six weeks later, the boat was all ready.

It was a beautiful morning in spring when they launched that boat. Everybody at the shipyard was so excited—it was the first launching of the year. And everyone was excited too because they were going to be guests at a wedding that very afternoon.

But just before the ceremony that young man's friend said to him,

"*Now I have a favor to ask of you. I know that this is your wedding day and tonight will be your wedding night, and you probably feel like being alone with your wife, but I wonder—would you mind inviting me to dinner tonight? And could we eat outdoors in the garden? And could we eat, just the three of us, you, and your bride, and myself?*"

"*I don't see why not,*" said the young man, "*but I'll ask her, just to be sure.*" *So before the ceremony he asked her, and she said,*

"Ah, bien sûr, *he's your best friend, of course he can come for dinner.*"

And so they were married.

And all the people who were invited to the wedding toasted the health of the bride and groom and much happiness abounded. But then it became late, it became dark, the shadows lengthened, the guests left. Then the servants were instructed to carry a table out to the garden, three chairs were arranged around it, places were set for three, and there the young man and his bride entertained the man's friend at dinner.

And it was a lovely dinner. The servants came and went with different plates of food and they [the three friends] laughed and talked together, and it grew even later. And finally the meal was over and all the food was cleared away, and they still sat around that bare table. The young man smiled at his wife and she smiled back at him, and he took his chair and pushed it closer to her, then he bent down and he put his head on his wife's lap and he closed his eyes, and he fell asleep.

Now that was when his friend got up and said to the girl,

"Don't be afraid. Just don't move and don't say anything."

And she looked at him in surprise, because just a moment ago they had all been laughing together but now her husband's friend seemed so serious. He came over to her and he picked up her sleeping husband in his arms, and he put him on the table. And as he did so, the girl noticed that the night sky was opening a crack, and out of a hole in the sky was descending a rope, a thick rope with a noose on the end of it.

She turned to her husband's friend
but he cautioned her not to move,
and not to speak,
so she obeyed him;
as the rope came down,
the friend took the noose,
and passed it around the neck of the young man,
tying a knot,
and when he let go,
the rope began to ascend,
pulling the bridegroom with it.

And the young woman watched in horror as her husband ascended into the dark sky.

How long she sat there looking upwards she had no idea, but she remained motionless, and she did not speak. Finally, she saw her husband coming down again—his feet, his legs, then the rest of him, and his neck was still in the noose—and his face still had the smile of a dreamer. And down, down, down he came, and the friend was waiting.

Once again he took him up in his arms,
laid him on the table,
slipped off the noose,
and the rope went up into the sky once more,
and disappeared.
Then the friend took the young man,
brought him back to his chair,
repositioned his head on the lap of his wife,
and then took his own seat,
at the table.

All at once the young man opened his eyes and he sat up and he looked around and said, "Oh, oh, I'm sorry. I fell asleep. I must have been dreaming. I had the strangest dream, and do you know what I dreamt? I dreamed that I was floating in the sky and there was something heavy on my neck."

"That is a strange dream," his friend said. "Tell me, I have a question for you. Do you know what day this is?" "Of course," said the young man, "it's my wedding day . . . Oh, wait a minute, wait . . . this is my 21st birthday . . . oh no, I'm going to be hanged today!"

"No you won't," his friend said, "I've already hanged you."

"You have?"

"Yes. You don't have to worry about that any more. But I do have another question for you. Tu me connais? Do you know who I am?"

"No," said the young man, "I don't know who you are."

"I'm your guardian angel," the friend said. "I brought you here, taught you your trade, and got you to meet your wife. Now you have a home, you have a future, you have a job, a trade, you don't have to worry any more. And God bless you both."

He got up, and he walked away, and they never saw him again.

But they prayed to him every day of their married life, which was long and happy.

THE THREE FEATHERS (STEWART CAMERON, 1988)

This is a transcription of Stewart Cameron's retelling of a Scottish variant of "The Three Feathers" (AT 402, "The Mouse [Cat, Frog, etc.] as Bride"), taped at the annual Toronto Festival of Storytelling in 1988. Variant texts are also in the Grimm collection, tales 63 ("The Three Feathers") and 106 ("The Poor Miller's Apprentice and the Cat"). We began the recording in an empty room but were soon joined by three boys, and later by one attentive adult who turned out to be Jim Strickland from whom Stewart had first heard the story. This variant is more than twice as long as the one I had heard in 1985, and certainly much longer than it might have been, due to Stewart's response at having an audience rather than just a machine and a curious folklorist. As with Marylyn's text, I have tried to capture Stewart's poetic phrasing at the end of the story; I also indicate his on-going responses to the other listeners—the boys and Jim Strickland—since these become part of his story.

Once upon a time in Scotland there was a king, and he had a very, very prosperous kingdom, and he had three healthy, strong princes, sons, to look after— and to look after him. Now he was getting on in years and his mind was bending towards just who he was going to leave this kingdom to. He wanted to leave it to the right man. Which of his three sons would do?

[Three unaccompanied boys now enter the room and I'm concerned that they might disrupt Stewart's narration, but they settle down to listen, whispering among themselves.]

Well I tell you, two of his sons were everything you could expect as far as princes were concerned. You couldn't tell one from the other. They were great at all of the things that princes were supposed to do. They went to the polo and they went to the tennis matches and they went to the horse races, and one thing and another. And they always did well in their lessons, as far as courtly bowing is concerned, and politics and everything of that sort. A-one students they were. You couldn't wish for better. And they dressed to the teeth. No doubt about it— they looked the role of princes. And all of the girls were falling head over heels in love with them, vying for them right left and center.

But the third son, if you must know, was somewhat different. Jack was his name. Now the king would say, ah, somewhat easily [uneasily] that Jack spent most of his time tending to the back garden. But truth be told the back garden was nothing but a marsh full of muck from rain and drizzle, full of frogs, toads, bulrushes, and all manner of weeds. And that's where Jack liked to spend his time, just mucking around in the back garden.

Well, the king made up his mind that, yes, he would have to decide, and he could not decide between his three sons—well, between two of them—just whom he was going to leave his kingdom to. So, as all good kings do, he had a number of good advisors, some wise men, and he assembled them around him and asked the big question of them.

"How can I decide who I am going to leave my kingdom to?"

And they gave it some long and hard thought and came up with a solution: "Just set your sons a quest."

"What's a quest?" said the king.

[Stewart is now beginning to tell the story to the boys off to our right as well as to me. They pretend to be uninterested, though they have become silent.]

"Oh, just send them out to do something or find something in a certain period of time, and the one that does it to your fashion is the one that wins the kingdom in the end."

"That's a great idea," said the king, and he summoned his three sons in front of him.

He had an idea in mind, yes indeed. They stood in front of him, and the king said,

"I am going to set you three lads a quest. Each one of you is to go off, where the winds will take you, and come back with the most beautiful tablecloth in the entire world. And the one who comes back with the most beautiful, finely made tablecloth—that is the lad that will be the king after I go."

[Here he turns and addresses the three boys as if he were the king, and at this they respond by giggling and pretending to take on the character of each brother. They actually leave the room briefly and return, still laughing.]

Fair enough. The three lads were ushered up to the topmost turret of the castle and each one of them was given a white feather. The first lad, the oldest prince [Stewart points to the boy on the left], *he was told,*

"Go over to the edge of the turret and cast that feather to the winds. And whichever direction that feather goes, that's the direction you shall go to find the finest tablecloth in the entire world."

Well, the eldest son, he took the feather and he threw it over the turret of the castle, and it caught in the breeze—ssshhhwwwssshhh—and off to the east it went. Fair enough. He saddled and he bridled his horse, and he got his bags of gold and his suit of clothes up on his back, and enough provisions to last him a good long time, and he set off to the east after that feather and after that prize of a tablecloth.

Well, the second son [he points to the middle boy], *he came to the topmost turret, and he too was given a feather, and he too cast it to the winds and away it went—ssshhhwwwsssshhh—to the west. He too saddled and bridled and dressed appropriately and away he went in search of the finest tablecloth in the west.*

And of course Jack, too, must be given a chance at this. After all, you have to be fair about these things. So the king calls,

"Jack,"

[Stewart indicates the remaining boy, who is already in character, acting silly and grinning foolishly.]

and up he steps, and he was given a feather too. Jack took the feather in his rather grubby hands and threw it over the edge of the castle. Ssshhhwwwssshh-hee, thunk—right down into the mud in the back garden. [The boy imitates Jack's actions.]

"Oh well," says Jack, but he didna' mind.

Well, I tell you, a year and a day was the length of time these princes had to fulfill their quest. And just about that time—it was just about a year later, Jack found himself mucking about in the back garden. [He addresses himself to the boys again.] *You know, he had his rubber boots off to the side there, and he was mucking around in this little pool of brown, yucky water, squishing the mud up between his toes . . . Och, there's no more beautiful feeling in the world than to have the squishing up between the big toe and the little toes. Just marvelous. So he was squishing around, and trying to do a sword fight with a little bit of a bulrush he had in his hand, slicing back and forth and pretending he was the prince he should have been, when there, in front of him, he hears this little bit of a voice.*

"Jack! Jack my man!" [He uses a higher, lighter voice.]

Jack looks around, you know, but there's nobody there whatsoever. So he says,

"Och, it's just the wind."

But then as he's mucking around, squishing back and forth, he hears the voice again:

"Jack, Jack my man! You've no left us much time!"

And Jack looks down, and sure enough it's a tiny, wee frog talking to him.

199

"Jack, Jack my man, you've got to hurry. What about your quest?"

And Jack, he'd never seen a frog talk before, but he said in answer, quite amiably,

"Oh, I've forgotten all about my quest."

[He looks at the three boys, who are paying somewhat closer attention, waiting to see what will happen next.]

"You've forgotten about your quest! Well your time is almost up. Follow me! Follow me!"

And the frog hopped over to the tail end of the garden and there was a great big rock. And the frog said,

"Tap that three times, Jack." And Jack took the bulrush that he was holding and tapped it three times, and—eeeaaaeee—the boulder opened right up and this great big tunnel went down, down, down into the center of the earth. And the frog said,

"Come on Jack! Come on Jack!"

and leapt and hopped right down the tunnel.

Jack followed after, for what could he do, you know. He was curious. He went down and down and down, and lo and behold, this tunnel opened up into a great big huge cavern, filled to the brim with frogs and toads and lizards and snakes. They were writhing about like it was Raiders of the Lost Ark [again, added for the benefit of the listening boys, to whom he nods], *and there at the farthest most end of it was this great huge bullfrog sitting on a stone throne and with a tiny wee crown on his head. And he's shouting from the back as Jack enters,*

"Jack, Jack my man, you've made it at last! You didn't leave us much time. Come here, Jack, come here."

So Jack steps forward, minding where he's putting his feet, and he bows before the king of the frogs, and the frog says,

"Jack, what is your quest? How can we help you this time?"

"Oh, my quest," says Jack. "Ahhh . . . well, I'm supposed to bring back a . . . a tablecloth. Yes, a tablecloth." "A tablecloth," says the frog. "My my my, we don't use tables down here. But I tell you what—we have this wee bit of a rag over the top of the walls just to keep the moisture in, you know. You can take that—I'm sure it will do. Over there, Jack."

So Jack goes over to the corner of the great huge cavern and takes down this cloth, bundles it up, and shoves it inside his shirt. And away he goes, to the cheers of the frogs, the lizards, and the toads, up up up the big tunnel.

And as soon as he gets out in the air again the rock closes behind him. And he is just in time, I tell you, because his brothers at just that moment have returned. And in fact, his eldest brother was up there in the throne room in front of the father himself, and spreading out on this table the most beautiful piece of Holland linen you have ever seen in all your born days. Not a stitch out of place, perfect in every regard, with a little trim of lace around the edge, and embroidery all the way through it. The king was feeling the texture of it—as fine as silk it was—and he says,

"This is the best tablecloth I have ever seen. Ah, it's going to take a heap of beating. But to be fair, we must see what your brother has brought in."

Well, the second brother with much ceremony came forward and spread out the most beautiful piece of Irish linen—lacework like you wouldn't believe, in and out woven with little bands of silver and gold. It sparkled in the sunlight.

"Och," said the king, "Have you ever seen a tablecloth so beautiful! That's marvelous, marvelous! I don't know how I can tell the difference between them. What a choice. But, to be fair," said the king, "we must give Jack his chance as well.

Jack had just come into the throne room, and he had his boots on—he shouldn't have, of course, because they were caked with mud and were leaving a track like you wouldn't believe across the velvet carpet. But the king ignored it as he usually did, and he said,

"Jack, Jack. Have you managed to complete your quest?"

And Jack said,

"Ah . . . I have something here."

And he opened up his shirt and took out the rag, and since all the tables were used he just sort of spread it out in front of the throne. And I tell you, it was beautiful! It had a picture on it like a mural, and every time you moved from one location to another, the picture seemed to move. The cloth was made of the finest, finest silk, never before seen in that land. Transparent, it was so fine. Not a stitch out of place. And the king stood transfixed. And the king said,

"Jack, my man, that's the finest piece of work I have ever seen. You've won!"

"Wait a minute! Wait a minute!" said the other princes. "No way is Jack going to win the kingdom! Now we've been away for a year and a day, and he . . . we don't know where he found that piece of rag. We demand a rematch! Another quest!"

"Well, it does seem a little peculiar," said the king. "Well, it's only fair. Okay. Another quest. Let me think now. Alright, alright. You three are to go out

and find the finest ring in the entire world. The most beautiful, the most price-less ring. Right enough!"

*Up to the topmost turret of the castle they went. Each of the sons was given a white feather. The eldest son [*he points to the tallest of the three listening boys*], the tallest one with the brown hair and the sparkling eyes, he went over there and very proudly tossed it over the edge [*the boy imitates the tossing*] and the wind caught it and—ssshhhwwwssshhh—off to the north.*

The second son, he took his feather and threw it over the turret of the castle and—ssshhhwwwssshhh—off to the south it went. [The second boy imitates the first, and follows his imaginary feather out of the room.]

And Jack, he took his feather and he threw it over the turret of the castle, and—ssshhwwwssshhh thunk—right down into the mud in the back garden.

"Oh well," he said.

Jack, of course, went down to muck about in the back garden.

[The third boy sits down on the floor and "mucks about in the mud."]

Now it was almost a year later, and Jack was there making a tiny castle out of the dried muck, and he was putting little flags of grass in all the turrets, and he was making it like so when, what do you think happened? This tiny wee frog hops right up to him and says,

"Jack, Jack my man! You've no left us much time!"

"Oh," says Jack, "Is that you again?"

"Yes, yes, I'm here to help you."

"Oh great! Would you mind getting a stick and pulling it 'round . . ."

"No, no! Your quest, Jack, your quest!"

"Oh, my quest. I've forgotten all about my quest," he says.

"Oh sure, Jack, now follow me, follow me."

So they go, hip hip hip hop hop hop over to the big rock at the end of the gar-den.

"Hit that three times with your stick, Jack."

And Jack did, one, two, three, and—eeeehhhheee—the boulder opened right up, and this great big tunnel went right down into the center of the earth, and . . .

"Come on Jack, come on Jack," called the frog.

And down he went, and Jack right after, lickety-split. And there he was in that great big huge cavern filled with all the toads and frogs and snakes and lizards, and the great big bullfrog sitting on his throne says,

"Jack, Jack, my man, it's nice to see you. Now what can I do to help you on your quest this time?"

Jack sat himself down, and he said,

"Well, I'm supposed to bring back, uh, I'm supposed to bring back . . . what am I supposed to . . . Och, a ring! A beautiful ring, that's what. Yes, I remember now."

"A ring," says the frog. "Well, I know just what to do now. See that big chest over in the corner? Bring it here."

So Jack goes and gets this great big heavy chest and carries it back.

"Well, open it up, Jack."

And Jack did. And oh, I tell you, the priceless gems, the rings, all of the things you wouldn't believe were there. And the frog says,

"Choose whatever you like, whatever you like."

So he fishes into the backmost corner of the chest and pulls out a ring, which he can't see very well because they don't have too many lights down there, and he sort of rubs it off and puts it in his shirt pocket. And to the cheers of all the toads and lizards he goes up the tunnel and comes out into the daylight.

And when he gets out the rock closes up behind him and he's off, up to the chamber of the king. And sure enough the eldest brother had just come back, carrying a velvet cushion, and was just kneeling in front of the king and saying,

"I've got the ring for you."

And the king picked it up and looked at it and said,

"That's a beautiful golden ring, it's marvelous." It was all inscribed with fine Celtic knot-work. "That's going to take a heap of beating."

[At this point I notice someone has come into the room and sits in the back, well behind us. I'm watching Stewart and do not realize that it is Jim Strickland, the man from whom Stewart learned the story, but I observe that Stewart seems to be searching more carefully for words and momentarily stops playing to the boys on my right.]

"You . . . " He calls his second son.

And with much ceremony, the second prince came forward and opened up this little jewelry box. And there, sitting on a piece of velvet, was the most beautiful silver ring, with a great big pearl sitting right in the centre. It was beautiful, and the king looked at it and said,

"Och, I don't know," he says, "I don't know which is more beautiful," he says. "My my what a decision."

Just at that point Jack comes through the door, and the king catches his eye and says,

"Jack, my man . . ." just to be fair, of course . . . "Have you got anything for me?"

"Yes, I do," says Jack.

[Stewart resumes the easy conversational flow of his story and is again including the boys in his audience.]

And he takes out this ring, polishes it off on his shirt and hands it to the king. And I tell you, it was the most beautiful ring the king had ever seen. It was a band of gold, true enough, but it was studded and encrusted with diamonds and pearls, and the inside edge of it was inscribed with the most beautiful flower pattern you've ever seen. The workmanship—why you'd need a magnifying glass just to see the detail in it. The king was struck dumb. Then he says,

"Jack my man, you've won again!"

"Wait a minute! Wait a minute!" shouted the two princes. "There's no way we're going to have the kingdom go to Jack just because he—we don't know where he found that ring down in the muck and mud in the back garden, but that's no fair at all! We demand another quest!"

"Wait a minute yourself," said the king. "For heaven's sake! I'm getting on in years and I'm going to die before you guys come back with your quests! No!"

"Yes!"

"No!"

"Alright, just one more quest. Just one. And that's it! I've had enough! I want you and you and you to go out and find yourself a wife. [He points to each of the boys, and they giggle about finding a wife.] *Yes, and the one that comes back with the most beautiful princess . . . after all, when you inherit the kingdom you're going to need a wife and the kingdom is going to need a queen. Therefore I give you one week."*

"ONE WEEK!" the older brothers shouted.

"One week to go out there and find yourself a wife, come back here and I'll decide."

Up to the topmost turret of the castle they went, and the eldest son he threw his feather—ssshhhwwwssshhh—and off to the east it went, and the second son he took his feather, and ssshhhwwwssshhh—off to the west it went. And Jack he took his feather and—ssshhhwwwssshhh thunk—right down into the muck in the back garden.

"Oh well."

Well, Jack, of course, he was about to go down into the back garden, but he was a little bit hungry, you know, so he spent his time in the scullery of the castle—because he, you know, well the people of the castle didn't mind having him there, he was an alright sort of chap, you know. And if they were making up some cakes and pies and whatnot they'd let him lick the spoon, and clean out the stuff from the bottom of the bowl. [He winks at the boys and says, "Hey, have you ever done that? Great."] *And when he was getting in the way they'd say,*

"Go away, go away Jack!" and they'd shove him out the door.

Well, no problem for Jack. He went out to the back garden to play a little bit further. He was going to make an entire village. And just when he got something interesting going . . .

"Jack, Jack my man!"

And sure enough, it was the frog, the tiny wee frog. "You've no left us much time! Come on, Jack, come on. Hurry! Hurry!"

So Jack, he goes over to the rock, taps it three times and it opens up and he goes down the big long tunnel and there is the bullfrog sitting at the back of this hall. And he says to Jack, "Jack, what is your quest this time?"

"Och, I don't think you can help me this time," says Jack.

"And why not?" says the bullfrog.

"Well. I'm supposed to come back with the most beautiful bride, the most beautiful princess in the entire world."

"No problem," said the bullfrog. "Ah, my daughter happens to be the most beautiful woman, the most beautiful princess you could ever care to marry. And I would be more than happy to grant my consent to your marriage."

Now Jack was sort of taken aback at the king's kindness, and said,

"Well . . . where is this princess?"

"Why Jack, my man, she's sitting right there in the palm of your hand. Isn't she the most beautiful princess you've ever seen?"

Sure enough, he had to admit that she was really beautiful—for a frog. And they left to the cheers of all the toads and frogs and lizards all the way up. They almost picked them up bodily, he and the princess, as they went up the great big long tunnel. And all Jack could think of was that he wasn't even sure that his father approved of mixed marriages. [He laughs at his own wit.]

So he got outside to the tumultuous roar of turtles and lizards—do they roar tumultuously? Well they did this time! Sure, you wouldn't believe it. And Jack, as he turned around . . . this great big huge turtle turned into a coach and four. A coach and four! He was dumbfounded! And then that tiny wee green frog

turned into the most beautiful princess that he had ever seen. Why she was
beautiful! His mouth dropped open and his tongue hung out. She says,

"Come along Jack," as she steps into the carriage, in her green gown.

And Jack followed her in and closed the door.

Well, I tell you. Just at that time the king was up in the throne room, and the
two elder brothers had come back with the most mean, miserable women you
could ever imagine. They, being princesses, wanted to buy all sorts of things
and wanted a big fancy wedding to invite their hundreds of relatives, just as
you would want. But in one week? You cannot do that in one week! It takes that
amount of time just to get the invitations printed, to say nothing about order-
ing the trousseau—so in one week they had to elope. And here they were, already
arguing with their husbands. And married only one week, for heaven's sakes.
And just then the butler said,

"Och! Stations everyone! I think we've got visiting royalty. Hurry! Hurry!"

And the king and the princes and their wives looked out the window, and
what did they see but this huge, great emerald carriage pulling up to the front
gate. And weren't they dumbfounded when out should come—Jack. Jack, little
tiny Jack, with the most beautiful woman, the most beautiful princess, anyone
had ever seen.

Well, there was no doubt about it—no doubt about it at all. Jack won the
day. And in time Jack became the king. And a good thing it was, too,
for his wife was as smart as Jack was a little bit—soft.
She was as industrious as he was, well maybe a tiny bit lazy.
And besides that,
every time when the affairs of state got a little bit beyond his control he would
nip out the back door and go play in the mud in the back garden.
But she let him do that because, you know,
considering her background,
she understood how that might be a nice thing to do.
And that's the end of the story.

[The three boys applaud and Stewart bows to them, then turns and addresses Jim Strickland, who now joins us to talk about the story for several
minutes.]

12

Old Tales, New Contexts

(1998)

Unlike the tellers in the previous chapter, Joe Neil MacNeil (Eòs Nìll Bhig), was a Cape Breton Island teller from Nova Scotia who grew up fully immersed in Gaelic tradition, but over the years he had lost his listeners. For him storytelling was indeed a dying art, but because he was a master teller, he was able to revive much of his material for Gaelic scholar John Shaw, who first heard Joe Neil's stories on archival tapes. Shaw soon realized that collecting more of Joe Neil's stories for an archive was not enough; he thought that Joe Neil deserved a living audience. The two went looking for listeners. When I met them they had found their way to the annual Toronto Festival of Storytelling for the first of three times, where Joe Neil narrated in Gaelic and John summarized the stories in English to listeners, who were gradually drawn into this seemingly awkward method of performance. Shaw later described it as "trying to play a tune you know on a fiddle left-handed," and that was also my felt experience in trying to write about their complex performances. A preliminary version appeared in *Who Says? Essays on Pivotal Issues in Contemporary Storytelling* (Birch and Heckler 155–76), and then rewritten for my

An earlier version of this chapter appears as "Old Stories, New Listeners" (Birch and Heckler 155–76), and is used with the permission of August House Press. I am grateful for the helpful editorial suggestions of Carol Birch and Melissa Heckler.

own book, *Burning Brightly* (117–33). For each of us, Joe Neil, John, and my-self, learning to play left-handed was definitely worth the trouble.

Since it had now become my standard practice to include a full text in writing about storytellers, I chose to include the first lengthy story I heard Joe Neil and John tell together, "The King of Egypt's Daughter," a fine epic tale that revealed not only the narrator's skill but also his light touches of humor.

On a February morning in 1986 I sat with dozens of other people at the annual Storytelling Festival of Toronto listening to a frail, elderly man reciting a long story in Gaelic. After a few minutes he stopped and sat down while a younger man stood up to translate a summarized segment of the story into monotonous English. "This isn't going to work," I thought to myself. "It's too tedious." We had heard the two men tell a livelier story the previous night and had come in anticipation of being entertained once more. Instead I was beginning to get a headache from trying to follow the complicated story in two languages, only one of which I understood.

I forgot my discomfort half way through the lengthy tale of a good-hearted young sailor and his encounters with pirates, a corpse, and the King of Egypt's Daughter, which turned out to be the title of the story. The chanted cadence of the Gaelic, the gentle intensity and non-theatrical style of both performers, and the story itself, were compelling enough to hold me and the rest of the au-dience for most of an hour. Also, it was obvious that the man speaking to us in an unknown tongue relished the tales he was telling—and eventually he also came to enjoy us, his uncomprehending but patient listeners, as the festival weekend progressed.

Later when I spoke with Joe Neil MacNeil, the narrator, and John Shaw, the translator, I did not know that they had not faced a formal audience together before, and had no idea what to expect. (I also did not know that Joe Neil's story, "The King of Egypt's Daughter," was the same narrative John Shaw first heard on tape and recognized as the work of a master storyteller.) I was sur-prised to hear that this was their first public performance, since they seemed entirely competent despite the occasional awkwardness of balancing narration and translation. I spent the remainder of the weekend following Joe Neil and John from one performance to another and talking to them informally about stories and storytelling. I learned Joe Neil had learned his stories in his own community as a young man but had ceased to be an active narrator when the Gaelic language declined. John found Joe Neil's earlier stories recorded on archival tapes and sought him out. Their work together over the next few years eventually led them to the Toronto festival, and here my story begins.

My interest is in Joe Neil MacNeil's return to active storytelling in the late 1970s and John Shaw's indispensable role in this personal revival. Joe Neil's memories of his own community is described in the book he and John Shaw published together, *Tales until Dawn: The World of a Cape Breton Gaelic Story-Teller*, in 1987, in separate Gaelic and English editions. John has been so directly involved in Joe Neil's success in reaching listeners beyond his own community that to describe just one of them is to tell only half of the story. What they have accomplished together is, in my experience, a unique approach to "tandem" storytelling.

My initial contact with Joe Neil and John was as an eager listener and not as a folklorist-researcher engaged in a careful study of narration. I emphasize this in hopes that others will find in my comments some useful information for their own work. My observations are based on attending every performance Joe Neil and John offered at four of the annual Toronto festivals (1986, 1987, 1988, 1990), from conversations with them during the festivals, and from letters exchanged with John Shaw over several years. I have been curious to know how they evolved from the more usual roles of informant/researcher into dual performers; why they chose to take their traditional art to a major professional festival; how this change of performance context has affected both the tellers and the tales. Joe Neil and John offer a manner of performance that touches on issues relevant to organized storytelling.

Joe Neil MacNeil—Eòs Nìll Bhig—was adopted into the MacNeil family of Middle Pond on Cape Breton Island, Nova Scotia, at the age of six months. At this time Gaelic was still a fully vital language in Cape Breton, and the only language spoken by Joe Neil's adoptive parents. He says of himself: "I spoke only Gaelic when I was young. I used to make some effort to pick up a bit of English here and there, though I spoke only the odd word" (3). His curiosity with language, and eventually with storytelling, was to lead him into a lifelong diversion that eventually caught the interest of scholars studying Canadian Gaelic.

Like Ray Hicks of Beech Mountain, North Carolina, he is not a casual teller of tales but a master performer with innumerable lengthy stories learned within a traditional oral community. Both men have succeeded in bringing an ancient body of oral literature to new audiences unfamiliar with the stories, the language, and the culture in which they were developed. However, neither teller initiated this on their own; both were "discovered" by outsiders who appreciated their stories and saw the potential for carrying them to a wider audience. In the case of Joe Neil, it was John Shaw, a Gaelic researcher, who "discovered" him in 1975. John was working in the archives of the College of Cape Breton in Sydney, Nova Scotia, when he heard a tape of a lengthy Gaelic tale and was impressed with the linguistic abilities and aesthetic sense of the storyteller: "A recording that caught my attention was a version of 'Nighean Righ na h-Eipheit' ['The King of Egypt's Daughter'], delivered with a sureness of detail and a command of Gaelic that I recognized as the work of a master storyteller. The same command of language—without apparent effort or limitations—impressed me again when I met Joe Neil some weeks later" (*Tales until Dawn* xv–xvi).

After this meeting Shaw recorded whatever Joe Neil could call back to memory of that story and others. The two men worked together for the next few years, patiently reconstructing fragments of tales that gradually returned to life as full, vibrant oral compositions. One concrete result of their collaboration was a book (actually two, one in Gaelic and the other in English) containing Joe Neil's wealth of oral lore arranged according to families and individuals from whom he had first heard the various items. Of the 52 full-length narratives recorded in the book (not the whole of his repertoire) there were only two for which he could not remember sources. He claimed not a one of them as his own, saying modestly in his preface: "Please do not regard me as deserving of any special praise but see this book as a tribute to those living in times past who were gifted, kindly and sensible, and generous with their store of tales" (*Tales until Dawn* ix).

Joe Neil was so modest that you might not guess from his own words that "their store of tales" was not so easily available because the stories were told only in Gaelic. He was in a rare position to hear and learn the stories since he began his schooling later than other children in his community. In school, children caught speaking Gaelic were vigorously punished by the teachers, and were also publicly embarrassed in front of their peers. Shame was a most effective weapon, so much so that many gave up speaking their own language in public, and gradually it died out in private as well. Joe Neil, however, clung tenaciously to his language despite retribution. He noted that an illness kept him out of school for the first year: "I am sure that is the reason even until to-day that I have such an interest in Gaelic, for Gaelic is my first language and it is still the language that I prefer" (*Tales until Dawn* 4–5).

There was no hint of bitterness in his words, rather a quiet pride in the beauty and strength of the language. He went on to suggest that he was differ-ent from other children in that he sought out older people instead of avoiding them, and this of course gave him even stronger connections to well-spoken Gaelic—and to the old stories. But as the older tellers died Joe Neil was left without sources for stories, and also without an audience, since many of his own generation could not speak the language well enough. Fortunately, Joe Neil had an excellent and active memory, which allowed him to call back the wealth of tales he had learned years earlier once he had a reason to do so.

In the years of careful work with John, Joe Neil regained his role as an ac-tive rather than passive tradition-bearer. He not only recalled and described what he remembered from earlier years, he was able to return it to life. Still, he no longer had any listeners—other than John—for whom to perform. There was still a handful of Gaelic-speaking contemporaries very eager and willing to listen to Joe Neil, but they could not function as a regular audience because they were too few and too scattered to form an actual community of listeners. John understood that such an audience was necessary for Joe Neil and began to seek out performance occasions in which Joe Neil might be comfortable.

In 1986 they traveled to the annual storytelling festival in Toronto to seek their fortune, in the manner of the folktale protagonist and a magical helper. Shaw comments on their debut in a letter I received in the fall of 1990: "You may have seen our first performance ever, in Toronto, in, I think, 1986. This was for an English-speaking audience. The manner felt, at least, to be *ad hoc*. I doubt this had ever been tried before, but this was the only way I could think to present the stories, Joe Neil, and the language to a mainstream audience. This was also the only active way that presented itself to bring the material to a larger audience" (Shaw, 1990 letter).

At their first night as participants in the pre-festival storytelling concert, some 75 people sat around small tables at the weekly gathering of 1001 Nights of Storytelling. Candles burning on each table provided the only source of light. Joe Neil and John were the first performers, invited by host Dan Yashin-sky to take the stage as the honored guests of the festival, which began officially the following day at a large old church on Bloor Street several blocks away.

The setting was anything but elegant and perhaps this was for the best, since Joe Neil seemed very much at ease in the casual setting. There was no formal stage, just a small space on the bare wooden floor, and no microphone to separate him from his listeners. After they were introduced, Joe Neil and John came to the front and sat down in gray metal folding chairs, bringing the chairs closer and turning them slightly inward so that the two men could see each other as well as their listeners. After exchanging glances and looking out to greet us with shy smiles, Shaw stood up and briefly introduced them and described what they intended to do: MacNeil would narrate in Gaelic and Shaw would summarize in English. They nodded to each other, a shared signal that was repeated each time I saw them perform; then Joe Neil stood up and began to speak in Gaelic. His focus was inward rather than out to us, though he acknowledged our presence with occasional nods in our direction. He told the story with a minimum of movement, facial expression, or voice changes, though his personal involvement in the story events was apparent from the calm intensity of his voice. Sometimes he looked out over our heads as if he were seeing the action of the story in the distance; other times he looked intently at John, the only one who understood his words in this audience of non-Gaelic speakers.

Despite the seeming distance between us, it was obvious that something interesting was taking place, as there were none of the usual signs of audience restlessness. There was a cadence and a power to his tales that seemed to break through the language barrier; and there was Joe Neil himself, so unselfconsciously immersed in his story that even an uncomprehending audience was no hindrance to his flowing words.

After a few minutes he stopped abruptly and smiled out at us, nodded to John, and sat down. John took the floor and began a brief summary of the exploits of the legendary carpenter and trickster Boban Saor, who exchanged clothing with his inexperienced apprentice in order to fool some strangers who had come to see if he was as masterful as people believed him to be. John sat down and Joe Neil continued the story of Boban Saor's clever prank with greater enthusiasm, responding to our growing interest in the story now that we had some clues to its progression. By the time John had summarized the final segment the audience as a whole was completely attentive, including the few youngsters, who had ceased fidgeting.

I later wrote to John asking about this story because I could not find it in *Tales until Dawn*. He sent the following detailed response:

The Boban Saor story we told on the first night was one of two that did not appear in *Tales until Dawn*. As far as I know it has been recorded only once in Scotland, and nowhere else in Cape Breton. My summary: Boban Soar hears that people were coming to put him to the test and see whether he is equal to his reputation as a carpenter. He sees them approaching from afar, exchanges place and role with his apprentice, begins planing an adze handle. He uses his eye to measure the handle for the adze head lodged in a vice at the other end of the work table. When ready he throws it and the handle fits perfectly into the eye of the adze head. The strangers walk out, saying to each other: "Did you see what his apprentice just did? Well, if the apprentice can do that, imagine what the master can do." They never returned to test Boban Saor. (1993 letter).

It was an excellent choice of stories; we, like the strangers who had come to test Boban Saor, were curious to know if this legendary master, Joe Neil, was as good as we had been told—and if his "apprentice" was worthy of his mentor. Translation alone would not have been sufficient to hold our attention. What John had accomplished was transformation, not merely translation. We, like the stranger, left convinced that we had indeed been in the hands of experts who were equally skilled in their work.

"Boban Saor" was much briefer and lighter than others Joe Neil and John told during the formal part of the festival over the next two days. The much more complex story of "The King of Egypt's Daughter," mentioned at the beginning of this chapter, seemed at first to be far less engaging than "Boban Saor." As a wondertale it was much longer and apparently more serious; both tellers were so caught up in the intricacies of the tale that they seemed less aware of the audience. At times we felt distant from them, cast adrift like the young sailor in the story. But like him, most of us found our way to solid land and were rewarded for our perseverance by following the adventures of the tenacious young protagonist.

Joe Neil was delighted by the warmth and receptivity of the listeners, and responded by coming further out of his stories as the weekend progressed. Instead of focusing on John, as he had been doing, he looked out at his listeners to note the reactions, both when he was narrating and when John was translating. As the weekend progressed both men were able to test their abilities as effectively as had the characters in their stories. One would not have guessed that Joe Neil's fine tales had been largely dormant for years and that John himself had no performing experience. John stated: "Joe Neil, as far as I know, was not an active storyteller before I met him, although he clearly had the capability to be so. He recorded some stories for an archive in 1975, and had recorded earlier for at least one Gaelic-speaking fieldworker" (1990 letter).

In my letter I had also asked John how they came to work together as actual performers rather than as informant and collector, which is the more usual relationship. He replied that he gradually realized that Joe Neil deserved a good audience, and the only way to find one was to agree to accompany him as a translator, since Joe Neil felt that the stories had to be told in Gaelic. Shaw understood that it was necessary to take Joe Neil and his stories into a new context. On his part he was willing to do the necessary work, including learning to face an audience himself, in order to do so:

> The crux of it is that this is the only real audience going for Joe Neil's material. Dealing with this new audience, I feel, has been an important experience for Joe Neil and has had a constructive effect on his understanding of the importance of his own tradition and the larger context of which it was a part. Now that nearly all of his own generation is gone, along with their acuity of mind and ability to listen well, the mainstream may be the source of people who are broadminded and thoughtful enough to relate to the material. (Shaw, 1990 letter).

Since both men were, by nature, modest and reserved, it was an even greater challenge to brave an unknown audience in Toronto. John described the difficulties of his own situation:

> I felt very much the mediator here between Joe Neil's very high standards of content accuracy/verbal skills and a well-disposed, expectant audience with no previous exposure and who knows what expectations. At first in my job there was not much room to move: It was all I could do to keep the details straight and put them into some kind of coherent English. My verbal understanding of the stories had always been as I had heard them in Gaelic, and giving them in English, especially at first, felt like trying to play a tune you knew on a fiddle left-handed. (1991 letter).

Learning to perform together was a great challenge for both men. Joe Neil would have been accustomed to an intimate setting where both stories and language would have been familiar; Shaw was not a storyteller at all and had to develop the basic skills of presenting a coherent narrative accurately and engagingly without imposing himself on the story. By the end of the 1986 festival it was obvious from the enthusiastic responses of listeners and the growing ease of these two tellers that they had accomplished their impossible task.

One of the festival organizers, Dan Yashinsky, recalls Joe Neil's comments at that first festival:

> I remember Joe standing up at a brunch at the Festival a few years ago and talking about how even he thought he'd forgotten all of his stories until John came around and started listening to him. His own community had stopped giving his story tradition much value, at least publicly, and had certainly stopped providing a continuity of listeners with whom he could exercise his powers of memory and performance. And as Joe tells it, they were both surprised by what came forth. "We were scraping the bottom of the barrel," Joe said—and then they seem to have turned the barrel into one of those magic fairy tale vessels which provides abundant, and always replenished, stores of good stuff. (1991 letter)

As his experience as a platform performer developed (not only in Toronto but also at the large Vancouver festival), Joe Neil continued to respond to the challenge of attentive but non-Gaelic-speaking listeners. Since he had no living oral sources he began to seek out stories in print in order to increase his repertoire. He read collections in both Gaelic and English, though until the 1990 festival he performed only in Gaelic. At this festival he chose to relate a 45-minute tale in English that he had found in a published Scottish collection. His task was doubly difficult: Not only was he drawing from less familiar material in written rather than oral form, he also chose to tell the story in his second language, and without John's help.

I sat directly in front of Joe Neil in the first row, eager to take in every word. At first he was obviously anxious about standing up there alone, without John sitting beside him ready to help. But once he had launched into his story he displayed the same unselfconscious concentration that he had in his Gaelic presentations—a calm intensity that demonstrated his deep involvement with the story and its characters. We now had the great privilege of hearing his eloquence and precision firsthand. Though he called it "reciting," the story was in his own words. As a folklorist, I was especially excited because I had read the epic poems of other master narrators but had never actually heard such an artist. I was thinking of the Yugoslav epic singers studied by Parry and Lord, who did not build their stories by rote memory, word-for-word, but relied on formulaic phrases and images around which they recreated their narrative anew at each performance (Lord, *Singer*).

John Shaw notes that each narrator had their own artistic techniques for bringing a story to life, some relying on language and style, others on elaboration of detail or vivid imagery, while some delighted in lively dialogue between characters. John elaborates on this: "Within the carefully transmitted framework of the tale, the story-teller was an active, frequently vigorous 'shaper of tradition' whose personal, creative role in telling the story was known to Middle Cape story-tellers as *Eideadh na Sgeulachd*, 'The Raiment of the Tale.' The devices used to achieve this differed from person to person, depending on a narrator's ingenuity and talents" (*Tales until Dawn* xxxii). Joe Neil, Shaw says, was particularly talented in both imagery and dialogue, as was apparent when we were able to hear him perform his own story in English. My handwritten notes scribbled on the festival program captures one of the many vivid phrases used in his lengthy story of a heroic quest. Here is a description of a threatening ogress his hero has encountered in a mountain cave: "She had one great eye in her head like a pool of deep dark water, and her gaze was as swift as a winter mackerel."

His very fine, dry humor was also apparent in his choice of words and phrases as well as in occasional glances at his audience to see how listeners were responding. For example, he commented on the raven who wanted a quid of tobacco as payment for helping the hero: "I guess he wasn't afraid of the cancer."

John emphasized that along with Joe Neil's artistic skills, his deepest interest in the stories was with the characters and their interactions: "His main concern is with the psychology of the story, using the relations between events to elicit the pathos or humour from the characters' situations with a frequent emphasis on the moral implications of the tale. This is all expressed through language which, although not ornate, is slightly formal" (*Tales until Dawn* xxxii–xxxiii).

We were able to experience Joe Neil's involvement with the tale firsthand, and to appreciate more directly the consummate artistry of his performance. The "slightly formal" language did not detract in the least from the listeners' enjoyment. We can also appreciate his personal involvement with each of the characters as he brings them to life in his stories. In this way Joe Neil resembles the skilled Siberian narrator Natal'ia Osipovna Vinokurova, studied in depth by Russian scholar Mark Azadovskii. In discussing skilled narrators like Vinokurova he cites a German scholar, Walter Berendsohn, who observed that "we are no doubt dealing with highly gifted people with rich fantasies and strong memories, with artistic types who are the equals of outstanding creative writers in the world of literature" (Azadovskii 13).

A striking example of Joe Neil's artistic gifts was his decision to narrate a complex tale in English at the 1990 Toronto Festival of Storytelling, without John Shaw on stage with him. When I later questioned Shaw about Joe Neil's response to his experience, he wrote that he thought it had been as significant for Joe Neil as it was for the listeners:

> Joe Neil viewed telling a full-length story in English as a challenge, and it took some courage to do this. I had encouraged him in this, and after an instant's confusion when I left him on his own, he went about the work quite naturally, as I knew he would. It seems to me that telling stories in English ["translating" is what Joe Neil calls it] is part of a constant effort to stretch himself and extend his skills. Since he was 80 Joe Neil has worked on and mastered, from books, at least two of the truly big Gaelic stories which to my knowledge have not been told anywhere for close to 40 years now [including Scotland]. (1990 letter).

Joe Neil might have called his performance "translating," but there was no sense of the story being consciously translated; it had the same sense of spontaneous flow as his Gaelic narrations. This is, of course, my own subjective response based on hearing Joe Neil perform in four festivals, and of course hearing many other tellers over the years.

John Shaw, too, has been willing to take up the challenge of stretching himself by learning and occasionally telling stories in a second language, one he learned as an adult, and not as part of his own background. He set off for Scotland as a young man, wandered about the more isolated regions learning Gaelic as he went. When he returned to the United States he began to study the language and culture formally, and in the 1970s succeeded in finding a research job in the only Gaelic-speaking region on this continent, Cape Breton Island.

Shaw, with his knowledge of Gaelic and his deep respect for Joe Neil and his stories, would seem to be the most obvious person to carry on MacNeil's tradition, but when he was asked by someone in the audience if he considered himself to be MacNeil's apprentice he said that he did not and that he *could* not. Later when I pressed him further he responded: "In order to be a true apprentice to Joe Neil a person would have to be training to be a full-fledged Cape Breton Gaelic storyteller with Gaelic as the primary language. Although I would view this as one of the more worthy and productive intellectual pursuits this part of the world has to offer, to do so would be unrealistic because these days there is no real audience for this" (1990 letter).

He went on to say that while the tales might be taken into an English language tradition they would, in his opinion, eventually lose their power: "The long tales, which are the heart of the tradition, have been unsuccessful at crossing the language boundary as active material." In their book he comments further that the longer narratives have not "crossed over into English," though some of the shorter and more humorous genres as well as a few belief legends, stories of strange happenings, have been more successful (*Tales until Dawn* xxv).

While the future of Gaelic storytelling in Cape Breton is in doubt, at least for a brief but significant time MacNeil and Shaw managed to breathe literal life into a great narrative tradition. Both men together achieved what neither could have accomplished separately. As Dan Yashinsky noted: "The thing is not to merely record the stories in a mechanical way, but to put yourself directly in the path of the tradition. What John's up to is the affirmation of oral tradition not only as an artifact but as a living source of value, something in need of live practitioners" (1991 letter).

John had no intention of becoming a performer himself but saw himself mainly as translator and as cultural broker between Joe Neil and "mainstream" audiences. He did, however, recognize improvements in his own presentations:

> Our performing has been sporadic, but within the last year or so [1989–90], due to practice, I've been able to do my part more easily, describing in English the visual scenes that Joe Neil gives through Gaelic. The feeling is one of more freedom in bringing across the nuances that I hear in Joe Neil's telling while giving the content of the tales. This is all easier and more comfortable than it was at first. In many ways my mind is able to work very easily with Joe Neil's; I think if I did the same kind of summarizing with another storyteller it would take some time before I felt comfortable. (1990 letter)

It was the experience of actual performances before living audiences, after 10 years of working together to reconstruct the stories, that allowed John Shaw and Joe Neil MacNeil to return an old art to full vitality. This is certainly a storytelling revival in the most complete sense, though both Joe Neil and John might have argued that the tradition and the stories had never quite died at all, and were in need of a healthy transfusion rather than full resuscitation. New listeners provided exactly that.

Traditional communities almost everywhere in the contemporary world have undergone rapid and radical transformations that have resulted in the loss of artistic forms and expressions like oral narration. We should remember, though, that changes in social and technological patterns have always been a natural part of human existence; tellers who wished to keep their art fully alive have met challenges with innovative responses, certainly including the use of "book" stories in their oral repertoires. I emphasize this to avoid the stereotype of oral tradition as an unchanging, "pure" expression that suffers from innovation. Quite simply, active narrators cannot survive without good listeners, and when their audiences change they must respond without losing the rich heritage on which they depend. It may even be necessary to seek out new audiences in unfamiliar contexts.

An example of narrators actively pursuing their own audience is described by narrative scholar Linda Dégh. She worked with two aging Hungarian women who had been active tellers in Hungary and then in their former ethnic neighborhood in Gary, Indiana, but now lived alone in separate suburban areas. They managed to keep their stories alive by telephone calls to each other but resourcefully sought out new listeners as well, regaling deliverymen, canvassers, postmen, or anyone else who turned up on their doorsteps. The fact that their hapless listeners could not speak Hungarian did not discourage the women, who were determined to maintain their legends and tales (*Narratives in Society* 306–24).

It is not so surprising, then, that skilled artists like Joe Neil MacNeil in Cape Breton and Ray Hicks in the southern Appalachian mountains succeeded in accommodating themselves and their stories to new audiences and new contexts. Listeners could not always follow the language of their tales, since Ray Hicks's Beech Mountain English is often as incomprehensible as Joe Neil's Middle Cape Gaelic; but the proficiency of these artists was compelling enough to carry over linguistic boundaries, to captivate audiences unfamiliar with the oral communities in which the tellers and their tales originally blossomed—even when listeners could not follow the words of a story.

They succeeded by meeting the challenge of entertaining new listeners in performance contexts quite unlike the more intimate settings of their original communities.[1] These tellers certainly had to make adjustments to unfamiliar situations, but their listeners also had to adapt; they had to relax their expectations of platform performing in order to appreciate understated performance styles and stories that were difficult to understand. Both Joe Neil Mac-Neil and Ray Hicks blossomed by meeting the challenges and enjoying the stimulation of festival audiences. Rather than maintaining the material with which they were most comfortable they sought out other sources for narrative material. Ray Hicks has added more biographical content to his performances while Joe Neil MacNeil, with John Shaw's help, sought out traditional Gaelic material from printed sources. In other words, they did not passively maintain oral tradition as they initially experienced it, but found new ways of keeping their rich legacies fully alive. Joe Neil had the benefit of John Shaw's generosity, perception, and good judgment.

Folklorist William Wilson's useful continuum of situational, conscious cultural, and professional storytellers is especially useful here. While less experienced situational and conscious cultural tellers might be easily discouraged by the loss of supportive and familiar listeners, active and experienced tellers are more ready for any opportunity to perform and are willing to adapt to new situations.

However, innovation is not subordinate to tradition. The sense of stories being part of a wider inheritance, not merely one's personal possessions, inspires a balance between traditional stability and individual innovation. Respect for the community of tellers and for the tales themselves is paramount. As Shaw notes, Joe Neil's only audience for a while was the occasional academic collector who came to listen respectfully and to record his tales. Joe Neil was willing to comply because he sensed this respect. John notes that "characteristic of outstanding Gaelic informants is their willingness to record for the serious collector. Once the informant's confidence is gained, such a task is perceived as a duty growing out of their unspoken role as guardians of their people's tradition" (*Tales until Dawn* xvii).

Ray Hicks, too, was more than willing to share his wealth of traditional and personal stories with collectors as well as large festival audiences. Like Mac-

Neil, he regarded himself as an heir to a rich local tradition. Folklorist Cheryl Oxford, who has worked extensively and intensively with Ray Hicks and his relatives Marshall Ward and Stanley Hicks, emphasized Ray's conscious sense of responsibility: "Perhaps because of his long apprenticeship in the communal wisdom of his mountain kin, Hicks is unwilling to relinquish his patriarchal role as storyteller to just anyone. He believes that these stories impart the collective memories of a kindred people" ("Jack in the Next Generation" 6).

Both MacNeil and Hicks were so completely immersed in their art that they sometimes seemed oblivious to their listeners, while at other times they responded directly and engagingly. Oxford described Hicks's penchant for fixing his total attention on specific listeners: "In contrast to these moments of reverie, however, are examples of Hicks' flair for showmanship and comic relief. He may emphasize a point in his telling by holding a member of the audience with a wide-eyed stare, leaning closer while watching for a reaction, as if daring her to laugh or express disbelief" ("Jack in the Next Generation" 13).

While MacNeil was less aggressive than Hicks since he was well aware that listeners could not understand his tales, he was still very aware of his audiences; he looked out at with occasional smiles and nods as his narratives progressed. Both tellers are also eager to talk about stories and storytelling before or after performances. They did not regard storytelling as an activity separate from other parts of their lives, nor something to be guarded as a personal treasure. They were fully aware of themselves as skilled artists and retained a keen sense of obligation to those from whom they learned their stories—and the art of telling them.

Part of this feeling of guardianship is a deep understanding of the inherent timelessness of the stories, a continuing relevance that goes beyond specific historical community and individuals. As Joe Neil remarked about some of the stories he remembered: "They were exceedingly lengthy tales and their subject matter was so strange. In a way they were just as strange as some things that could happen today, but at the same time so understandable; you could understand everything that was there—every misfortune and hardship that they encountered" (16).

Toronto storyteller and author Celia Lottridge recognized what Joe Neil and John had accomplished, and acknowledged their impact on her as a storyteller:

You know, when we had Joe Neil here, it was significant. He does come out of oral tradition, and he's made himself a person who takes that tradition he really grew up with and the stories he heard orally, and he's seeing himself as the lone person who's really doing that. I mean, he's gathered up stories that maybe he wouldn't have told if he had just gone on in an oral culture. But he still comes out of that background. I've found that listening to those people [Joe Neil and John] to be extremely illuminating, and it puts what I do into a much broader context. (Lottridge)

As Celia and others noted, both men were so fully engaged in the stories as lived experiences that their sense of presence invited audiences directly inside their tales. I overheard one listener remark to a friend, "Well, now I know stories aren't just something you tell or hear—they're something that happens to you when you tell or hear them."

In the four years I observed Joe Neil and John at the Toronto festival, it was apparent to me that they had altered the context as much as they had been altered by it. This is significant in a performance milieu where many modern tellers feel that traditional material needs to be dramatically transformed (often through parody) to suit contemporary listeners. On the other end of the scale are those who feel that traditional tales are to be told in their "original" form (that is, word for word as they exist in print) in order to retain their purity. For Joe Neil, stories, even those he sought out in books, were always alive and relevant and authentic. They did not require purist preservation nor heavy-handed modernization.

Joe Neil MacNeil reflected thoughtfully on storytelling as an immediate experience, even when he was speaking nostalgically of his own difficult early years. What he remembered most clearly was the immediate personal face-to-face exchange: "You were alive with them [the tellers he recalls by name] there in the flesh and participating in the whole event. You could talk to them right there, but if you ever chose to address the gadgets I mentioned [radio and television] they could never answer you. So there was the pleasure and a sense of unity. I think that people felt very united, united physically and united in spirit" (10).

For Joe Neil, of course, unlike most of us who bring stories to a stage setting, storytelling grew from a communal base rather than from individual efforts. He modestly stated, as Shaw said earlier, "My own experience was ordinary enough," meaning that he had been only one of many narrators who felt a deep connection to their tales as part of a much larger whole. His devotion as a "conscious cultural storyteller" inspired him, when the opportunity presented itself, to evolve into a fully skilled platform performer—with the help of a scholar who wanted to record as well as to bring to full life the verbal artistry of a master narrator.

This article is an attempt to recreate in words what has been only partially verbal. Anyone who has tried to transform spoken words into print will understand my sense of dissatisfaction with the one-dimensional results that can only hint at the exhilarating reality of being there at the re-living of a traditional art.[2] I learned more deeply from my experiences with Joe Neil and John that both scholars and storytellers are professionally engaged in a revival, each in their own way trying to bring life to stories that originated in another medium. Scholars, in this case folklorists and anthropologists, try to replicate the event as accurately as possible by describing it in ways that capture the actual spoken words so they can, if it is desired, be measured, weighed, compared and contrasted. The highest ideal is to present in words, sometimes with the addition of charts, graphs, and other statistical methods, what existed orally for a few fluid moments, not only for the scholarly viewer but for the participants, both tellers and listeners.

It is easy to forget that measuring and weighing can get in the way of appreciating artistic creativity. Linguistic anthropologist Del Hymes, who spent much of his career exploring the complex narratives of Northwest Coast native traditions, counseled readers to remember that whatever the other function of stories they were also entertaining: "Scholars are sometimes the last to understand that these stories were told and told again, not simply to reflect or express or maintain social structure, interpersonal tensions, or something similar, but because they were great stories, great fun" (22).

Storytellers have another challenge, being attuned to the living storytelling event in a different way—as a model for presentation within their own experiences and interests as platform performers. They recreate an oral experience by retelling the story they have heard to another audience in a different context, instead of attempting to describe it accurately and objectively as an event. The danger here is that ignorance of the rich soil in which any given story took root and flourished can lead to misunderstanding, unless a teller has taken care to do a bit of research on a story and to appreciate and respect the generations of actual (not idealized) people who contributed to this continuing artistic creation. An anti-historical perspective can result in egocentric claims that a story "belongs" to them simply because they have recreated it in their own words.

Any story text is only a part of actual creation, one link in a long chain of human interaction and reflection that does not stop with any individual teller. Joe Neil, a master of the art, did not claim a single traditional tale as his own; he recalled them as belonging to the families in which he had first heard them, and that is how the tales are presented in his book.

I have learned a great deal from the combined performances of Joe Neil MacNeil and John Shaw. As a folklorist I was impressed with their dedication to storytelling as the living legacy of both a community and an individual artist, and also with the careful way in which they brought this art into a new performing context without losing the integrity of the tales or the telling of them.

As a storyteller I gained new perspectives on issues now central to platform performance contexts: that is, conscious standards of excellence in training and expression; the ethics of public presentation (notably "ownership" of tales); relations between tellers and listeners before, during, and after performances; the individual artist's commitment and responsibility to a wider community as well as to the stories themselves. Any one of these topics would require another full chapter, if not an entire book, so I only mention them here to suggest further possibilities for exploration.

Joe Neil MacNeil died in 1996, at age eighty, and thus he never saw this article. I had sent a preliminary copy to John Shaw at the School of Scottish studies, and in his return letter he included his eloquent tribute to Joe Neil that was published in a Scottish newspaper. He also commented that "it's not easy to measure success in a game like storytelling for an urban audience arriving with occasionally bizarre expectations, but from a purely personal standpoint the best thing about your article was that someone noticed that we were trying out and took the trouble to think about it. I'm sure Joe Neil would have felt the same way" (1996 letter).

Joe Neil MacNeil's deep attachment to storytelling as he knew it is best expressed in his own words. In describing one of the tellers remembered from childhood, he echoed his own joyous approach to storytelling: "Angus [MacIsaac] was full of a kind cheerfulness. He used to tell stories and he could make them up as well. He made them up in great numbers and with ease. And he could invent long ones, too; some of his tales were extremely long. He knew himself that they were not true and when he was finished telling one of these big stories, after he had let out a little laugh, he would say, 'And that's no lie'" (95).

He was well aware of the deliberate ambivalence here, that wondertales are both truth and lie at the same time, but he himself had no such ambivalence. He and his listeners found ways to solve this apparent dilemma.

Whether storytellers have learned their stories from an oral tradition, like Joe Neil MacNeil or Ray Hicks, for example, or from printed sources, every teller addresses this challenge while trying to keep old stories alive in new contexts. As an illustration, here is the text of Joe Neil MacNeil's telling of "The King of Egypt's Daughter."

THE KING OF EGYPT'S DAUGHTER (JOE NEIL MACNEIL, 1978)

This was one of the Gaelic stories recorded by John Shaw in 1978, which he later translated for Joe Neil's collection of stories in Tales until Dawn. *"The King of Egypt's Daughter" is a lengthy and detailed story that I find almost as delightful to read as it was to hear, because of MacNeil's fine narrative skills (*Tales until Dawn *121–27). It is reprinted here with the permission of McGill-Queen's University Press. John's notes to the story identify it as having been told by Angus MacMullin and Alexander MacLean. Joe Neil remembered hearing it from the MacMullin family years earlier. As I noted earlier, this is the story I first heard them tell at the Toronto festival in 1986. It is AT 506, "The Rescued Princess."*

There was once a young man, Jack, in a certain part of the world and, since employment was scarce and work could not readily be found, he decided one day that he would go down to the pier to see if there were any sailing vessel in hopes that he would be able to strike a bargain with a captain. And it happened that there was a sailing vessel in at the time, so he went to talk with the skipper of the vessel and was hired on. He was to stay on the vessel for a certain number of years—some years and a day—and a wage was settled, conditions were agreed on, and when they were ready they sailed.

And however many years he had sailed, when that number of years and a day had passed, the sailor said that his tour was now completed and that he wished to leave. Well, the skipper was unhappy to see him leave because he had been so good on board, but he would not oppose him. But he asked him how he intended to leave now that they were out at sea.

"If you give me," said the sailor, "the longboat with a sail, a compass, and a little food to put on board, I will be able to sail right from here." So everything was fitted out and the sailor was given his wages, and he took leave of the skipper and the others on board and set sail.

Whether a storm arose or he went off course, whatever happened, he sailed for some time before he reached an island; I'm certain that he did not know at the time that he was on an island. He landed and beached the boat, pulled it up, and went walking around. He climbed up in the mountains, noticing then that he was on an island, and he saw a hut on the other side of the island and made his way down to it. When he reached the hut he beat on the door and a young woman opened the door and looked at him.

"Isn't it an unlucky thing for you," said she, "to arrive here!"

"Yes, indeed," said he. "And what is the reason for that?"

"The reason," said she, "is that this is a sea-pirates' lair. The ship on which we were sailing was caused to founder and they took everything that was on her and took me along with the rest. All the others on board were put to death, and they sent the ship down to the bottom. I'm the King of Egypt's daughter and I'm being held a prisoner here by the three pirates. Right now they are out at sea, but when they return you are not going to be safe at all."

"Well, be that as it may," said he, "I'll stay here until they return."

Whether the passing time was long or short, one of the pirates came down to the hut and saw the man sitting inside and asked him where he had come from. The sailor replied that he had come off a wrecked ship which was torn apart in a storm, and that he had been fortunate enough to cling to a piece of wood that was floating on the surface. He had kept hold of it and was driven around the ocean until at last he came to rest on this piece of land.

When the second pirate came home, he questioned him, and the sailor gave him the same story that he had told the first pirate, and when the third pirate arrived he had the same story for him. So they agreed that since he had come to them in those straits he could stay. So one of them said that they were going out to sea to plunder and that he was to stay on land to walk the shores to see what he would come upon there.

"And we have," said he, "a rule here on this island: the man among us who does best during the week becomes lord or king of the island until someone else does better than he. And whoever does, the title goes to him."

The pirates took off on the ocean, and he was going around on the shore, and I'm sure with what he had hidden—the little bit of money that he had—when they returned home in the evening he had gathered more along the shore than they had out on the ocean. And by virtue of this it was agreed that he would become king of the island for the week.

So they continued going to sea and he remained on land. But one day he began thinking that the time was right; he had begun to reckon the length of time they were out at sea, so he said to the young woman that it was time for them to be taking off. They got ready, though she wasn't all that eager to take this opportunity in case they might be captured, but at last she agreed to go. They were only a short distance out to sea when they heard the stroke of an oar, and when they looked the pirates' boats were coming after them. Well, she began crying and lamenting, saying that they were now worse off than they had been before.

"Never mind," said he, "we are not lost yet."

And before the pirates caught up with them they entered a bank of fog and he put the boat onto another course; he changed course when he entered the fog patch, and they could no longer find him. But the young woman was even worse off once they entered it; now they were lost and she thought they would never get out. He told her not to worry at all about finding their way out and that he would continue on course with the boat.

Whatever length of time they sailed, they reached a seaport. He brought the boat into the wharf and went up to an inn to spend the night there. They intended to stay there until they could see whether they would find a chance to go to Egypt. Anyway they went to the inn and engaged rooms and, as they were on their way up to their rooms, they noticed a corpse hanging up there. The woman took to yelling and crying loudly.

"It was bad enough," said she, "to be with the pirates, but isn't it terrible to be with murderers now?"

"Never mind," he replied, "I will find out the meaning of this before we go a step further." He went down to the proprietor of the inn and asked him what was the meaning of the corpse hanging there.

"Well," said the proprietor of the inn, "it is always the custom in this town— it has been a rule for some time—that the body of anyone who leaves the world with debts is to be hung in the inn for so many days as a visible example to those

passing back and forth so that they will be sure to settle their own debts before they leave this world."

"And," said the sailor, "would it be permitted or regarded as correct for another man to pay those debts off?"

"Oh, yes indeed," replied the innkeeper. "That would be all right."

"Well," said he, "we will take it upon ourselves to pay the debts that this man has incurred, whoever he may be."

"Very well," said the innkeeper, "I will send for the merchant to come here tomorrow morning and we will settle the matter."

They retired that night, and in the morning of the next day the merchant was sent for and arrived at the inn. The sailor asked him what debts were owed by the man, the merchant told him, and the sailor agreed to pay them. "Very well," said the merchant, "I am well satisfied."

So the sailor settled the debts owed by the poor man and sent for a grave-digger and told him to clothe the body and to give him a gentleman's burial, and that he would pay the costs. That was done, and however long they stayed in the town, he would go down to the wharf daily to see if there were any sailing vessels coming around. One day a great sailing vessel came in and he went to speak to the skipper. He found out from the skipper that they were about to sail, and he obtained passage to Egypt on the vessel, mentioning that there was someone accompanying him. And that was all very well, they were to set out on their journey the next day.

He and the King of Egypt's daughter went down to the wharf, and when the skipper of the vessel saw the girl, he thought that he ought to recognize her. He went down to his own room where he had a picture of the King of Egypt's daughter, and sure enough it was she. But he did not let on at all.

They went on board and set sail. But the skipper gave an order to one of the sailors on the vessel to throw him overboard at the first opportunity. It was not advisable for that sailor to challenge the skipper, but he conveyed to the other man what was supposed to happen, saying that he would not do what had been asked.

But in the end, Jack the sailor went overboard, and down he went. He caught hold of a connecting rope that was underneath between the boom and the bow of the vessel, and there he remained. And the story went around that the sailor had fallen overboard, and when she heard the news, didn't the girl take to screaming and complaining, but the skipper told her not to be upset at all.

But the boat became becalmed. It was not moving—there was a dead calm—and Jack was seen swimming alongside the vessel. Right away the skip-

per gave the order to throw him a rope to try to bring him aboard. And sure enough he managed to grasp the rope and came aboard quite smartly. So that was settled. But one night when he and the skipper were up on the top deck keeping watch, the skipper saw his chance. The ship was tacking back and forth and on one of her tacks across, the skipper gave Jack a shove and out he went into the sea. He knew then that there was malice behind the skipper's actions so he did not attempt to return to the vessel, he struck out from it, calling out to the skipper, "I will be in Egypt before you."

And he kept on swimming. Whether the time was long or short, he kept on at his own pace until at last he gave up. He couldn't swim any further; he was just trying to stay above water as best he could. It looked as if he had just about given up completely, lying on the surface between two waves.

"Is my plight not a pitiful one!" said he. "All the big waves I have surmounted during my time at sea, and now it seems my lot to sink down between two of them right here."

Then he heard a blow or a noise as if from a boat, and when he looked, there was a black longboat beside him and a middle-aged man sitting at the oars. "It seems to me," said the man, "that you're in a fix."

"Oh," replied Jack, "I am in a fix. My time has come."

"Oh, I don't know," replied the older man, "that your time has come yet. If you were to make an agreement with me," said he, "I will take you safely to harbour."

"It is difficult for me to make a deal with anyone in my present circumstance."

"Well, if you promise to do what I ask of you, I could see that you were at a harbour in time."

"Well," replied Jack, "how can I promise something that is neither there nor within my power?"

"Well," the man replied, "the promise I'm asking is to give me your son on the day that he is three years of age."

"It is difficult for me," said Jack, "to give someone my son or my daughter at any age since my life is at an end and I have no wife, son, or daughter."

"Well," the older man said, "if you promise we will see about the rest."

So Jack got into the boat and stretched himself out on the deck, so exhausted that he fell asleep. And however long a time he slept or however long their journey too, at last they reached Egypt. They came into port and Jack was there a number of days before the skipper landed. He had found employment and was *working at the shore around the wharf when the big vessel came into harbor. The King of Egypt came down with his servants and they went down to the wharf, and the skipper of the boat came in with the king's daughter, and she was received with great pleasure.*

"I see," said the king, "that you have found my daughter."

"I have," replied the skipper.

"We will go up now," said the king, "to the castle, for there are agreements to be kept. I promised that whoever should find my daughter would have her in marriage."

"May I," said she, "say a few words?"

"Yes," replied her father. "You have my permission to speak at any time at all."

"This is not the man who found me. I was found by the man you see working over there."

"Oh, indeed. We would require some proof of that."

"There can be no such thing," said the skipper.

"Oh," said the king, "we must settle the matter somehow."

"Go over there," said she, "or call him over here, so that he may give you a little of his life story, and you will learn that things are different from what you believe at present."

The man was called over and was asked where he hailed from and the way the world had treated him, and he began telling his story, I believe, from the time he went on the sailing vessel until he was thrown off the vessel by the skipper. When the King of Egypt heard what had been done to him and all the rest, he ordered that the skipper be shackled and deprived of his freedom for the rest of his days, and that the sailor be taken to the castle, and that he be dressed in garments suitable for a person of his quality. A great wedding was arranged, and Jack and the King of Egypt's daughter were married.

But, with the passing of time, she grew heavy with child and gave birth to a baby boy, and there was much more happiness and rejoicing. But time passed and passed swiftly, and soon the period of three years had run its course. And the day arrived at last when the young lad was three years of age. The older man came around, he knocked on the door, was invited in, and entered. When the older man had been sitting inside for a while, the sailor told his wife the conditions to which he had agreed in order to save his own life while he was at sea.

"Well," said she, "hard as it is, a promise must be fulfilled."

So the lad was brought to the older man. And he lifted him up and placed him on his knee and said, "You have been as good as your promise, which promise has been fulfilled tonight. It is in fact a long time since you paid me."

"I don't understand," said the sailor, "how I could ever have paid you."

"Oh," replied the older man, "you may remember when you were at the inn and took down the corpse that was hanging from a rope and gave it a respectable gentleman's burial and paid off the debts. Now the lad is going back to you as he should. And he has my blessing that every good fortune will meet him and the rest of you."

And there you have the story that I heard about the sailor and the King of Egypt's daughter.

13

Fire and Water

In Joe Neil MacNeil's story from the previous chapter, the heroine bravely held off her pirate captors as well as the captain of a sailing ship, and even demanded her rights from her own father, the King of Egypt. With her determination in mind, I met my own challenge when I was asked to contribute an article on feminist folklore scholarship for the book *Fairy Tales and Feminism: New Approaches* (Haase). I had retired by this time and was no longer focused on feminist approaches, nor had I kept up with the scholarship since my interests had shifted to contemporary storytelling. I began to read what I had been missing, and decided to see if I could use a story as a metaphor to put the development of feminist folktale scholarship in a different perspective. I had been working on an unusual Mediterranean version of "The Water of Life," with a heroine who outdoes her brothers. An apt analogy for scholarly feminist writing, I thought. Once again I was able to include a full story text that readers could use for gaining their own perspectives, or could read just for the fun of it.

I began the article with summaries of two stories that seemed at first glance to present polar opposite: the girl in "Frau Trude" who was thrown into the fire, and the sister in "The Water of Life" who succeeded where her brothers had failed. My intention was to show how these two stories revealed the complex development of feminist commentary on fairy tales, from its beginnings in the 1950s and 1960s and its continuing evolution into the 1990s when the article was initially written. The combined stories would, I hoped, make clear how a wondrous and varied forest grew and blossomed from a few early seeds.

Here are two very different story scenes:

In a dark forest an old woman—a hag, not a granny—sits beside her fire awaiting a rebellious girl. When the girl arrives, the hag will turn her into a log and throw the log into the fire.

In another forest, a sister and her brothers are seeking the Water of Life. The brothers will fail and be turned to stone, but the sister will succeed in the quest.

The creative tension between these stories has fueled feminist studies of folktales for the last decades of the twentieth century. They seem diametrically opposed, victim and victor, but it is not so simple given the deliberately enigmatic quality of wondertales. The mysterious nature of this genre endures, even after long years of attention by a host of writers offering their own particular interpretations. Feminist scholars in particular have criticized the overabundance of passive victims and sought out more active and resourceful women. Each new study and every recreated story opens up new patterns, perspectives, and constant variations on themes. Jane Yolen's stories, for example, always make me look again at my own favored traditional tales. Even with all of this attention, no single outlook or approach offers a final answer to the mystery of this genre, because the wondertale at its best is multi-faceted in depth and meaning, always open to new breath and breadth.

Like others who followed a feminist path, I was lured into the enchanted forest of wondertales by an interest in the good and bad women who peopled them. I read story after story to see how folktale women fared or failed in their adventures. I was studying stories from a safe academic distance, making my own observations and categorizing heroines as Persecuted, Trapped, Tamed, or Heroic. But when I stepped over the threshold and started *telling* the tales, strange things began to happen. I could not avoid experiencing a few transformations myself, and from coming out of the hag's metaphorical fire somewhat different from what I was before I was thrown in. As I write this article I balance metaphorically somewhere between the hag's fire of death and the Water of Life, with the ever-growing understanding that this enigmatic position offers me the fullest potential for insight. But I am getting ahead of my story.

My first steps on the feminist path began with an article, the first I ever wrote, titled "Things Walt Disney Never Told Us." At that time, in the early 1970s, I was a graduate student researching my dissertation on women in folktales. I have written many articles on women and wondertales and have since moved on to explore contemporary storytelling and tellers, but it is still that first article that continues to interest readers. This has been both blessing and curse: a blessing because it set my direction as a feminist folklorist; a curse because it seems to have cast a spell by keeping my academic image preserved like Sleeping Beauty, forever young and eternally unchanging. My original intention was to try and break this spell by exploring where I and others have been these past few decades. However, the computer intervened by wiping out my first draft with its reflections on feminist work, expansive explanatory notes, and careful citations. It all vanished like the golden ball in "The Frog King." After a rage worthy of the elder sister that I am, I took it as a message to let the original article go, focus on the two opening stories and see what happened next. I was prepared to expect the unexpected.

Expecting the unexpected is central in both stories whose scenes opened this article. Both were memorable tales that stood out from the hundreds of others I read in the 1970s, but for very different reasons. The first one, a distressing Grimm tale called "Frau Trude," enraged me; the second, an unusual Catalan variant of "The Water of Life," delighted me. They seemed like perfect opposites, one ending in destruction and the other in re-creation. Each in its own way has made its mark on my evolution as feminist, folklorist, and storyteller, and they continue to do so. Because they still speak to me I will explore them here as literal and figurative examples of this evolution, my revolution around the figures of the victimized and the heroic women of wondertales. Let me begin by returning to the hag as she waits for the trespassing girl.

The girl in this brief Grimm cautionary tale has been sternly forbidden by her parents to seek out Frau Trude, an evil woman with a wicked sense of humor (it took me a while to appreciate this potential in the old hag). Of course, the girl disobeys, goes off through the forest to find the crone, and on her way sees three strange men—green, black, and red—whom she describes to Frau Trude. Her big mistake is to admit that she has looked through Frau Trude's window and has seen a distressing sight, "the devil with a fiery head" (Zipes, *Complete Fairy Tales* 174). She learns too late that she has seen the forbidden, "the witch in her proper dress" (174), and is promptly turned into a log and fed to the fire. There is no redemption here. Frau Trude sits down to warm herself beside her fireplace and says sweetly (I can see her smile as I write these words), "Indeed, she does burn brightly." The story as I initially read it was a paragon of the worst victim tales. Even in one of the most abusive of the Grimm tales, the "Maiden without Hands," the heroine survives mutilation and gains independence. But in "Frau Trude" the girl who is simply curious and disobedient is destroyed. I was enraged with the story, and unaware of how deeply I would also be engaged with it over the years.

I see now how this brief little story has paralleled my own work. When I began my dissertation research, women in folktales had hardly been explored in depth, and I knew of no academic models to guide my curiosity. In my quest I was going against the wishes of one of my dissertation committee members, who wanted me to do a topic on heroines in legends of the American west. But I had already been lured into the world of folktales and I was determined to go on, even if it meant I was being disobedient, and trespassing in forbidden territory. It is hardly surprising that I was distressed by the story of a girl who is destroyed for being too curious. I pushed on, as she had, but I was luckier; I survived the fire and completed my impossible task, with anger as my fuel.

Now, almost three decades later, I have become the crone who waits. I ponder the scene at the fireplace rather than reacting with rage. Why was Frau Trude so unforgiving? She herself admitted that she had been waiting a long time for this particular girl. Only to destroy her? (She is lucky to have missed Gretel, who would have pushed her into her own fire.) But from the crone's point of view, and my own all these years later, perhaps what she really wanted was new energy, an apprentice who could learn whatever she had to teach. That sort of girl would have to be disobedient or she would never visit a witch's hut in the first place. So I look back on that curious girl that I once was and wonder where she is now that I need her fresh energy. I imagine Frau Trude whispering, "Now dear, remember that fire can be a transformative element. Just stay a bit longer and warm yourself." If that girl *had* survived the fire, we can imagine her going on to new adventures, as she did in my various retellings of the story.

That brings us to "The Water of Life," a grand adventure indeed. The story as I first read it is a Catalan variant published by Andrew Lang (184). It is a complex tale, so I summarize it more fully than "Frau Trude." A sister and three brothers decide to better their lot by working hard, and manage to build both a fine palace and a handsome church. They are told that in order to make these complete, they need to find "a pitcher of the water of life, a branch of the tree . . . whose flowers give eternal beauty, and the talking bird" (185). Each brother sets off in turn to find these objects on top of a mountain, each meeting a giant who warns them about the speaking stones on the mountain path. All the brothers hear the stones scoffing and mocking, stop to respond, and are turned to stone themselves. The sister now sets off alone on the same path, gets the same advice, and succeeds in walking over the stones even though "it was as if each stone she stepped on was a living thing" (188). She reaches the top and finds the three precious things, but as she starts down the path she accidentally drops water on some of the stones, who take their human shape again. She continues downward transforming the stones, and returns home with all of the people and her brothers. They plant a branch of the flowering tree, watering it with the magical water and releasing the talking bird from its cage to settle on the branch. A wandering prince hears of these wonders, comes to see for himself, and falls in love with the sister. You know what happens next.

Despite the inevitable concluding marriage, this story moved me with its unusual plot. I placed it in my highest category, Heroic Heroines, quite the opposite of "Frau Trude," whose failed protagonist was relegated to the lowest one, Persecuted Heroines. When I began to perform stories some time later, this one came to mind immediately. I could not find the printed text at first but I trusted my memory, since the story had been so striking. Months later I found the text again, and saw with surprise how far my variant diverged. I had accurately recalled the magical power of the bird and the flowering tree, how sister and brothers walked over the talking stones to find the water of life, and how she transformed the stones on the mountain. But the order and significance of these motifs had changed as my story evolved, and there were other surprises as well. Somehow a dragon had come into the story, and the prince had left it. After several years of oral telling, the story took its own shape, though its emergent quality continues each time the story is told. (A full text of the story, as it existed when this article was written in 2004, is included at the end of this chapter.)

I offer a brief sketch of how this evocative story has matured over a decade of oral performing, in order to reveal how it has come to reflect the evolution of my ideas about women and folktales. As I have already said, I was startled to see how far it had moved away from the printed text. The characters were similar, but the events had changed, though I was not conscious of altering the story significantly. Three changes were surprising: There was a fox instead of the giant; a golden dragon appeared where there had not been one before, and I wondered where the prince had gone. The fox as helper and the dragon as tester seemed so natural to the story that I could not believe they had not been in the story as I had first read it. Foxes can be accommodating, and dragons guard treasures, as we know—and what greater treasure is there than precious water? Such a prize could not be taken without a challenge of some sort. Yet in Lang's variant there is, surprisingly, no dragon, and thus no challenge.

And the prince? When I reread the story he seemed so superfluous that it felt as if he had been added for a romantic conclusion. I simply had not remembered him at all when I began to tell the tale, so he vanished without a trace, and without protest. This was a clear reflection of my own inclinations at that time, my strong preference for heroic women who were more in need of dragons than of princes.

These were not deliberate alterations. I stress this because much of my folkloric work has emphasized the natural integrity of wondertales, their deeply evocative and enigmatic essence. As archetypal literature I insisted that they needed no conscious modifications to render them contemporary and relevant. My position was a reaction to overly zealous modernizers, including some feminists, who were often too quick to transform stories to fit new sensibilities and polemical positions. I found that if someone worked only from the surface of a tale rather than from its depths, the story invariably lost something in the translation. Archetype became stereotype and the mystery was gone. This is the problem with all of "the Disney versions," for example.

It was a shock, then, for me to see my own unintended meddling. I had thought I was telling the story as I had read it rather than deliberately changing it to fit my preferences. This is a fine line to walk, since tellers and writers by nature are guided by their own predilections. But at that time I was more scholar than teller, still anxious about interfering with a traditional story. I could see that the tale as I had been telling it made narrative sense, and did not seem unfaithful to the spirit of the text since it rose up from the depths of the tale as I remembered it emotionally. Nevertheless, I felt uncomfortable with it because it was somehow not "true" to the text, so I tried to re-form it by returning to Lang's sequence of events. I removed the dragon and reinstated the prince, and allowed the wedding to take place. After several attempts at telling the "true" tale, I gave up on this impossible task; the story had become as petrified as one of the stones on the mountain path. It had lost its power over me so I stopped telling it.

A year or so passed before I was motivated to tell the story again, this time as part of a workshop sponsored by a Christian feminist gathering in Toronto. I decided to take an artistic leap and return to my own variant to see if it was still capable of any life. Interestingly, when I told it to this particular group, the blossoming tree took on its own role, sharing the center of the story with the courageous and once again prince-less sister. In the context of a Christian-centered context the story revealed itself—naturally, not through my intentional manipulation—as a redemption from "the fall." The fruit of knowledge brought joy, and the serpent-like dragon was a source of power rather than an evil tempter. What he says to the woman is a question I have asked myself often: "Why did you come here and what do you want?" If she had failed to answer, her story would have ended quite differently. I, too, had to answer the question for myself. She sought the Water of Life for the tree, I sought the breath of life for the story.

I began to tell the story more regularly again, and found that the sister's heroism became less of an issue for me. I saw that her test was not so much climbing a mountain and facing a dragon, but walking over the stones without letting them stop her. At this point in my told story, the stones began to speak more forcibly, and in specific voices. She almost stopped for the stones that flattered her for having come so far as a "remarkable" woman, and then for the weeping stones that begged her, implicitly, to be a more traditional woman and not abandon them on the mountain. She had to leave these stones behind without seeming heartless and opportunistic, not by ignoring them but by hearing their cries and still going on, realizing that she would be unable to help if she stopped. This has been a very powerful moment for many who have heard the story.

The metaphoric image of living things that have been paralyzed, petrified, caught alive on their own rigid paths, became increasingly central to the story. I saw, too, how important it was that the eventual transformation of the stones comes about by accident, not bold action. The sister does not have a plan; she simply trips, makes a mistake, and from this learns the full power of the water. The stones find themselves alive again, no longer paralyzed by rage and despair. As a teller, I tripped when I "forgot" the Lang variant. More by accident than by deliberation, the tale took on its own life again.

After several years of telling this story in a wide variety of contexts, each one with new revelations, new perspectives on the twists and turns of the quest for the magical water, I came to a much deeper understanding of what held a wondertale together and brought it ever-renewing life. As in a meaningful dream, all the elements of the story were necessary for its ripening, none were trivial or meaningless. As I learned from tellers I interviewed for my study of storytelling, *Burning Brightly,* a told tale is always new, always unfolding again and again over the years of its life. This variability inspires ever-new paths of narrative investigation, arising from professional training in either (or both) artistic and academic disciplines. A story can begin to grow from within, like the fruit on the tree, guided in its development as much by intuitive narrative sense as by abstract rationale.

My long experience with "Frau Trude" and "The Water of Life" as told stories allowed me to experience the very real metaphoric correlations of folktale magic and mundane reality. Let me be more specific here, and playful, by using my telling of "The Water of Life" as an allegory of my work. When I began my work on women and folktales, I was following a trail first blazed by feminist writers who criticized fairy tales as sources of negative stereotyping. Like the bird in "The Water of Life," they revealed what and where the problem was and gave some idea of the path ahead. Simone de Beauvoir and Betty Friedan, for example, identified and firmly rejected the overly feminine model projected by the pretty princesses who seemed to dominate so many fairy tales. These critiques kindled fire in my soul. But their images of figures like Cinderella and Sleeping Beauty were too generic, popular stereotypes rather than archetypal characters from specific stories. In contrast, later writers like Alison Lurie and Marcia Lieberman presented impassioned critiques of submissive heroines, and surveyed them more comprehensively by using specific examples from popular collections. Lurie focused on the Grimms while Lieberman sought her women in the multi-volume Lang "fairy books." They found that heroines like the woman in "The Water of Life" were much outnumbered by their passive sisters and they were angry about it. This further fired my own work, making my path more apparent. They functioned for me like the fox in "The Water of Life," by providing more specific information about the difficulties of the path ahead.

In the following decades other scholars, among them Karen Rowe, Maria Tatar, Ruth Bottigheimer, and Jack Zipes, carried this work even further in publications exploring traditional heroines, while creative writers like Jane Yolen, along with Tanith Lee and Angela Carter, created new ones. Poets Anne Sexton (*Transformations,* 1971) and Ralph Mieder (*Disenchantments,* 1985) also found ways to give a new spin to fairy tales. Some of these stories and poems gave me the creative energy to go on with my own work, and challenged me as directly as had the dragon in "The Water of Life." I felt that I had an obligation, through my writing and storytelling, to carry the water of life back down the path.

Many feminist writers and authors, myself included, continued to hold fast to the dichotomy between negatively passive and positively active heroines. I still regarded "Frau Trude" and "The Water of Life" as opposites, even after I had managed to bring "The Curious Girl" out of the fire—until I eventually rethought my firm categories that held victimized heroines in disfavor. In this I was motivated by two very different story tellers, Susan Gordon and Carol McGirr. Gordon wrote about her understanding of the Grimm tale, "The Maiden without Hands" (AT 706), gained through her retellings ("Powers"). This heroine, threatened by the devil, mutilated by her own father, sent into exile to suffer alone, was one I had firmly classified as "Persecuted," an example of the most abjectly abused of all heroines. Gordon's words made me look again at a heroine she viewed as heroic, a resourceful woman who does not, in fact, submit passively to her fate. This was an opinion I had already heard, and ignored, from a few of the girls and women I interviewed during my early research. I had glossed over these responses as aberrations, but when I reread the interviews, I was compelled to see how earnest these respondents were in insisting that "persecuted" heroines were, in fact, heroic.

Similarly, Toronto teller Carol McGirr insisted that the persecuted sister, Tanya, from the Russian tale "The Rosy Apple and the Golden Bowl," was dauntlessly heroic. She survived the benign neglect of her parents and the fearsome greed and murderous cruelty of her sisters. I had to admit that she was certainly dauntless, overcoming even her own death to triumph fully over her cruel sisters in the end.

This shift of viewpoint blurred the distinct boundaries of the four categories I set up in my dissertation, most notably those that placed persecuted and heroic women at opposite ends of the scale. Telling stories for 25 years further softened the firm lines I placed between categories. Having brought

"Frau Trude" and "The Water of Life" together here, I am startled to see how much these two have grown together over the years. The two protagonists have become more sisters than opposites, experiencing the elemental forces of fire and water. The antagonists, too, are less disparate, the crone now cousin to the golden dragon; both are awesome figures who offer challenges that open the possibility of renewed life.

You will recall that the unexpected is to be expected in fairy tales. Just when you think the path is clear, something happens that turns everything around again. So it is in the telling of tales as well. On one occasion, the prince managed to slip back into "The Water of Life," though in somewhat altered form. It happened in this way. Almost at the moment I called up the story text to begin revising it for the eye, I had a phone call from a friend asking if I knew "something ecological with a love theme" for her daughter's wedding in another city. I said that the story I had just started to edit was certainly ecological, with its theme of a tree that needs pure water in order to live again, but I was not sure about a "love theme." I was willing to play with the story for a few days for this special occasion, and as I tried it out with friends the prince did indeed find his way back. This time, however, he was a commoner, a wandering musician who was more interested in the heroine's accomplishments than in her beauty. I was intrigued to see, when I reread Lang's variant, that even in the printed tale the prince/musician had the good sense to admire "the courage of the maiden" and not just her beauty. This gave him more potential.

I finished this special wedding gift and went back to work on the story. The prince, I found, wanted to stay, and I saw that he had opened an archetypal slot for a character—not necessarily male—who could carry the story further. I did not want a love story with a concluding wedding celebration, but I was curious to see what might happen if I left the slot open. I wondered who might wander in. After telling the story to friends, this unknown figure became a simple traveler of unknown gender or age, with no overt romantic expectations. This left the story open-ended, with further interpretation left up to the reader or listener. The 10-year-old friend I read it to was intrigued by this unusual resolution. She still called the traveler "he," but said she could see how it could be "she" or even "it." She also thought it could be the fox who came back into the story. A mature friend about to set off on a solo kayak voyage envisioned an older woman looking for new adventures. Others, already familiar with the story, heard the new ending and found it intriguing.

The story as I had been telling ended in this way: *The sister and brothers divided all the fruit and shared it with every person there. Each who tasted it found that their new year was filled with joy, which didn't mean they had no sorrows, only that their troubles did not overwhelm them. Trees began to grow in that stony land again, but only one tree bore the fruit of joy.*

So it was, and ever will be, even now to this very day.

The version I played with brought a wanderer back into the story, taking it closer to the version in Andrew Lang, though, as I said, gender is deliberately not specified here, and no marriage is indicated:

The fame of that tree, and of the sister who found the water that renewed it, spread through that land and beyond. One day someone from far away heard this remarkable tale and came to see if it was true. When this curious one arrived at the place where the sister and her brothers lived, they were happy to show the tree and to tell how it came to bloom again. The traveler admired the strangeness and beauty of the tree and the truth of the tale, but even more than that admired the courage of the woman who had climbed over the speaking stones and touched a dragon to win The Water of Life.

"I will play you a song in exchange for the story," said the stranger, who took out a small flute and began to play.

When the sister heard the song, she recognized the melody that had accompanied her all the way through the forest and up the stony path. She admired the strangeness and beauty of the music, but even more than that she admired the skill of the one who played it. She asked where the song had come from.

"You'll think it's peculiar," answered the traveler, "but I'll tell you. One night I had a curious dream about a fox playing a flute. My tune came from this dream."

"I see," she said, smiling. "I know that tune."

And it was true.

So it was, and ever will be, to this very day.

This story, and wondertales in general, continue their emergent quality, to grow as long as the telling of them goes on. (As I continue to tell "The Water of Life" at this time, in 2006, the wanderer/prince/musician has left the story again, not through any conscious decision but, I supposed, because this character had said all that could be said.)

When I consider how long I have contemplated folktales and heroines, I see that the lifeblood of my work has been a deep interest in resourcefulness and transformation. These features are central to the mystery of wondertales, true even for the most downtrodden or the most aggressive of heroines. By using two very different stories as examples, I hope I have been able to show the resilience of old tales and their heroines as they continue to live and to interact in the modern world, told and retold in contemporary contexts.

Composing stories orally is as ephemeral as writing in air, and writing them is, for me, like trying to carve words into solid rock. Both are frustrating and rewarding, in quite different ways. Much of the time I have felt more like a stone on the mountain path than the woman who touches each of them with transformational water. It is a struggle to keep going, keep writing, keep telling. Sometimes I have to wait for that single drop of creativity to get me rolling again. This is a challenge for us as feminist scholars and writers and tellers—keeping our voices alive even when we feel petrified, unable to continue on the path or to face the dragon even when we succeed in climbing the mountain. Eventually we find our way, meet our witches and dragons, pass through fire, and carry water back down to other thirsting stones.

THE WATER OF LIFE

Once there was a land so barren that in some places only stones seemed to grow, and only the hardiest trees could survive. A sister and her brothers lived there. They had little between them, but they did have one very precious thing, a tree unlike any other. This tree bloomed just once every year, in the darkest time. It put out one perfect flower on the highest branch, and every year this flower slowly formed a single flawless fruit. On the first day of each new year when the fruit was ripe, the brothers and sister would take it down, divide it, and eat it. The rest of their year would be filled with joy, which didn't mean they had no troubles, only that their sorrows did not overwhelm them.

One day everything changed. The tree did not bloom. It had no leaves, no blossoms, no fruit. The sister and her brothers stood at the base of the tree looking up, not knowing what to do. As they watched, a strange and wonderful bird flew out of the clear blue sky and settled on the highest branch. It began to sing a haunting song that entranced them all with the rise and fall of its melody. Beautiful as it was, the sister heard something more, like a soft voice whispering. "Listen!" she said to her brothers. "The bird sings that our tree has stopped blooming because we didn't share the fruit with anyone else." They heard that it would not bloom again unless they found one cup of the Water of Life and brought it to the tree. "Where?" said the older brother, and when he heard that this precious water was in a well on the top of the mountain beyond the great forest, he announced that he would go and find it.

"You all stay here and tend the tree," he said confidently.

"No," said the younger brothers. "We want to go too."

The sister agreed to stay and tend the tree, but she was careful to notice the path they took so she might follow if they failed. The three brothers set off together. She watched them disappear down the long path that led to the great forest.

They walked on and on, further than they'd ever gone in their lives, and after some time they came to the forest. There beside the path at the edge of the woods, a red fox crouched, gnawing on a white bone. The fox looked up at them and said politely:

"Where you are going and what do you seek?"

"We've come to find the Water of Life," the first brother answered brusquely, "on the top of the mountain beyond this forest."

"I see. But do you know that this is a dangerous road—and that the path up the mountain is even more dangerous? I've never seen anyone come back in all the time I've been here."

"Why?" said all the brothers together.

"This is what I know. When your feet touch the stones on the path leading almost to the top of the mountain, those stones will call out. They'll insult you and challenge you and flatter you, and they'll even weep and wail. But anyone who stops to answer the voices becomes one of the stones. They do not return on this path."

The brothers were disturbed to hear this but determined to go on. They hastily thanked the fox and set off into the great dark woods. The path led them through shimmering light and shadowed dark as they walked together. At last they stepped out of the forest into bright sunlight, where they could see a mountain covered with evergreen trees. A narrow path of stones wound up through the cool green woods, almost to the top of the mountain.

"The fox was right," the first brother said eagerly, and he ran to the base of the mountain and began to climb. The very first stone he stepped on spoke to him. "Stop!" it called. He went boldly on, and when he didn't stop, the stones began to insult him. He grew angry as he heard the voices, but he went on. At last their words made him so furious that he forgot the words of the fox and turned to answer them. He stopped. He became one of the stones.

The other two brothers, each in turn, started up the path, and each climbed a little further than the last. But they both suffered the same fate as their brother, the second giving in to the voices that challenged, and the third to those that flattered. None of them come back down the fox's path.

The sister waited at home for some time until she was sure that her brothers were not going to return. She prepared herself, and then set off on the path her brothers had taken. She too met the fox, who asked:

"Where are you going and what do you seek?"

She answered the fox politely, and listened thoughtfully to what the fox said in response. She learned that the long path was dangerous, that anyone who stopped would become one of stones. She guessed what must have become of her brothers. As she listened closely, she felt that she could hear behind the fox's words the faint echoes of a tune that reminded her of the bird's strange melody. She said good bye and went on her way.

The song cheered her as she passed through the great forest of shimmering light and shadowed dark. At last she came out into the open and saw the mountain and its stony path. She walked toward the mountain, still listening for the faint strains of melody whispering in her head.

Soon enough she came to the first stone of the path and heard it call out "stop!" but she went on, and the music came with her. When she didn't stop the stones began to insult her, and then to challenge her, and at last to flatter her.

"Do stop!" they called in sweet voices, "You're a remarkable woman to have come this far. Stop and share your secret with us." She was tempted to help, but even when she heard her last brother's voice among them she went on, sorry that she was now completely alone. Then the stones began to wail and to cry out in pitiful voices:

"Oh please! Stop! Stop! Please don't leave us here like this, all alone. We've been lying here for so long, so very long."

She heard their anguished voices and now she really wanted to stop and help them, but she remembered the fox's words. If she stopped now she would become one of them, unable to help at all. In tears, she willed her feet to move over the weeping stones one step at a time, up and up, with their sad voices calling out behind her as she went on.

Finally the path ended and she found herself at the top of the mountain, with the world spread out below. At her feet lay an ancient well, and on the edge of the well was a small silver cup. She reached down to pick up the cup, but as *her fingers touched it she heard a deep hissing sound. The earth under her feet began to tremble and shake, then the well was filled with a deep roaring like the sound of a fierce storm approaching. She stood there watching, and before her startled eyes the head and neck of a great golden dragon rose up slowly from the well until it towered above her. The dragon spoke in a voice filled with rolling thunder:*

"Where you are going and what do you seek?"

"I've come for the Water of Life," she stammered, "just one cup, for the tree."

"One cup, you say? That is much more than you think. But I will allow you to take one cup . . . if you do something for me."

"What could I do for you?" she said, her voice full of fear.

"You can polish the scales on the top of my head until each one glows like the sun. If you do that, you may take one cup of the Water of Life."

She looked at her ordinary hands, and, with nothing else to offer, she agreed. The dragon bent down his great golden head and she began to polish the scales, each one carefully. When she finished, he lifted his great head and hissed slowly, carefully,

"One cup is yours—and take care how you use it."

As the golden dragon sank back down, the well filled with surging water. She seized the silver cup and filled it, turned quickly, and started back down the mountain.

When she came to the first stone she tripped, and one drop of water fell from the cup onto the stone. Before her eyes that stone turned into a human being. They looked at each other in amazement, then she looked at the water in the cup. She touched the next stone with the water. This stone, too, became a human being. And the next . . . And the next . . . And the next.

She noticed that the water in the cup did not diminish, and then she understood the dragon's words. One cup was much more. She moved down the path touching each of the stones with one drop of precious water and watched as each stone took its own human shape again. Happiest of all to see her were her own brothers. The four of them together, followed by all the people who had been stones, carried the cup back to the tree.

The people gathered in a great circle and watched as the four poured out the precious water at the base of the tree, and as it sank slowly into the earth the tree began to put out new leaves, then blossoms. As they watched, each blossom turned into perfect fruit, exactly enough for all who were there. The sister and brothers divided all the fruit and shared it with every person there. Each who tasted it found that their new year was filled with joy, which didn't mean they had no sorrows, only that their troubles did not overwhelm them. Trees began to grow in that stony land again, but only one tree bore the fruit of joy.

So it was, and ever will be, even now to this very day.

III

Fairy Tales and Dreams

14

In My Mother's Garden

(2004)

This was one of the first pieces that came to mind when I thought of working on a book that brought together dreams and folktales. I presented it orally several times as it developed over the years, and contributed it as an article to *Marvels & Tales* before it achieved finished form in the completed book *The Golden Woman*. My mother died in 1991, several years before this article was published, and when I began to bring it to life, the challenge was to recreate, from sparse memory, a small part of her life as a gardener, a dream I had about her garden, and a folktale one of my university students told in class. Because these various elements took place at different times and depended on my memory rather than on immediate contact, I was not able to review them more objectively with a folklorist's eye. Thus the article was not written as an academic piece. Instead, it grew somewhat erratically, like a garden in need of a lot of weeding and careful tending. In many ways, then, it served as a model for other chapters in *The Golden Woman,* which brought together a complex garden of dreams, folktales, and personal stories intertwined and cross pollinating.

An earlier version, with a slightly more academic slant, appears in the 1997 edition of *Marvels & Tales* (Stone, "Inside Out").

In many ways this chapter makes a fine bridge for all three sections in this book; it echoes my early work in section 1, since the protagonist in the tale, usually a sullen old man, becomes a wily crone, an enterprising woman who tricks herself into heaven. The article also continues the pattern set in section 2 by building itself around a full fairy tale text and commentary, opening many other possibilities of association for those who read it. And, as I have already said, it is probably the quintessential piece for section 3, since it balances story, dream, and life experience. If I were writing it today, I might put more emphasis on how and why certain stories stay alive for us at different periods of our existence, transcending the boundaries of time and space and personal challenges. And if I had a single wish from one of the wish-granting figures in fairy tales, it would be that those who most want and need to hear this story of regeneration will somehow find it.

As a child I sometimes dreamed that my mother was a witch who was chasing me, and I escaped her by flying off the roof of our house in Miami. I grew up certain that my mother the witch preferred Janet, the good girl whose half of our shared room did *not* look like hurricane damage. This misconception colored my relationship with her well into my adult life. I was surprised, then, to learn, late in our up-and-down relationship, that she had warm memories of my early stories of "Snakey" and that she was proud and delighted that I had become a public storyteller. She herself was not at all a public person, choosing to hide behind the scenes, usually in the kitchen, where she could watch what others were doing and attempt stage directing, especially of my father.

Her interest in my stories gave us a long overdue channel for communication. I learned to appreciate her understated cronish wisdom and humor as we talked about folktales, dreams, and life, and she heard many of my stories over those last few years we had together. Her favorite, especially in her final months of cancer, was "Jumping Mouse," about a curious desert mouse who is determined to find the sacred Blue Mountain (Storm 68). While the collector of the story has been criticized by anthropologists as well as by the Cheyenne people, the story is still compelling. I told it to my mother whenever she asked. This is a considerably abbreviated version, with a gender change to suit my mother.

A desert mouse disobeyed her elders and kept jumping too high, risking being caught by eagles. One day her joyful leaps took her up so far that she saw a blue mountain far off in the distance, and yearned to find it. She was guided by other creatures who knew the way: a frog who repeated the warnings about eagles but told her how to cross the desert; a buffalo who protected her and accompanied her to the base of the mountain in exchange for her right eye; a wolf who carried her almost to the top, but at the cost of her left eye. "How will I know I'm there if I can't see?" Mouse asked. Wolf explained that she would feel the winds blowing from all four directions at the top of the mountain, and that she should leap up as high as she could and let the winds carry her. Jumping Mouse reached the top, felt the winds swirl around her, and leapt into them. As she was carried down on the wind, expecting to die, she began to regain her sight, seeing more clearly than she had ever seen before. As she floated over her helpers she called down to each of them in turn, "Hello, Brother Wolf! Hello, Brother Buffalo! Hello, Brother Frog!" Each looked up, and called out, "Hello, Sister Eagle!"

My practical mother, the gardener, said that she usually did not enjoy "stories that couldn't happen." She liked this one because of "the stubborn little mouse who didn't do what she was supposed to." She was intrigued by the enigmatic conclusion: "What's happening?" she asked. "Did the eagle eat the mouse or did she turn into an eagle?" Since she was facing death herself, this mystery was very real, more than "just a story." I told her it was up to her. She smiled, and chose transformation.

Dreams, too, often leave us wondering "what's happening?" My mother understood that "Jumping Mouse" was a very human story, and that the ending is not about death but about rebirth. She found that message moving, comforting, and all her own; I had declined to interpret the story, wanting it to remain open, though of course that's exactly how I saw it myself. And I did truly *see* it. In a different way it is the story of anyone who has struggled to find their own creative path without being turned aside by discouraging voices, that "petty criticalness" as described earlier by Brenda Ueland. Flying in this sense is not at all an escape from adventure, it's a joyful leap deeper into it.

My mother said that this little protagonist reminded her of me as a girl. "Her name could be Kay Francis," she suggested once with a smile. I thought the mouse was also like that fun-loving girl who was my mother, who met her husband-to-be at a church Halloween party.

She was fond of all the stories I told with resourceful protagonists, but she probably never heard the one I most wanted to tell her. It came too late, when she was in the final stages of cancer and lost on pain killers, though a friend assured me that she might be able to hear it even in this state. I will try to recreate the sequence of events that brought the story to a new shape, but this is difficult because it is not, in fact, a simple sequence of events. I struggled with this in a preliminary article about my mother and her garden in an earlier article, "Inside Out: Folktale and Personal Story," and am still trying to piece it all together from faulty memory aided by responses from my sisters. While the story was coming into being in relation to my mother and her garden I was a daughter and storyteller, not a folklorist, so I was not studying its gradual development. Let me begin my exploration now in a dream I had that showed me how important that garden had been.

Late in her life my mother became a gardener. Wearing a battered hat to protect herself from the Miami sun, she began to plant a modest vegetable plot to supplement their diet, since they were living on my father's small pension and occasional contributions from the family. That was her practical reason, but in fact she had always loved working outside and trading plants with Mrs. H. across the street. I just never paid much attention when I lived at home. She began the garden after we had all left home, and after all of her grandchildren had grown beyond babysitting age. As far as my sisters and I can figure, this was sometime in the late 1970s and early 1980s. Theoretically Florida has a year-round growing season, but she still did much of her gardening in winter (in Miami, the season of brown grass) because summer was too hot for her, even in her gardening hat, and for many of the vegetables as well. I am sorry that I paid so little attention to her garden. I had married and moved to Canada by that time, and we visited only once a year, usually in the Christmas season when we had time off from teaching. I remember that our children, Nathaniel and Rachel, were excited at being able to go out to her backyard and pull up vegetables for their supper, the only time I could get them to eat carrots and peas willingly.

For about four or five years the garden was larger every time we returned. It had begun as a small patch between the clothesline and an old grapefruit tree, and ended up covering half of the back yard. She even had my father move the clothesline to another part of the yard to accommodate the garden, and considered cutting back the grapefruit tree to provide more light. In the end she let the tree grow, because it had been "a friend" from our first difficult days in

Miami in the 1940s. My mother was modestly proud of her very ordinary vegetables—carrots, beans, peas, two kinds of peppers (the hot ones to discourage bugs), green onions, and of course tomatoes. But she was especially happy with her old southern favorites that none of us would eat as children because they were "hillbilly" food—things like collard and mustard greens, and others I couldn't even identify. She remembered them from her childhood in Melvin Hill, North Carolina, which she had left at age eight when her family moved north to Windsor and then to Detroit. She even tried to grow a small cotton plant once, as a joke, in memory of her hard work picking cotton as a girl. "We all had to work when we weren't in school," she told me, as she showed me the souvenir cotton boll she'd brought back from a family visit in the 1960s.

We all took that garden for granted. It seemed like a perfectly natural thing for her to be doing, since she'd always loved growing things indoors and out. I learned to appreciate her green thumb when I left a spindly house plant with her once and found that it had become a tree when I returned to get it. Because I took her green thumb for granted, I don't remember now when the garden began its decline nor how long that took, perhaps only a year or two. I only remember, sadly, that one year when I went home it was gone. Only a bare patch of grey South Florida sand was left, not yet reclaimed by crabgrass. Even then, I did not understand just how important that garden was to her—or to me— until I had a remarkable dream a few years later.

In the dream I was visiting Miami, walking up the familiar cement driveway to the front porch of the house I grew up in. When I entered the porch my mother came out to greet me. She gave me the usual hug and then said, "Go out back and see what I've done with the garden." I dropped my suitcase on the porch and walked directly through the living room, kitchen, and back porch, and opened the rear door. I stepped down onto the green cement steps my father had built and painted in my mother's favorite color. I was stunned at what I saw. The garden began right at the base of the green steps and went on and on and on, right to the horizon. I woke up in surprise, amazed, feeling as if I had actually been there. My mother's garden covered the earth.

Obviously the garden was much more than a practical vegetable patch. When I visited my parents later that year, I told my mother the dream and said, "I had no idea how important that garden was to you." She just smiled and nodded. But I still did not fully understand how much of her creativity and her love had gone into the garden, where she could justify such "indulgence" (she was having fun) by growing everyday food. Flowers would have been too much of a luxury, I think. But in the dream garden there were both flowers and vegetables together. The memory of this dream and the actual garden it evoked was in my mind when I heard one of my university students tell a folktale about a grouchy old man who fools death and the devil. It took a hard blow to bring garden, dream, and story all together. In the late 1980s my mother was told she had cancer. My visits became more frequent, two or three times a year instead of once at Christmas, and during my visits she asked me to repeat some of the stories she had heard me tell in the past.

The one story I wish I had told her was an odd one I had just heard from a student in my folklore class. At first I didn't connect it with my mother or her garden, because this was not implicit in the folktale as it was told. I was slow to see the possibilities, but as I understood them the story began to bloom.

The folktale is popularly known as "Wicked John and the Devil" (AT 330). There are hundreds of similar stories collected in Europe and Euro-America. One index lists titles of 24 collections with variant texts, from England and Ireland, France, Italy, Norway, Iceland, the southern United States, and Maritime Canada (Ashliman 72). Two southern variants follow the usual pattern of the story (Chase, *Jack Tales* 172; *Grandfather Tales* 29). In these a crotchety old man uses wishes granted by St. Peter to outwit both death and the devil, but as a result he is not permitted to enter either heaven or hell and must wander the earth forever, carrying a coal from hell.

The story told casually by my folklore student, Chris Barsanti, was unusual. He identified it as "a gypsy story," but did not list his source and has since left Winnipeg, so I have been unable to identify the exact text. It does not match any of those I have explored, so I assume that it was his original interpretation—and I so credit him here.[1] His story is atypical because the protagonist is a more pleasant character, and also because he manages to trick his way into heaven by using a fourth wish, one more than what we expect in folktales. This intrigued me, as did the nature of the wish: The man says, "Where my old hat is, there I will be."

There are some folktales that reach beyond the entertaining qualities of the story, and we may be unaware of why a particular tale is so instantly absorbing. This was just such a story for me, and I began to tell it soon after I heard Chris Barsanti's version. It took many months of performance for the story to begin to reveal its connections with my own life, and even longer to find its connections to my mother and her garden. Since I was telling the story rather than studying it, I cannot remember quite how and when my mother and her garden began to influence it. The old hat offered me a clue, since it is in both the story and in my mother's life, and probably in the dream too if I had looked at the peg it hung on before stepping out the back door.

By the time I sent my mother a tape of the story, the old man had been firmly replaced by an old woman, less crotchety but no less wily. I put her in to amuse my mother, but that woman has refused to leave, being entirely comfortable with her place in the story as I tell it now. She is not my mother, but for me she is a kind of memorial to my mother. (The full text of "The Old Woman and Her Hat" is included at the end of this chapter, along with a poem, "Horizon," by Tanis MacDonald.)

I am not at all certain that my mother ever heard this story, as we never had a chance to discuss it. I do know that she never felt as confident as the old woman in the story. I think of her now as always wavering firmly between decisions. Perhaps six children would bring that out in a person. She had told me, when I visited her last a few months before she died, that she had been agonizing over heaven and hell. She said, with an embarrassed smile, "I haven't thought about that since Sunday school. Now isn't that silly, to be worried about that old Sunday school story?" Her words stayed with me when I returned home. Soon after this visit, as I was telling the story of the stubborn old man, I saw how it addressed the issue of finding one's place in the afterworld. Other connections with my mother began to fall into place.

Several aspects of the story as I had heard it opened to new possibilities. There was the unusual granting of a fourth wish, which gave the protagonist another chance to save himself, and with an ordinary and familiar object—an old hat. His tenacity evoked my mother's determination to go on under adverse conditions: past illnesses, the early deaths of two of her eight children, constant economic hardships, the suicide of her nephew, and now a fatal disease that she had long feared. She had lived her own hell and could still hold up her head. I tried to imagine her confronting St. Peter with wishes that seemed foolish to him but very down to earth for her: Don't climb my tree, don't sit in my rocking chair, stay out of my rain barrel. And of course, the hat used to gain entry to heaven conjured up a battered cloth hat that hung on the back porch long after my mother no longer used it. But she herself was not yet "in" the story for me until I had told it for a while, with the clear image of her old gardening hat. Even though it is most likely that she never heard it, telling the story with her in mind permanently altered it for me. It became a living story instead of an interesting folktale. I must emphasize that it is a story inspired by my mother, not about my mother.

As I have already said, folktales and other metaphorical expressions do not share a one-to-one relationship with ordinary reality. Yet they still can, like dreams, speak deep truths about lived experiences. People have been exploring the deeper meanings of folktales for more than a century and from many different points of view—artistic, historical, social, psychological. I suggest that no final interpretation is possible because every response is unique and personal. Even a single tale type like "The Smith Outwits the Devil" has as many possibilities as there are people who have heard and told it. Mine is only one of countless interpretations, and it evolves as I continue to tell the story. And, of course, this is exactly how new variants and versions arise throughout human history.

I did not consciously rework this story with the intention of transforming it into a story about my mother. I am aware, however, of the changes that have arisen through the actual telling. The apple tree, incidental in the story as I heard it, takes a more central role, echoing the grapefruit tree that grew for 40 years in the back yard. The old woman's memories of her garden shifted my view of the protagonist's character; I thought of the unending care and patience that a garden requires, and realized that a gardener would be practical and down-to-earth rather than mean or greedy, as the hero (often a blacksmith) is typically depicted in this tale. Story characters become real to a teller as a story becomes familiar. This does not mean they take on the personas of known people, which could in fact limit a story, but rather that they take on their own lives. When this happens, in oral and written literature, it is a gradual and often unconscious evolution. It was only after many tellings that I could see, through the story, my mother's actual cronish qualities in a positive light. Crones know what they want and they aren't worried about their feminine image. They know how to work with earth and plants, and they are not overawed by supernatural forces. Why not capture the Angel of Death in an apple tree and the devil in a rain barrel? At the end of this story it is the woman's choice to seek out her fate rather than having it forced upon her. I can imagine my mother smiling when she heard how the old woman was banned from hell, since she herself was worried about ending up there, in "that old Sunday school story."

For me this story of wishes, gardens and trees, helpful and threatening figures, and the old woman who succeeds in finding a path into paradise is a living story. It reveals my mother's struggles with adversity, in growing her garden and in facing death; it is exactly this reality, this actuality, that allows me to continue telling it with a sense of integrity, not as lived history but as living metaphor.

I do not have a sentimental image of my mother sitting under an ancient tree in paradise, planning her new garden. That is not the point of the story, and would narrow its meaning rather than broadening it. For me the story echoes her difficult life, her garden, and her love and respect for stories as well. All of these factors continue to provide living energy for an old tale that is entirely relevant today, not because it is a consciously re-formed "modern" folktale, but rather a traditional story that continues to speak in a new voice. This is how folktales express truths that both encompass and transcend personal history.

Here is another example of how archetypes challenge our too-narrow perceptions. In the dream I am walking down a long hall with a friend and say to her, "Oh, this is another one of my hall dreams." In other words, I begin to recognize that I am dreaming. She looks at me and smiles in recognition, as my daughter Rachel smiles in my lucid dream of "The Golden Woman." I notice my friend's smile, and try to explain the situation to her. "Listen! I know this is a dream and we can ask for something we really want." I think about it carefully and realize my mother has not appeared in any dreams lately, so I say with resolve, "I know what I want! I want to see my mother." Instantly the scene shifts and I am looking into a dimly lit space that seems to be a small domed room or a cave. I can see the figure of a robed woman, her face covered by a cowl, seated in a chair right in the center. It is too dark to see who this is but I am sure it is not her. I reject the image, saying in a disappointed voice with a touch of anger, "That's not my mother." As the scene fades and I move toward the waking world, I vaguely notice that this robed woman is somehow connected with a crescent moon and, I think, stars.

I suppose if I had been raised as a Catholic I would immediately identify her as Mary, but that does not feel right to me, somehow. This is a darker archetype, deeply earth-connected in spite of the moon and stars she seems to be associated with. Her bare feet are firmly on the ground. I feel the same dual sense of elation and frustration as in other disturbing dreams that I was not ready to accept. The frustration arises when I send away a powerful figure, as I sent away my dream buffalo in adolescence, and lose whatever they might have to offer. The elation comes from knowing that such figures do not give up easily and will eventually return in an altered form. We meet her in the guise of various crones, in stories and in dreams. Indeed, the witch *will* come one day.

I have waited for another chance for the seed that wants to be planted, and perhaps that is how I finally experienced "The Golden Woman," who passes through all four elements and rises transformed. With this in mind, I can see how my mother's garden covers the earth. And of course the tree that grows there can be found in "The Water of Life." The connections go on and on, right to the ends of our imagined inner earths.

THE OLD WOMAN AND HER HAT[2]

An old woman sat under her old apple tree, enjoying a bright fall day. She was remembering the vegetable garden she once kept before age and infirmity caused her to abandon it. She thought about all the things she had grown. "Ah, those ripe red tomatoes and the crisp green lettuce—I can almost taste them right now. Oh well, I still have my crisp juicy apples, and I'm sure this old tree will live well beyond me."

Suddenly a voice broke into her thoughts: "Kind woman, may I have one of your apples? I'm so hungry and weary, even an old dry one would nourish me." She looked up and saw an old man, a beggar, leaning on a gnarled walking stick. Now, no one had ever called her "kind" in her entire life, and indeed she was not. In fact, she was known to be a bit sharp-tongued and short tempered. His voice, and the memories of her garden, made her feel warm and generous. She said to the ragged man, "Take what you want. I have more than enough for myself." She even stood up and picked three of the ripest apples that hung just within reach.

The man took the smallest of the apples and ate it slowly. As he swallowed the last bite, a strange thing happened. She watched in amazement as the old beggar began to transform. His bent back straightened and he grew taller, his shabby clothing began to fill with light, his face glowed like the full moon. He smiled down at the woman as he spoke: "As you can see, I am St. Peter, the guardian of heaven's gates. I walk this earth looking for acts of kindness and generosity, and when I find them I am delighted. Old woman, I offer you three wishes, one for each of these apples."

Being a practical woman, she began to look around her small yard and inside her small house. She chose her wishes from what she saw. Her first wish was that anyone who picked an apple from her tree would be stuck fast until she released them. Her second was that anyone who sat in her favorite rocking chair would be unable to rise until she permitted them to do so. Her last wish was that anyone who looked into her rain barrel would be pulled in and held there until she let them out.

St. Peter, exasperated that she hadn't wished herself into heaven, cried out, "I've never done this before, but I'm going to give you one more wish. Use it well!" Again she looked around her, and when she saw her old gardening hat hanging on a peg beside her door, she said, "Ah, there's my fourth wish—wherever my hat is, I will be." The glow left St. Peter's face. He frowned down at her. He grumblingly acknowledged her wishes with a gruff, "So be it." He stalked off without a backward glance, muttering to himself as he went. "Silly old fool. She'll get what she deserves."

More years passed, and the old woman went about her life from one day to the next, as she had always done. One bright morning a knock came at her door. She slowly opened the door, and there stood the Angel of Death. She was surprised to see that the Angel of Death was a young woman, who said to her in a calm voice, "I've been sent to claim you now. Please come." The old woman, thinking quickly, said, "I'll be right with you. I just have to find my old gardening hat. But you must be tired after such a long journey. Why don't you refresh yourself with an apple from my old tree?" Death, who was rarely greeted so politely, was happy to oblige—and was soon stuck fast to the tree. "Let me go!" she demanded. "I have many more people to visit today. "Oh yes, I can do that," said the old woman, "but only if you grant me seven more years." Death had to agree. When she was freed she went away, grumbling like St. Peter, and vowing to return.

Indeed she did return, exactly seven years later. When the old woman opened her door she saw that Death was now older and wiser. "I won't touch that tree," she snapped. "You'd better come with me straight away." "But of course I will," the old woman answered. "I've been waiting for you—I just have to get my old hat. I'll be only a moment, so why don't you rest in my rocking chair while you wait." Death sat down, and rested much longer than she wanted to. She only won her freedom by promising the old woman seven more years.

Time passed as it always does. The old woman was too busy to notice, except for her growing aches and pains. At the end of seven years the apple tree still bloomed, the rocking chair still rocked, and her rain barrel was full of fresh water. This time when the knock came she opened her door expecting to see Death even older and warier, but it was not the Angel of Death who stood there. It was the Devil himself. "Death has given you up, so now you belong to me. Come along now, and no tricks! I know all about the apple tree and the rocking chair." "Oh, I wouldn't think of it," she said. "But if you know about the apple tree and the chair, then you must also know that I never go anywhere without my old hat. While I get it, why don't you take a nice cool drink from my rain barrel? You must be thirsty after such a long journey from such a very hot place." The Devil, who was rarely offered anything so pleasant, was happy to accept. And when he lifted the wooden lid and reached in for a sip of fresh water, into the barrel he went. "You crafty old woman! Let me out immediately. I have important souls to claim—politicians, for example, and others more important than a silly old woman!" And so she won another seven years.

"Perhaps I could start another garden, just a small one," she said to herself. But she forgot, too busy enjoying the days and weeks and months of that seven years. The apple tree went on bearing fruit, losing leaves, blooming again, and putting out more fine apples, for seven more years.

At the end of this time no one appeared. She waited for that last knock at the door, but it did not come. She was weary of life, having lived far beyond her years, and found herself actually wishing to see the Angel of Death again, or even the Devil himself. But finally she understood that neither Death nor the Devil would come to her now. "Oh dear, she said, I'll have to find my own way to the other world." And being a practical woman she set off right away, taking only her old gardening hat with her, and one fine ripe apple to eat along the way. She walked farther than she had ever walked in her entire life, and at last came to a crossroad. She set off on the road to the right, and gradually it began to descend. After some time she found herself at the gates of Hell, and knocked loudly. The Devil himself answered and saw who was there. "I forbid you to enter here, old woman. You don't belong here. Go away! Go up to the other place."

She retraced her steps and eventually found herself back at the crossroad. This time she took the road to the left, which led her up and up to the very gates of heaven. St. Peter answered her knock, but when he saw her he called out, "Old woman, you had four chances to wish yourself into heaven and you refused. I cannot let you in." He began to close the great gates of heaven. They moved slowly together, and just as they were about to swing shut the old woman remembered the hat on her head, whisked it off and tossed it inside. It rolled and *rolled until it came to a stop at the base of an ancient tree. And that is where she found herself, standing in heaven looking up at that towering tree that seemed to have been there forever. Slowly she sat down under the tree, reached over and placed her old hat on her head, and leaned back against the warm bark of the tree, enjoying the beauty all around her. She felt the seeds of the apple in her pocket and remembered the tree in her front yard.*

"Well now," she said, smiling to herself, "this looks like a fine place to start a new garden." And she was surely right.[3]

[*Here is "Horizon," a poem based on this dream by Tanis MacDonald, a fruitful way to carry this story further on its journey. Her words transform the dream in ways that I resisted at first, since they were not "correct" in terms of my dream details. I reminded myself that artistic re-creation is what I am exploring here, and I let the dream go free.*]

I'm not over the swept threshold
of my mother's house when she says
come see what I've done with the garden.
Treading through the cool dark rooms,
I am a needle steadied for darning,
the fuss-and-fix-it that made me,
that chafed me. But by the back door,
on that single step that passes as a porch,
I stop, rooted, because
my mother has finally done it.
She's gardened the surface of the earth entire,
hoed and watered the world into neat rows,
tinkered the planet into good working order.
She's planted all the way to the horizon,
its calm line drawn perpendicular to
sixty staked rows of stringbeans,
pulling the sun down each night,
yanking it up each morning. Raspberry canes
swarm in the middle distance, snarling
their fruit forward. Rhubarb begs

for pies, heliotrope dogs the sun,
the spider-spread of portulaca
webs the soil at my toes.
My mother walks the rows,
bends to turn a tomato and show
me the blush, how the sun ripens
one side first

(MACDONALD, *holding ground* 69)

15

The Golden Woman

A DREAM AND A STORY (2004)

The subject of this article, a single profound dream, became the heart of an entire book. It was actually meant to be an epilogue for my previous book, *Burning Brightly*. However, it did not fit easily into a book about storytelling and storytellers, and hence *The Golden Woman* came into being in 2004. I have made slight changes here to adapt it to the present context, since as a book chapter it does not quite stand on its own. For example, I add a reference to a previous chapter from *Golden Woman* in this present book, and remove other unneeded references. Since I already included the full text of "The Water of Life" at the end of section 2, I summarize rather than repeating it here. I do retain the evocative poem of Tanis MacDonald, whose compositions on several dreams appear throughout the full book, illustrating my thesis that dreaming, as an art on its own, can also inspire further creativity.

There are comments on both Grimm and Disney heroines here, which is one of the many connecting threads I discovered as I reread each of the pieces I include in this present book. I note that in the dream of "The Golden Woman" I am, like Snow White's stepmother, looking into a mirror. Unlike her, I choose my older, less beautiful face over the enticing younger face the mirror first presents, and thus unwittingly become the crone herself—but this time with positive results. In my exploration of the dream, I connect the concept of cronehood to a variety of other folktales in which witches or other powerful figures act as testers of the protagonist—as does the dragon in "The Water of Life."

———

A rare dream illuminates much of what I want to say here about the artistry of dreams and their transformative quality. The dream is unique because it is a complete story from beginning to end, instead of the usual fragment with incomplete openings and closings. "The Golden Woman" led me deeper into dreams and folktales as a whole, revealing the intricate interweaving of biography, dream-life and story-life as artistic visions.

In a dark period when my writing was not going well, I had a surprising dream that filled my gloomy emptiness with unexpected radiance. The subtle colors, sharp images, the smell of earth and water, and the feeling of movement as graceful as a slow dance, are as immediate as they were when I experienced them several years ago. Jung might have called this a "great dream," one that goes beyond personal biography and into archetypal consciousness. That is, it is not just my personal dream, it is a dream for anyone who senses the pull of movement and the immediacy of imagery in "The Golden Woman." The dream begins with a familiar folktale motif, a mirror that reveals the truth when requested.

My daughter Rachel and I were standing together in the hall of our Winnipeg house, looking into the round, blue-framed mirror we saw every day. I did not recognize this as a dream because there was nothing dream-like about its setting or situation. Except for the mirror, which was larger than usual and on the opposite wall, everything was exactly as it was in the waking world: the dark blue of the frame, the off-white walls reflecting light from the front door, the dimly lit basement stairs to our right, the open kitchen door just beyond that. Also, I could see and hold my reflected image as clearly as if I were awake. In dreams my image faded if I looked too closely, so again I had no clue that I was not awake. I could see eighteen-year-old Rachel with her smooth face and her long, honey-brown hair, and saw that my mirrored image was also young, about twenty-five, with long, wavy brown hair. I felt a surge of joy, a strong feeling that somehow I had another chance at youth. It was a very convincing feeling, but almost immediately, for no reason I could identify, there was a warning twinge that something was not quite right. The image I saw was so deeply satisfying that I did not want to let it go, but I needed to know why the glimmer of doubt arose.

Because I did not shut out this vague feeling of unease, the dream could open to its lucid potential. I began to understand that I was not actually in the front hall seeing my true face. I turned to Rachel's mirror image and said, "This must be a dream," and she smiled at me enigmatically. I turned back to my own image and said in a firm voice that seemed to come from outside of the dream, "I want to see what I look like right now." Immediately my image began to shift and I saw myself as I was in waking life, older and rounder, my face fuller and square-jawed like my father's, my hair short, straight, and silvery white.

As I studied this face and accepted the image as true, I felt a shift in the dream. I had a conscious body sensation of subtle change, and I actually shifted to the right, taking a side step into the kitchen. Still aware that I was in a dream, I saw that our oak floor was now covered in old black linoleum with random white spots, an echo of the kitchen floor from my early Miami childhood. I knew from a previous dream that the spots in the floor might be passages into another reality, and allowed myself to sink slowly through one of them right through the floor. I did not resist the movement as I descended slowly and steadily downward through the air into a crawlspace and then into damp, dark earth. I could (and still can) smell the richness of the moist living soil pressed against my nose. This seemed to go on for a long time, but I felt no anxiety. All at once I fell gently out of the earth and into a deep green underground sea. In many of my dreams water has been a frightening element, but here I had no fear. Flashes of light revealed color and motion in the darkness. This moving sea was warm, dense, alive, my welcoming birthwater, and I was a natural part of its languorous movement.

As I sank, I became encrusted with the kind of growth that covers objects that settle to the sea bottom—barnacles, coral, other kinds of sea life. Soon I was completely enclosed in a solid cylinder that was a protection but not a confining shell, giving me firm weight in the heavy water. Inside, I was fully alert and could still sense the world around me, could experience the shifting light and the warmth of the water, and the slow movement down and down as I continued to sink.

Eventually I settled to the bottom of the sea into soft sand, where I could feel myself rolling gently back and forth with the natural surge of the water. I perceived four beings of some primal sort, more or less human, moving through the water and positioning themselves around my cylinder, two on each side. They used the motion of the sea to gradually roll the cylinder toward the shore, out of the water, and onto an island.

On the shore, a semicircle of people stood waiting around a large bonfire. The cylinder was slowly rolled right into the center of the fire while everyone watched quietly and calmly, waiting for what was going to happen. I understood that this was a sacred ritual of some sort and did not resist the flames.

Inside the cylinder I could feel the heat of the fire as it began to penetrate through the hard exterior, growing hotter and hotter. This was a strong physical feeling, not a vaguely dreamy warmth but real heat. I understood calmly that this heat would eventually become unbearable, knew intuitively but without apprehension that something would have to happen soon, that my situation would inevitably change profoundly. I waited. The others waited. When the heat inside the cylinder was at the point of becoming unbearable, my dreaming mind suddenly split: "I" was both inside the cylinder directly experiencing what was happening, and outside with the others observing it vicariously.

At the very instant of that split in consciousness, at the peak of pain, the cylinder itself split into two perfect halves. I felt myself lying there in the full heat of the fire, glowing hot, molten gold, transformed. At the same moment, the other aspect of me as the outside witness looked into the divided cylinder and saw the living gold in the shape of a woman, free from her mold. As the Golden Woman, I sat up and observed the semi-circle of people. As the woman in that circle, I witnessed the rising, and simultaneously saw and felt what the golden woman saw and felt. We became a single consciousness again as the Golden Woman began to move. I awoke rising.

When I woke, I kept my eyes closed and lay without moving for a few moments, allowing for a less abrupt passage from fragile dream consciousness back into the waking world of morning traffic and the neighbor's dog barking and dishes clinking downstairs in the kitchen as my husband made coffee. These small moments between sleeping and waking invite a dream to present at least a fragment of itself, and sometimes I can trace that fragment further and further back into the dream. But this time I had the entire dream, intact from my first gaze into the mirror to the rising of the Golden Woman. I was amazed, since I usually only manage to call back the last fading bits of a dream and have learned to appreciate even this much. Even if I had retained only that final image of the woman rising from the fire-encircled cylinder, it would have been enough to inspire imagination. But to have the full composition was a great gift.

In the bright light of that ordinary morning I allowed the dream to play and replay in my mind until I was certain I would not forget it. As I began to write it down, I could see how artfully my present and past experiences in the waking world had provided the rich soil for the rising of the Golden Woman. It was significant that the dream began in our actual home and not in one of the countless more appealing dream houses I have passed through over the years. I felt I was rooted in my mundane waking life with all its mental and physical associations. I was delighted that Rachel was with me initially, acting as a silent witness in much the same way as my dream-self later witnessed the golden transformation.

The mirror, too, was from the waking world, but subtly changed in size and position, another hint that this was a dream: I catch this hint and do not reject it, thus providing the conscious mind with a small place to enter. In this brief lucid state I know that I am dreaming and say the words instead of just thinking them. I give up my enticing youthful image, allowing the dream to free itself and move on.

Biography influences the dream in other ways as well. There is a brief flash of my childhood kitchen linoleum not seen for more than fifty years, with white spots offering passage into another world. The underground sea, unusually benevolent in this dream, evoked childhood memories of swimming in the Atlantic waters of Baker's Haulover in north Miami, and also, I believe, the body's memory of birth waters.

Since this single dream arose from the dream-treasury of my whole lifetime, I also looked for previous dreams that spoke a similar language, revealing variations on a theme. In one from some years earlier I had also passed through a linoleum floor, guided by voices to a lake where I was told I would "see the face of god." When I looked into the dark water I saw a faintly glowing face that seemed to resemble my father but one that I knew was divine, beyond the personal. A friend who read my description challenged my interpretation: "Think about it. Whose face would you expect to see reflected in water?" With the mirror in the "The Golden Woman" in mind, and the realization that my face resembled my father's, the answer was clearer. The dark lake water reflected my own glowing face, that is, the face beyond my face. I see this early dream as preparation for the later one, a fine variation on the theme of our innate sacred selves.

Everything that I have said to describe this single dream of "The Golden Woman" points to its elegance and eloquence as an artistic creation. It is my strongest evidence that dreaming is an art. Let me then show what art lessons I learned, first from classes and then in the dream. When I was an art major at the University of Miami in the late 1950s, the instructor of my first class taught an effective means of going beyond what is merely pleasing to the eye. We worked for a few weeks on pencil drawings, and when we were satisfied with whatever we had drawn we were instructed to erase it. Some people were annoyed by this task, which seemed to echo that of Sisyphus in Greek myth continually pushing the boulder up the mountain and having it roll down on him time and again. But for me it was an intriguing exercise that moved me beyond "drawing pretty," of being too attached to artistic results. I learned to value and enjoy the process of creation and to worry less about its outcome and its permanence.

Years later I witnessed the creation and dissolution of two different Tibetan sand mandalas (sacred circles) in Manitoba, and remembered my art lessons. In the dream I let go of my own pretty image and was rewarded by being carried deeper into the imaginative process. Because I rejected the surface image, my dream self could evolve, transformed by air, earth, water, and fire into the golden woman. I became my own artistic creation and was fully aware of the process, even witnessing it at the same time as I experienced it. This is one of the fine gifts of dreaming, being in two places at once without being disconcerted or disjointed by the experience.

This dream is a poem of the soul, rich in archetypal symbolism that carries it beyond the personal. The reflected image, the passage through the four elements of air, earth, water, and fire, the protective cylinder that acts as a transforming mold, the primal figures who roll me out of the water, and the phoenix-flames that bring about the alchemical change from base flesh to molten gold, each of these echo motifs in mythology and folktales. Tanis MacDonald captures the earthy, archetypal nature of the dream in her recasting of the dream in her poem, "Golden Woman."

The mirror lied, flattered me
with plum-smooth skin and a dewy

mouth—what I thought I wanted until
I saw it, too late and false beside
my daughter. No queen born of venom
and cowl wants the truth, but I
stared the mirror down, stared
hard enough to grind it to sand
and it gave up my real face like
a hostage.

Drawn down like water, the earth
thirsted for me, pulled me
through the linoleum, past
crawlspace, foundation, worm-scented soil
pressing my nose flat,
drawn down through the earth's tap
into a dark sea and sky. I lay
white and calm as the moon
beneath the water. Barnacles sang
my praises, their small mouths
firm against my flesh, linking
lip and leg into a breathing armour.
Waves rolled me along the sea floor,
past coral and ray, into the arms of
four gaunt figures, gilled giants
beneath the waves. They bear me
on a watery bier in my sarcophagus of
salt and sea creature

to the night shore, where flames
crackle, a crucible to burn away
my dross, split my shell, pour me
honey-limbed, incandescent, golden.

Tanis's artistry in moving from my vision into her own poetry brought this
dream out to the full light of day, available to anyone. I learned things about my
own dream that I had not noticed before. Tanis's conscious composition ex-
tends the power of the dream so that it frees itself from my limited unconscious

mind and reaches out to touch other imaginations through her poem. We can break away from literal interpretation, free ourselves from being tied too unimaginatively to the unconscious, build on what our dreams suggest to our waking selves. As fellow dreamer Kira Van Deusen put it, "I'm giving myself more permission to continue the dream story while I'm awake, no longer a slave to what comes from the unconscious" (E-mail to the author).

This is how Tanis and I worked: I told her a dream, she let it brew in her imagination for a while, and gradually a poem began to suggest itself. Her poem stays true to the dream and yet takes it further, adding another perspective by weaving new details into the pattern—the worm-scented earth, barnacles that sing, and the awesome gilled giants. The poem also wisely observes the intimate affinity of birth and death, using the images of bier and sarcophagus that contain both dross and pure gold. And of course there is the truth-speaking mirror that calls up that "queen born of venom," the archetypal wicked mother/stepmother of the Grimm tale "Snow White." Here the motif is reversed: the queen in the tale wants only her own beautiful image and cruelly rejects that of her daughter, while my dream self celebrates the reality of my daughter's image and finally insists on seeing my actual face, for better or for worse.

That mirror-mirror-on-the-wall reveals who is fairest of them all and cannot lie once this information is commanded. It is clear that my daughter is more beautiful than I am. Even the venomous queen cannot make the mirror speak falsely, and thus she learns that Snow White is still alive and vulnerable. To carry the metaphor further, the dream itself is a magic mirror for the creative psyche and will show us what we most deeply wish to see, take us as far as we wish to go. That is to say, this mirror responds to what the heart asks rather than what the thinking mind asks. When heart and thinking mind, unconscious and conscious, both request the same thing, dross becomes gold.

Folktales, particularly those popularized by the Grimms (not to mention Disney productions), often present young and old women in opposition, but older women also function as guides. The fact that I chose my older over my younger self in the dream allowed my dream-self to break free of the mirror image. I became my own cronish wise woman. This time, unlike an earlier passage-through-linoleum dream in which a voice told me I would see "the face of god," it is my voice and not another that speaks of a divine image—my own face.

The otherworld journey is so familiar in folktales (and of course in dreams) that it hints at shamanic influences. There is a wealth of work on shamanic dreaming and practices, but these rarely focus on folktale connections. Kira Van Deusen is an exception, having explored living Siberian narratives in terms of shamanic motifs (*Flying Tiger, Raven, Shyaan am!*). In both folktales and shamanic journeys, one travels to another world through a passage of some sort: One might cross over or fall into water, wander through dark forests or wastelands, climb a mountain or a tree, or be carried off by an enormous bird or a powerful wind. On the other side of the archetypal passage is another world where one can experience transformation. In the Grimm tale of "Frau Holle," for example, a girl falls down a well into the magical world of a crone, Frau Holle. She returns home covered in gold, a golden woman. Gold is a common folktale element. We think of it in terms of wealth, but as an archetype it denotes absolute purity, often of the inner sort. Archetypally, gold is often a symbol of inner purity. Kira Van Deusen told me that in Tuvan folktales, for example, the Golden Princess is a paragon of womanhood who shines with the light of both sun and moon (*Shyaan am!* 35).

Compliance, which on the surface looks more like passive surrender than willing participation, is another central motif in folktales. Cinderella does not openly challenge her sisters, for example, nor does she resist her magical helpers. While she seems to do nothing much, in fact she willingly participates in her transformation from ash-girl to queen. She knows what she wants, and she accomplishes it without being as opportunistic as her sisters. (I am speaking here of the more traditional oral tales rather than the seventeenth century literary version of Charles Perrault, popularized by Disney and many other Cinderella revisionists. More resourceful heroines need neither fairy godmother nor glass slipper.)

Like many "Cinderella" figures, the girl who falls down the well in "Frau Holle" also accepts the movement of her life adventures, which include obeying both her mean stepmother and the intimidating Frau Holle. The message of many folktales, and of many dreams as well, is to allow things to reveal themselves instead of always trying to control the outcome or, conversely, to avoid what is unpleasant. If I had rejected my aging face, resisted the sinking movement, or avoided the painful fire in "The Golden Woman," I would not have been transformed.

The triple challenge in "The Golden Woman" is to see the true face in the mirror, pass through the four elements, and survive a fiery transformation. The folktale that most reverberated with this dream was "The Water of Life" discussed earlier. Of course, the heroine in this tale has more perilous tasks than my dream-self in "The Golden Woman." In order to obtain the water of life for a dying tree, she must find her way through a forest and up a mountain, walking over a path of speaking stones who try to stop her and turn her to stone. This is challenge enough, but she must then face the dragon who first challenges her and then demands her touch in order for the transformative water to be released.

Just as the "Golden Woman" opened out as I continued to tell it and to hear other's responses to it, so "The Water of Life" evolved after several years of telling and listening. Some elements of the story became more explicit after listeners' reactions: the stones gained words of flattery as well as insults, challenges, and supplications; the dragon now calmly said, "What have you come here for," instead of belligerently accusing the woman of coming to steal his water.

Some of the most insightful responses came from the classes of troubled students I met over the years. For instance, I learned from eleven-year-old girls from a class in a core area school, who insisted on acting out the story and speaking in the voices of the angry stones, that the verbal assaults were specifically personal and not generic: "You're ugly, you're stupid, you'll never make it!" The boys, responding from their various roles in the story, added, "What? A girl! Forget it!" These were familiar insults, heard in the schoolyard every day. The boy who took the role of the tree thought that it should have a name, and they all agreed that it should be called The Tree of Hope.

I learned more from the small groups of troubled ten-year-olds in a suburban Winnipeg school where I worked with the guidance counselor and social worker for three years. Let me describe one of these occasions to show how a story opens out in the same way a dream does. On a Thursday morning in April (it was still snowing outside), about a dozen students sat in a rough circle on couches and chairs in the guidance counselor's office. As storyteller I sat in the circle, but the other two adults sat just outside where they could both observe and take part. The basic rule at every session was that the story was not to be interrupted once it began, no small feat for children who could not sit still for the ten to twenty minutes it took to tell most stories. On this particular day, the four most disruptive attention-deficit-disorder boys sat together on the sofa, playfully kicking and punching each other and grumbling about school. The other two boys sat across from them, fidgeting a bit but remaining silent and attentive. The only two girls in the group sat utterly quiet and immobile in chairs next to each other, looking straight ahead and pretending not to be part of the "gang." In this unpromising but familiar atmosphere I began the story. Attention gradually shifted until everyone was listening, not without occasional small shoves and kicks, but no interruptions. They even gasped when the heroine tripped as she started back down the mountain.

It was our practice to retell a story as a group as soon as it was finished, with each person, adults included, contributing a sentence or two of the story. After the usual grumbling one of the boys on my left began hesitantly, and the story was off and running. The two girls, who had almost never taken part in previous group stories, were completely active this time, perhaps because the protagonist was a courageous young woman. The groups' attention to detail was impressive, and their involvement with the story was enthusiastic enough to arouse their questions: "Why did they trust a talking fox?" "How did they know he wasn't lying to them?" "How did the first stone get on the path?" "Could some of the stones be animals instead of people?" One of the quieter boys who loved mythology asked if the bird at the top of the tree was related to a Roc or a Phoenix.

The ensuing conversation on these topics cast new light on this familiar story. I pondered each query carefully, discussed them in a casual conversational way that kept our dialogue open. I thought it was interesting that some stones might be animals, and asked what animals might be on such a quest. I suggested that the fox might be our own trusting voice that we need to hear above all the other negative voices that try to turn us to stone. They, even more than I, were all too familiar with such voices inside and out. I wondered about how they might be able to identify their own "fox" voice that could be trusted, and how failing to hear it might turn you into the first stone on the mountain path. We agreed that the first stone must have stopped itself with its own voice and then decided it wanted company. We played with the image of the singing bird as a small cousin of phoenix and roc, and I noted that sky creatures like these mythical birds were often associated with earth-based serpents and dragons. They were intrigued. It was interesting for me to see how they took the story into their own lives. I told them their questions would keep me thinking about "The Water of Life." I know that all of these collective reflections will inform future tellings of "The Water of Life," though the fundamental story itself will not change.

Because I already know that this story—and all others—will go on evolving in depth and meaning over the years, I see as I write it down here how it has taken on increased familiarity from my mundane life. The Tree of Hope now echoes the old grapefruit tree in my childhood Miami backyard that grew from a sapling into a magnificent tree with fruit too high to reach—except by birds. The modest house of the sister and her brothers has become the white frame house my five siblings and I grew up in, and I can see the sister looking out the back bedroom window to see where her brothers are going. The silver cup that will carry the water of life has taken the shape of the engraved baby cup of our son, Nathaniel. The brothers, of course, speak in the voices of my brothers, Allen and Terry, and perhaps—now that I think of it—my deceased brother, Kenneth. These changes have evolved slowly and spontaneously, not by conscious design on my part, and while they do not alter the basic shape of the folktale, they certainly transform my understanding of it.

My understanding of dreams and life memories evolve as I age, much as the folktales I tell deepen with experience. I find that the dream of "The Golden Woman" and the story of "The Water of Life" bring a transformational touch to my thoughts on dreaming as an art. Just as a drop of water contains the ocean, each dream contains the whole of all your dreams and a single folktale echoes every other story. For each of us, everything begins when we begin, and expands out as we live and re-form our life stories from day to day.

16

Follow Your Frog

(2004)

This article, chapter 7 from *The Golden Woman,* was an exploration of the fools and simpletons of dreams and folktales, the unpromising protagonists who often ended up with half the kingdom and a royal marriage despite their apparent handicaps. I had often wondered why these characters were rarely female, and remembered that I had identified strongly with them as accidental heroes when I was a child looking for someone more interesting than the too-good fairy-tale princesses. Later in life I found such heroines in various Anglo-American collections, but they were usually clever rather than foolish. With this in mind, I found myself retelling Stewart Cameron's story from chapter 11 with greater emphasis on the canny female frog. My story evolved with the help of a group of sixth-grade girls who challenged the quest of finding the most beautiful woman in the world when they asked, "Why couldn't she be the smartest woman in the world?" I wondered how we would be able to tell who was smartest. Jack's frog bride took on new life as she herself responded to this challenge.

In a Grimm tale aptly named "Lucky Hans," a foolish young man wants to go out into the wide world to seek his fortune but has no idea what this means. In order to finance his adventures he works hard for a stingy farmer for several years, and is rewarded with a sack of coins too heavy to carry, so he trades what he has for less valuable things—the coins for a horse, the horse for a calf, the calf for a pig, and so on. He finally ends up with a stone that he accidentally drops down a well. Instead of being dismayed, he says to himself happily, "How lucky I am! That stone was too heavy anyway." And he sets off once again to seek his fortune.

This popular tale is Grimm number 83 (Zipes, *Complete Fairy Tales* 329–34) with similar stories (AT 1415) found across Europe and North America. There are some good Appalachian variants: for example, a Kentucky story called "Foolish Jack" (Roberts, *Old Greasybeard* 143–47).

Hans is the epitome of the fool who seems destined to fail in the practical terms of the materialistic world of ambition. His common name is typical; depending on what country the story comes from, he can be Jack, Ivan, Ti-Jean, or Jan, for example. One author has published two books of his own retellings of Jack tales from the southern United States (Chase, *Jack Tales* and *Grandfather Tales*). A more recent book (McCarthy, *Jack in Two Worlds*) examines tellers of these kinds of stories in North America today. Jack and his cousins are still alive and well.

We know Jack well from "Jack and the Beanstalk," a story so familiar that it still inspires jokes, cartoons, and various other modern reworkings. For example, in the Disney version Mickey Mouse takes the role of Jack, while in a Bugs Bunny cartoon Bugs is Jack and Elmer Fudd is the giant. No matter what form the story takes, the foolish character is as fortunate as Lucky Hans.

I used this story when I was interviewing children and adults during dissertation research in the early 1970s. Invariably people got into debates about Jack's silliness. One group of twelve-year-old girls jokingly suggested that a girl might do things differently: "I bet she'd ask for more beans," said one, and another added, "Yeah, girls expect more for their money!" They all agreed that a girl "wouldn't just count on luck, she'd plan everything out" ("Romantic Heroines" 365–66). They not only talked about the girl's practicality but also on the problems she might have climbing the bean stalk in a skirt, and whether she would kill the giant or let him live. Yet if Jack had indeed decided to plan everything out and decided not to trade the cow for a few special beans, there would have been neither beanstalk to climb nor the giant's treasures as a reward.

Over the years I had similar discussions with my university students, who wanted to know why characters like "Jack" won out in the end even when they seemed to do nothing to deserve success. Their achievements were popularly described as arising from "dumb luck." Many students thought that winners should be those who went after what they wanted, the kind of heroes who got ahead of the crowd by being active and independent. But others were delighted by the Jack-like characters whose very foolishness was a defiance of conformity, the very opposite of doing what was expected.

It is no accident that traditional tales throughout the world favor characters who win out over those who are practical and ambitious, like Jack's older brothers. One student who pondered Jack's situation decided that he had a lot more than dumb luck going for him: "for results that are truly amazing, fantasy and imagination are needed, not just hard work" (Pound 7). He was inspired by a variant of a "Jack" tale I told in class, a Scottish variant I had heard from Stewart Cameron at the Toronto Festival of Storytelling in 1985; his text and commentary is included as chapter 11 in this book. In this widespread European story, three brothers are given feathers as guides on their quest for magical objects. The final quest is often for the most beautiful woman in the world, and her identity is always a surprise, as we can see in the title of AT 402, "Mouse (Cat, Frog, etc.) as Bride." Here is a summary of Stewart Cameron's story (full text in chapter 11):

A king called in his three sons in order to determine which one would be resourceful enough to inherit the royal realm. Three times they were each given a white feather and told to follow it and to bring back three objects: the most prized ring, the finest tablecloth, and the most beautiful woman in the world as their bride. Each time, Jack's feather fell into the mud, where he loved to play, and each time a small green frog hopped up and offered to help him. Though he goes nowhere very far, he succeeds in bringing back the winning things, and he and his transformed frog princess eventually rule the kingdom, much to his ambitious brothers' annoyance.

When I began telling Stewart's story in Winnipeg, a group of twelve-year-old girls in one school had been bothered by the final task of finding the most beautiful woman in the world and wanted the brothers to find the smartest woman in the world instead. We brain-stormed on riddles that could be used to test the women, and these are now part of the story. This put the heroine in a much stronger position in the story, and when Stewart heard of these changes, he decided to include them in his own future tellings.

Most students who heard me tell this story in my folklore class were more practical. They seemed to agree with Jack's ambitious brothers who complained,

"We went all over the world searching while Jack just sat here and played in the mud," and were unwilling to accept the possibility that Jack's good-hearted nature was revealed through his seeming inability and lack of ambition. Richard Pound was an exception. He insisted that Jack went well beyond what the king demanded, and that more than luck was involved: "In one sense Jack is lazy and lucky—his friend the frog bails him out. But in a different light Jack somehow transcends the competitive structure of the quests and achieves magical results. The hard-working brothers do find nice rings and good table-cloths with much toil, but Jack—by focusing on enjoyment and imagination—delivers to the king unbelievably fantastic works of art" (6). Pound concludes that the moral of the story is "that imagination does have a place in the world." He was so inspired by the story that he reviewed his nightmares of working in a demanding restaurant called Earl's (he called them "earlsmares") to see if these dreams could be transformed by active imagination, since his dreams were unpleasant replays of his daily work. "In the dreams everything seems very real to me, so real that my body reacts to being out of control in the dream in the same way it reacts in my real job. I'll wake up from an 'earlsmare' with my hands clenched, my jaw tight, and that same gnawing sensation in my stom-ach. As a result of believing in dreams I feel very real tension" (Pound 3).

While working on his class essay he began to challenge these dreams: "If the dreams themselves refuse to be out of the ordinary, it doesn't follow that I must act realistically as well—I myself can be what is exciting and odd in the dream." The story of Jack, who was certainly what was exciting and odd in his own story, inspired Richard to give his imagination a freer rein. He found that his dreams did indeed transform: "I realized for the first time not only the an-noyance of an earlsmare but also the opportunity it offered. It is, quite literally, a server's dream to be able to act in any way they desire while dealing with cus-tomers. As long as I was able to realize I was dreaming, I could now strip naked in the middle of the restaurant or paddle a canoe through the prep kitchen. I could do anything my mind could think of" (Pound 4). He became increas-ingly excited by the potency of imagination in the story, his dreams, and his daily work, sensing that even mundane work could be an expression of artistry:

> With the story seen from this viewpoint, the frog that seems so instrumental in Jack's success could be read as Jack's faculty of imagination—the extra in-gredient that was lacking in his brothers. This helps illuminate my dreams

[and reality] of working at Earl's. I try to work as hard as I can and I never seem to live up to my own standards. Seeing those dreams as opportunities for creativity will, I hope, shift the whole framework of emotions around. I can see now how I should be able to enact the same sort of transformation in real life. (6)

Richard reported with a smile that he actually felt "a bit like Jack." He was following his frog. I have quoted his words at length because they are such evocative examples of my point that we can be artists in life and in dreams, and that other forms of creative expression, like folktales, for example, can affect us positively.

It seems that these old traditional stories of apparent fools are more than wish-fulfilling escapist fantasies (unless the Disney corporation gets hold of them). Their purpose is more soulful, directing us to less materialistic and opportunistic views of life. Also, they emphasize the value of doing things your own way even when others might consider you odd, impractical, lazy, or just fooling around, accomplishing very little in a goal-oriented "real world" where success is measured by external things. Sometimes playing around in the mud, metaphorically speaking, is exactly what we need to do.

The complaints of Jack's brothers that he is only playing around are familiar to artistic creators, who have to spend a lot of time "messing about in the mud" like Jack in order to bring their work into being, whether in dance, music, drama, writing, painting, cooking, or any other creative art. To be recognized for our true nature as artists is deeply satisfying, but not more important than our self-recognition and trust of what we are doing. Like Jack, we sometimes have to follow the unlikely frogs in our lives and go on with things when others disregard or even denigrate our actions.

Another aspect of these stories, of course, is that Jack and his counterparts would undoubtedly be the troublesome kid in the classroom, suffering from various modern ailments that result in learning disabilities. I have learned a lot in the few years of telling stories to the group of troubled ten-year-olds at a Winnipeg school I mentioned earlier, so I know these are very real problems that create significant disruptions. But I also see the spontaneous creativity that often emerges when these students begin to trust their own out-of-the-ordinary way of seeing and doing things. One extremely insecure girl who barely said a word the entire year—she was doing her own version of Jack's silent playing in the mud—presented me with a gloriously colorful and joyous drawing inspired by one of the stories I had told. She seemed to have found her frog, at least temporarily.

The frog is an utterly common creature, lacking the dramatic character of a dragon or a beast, and perhaps that is exactly where the frog's power lies. It takes an unusual person to treat a talking frog with respect, as Jack does. Ordinary things like tablecloths and rings, for example, challenge protagonists to see that these might be much more than they seem. This is true of people in ordinary waking life as well, as I discovered in working with the various children in schools. I was looking for treasure in hidden form. It is no wonder that some of the magical characters in stories appear as ragged old men or ancient crones, not to mention frogs, waiting to reward those who see more than Jack's brothers were able to see.

Similarly, in some stories the protagonist receives a mundane inheritance that seems utterly without value. This may be small and insignificant, like a doll (in the Russian tale "Vasilisa"), a crude cloak (in an English "Cinderella" tale, "Mossycoat"), or an ordinary animal like a cat, a dog, or a horse in various tales. If there are older siblings they usually refuse the objects, but the fools take what is offered and go out into the wide world with curiosity rather than ambition. Even when they set out to "seek their fortune" they are looking for adventure rather than material gains, often not understanding what "seeking one's fortune" means.

In variants of the popular "Puss and Boots" and "Dick Whittington's Cat," the hero is left with only a crafty cat who succeeds in gaining fortune for his guileless owner. Variants are found throughout Europe, with different animals as helpers. "Puss-in-Boots" (AT 545, "Cat or Fox as Helper") and "Whittington's Cat" (AT 1651) turn up in Finland, Estonia, Sweden, Denmark, Ireland, Italy, various Slavic countries, and of course France, Germany, and England. In other tales it is an unlikely horse who guides the hero to success. My favorite is "The Golden Feather," an unusual Jewish variant of a complex European tale known in Russia as "The Little Humpback Horse" (Weinreich and Wolf 142–47). The unpromising youngest son is given the youngest horse as his inheritance. Both are seen by others as ugly and witless, but the horse's wise guidance leads the inept young man to unexpected success over a threatening witch. The story concludes with man and horse farming together and providing their neighbors with the fruits of their labors.

With all the horses in my background it is not surprising that I am fond of stories where horses play a role. In the tale "Öskus-ool and the Three Arts," from Kira Van Deusen's collection of Siberian tales, horses are secondary, but still important (*Shyaan am!* 31–34). The Tuvan hero, Ösküs-ool ("Orphan Boy"), is so unsophisticated that he does not even know how to count the small collection of animals he has. He only knows that his favorite horse is important. Though this horse does not speak or guide him, unlike the one in the Jewish tale, somehow his relationship to the horse plays a part in his eventual success as he trades the animals—except for the one horse—to gain wisdom. Here is a summary:

When his father died, Ösküs-ool was left with a small herd of animals—10 goats, 10 cows, and 10 horses. Since Ösküs-ool could not count it seemed like a lot to him, though it was not much by Tuvan standards where a herder might have hundreds or thousands of animals. He did not know what to do with his animals, so decided to trade them for wisdom, which his father had told him was precious. He had no idea what wisdom was so he set off to find it. Like Jack and other European characters of similar nature, he was going out "to seek his fortune" without any idea of what this might be.

He visited three different domed yurts in succession, where he traded his animals for the wisdom of chess, the wisdom of sleight-of-hand magic, and finally the wisdom of counting. Because he had learned to count, he understood that he could subtract one horse from the ten. As he continued his journey on this horse he met the cruel Karaty-khan, who owned huge herds of animals and many enslaved herders, all of whom he had defeated at chess. Ösküs-ool was the first to best Karaty-khan, using his newly learned skills in chess and sleight-of-hand magic to defeat him at his own game. Ösküs-ool won all of Karaty-khan's sheep, which he joyfully counted and then presented to the herders, whom he freed. Both the Jewish and the Tuvan tales focus on the relations between human and animal; romance is not an issue in either one. Instead, the heroes benefit others instead of living happily ever after with a bride.

Characters like Ösküs-ool are appealing not just because of their role as apparent losers—what we feel like on our bad days—but also for their resourcefulness and tenacity. They are often misjudged by other story characters, Karaty-khan for instance, but their openness, patience, generosity and ingenuity turn the tide in their favor. Like Jack in the earlier story, imagination is the key to victory over an apparently superior force. Ösküs-ool exemplifies the type of character who progresses from inexperienced novice to knowledgable initiate, now able to face the world successfully with new understanding and skills.

This is often the case in dreams as well, as we find creative solutions to symbolic issues. In 1983 I had an unusual two-part dream, "The Cave," that covered different time periods: I was an anxious teenager in the first part and became a more confident adult in the second, though not without a bit more Jack-like ineptitude.

I was standing with several other young people in a large cave filled with amber light, looking into a deep pool that the others had already leapt into. Although I was apprehensive, I was about to follow them into what seemed to be an initiatory rite of passage. As I prepared to jump, I heard an older woman's voice telling me not to jump, and I trusted her. The voice directed me to a flat, white stone that seemed to glow as I touched it and picked it up.

Suddenly the dream skipped ahead, or I might have unconsciously connected two dream-stories while asleep. I was now an adult, attending some kind of conference, still carrying the stone in my pocket. I felt warmth there and reached in to touch it, and somehow knew that it was now time for me to return to the cave. I perceived that this was to be some sort of test of my abilities and was anxious again, so I asked a male friend to accompany me. Using the white stone as a guide I found the cave but entered through a different passage this time. I was guided by the same woman's voice to a narrow rocky arch over a bottomless chasm. I was directed to pass over this bridge with my eyes closed, but I was terrified of falling and asked the man to cross first. He walked safely to the other side but I was still frightened. Humbly, I knelt down and closed my eyes, wrapped my arms and legs around the narrow arch, and inched slowly across. I reached the other side exhausted but relieved, sensing that this was literally a rite of passage, a bridging of a gap between youth and maturity. My success was not in the least dimmed by my lack of boldness. As I reached the other side I saw that the white stone had become smaller and dimmer, and knew that I no longer needed it. Instead of clinging to it as a symbol of my success, I put it on a ledge where it could be found by someone else who needed it.

Like Jack in Stewart Cameron's story, I was willing to look foolish and not be stopped by it as I crawled across the stone bridge. Also, I found something in a cave that seemed common but turned out to be precious—not a ring or fine silk or a frog princess, but a glowing stone that seemed to guide me and give me strength. And like Ösküs-ool, who frees the shepherds and gives them the sheep he has won, I gave up the magic stone for the benefit of someone else who could use it.

Incidently, fear of falling—of failing—is a very familiar theme, as I discovered after hearing similar dream situations described by other dreamers about crossing bridges, mountains, rivers and other daunting obstacles. I was interested to find an example reported in a book on lucid dreaming:

> I was walking along a gradually ascending mountain path with a friend. As far as the eye could see, the only thing moving was the silent mist that veiled the majestic peaks in mystery. But suddenly we found ourselves before a narrow bridge that precariously spanned a chasm. When I looked down into the bottomless pit beneath the bridge, I became dizzy with fear and could not bring myself to proceed. At this, my companion said, "You know, Stephen, you don't *have* to go this way. You can go back the way we came," and pointed back down what seemed like an immense distance. But then the thought crossed my mind that if I were to become lucid, I would have no reason to fear the height. (LaBerge 100)

At this point he began to realize that he was dreaming, and in this lucidity regained full confidence and crossed the bridge, back into his waking world. If I, too, had realized I was in the dream world, I could have walked easily over the narrow bridge without fear—or even danced across.

My real-life experience with fear of falling happened on our honeymoon hike, when I tried to follow my husband up a rock face on Mt. Washington in the White Mountains of New Hampshire. I had never ascended anything higher than the hill in Greynolds Park in North Miami and found the real mountains entirely daunting. My husband still insists that the "cliff" we were climbing was only twelve feet or so, but in my memory it was Himalayan. He scaled it easily, like the man crossing the chasm in my cave dream, but I crawled up slowly, hanging by fingers and toes and growing increasingly panicked but unwilling to admit it. Halfway up my panic became full blown hysteria as I was certain I was going to fall and die. I was entirely unheroic in my screaming at Dan for bringing me up the mountain, and he managed to calmly talk me up, pointing out where I could find finger holds. Though I was still sure I was going to fall, I managed to hold my hysteria back long enough to finally crawl humbly to the top, undignified but alive. All was well until I discovered that I had lost my wedding ring, which I had put in the kangaroo pocket of my jacket to protect it from scratches. It is still there somewhere on Mt. Washington, waiting, like the white stone in my dream for someone else to find it.

Perhaps it was this stone that attracted me to the speaking stones on the mountain in "The Water of Life," though of course these stones were anything but helpful. With Jack in mind, too, I can see more clearly how the youngest sister in the story succeeds where her brothers fail precisely because she does not listen to the voices of challenge and despair. She makes her own stumbling way to the top of the mountain, but while she does not allow the stones to stop her, she does hear their voices of suffering. And also, she has her "frog" in the form of the small red fox who tells the truth about the talking stones. Both fox and frog speak in that still, small voice that can be heard through the cacophony of inner and outer voices that can persuade us to stop ourselves, and bring about our own stuck-in-a-rut suffering.

And that reminds me of another story. Suffering abounds in folktales and sacred legends as much as in dreams and in life, and following one's frog can certainly lead to difficulties. In one particular story, "Sorrow in Youth," misfortune is at the very heart. This is my version of AT 938A, "Misfortune in Youth," developed from a single variant (Lang 167). The woman, like me, had to scale a cliff, but with quite different results.

A rich merchant whose wife had died giving birth to their child was determined to protect his daughter from sorrow. He kept her confined to his large estate, allowing her to explore a bit more widely each year. On her sixteenth birthday he gave her a ruby ring belonging to her mother and allowed her full freedom on his vast estate. While exploring far from the mansion one day, she found a young eagle crying in distress and carried it back up to its nest high on a cliff. In gratitude the eagle-mother offered to reward the young woman by giving her the choice of having her sorrow in youth or later in life. Since she did not know what sorrow was and was curious, she chose to have sorrow in youth. "So be it," said Eagle, telling the young woman that she would reappear when the sorrow was coming to an end.

When she climbed down, she discovered that she was lost, and by the time she found her way back to her father's home he had left, fearing that she was dead and would never return. Not knowing what to do, she left her father's gates for the first time and sat down outside and began to weep in desperation, feeling sorrow for the first time in her life. A woman passing by offered her work, and she gratefully accepted, learning everything she was taught and working very diligently. All went well, until one day she broke a fine crystal bowl and was so distressed that she left without a word, filled with sorrow. After this, she went from one place to another for some years, leaving each time as she had made one mistake after another. Now she certainly knew what sorrow was.

One day as she was wearily on the road once again, she decided in desperation that no matter what happened she would not run away again. She soon found a job at a bakery where she worked hard, getting up early every morning to light the ovens so that she and the baker's wife could bake the bread. As they worked they talked about the dreams they had each night. Early one morning she dreamed she saw a woman with outspread arms standing at the top of a tall tree, and woke up mystified. When she told her dream to the baker's wife, she was instructed to leave immediately in order to find that tree. After searching far and wide she found the tree behind the bakery, and was this time instructed to sleep under it that night.

In the early morning she had the same dream of the woman with outstretched arms at the top of the tree, and awoke to find Eagle with outspread wings calling to her. Eagle dropped her a ball of silk thread, which she took to the old king in exchange for its weight in gold. Light as it was, the silk did not balance on the scale until the king put his crown on top of the gold and silver he had heaped there. He held out the crown to her, and when she accepted it he saw the ruby ring. He looked at her more closely and asked, "Who gave you that ring?" When she told him, father and daughter were joyfully reunited at last. She became queen of her own realm, all the wiser because of the sorrows she had suffered.

This struggling woman makes an interesting contrast to the playful Jack whom we met earlier. In the first part of her life she seems more like Jack's hard-working brothers, striving to do things correctly and giving up when she fails. Still, she is not an ambitious opportunist, and thus is willing to do whatever work is offered, not worrying about rewards. Only when she finally decides to stop running away is she able to experience a prophetic dream that leads her back to the eagle. Like Jack, she is rewarded because she is willing to follow the guidance of a creature, and also because she does not reject the seemingly ordinary ball of thread she receives, and with this fulfills the king's request.

This story seemed to have unusual depth and breadth to me from the first time I read it, but for several years it resisted my attempts to retell it. I was stopped by these failures and kept giving up, as the woman in the story did.

One day I was looking at one of Henry Moore's strong, flowing sculptures in Toronto's Art Gallery of Ontario and had a flash of realization that stories, like Moore's challenging sculptures, needed to be viewed from every angle. I returned to the folktale with Richard Pound's enthusiasm about re-viewing his frustrating dreams of restaurant work in mind, determined this time not to be so discouraged. I played around with different images and actions until the story began to come alive and gradually took on its present form. Like Ösküs-ool, I had figured out how to trade what I had for wisdom, giving up old ideas to see new facets of a story I thought I knew. In this long period of experimentation, I gained more respect for the woman's apparent foolishness. One thing I know about fools in folktales, dreams, and in life as well, is that things happen when they are meant to happen. That is, it seems to me that ineptitude, lack of ambition, and other seemingly negative qualities that make us look foolish might eventually lead to unexpected outcomes. Some of these are positive, all of them are challenging. One example from my own life is the long passage in academic life from sessional part-time lecturer to part-time tenured full professor, as much by accident as by design. But that would be a very long story.

I am wondering what might happen next to Jack as the King, Ösküs-ool with his new wisdom, or the woman now queen of her own realm. In many stories, characters who have risen above their hardships and gained wisdom might begin to practice their skills in unexpected ways.

17

Some Day Your Witch
Might Come

(2004)

With this chapter, adapted from *The Golden Woman,* it seems that I have come full circle in my long adventures with fairy tale women. Here the witch has her day—many days, in fact. If you count my beginning as a five-year-old listening to Snow White singing prettily, "Some day my prince will come," pass through my years of wondering about good and bad women in folktales, and then enter the story of "Light Kate and Dark Kate," which I composed decades later, it seems that I've been waiting for my witch to come all along. After I had already finished writing, my daughter Rachel gave me an intriguing book, *Kissing the Witch* by Emma Donoghue. In it, witches, crones, and wicked stepmothers are transformed, as are their supposed victims. These crones would have made a fine coven in my story "Light Kate and Dark Kate," and I'm sorry I did not meet them earlier.

My original chapter title provided the name for this present book, though its more gentle "might come" became the more assertive "will come," more closely paralleling Snow White's song and more in keeping with my long search for strong women. Once again I found myself agreeing with those I had questioned three decades earlier. When I reviewed my dissertation interviews once again, this time focusing on the crones rather than the princesses, I saw that several had recalled witches, stepmothers, and other dark women as powerful. Some approved, others did not, but they all agreed that these were the potent women in fairy tales.

I begin the chapter by introducing a number of threatening figures from folktales, then discuss dark forces in dreams, and finally suggest that my own fascination with folktale crones arose from these dreams, evolving gradually from fear to fascination as I came to see that the light side was only half of the story. We meet Frau Trude again here, along with a few crones from my waking world and significant examples from my dreams. Of these, my favorite is still Nameless Dread, a threatening witch who smiles up at me calmly as I try to strangle her. Without Nameless Dread I doubt that I could have brought to light the story I'd had in mind for years, my original composition, "Light Kate and Dark Kate," included at the end of the chapter. Here, the "bad" stepsister not only gets her comeuppance but eventually her wisdom as well, from three different fairy tale crones who already have menacing reputations in traditional tales.

It seems to me now, as I look back on my work, that the crone/witch/hag has been my companion all along, prodding me on and refusing to be silenced. Anger is a helpful quality here, but only if it adds necessary fuel to the transformational fire rather than sending it raging out of control.

I remember that stage of childhood dreaming where I could actually feel myself falling into sleep and trying to fight the sense of being enchanted by some unknown force. I also recall occasionally finding myself paralyzed and unable to fully wake up, and in that state seeing odd things floating around in my dark room. There is one very clear memory of a hideous green face up in the left corner where the walls and ceiling met, a face that leered at me with the malevolence of the queen-witch in Walt Disney's *Snow White and the Seven Dwarfs,* which I had seen at age five. I knew I was awake, but I could not move out of the spell of that glaring gaze until I finally managed to move the little finger on my right hand. I used that spell-breaking method any other time I felt myself caught between sleep and waking, a state I later learned was called "dream paralysis."

Perhaps my long fascination with witches, crones, and hags arose from this very real experience. In waking life, dreams, and folktales, I was both drawn to and repulsed by older women who seemed overwhelming. While I was afraid of them, their fierce negativity always seemed to be only half the story, only one side of the coin, and I was curious about the other side. My fierce ambivalence was unconscious for a long time but finally rose to the surface when I began to work on "Frau Trude." As I have noted elsewhere, this folktale became very central for me, personally and professionally, and compelled me to explore my love-hate affair with powerful, threatening women. The story had double enticement: I strongly identified with the doomed girl when I first read the story, since she was the epitome of the "bad" girls in folktales even though she had no younger sister to mistreat. I *was* that girl, at least in my imagination. It seemed to me that she was being punished for her curiosity about the world, as I felt I had often been. Later, when I was old enough to be the crone herself, I wondered who she was, how she gained her power, and whether she always used it so destructively. My partial answer was in the bare bones of the Grimm tale and what came out of it after some months of grappling with the story in performance. This story bedeviled me enough that I have told it in various ways over the years, as I have already discussed in earlier chapters. As my story evolved, the girl was freed from her enchantment, but what happened next? That is another story altogether, and one that has its echoes in the story of "Light Kate and Dark Kate" that I include later in this chapter.

As an artist I sensed great potential in the archetypal figures of the naive girl and the all-knowing crone who find their way into many world tales. I knew I would not get at this through deliberate manipulation of dreams and folktales because these creations have their own voices, and leaping in too consciously with changes interferes with a more natural transformation. Patience is definitely a virtue, and not one of my stronger assets. The cruel tale of "Frau Trude" took quite a while to transform itself into the more promising story of "The Curious Girl," and it was worth the wait. Only after a story has found its own shape can I look back and see what influences arose like sparks out of the fire of imagination and memory. I was delighted to notice that the girl's finding that she could not speak evolved from a dream of finding myself completely without words. In the dream and in the story, words fly out on their own and an unknown story comes into being without conscious effort, as much a surprise to the teller as to listeners.

I saw, too, that in the figure of Frau Trude there were aspects of various cronish women I had known in my waking world, especially the woman across the street, Mrs. H., whose garden had seemed to me as a child to resemble the dark forests of folktales. I also saw aspects of my mother, of course, both as the story-mother who forbids her daughter to seek out the witch, and as the "witch" herself who punished the girl's disobedience and curiosity. What was more shocking was to see *myself* as the witch. You might think that now that I have entered the cronish half of life I might be free of the witch's threatening power, but apparently I have not yet faced up to this enchanting artistic potential in myself. I am not free of distressing dreams with threatening older women, and maybe I do not want to be. Here is one that was so disturbing that I woke up filled with both with rage and terror.

In the dream I heard that a dangerous witch was threatening people and was looking for me, and I realized I had to seek her out before she could hurt anyone. I found her in bed, a wrinkled old hag with covers pulled up to her chin, a menacing figure with an ominous leer. I wanted to run but compelled myself to stay, as I had in other threatening dreams. I reached down and began choking her but she just smiled up at me, and I understood that I could not destroy her no matter how hard I tried. I woke up with her calmly intimidating smile still in mind, wondering who she was. Just before I reached full consciousness a name floated into my mind—Nameless Dread. It was so perfect that I laughed, and then saw the humor in the old hag herself. She was playing with me, waiting patiently for me to challenge her, and I had finally done so. She seemed like a deliberately ambivalent figure, waiting to test me and see if I was worthy, like many of the crones in folktales. Baba Yaga from Russian tradition is a very fine example. In two different variants of a folktale featuring the Russian Cinderella, Vasilisa, the witch challenges but does not destroy the young woman. In "Vasilisa the Beautiful" she is sent by her stepmother and stepsisters to bring fire back from the witch, who agrees to help if all the work is accomplished. Not only does Vasilisa work as well as the good sister in "Frau Holle," she also feeds the dog and cat, who then help her escape safely. She carries home a skull with fiery eyes that are so bright that the cruel stepfamily is destroyed (Stevens 90–105).

Nameless Dread, far less challenging than Baba Yaga, had disappeared from my dreams after I called her name and thus had power over her. Or so I thought. My ambivalent crone was still with me and made a return visit as a crudely disguised parody of my mother.

In the dream I was visiting my family home in Miami, trying to find my mother. I finally saw her resting in bed, then discovered to my horror that it was not my mother at all but a menacing hag with dyed black hair and sharp features. I immediately decided that I was going to sneak away before she noticed me. When I got to the living room I found that she had hidden my car keys, so I had to go back and confront her. Like Nameless Dread, she was lying there waiting for me with open eyes, the blanket pulled up to her chin and her gnarled hands lying serenely above the covers. I must have learned something, because instead of trying to choke her, I told her openly that I was planning to leave and asked if she had seen my keys. She smiled a Nameless Dread smile as she lifted her right hand to reveal them. She picked them up and tossed them to me with a laugh, saying cheerily, "I guess I'm just a selfish old bitch." I was amazed to hear myself answer, "Okay, Selfish Old Bitch." I woke up with a feeling of lightness and freedom, having given her a name within the dream, and accepted the crone once again.

I began to recognize her archetypal form from earlier dreams: a threatening woman prevented me from crossing a bridge because I did not know the password; another woman kept me from going through a special door because she said that I was not ready; still another deterred me from packing a suitcase for a planned escape because I was not putting in the "right" things, whatever these might be. A particularly annoying woman informed me that my dream house was not perfect after all, but did not tell me what she meant. In general these women restricted my movement again and again. Twice they appeared as Darth Vader with that menacing heavy breathing and a threatening stare. But none of them ever attacked, or even threatened to do so. Instead they seemed to be waiting for me to do something. Tell them a story they had never heard, perhaps.

Jung described shadow figures that embody all the darkness that we reject in ourselves (*Man and His Symbols* 144–48). Nameless Dread and Selfish Old Bitch and their many sisters represent her well. She will not go away, she cannot be destroyed, and she has the car keys. We cannot move without her, but we need to get our keys back. The only way to transform her is by accepting her, finding the story she wants to hear, and releasing her potential as a wise woman and muse. As I pondered Selfish Old Bitch masking herself as my mother, it occurred to me that perhaps her inadequate disguise was deliberate, that she wanted me to see through to the other side. I recalled my mother in a dream from years earlier, this time entirely recognizable and positive, and appropriately reading her favorite magazine, *True Story*. I was terrified by a bear who was chasing me and went to her for help. She was lying in bed, much like Nameless Dread and Selfish Old Bitch years later. She looked up from her magazine and calmly told me that the bear would not hurt me. She was speaking the true story, telling me something I needed to know about threatening figures. Accept them and they do no harm. Lessons like this apparently need to be learned over and over again, hence the hag was not finished with me in dreams. It was my choice whether she told me the true story or stole my car keys.

This works in folktales as well. The hag can turn you into a toad or instead provide much-needed help, depending on how she is approached. And in the waking world? Two figures from my past come immediately to mind. One of them, as I mentioned earlier, was Mrs. H. across the street from my childhood house in Pinewood Park, who seemed to love her garden more than she loved people. For me and my sister Janet, she was "the crazy old witch" on our block, though I no longer recall what she did to deserve our misgivings, other than water her garden early in the morning wearing her bathrobe outside. We avoided her house on Halloween and sometimes tossed things into her yard that we knew she would never find since her yard was so covered with trees, bushes and plants that it was like the enchanted forest of folktales. I suppose, now that I am a bit of a neighborhood crone myself, that we were disturbed because she did not seem to be like the other mothers we knew. I only found out as an adult that she was a good friend to my mother and provided her with many of the plants in her yard and garden, and taught her how to grow them. When I was an adult, I went over with Jolene to collect her mail when she was hospitalized after a heart attack. We almost went astray in her overgrown garden-grove, and I understood what it was like to lose oneself in an enchanted forest. While I never resolved my feelings of discomfort with her face-to-face, I feel that I have partly redeemed her (and myself) through the challenging figure of "Frau Trude." The story encompasses the forest-garden she struggled so hard to maintain, complete with unearthly servants.

My second cronish figure was "Harriet," an older woman I worked with at the encyclopedia company in Chicago. She took me under her wing, as she did all new employees, helping me find an apartment that she approved of, accompanying me in shopping for acceptable winter coats and boots (what did I know, coming from Miami?), and providing a constant flow of advice at work. Eventually her unrelenting advice became overbearing and I had to escape, rather rudely, as I recall. We had more or less reconciled when I left Chicago two years later, but I never felt I had succeeded in seeing the other side of the coin. I had not faced up to what bothered me most—a woman who was, unlike my mother, unabashedly bold and confident, unafraid of what anyone else thought of her.

Where does artistry come into this? With understanding and acceptance of one's own fears and one's own dark side, the force that Jung identified as the Shadow. If the Shadow is denied, it will find ever darker ways to make itself felt. If it is recognized, it might have something to offer. The writer Brenda Ueland, whom I have quoted earlier, is a fine example of a woman who accepted her cronishness and was quite willing to be outrageous in her defense of enthusiastic artistry. Her comment on a man who was proud that he had raised his children to be rational skeptics was that "he might as well have taken them out in the backyard and killed them with an axe" (173). If Ueland ever appears in cronish form in my dreams she surely would not deny me passage. Quite the opposite. She thought that we should all follow our creative bents in order to "learn about the powers that are in you, all the endless stories not only from this life but from all your former incarnations" (163). For me, all past selves from the present life are former incarnations, and they all have their own stories and dreams waiting to get past the censor, the shadowy gate-keeper.

We learn from our mistakes, in dreams as well as in life. Looking at stories and dreams as on-going created works with limitless possibilities, you can see how re-viewing can be fruitful. For instance, here is a dream I had in 1984, "Old Woman," where I met an early version of the hag, this time testing me for generosity. I failed the first test.

I was lost after visiting a friend in the city and leaving with food and other gifts in paper bags. It was dark and I could not find my car, could not remember where I had left it (all too familiar from waking life). I gave up and started walking down a long road, now out in the country instead of the city, wandering aimlessly in the dark. I stopped, admitted that I was lost, and said to myself, "Where am I?" This was an invitation for help. I saw now that the road and the surrounding area were faintly silvered by a full moon that I could not see. A mist began to rise and I thought to myself, "This looks like Scotland or Ireland." I recognized the otherworldly quality of the surroundings and wondered where I was.

I now came to a fork in the road and stopped, not knowing which way to go and vaguely sensing that this was a significant turning point. Like the curious girl, I thought I should turn back, but really wanted to find out what was ahead. I heard a woman's admonishing voice from behind me saying, "You shouldn't be out like this. You'd better come home with me." I turned to see a sturdy old woman approaching on my left. She silently beckoned me to follow her. I obeyed, almost as if I were under her spell like the girl in "Frau Trude." We came to a small house in a forest clearing and went in. I put my paper bags of food and gifts on the wooden table in the kitchen. The old woman offered me a safe place to stay for the night and asked if I had food to share. Here my "bad girl" came into play. I took a small amount of meat and bread out and we both ate, then I began to put the rest away. "I want more," she said, but I did not want to give it to her. "I can take what I want," she threatened. I was annoyed, thinking I had shared enough already, but I grumblingly took out a bit more meat and bread and began to prepare it for her. "I'll do it myself," she said, and I figured she wanted to take it all. I was stingily trying to figure out how to give her more without really being generous, hiding food in a corner of the bag. In the middle of my silent grumbling I woke up with a feeling of loss, not for the food but for the old woman. I wanted to go back and try again, but could not get back to sleep. Instead I stayed awake quietly and let the dream come back to mind.

When I understand a dream as an open creative expression, I feel freer to see its potential for further development. In both folktales and dreams (and of course memories), there is a fine line between allowing other possibilities to arise and manipulating outcomes. When I allowed this particular dream to come back to mind, I tried to keep myself balanced on that fine line, truly wishing the dream to suggest its own alternative outcome. Like the girl who brings stories to Frau Trude in "Curious Girl," I wanted to bring something to the hungry hag. As I re-imagined the dream, here is what happened:

When the old woman asked me if I had anything else to eat, I decided to put all of my food on the table, and we both ate the entire feast. When we finished the old woman said, "Bring me one of the coals from the fire to light my lamp. Take the spoon to carry it in." I obeyed, taking a glowing coal out with the spoon and trying to carry it back to the table, but found I could not keep it balanced. It seemed to have a life of its own, suddenly flying out of the spoon and filling the room with blinding silver light that hurt my eyes. It flew right up the chimney and disappeared, taking the light with it. The room was now utterly dark and I could hear the old woman chuckling. "Well, you got the coal further than I thought you would. It doesn't matter. It's safe to go now." I left happily without even a thought of my bags, starting down the same road again. This time it was brilliantly lit and I could see the moon in the sky, just above the trees behind the hag's house, somehow connected in my mind to the glowing coal that escaped from her chimney.

One thing that allowed this dream to develop further was my acceptance of the hag as an enigmatic character. Witches can have transformative potential, as I learned from my son Nathaniel. My husband and I had taken him to see the Disney version of "Snow White" when he was almost six, the same age I was when I saw it in 1944. He found it as distressing as I had, but for different reasons. He asked me to tell him the story in my own words, knowing already, from hearing stories both told and read, that oral tales have lives of their own while written ones do not change. As I had in the "hag" dream above, he sensed further possibilities and patiently let them develop. After a week of hearing me tell "Snow White" every night, he said, "Tell me that story one more time. But this time I want the bad mother to go to sleep for a hundred years and wake up a nice lady." As a storyteller I saw how he had creatively worked out a transformation, and as a mother with a short temper, I was touched by his generosity.

At this same age, five, I was seeing the green face floating in my room after a dream. If I had been able to see the face more than once, and perhaps have my mother telling me not to be afraid, maybe I too might have been able to see possibilities of its transformation into "a nice lady." The problem with witches, though, is that they do not transform. They are what they are, unlike the beasts who become men or the ducks and swans who become women. No self-respecting witch would want to become a nice lady no matter how long she slept. Perhaps that was the living center of my fascination, that the witch could not change but somehow still had another side, some essential aspect of her character that allowed her to share some of her powerful art under the right conditions.

I had accomplished part of my quest through the evolution of "Frau Trude," where the girl was not destroyed in the end but gained her own shape back. This led me into the adventures of "Light Kate and Dark Kate," a story I had had in mind for several years, in which it is the "bad" older sister who has the adventures. I was now on new ground, moving further away from familiar folktales, with no idea, but a lot of excitement, how things might go. I kept reminding myself of the inspiration I felt when attending a piano concert and listening to the soloist reading from Beethoven's letters concerning composition—how long it takes to bring a work to life, beginning with an idea that is carried around in the mind, taken on walks, played with, gradually written down, and then treated to a lot of changing. The words of Beethoven's letters encouraged me to try out my long-imagined story.

"Light Kate and Dark Kate" is quite a different telling of a familiar story, using bits and pieces from various folktales in which the younger sister usually triumphs over her lazy, greedy stepsister. While she might be singing "Some day my prince will come," her older stepsister is humming the title of this book, and indeed her witch is about to arrive. The ambivalent crones in this story, and in most of my dreams, have one foot very strongly planted on the dark side, and perhaps only the toes of the other pointing to the light side. There is a balance, but one that is easily swayed depending on the nature of the person who approaches the crone. Dark Kate, who in other stories would come out badly, earns her magical powers by discovering how to listen and learn. Since she is rash rather than dark-hearted, she can survive the triple crones' threatening ambivalence instead of being destroyed, turned to wood, or covered with tar like her less resourceful counterparts in other fairy tales. (See the end of this chapter for the full text of "Light Kate and Dark Kate.")

As for me, I am respectful. I have sensed the dual nature of the various crones I have met in dreams and stories and note a bit of the trickster in Nameless Dread and Selfish Old Bitch, who challenged me with their wicked smiles. But until one significant night of dreaming, I had received no special gifts (getting your own car keys back does not count). Crones, of course, can take positive as well as negative form. I found this when I began to have dream visits from an old storytelling friend, Katy Simons, age ninety-one when I met her in the dream. Katy had been a mature student in my folklore class in the mid-1970s, but had disappeared from my life except for infrequent spontaneous meetings. The last time I saw her, she was touring a public building with a group of seniors. I greeted her warmly, but she did not remember who I was. We had both aged, but she was more easily recognizable to me than I was to her, with my long brown hair now short and white, and my figure predictably less girlish. She acknowledged me politely, and when I said good bye I thought it might be the last time I saw Katy. I was wrong. The next year an article on her appeared in the University of Winnipeg alumni journal after she had been honored with the prestigious Righteous Among Nations award from the Holocaust Museum in Jerusalem for her family's part in sheltering Jews during the war years in Holland. I was delighted to see that she was still very much alive, but also a bit guilty because I had been unable to edit a rambling memoir she had written years earlier.

In a space of two months Katy visited me in three dreams, always in a public place (my other crones were always private), and always without the two aluminum canes she has used for years after failed hip surgery. In these dreams she was entirely articulate, knew exactly who I was and greeted me warmly, and had all of her old spark and boldness. In the third dream, Katy revealed the radiant aspect of the crone as an archetype of gift-giving power.

In the dream I was at a conference or a storytelling event and was going up a flight of stairs to meet some friends. On the fourth floor I heard someone call my name, and turned around to see Katy approaching in one of her usual blue print dresses. "Kay, I brought you something," she said, as she handed me a glass box the size of an old glove box. The crystal clear box was transparent but its contents were obscure. Still, I knew that I was receiving a significant gift as I held it in both hands. "Katy, you always find such beautiful things," I said. "Oh yes, I know where the beautiful things are," she answered simply, and with a smile that was not ambivalent in the least. I awoke with a distinct sense of having actually received a fine gift, and when I told the dream to my friend Morgana, she pointed out that the crone who "knows where the beautiful things are" is me, of course. The gift is real.

When any archetype appears three times, an important change is taking place. With the appearance of a gift in this particular dream, maybe I have at last discovered how to listen and learn, how to accept what the crone has to offer, even when I cannot see what it is. Perhaps it is not meant to be seen, but felt in some other way. I want to emphasize here that familiar figures who appear in dreams are not actually the people we recognize from our waking world, but archetypal images taking on the appearance of those we know. Katy the woman is not a crone, but Dream Katy is. That is, she fills the open archetype of the crone, much like Selfish Old Bitch is an archetypical figure trying to look like my mother.

Like other gift-bearing dreams, this one asks to be brought to light in the waking world, and the dream was a reminder that I could do so. I finally completed her roughly written memoir, determined to find the art in Katy's life and release it from the clear box. And I did. With this, the dreams about Katy became real, out into the waking world, transformed into the written word. Crones, skilled in true magic of all sorts, are at the heart of many such transformations. They come when they are called up, wished for, or dreamed of, as they were for Dark Kate.

LIGHT KATE AND DARK KATE

Here it begins, in a time that never was and always is. There was a man who had a daughter named Kate, and he married a woman who had a daughter with the same name. Since the man's daughter was fair and fine he called her "Light Kate," and called his brown-haired stepdaughter "Dark Kate." Now, Dark Kate's own mother did not like this, and decided to punish the fair one by making her life more difficult. Light Kate did whatever she was told and did it well, and never complained a word to her father. Dark Kate paid no attention because she was too busy with her own things. She preferred black nights to sunny days, and loved to walk in the darkest part of the woods where she could catch the odd creatures who lived there, toads and snakes and strange beetles. While Light Kate's room was always spotless, Dark Kate had bags and boxes and dusty jars filled with all sorts of things that she gathered in the woods. Her stepfather complained, but mother said, "She's just being creative."

One day the mother gave Light Kate a bucket and said, "Go fetch me some water from the well at the world's end. We need it for cooking our supper." Light Kate asked politely, "But where is the well at the world's end?" Her stepmother growled, "If I knew that I'd get it myself, you silly girl. Out with you." So Light Kate obediently picked up the bucket and went out the door of their small hut. She wanted to ask Dark Kate where the end of the world might be because she was sure Dark Kate would know, but her stepsister was nowhere to be seen, and might not have told her anyway even if she did know.

Light Kate carried the pail for a long way, growing more and more tired and hungry and frightened with every step, but she went on. Soon she came to a fast moving stream, and saw that she could cross safely by stepping on the rocks that made a path through the water. When she came to the other side she saw a small apple tree growing beside the road. Its branches drooped with the weight of the ripe apples, but they were too high to reach so she sat down to rest in its shade. The tree called down to her, "My branches are too heavy from all these apples. Shake me until they all fall, then take as many as you like." Light Kate said that she wasn't strong enough, but the apple tree encouraged her, so she be-gan to push and shake the tree as well as she could. Apples fell all around her, and when the last one had fallen, she picked it up and ate it. It was a very sour crab apple, but Light Kate didn't complain, she simply thanked the tree. "And thank you as well," it responded. Then it said, "Now, can I help you as much as you've helped me?" "Oh yes, do you know where I can find the well at the world's end?" she asked courteously. "Of course, just go back to the stream."

Light Kate went back to the stream, and thinking that this must be the well itself she dipped her bucket into it. Instantly the water pulled the bucket out of her hands and swept it way. Poor Kate. She ran along the bank trying to grab the bucket back but the stream was much too fast. As she ran, she tripped on a rock and the next thing she knew, she was in the stream herself, being pulled down and down. She fainted in terror, and when she awoke she found herself in a strange land. In the distance she saw a strange little house, and in it, an even stranger old woman who invited her in. "Are you a hard worker?" the woman asked? "Oh yes," said Light Kate.

She was fed and given a bed to rest in, but in the morning the crone commanded her to clean the house, cook the meals, and feed any animals she met. She did exactly as she was told, and the old woman smiled and invited her to choose her reward. There were two small chests equal in size and shape, but one was made of battered tin and the other was of dark wood with elaborate carvings of peculiar creatures. She chose the modest tin chest and was told to open it only after she had crossed the stream again. "It's so heavy. How will I carry it home?" she sighed. The old woman told her to close her eyes and spin around and around until she fell down in a faint. She obeyed, and she woke up, finding herself beside the stream. The crab apple tree she'd helped pointed the way home. When she crossed the stream again she obediently stopped and opened the tin chest. Inside she found a fine silken sack full of gold. Her bucket was nowhere to be seen, and she was sure she would be punished for losing it. When she came safely home with a fine silk sack full of gold but no bucket, she told her stepmother how she had fallen in the stream and found another land, where she'd worked for a strange old woman who rewarded her with gold.

The stepmother, entranced by the treasure, called her own daughter intending to send her off to find more gold. Dark Kate was far off in the woods collecting toadstools and didn't hear her mother until an owl, awakened by the yelling, hooted in surprise. Kate looked up, listened carefully, and heard her mother's angry voice. She put the toadstools in her pocket and went home. "Now listen to me," her mother said, "I want you to take this bucket and get water from the well at the world's end, and come back with a sack of gold like your sister did." Kate grumbled, but when she saw the gold she thought she could certainly do as well as her silly sister. She set off dragging the heavy bucket along. She crossed the same stream and splashed through it, and saw the small apple tree, once again covered with ripe apples since it was no ordinary tree. "Good. I'm hungry." She set the pail down and climbed right up into the little tree, paying no heed to its shouts to shake its branches free of apples. At the top she found the biggest and ripest of the apples, and sat up there eating it. "Oh, too sour," she said, but she was hungry. When she finished she jumped down, her movement knocking off all the apples.

"And now off to the well," she said as she stood up.

"This is not how I like it," the tree grumbled, "but I guess I'll tell you anyway that you'll find the well at the world's end if you go back to the stream." Without a word Kate picked up the bucket and went back to the stream, thinking, as her sister had, that it must be the right place. She tossed the bucket in and dove in after it, felt herself pulled down into the water that grew darker and colder as she sank. When she touched bottom she went right on sinking down into the earth, until at last she found herself in another land. She, too, saw the odd little hut and met the same strange old woman who asked if she was a hard worker." "Sometimes," Dark Kate answered honestly. She was fed and given a bed to rest in, and in the morning told to clean the house, cook the meals, and feed any animals she met. She began to work, but didn't do anything very thoroughly because she was too busy looking out the windows of the hut and wondering what animals might come to be fed. She didn't care much about the hens and geese and chickens and pigs, but when a bear came she fed it well, and even found food for an old warty toad, just in case.

"Not quite what I expected," the old woman said, "but your work will be properly rewarded." She led her to two small chests and said she could choose what she deserved. Dark Kate did not hesitate to choose the fine wooden chest with its elaborate carving of peculiar creatures. "To each her own," said the old woman, and sent the girl on her way, telling her not to open the chest until she'd crossed the stream.

With no delay Dark Kate set off. She could hardly wait to open the chest and find her reward. She hadn't even gone as far as the crab apple tree when she stopped, sat down beside the path, and threw back the lid expectantly. Inside was a rough woolen sack that seemed to move when she lifted it out. She didn't mind that it wasn't fine silk. She pulled the sack open and jumped back in surprise when snakes slithered out and ugly toads leapt away in all directions. The largest of the toads headed back down the path in the direction of the old woman's hut. Kate yelled, "Hey, come back here! You belong to me!" And off they went together, with the toad in the lead and Kate running after.

Kate galloped after the toad, catching it by its right front leg just as it leapt to the threshold of the crone's hut. Kate was astonished to find herself holding the right hand of the old woman, who smiled darkly.

"Welcome back, my dear. I've been waiting for you for a long time now."

Kate, terrified for the first time in her life, found that she had no control over her feet. She was compelled to follow the crone back inside.

"You've passed my first test, let's see how you'll do on the next one," said the crone. "I tried this on another impudent girl once, a long time ago."

Dark Kate was too frightened to move. The crone passed her hand over Kate's head and chanted strange words. She felt herself growing stiff and hard, unable to lift even her smallest finger. The crone had turned her into a log, which she then tossed casually into her fireplace. "Let's see what happens now." She cackled when a shower of sparks flew out of the fire and landed on the floor. Before they could scorch the wood, the crone transformed the sparks back into Dark Kate.

"Interesting," she said. "Have you met . . . no, that's impossible. No matter. You have fine potential, and I have a lot to show you."

Dark Kate did not go home again. Her mother wouldn't have liked the toads and snakes anyway. So she stayed to learn all there was to be learned from the odd old woman in that curious place beneath water and earth. Then she was sent on her way.

"My sister Frau Holle can teach you more. The apple tree might tell you where you'll find her."

Kate, older now, remembered with some regret that she hadn't treated the tree very well and expected no help at all. This time she approached it more respectfully, but still couldn't resist reaching up and taking one sour apple without permission.

"Ah, you again. I see you still have your old spark."

"More than you know," Kate answered evenly. "You have no reason to tell me, but do you know where Frau Holle lives?"

"Oh indeed, she's the one who turned me into an apple tree. I'll tell, if you promise to find what spell will disenchant me and then come back here."

Kate agreed, intrigued with this challenge and certain that with her own new powers she could accomplish the task easily.

"Good. Follow the stream until you come to a hedge of brambles. Pass through them and you'll find yourself at the other end of the world."

"But where is that?"

"Just go on a bit further. It's right down the path."

Kate was skeptical that the end of the world was so near, but she followed the directions, came to the bramble hedge, spoke a spell that turned its thorns into blossoms, and passed through. On the other side she saw an old stone well.

"Oh no, not the well at the world's end again," Kate murmured. "Well, at least I know what to do. Here goes."

She dropped down into the well, heard the air whistling in her ears as she fell into darkness, and the voices of frogs and toads singing as she went. "Maybe one of them's a prince," she chortled to herself. For a long time, forever, it seemed, Kate's plunge continued, so long that she forgot where she was and where she was going. At last she plunged into the water at the bottom of the well, sank until she felt solid earth beneath her feet. It seemed to be dry ground.

"Now what?" she said out loud, and was startled to hear a voice answer her. "Over here, over here."

She turned toward the sound and saw the merest bit of light, and in it a tiny brown toad that was beckoning her to follow.

"Well at least it's not a white rabbit," she grumbled as she found herself once again following a toad. "My cousins told me to watch out for you," the toad said cordially.

And that is how she came to Frau Holle, was taught to shake the crone's feather bed so that snow fell in the right season, learned the language of the birds who could hear all the sounds of the world, and discovered which stones were the keepers of stories. There were other things as well, but she was diligent and mastered them all, and was even beginning to do things that her teacher had not taught.

"That's it. You're ready to move on. I have nothing more for you. You're finished here. Go on to my sister, Baba Yaga."

Kate was about to ask where she should go next when, all at once, the apple tree's request came back to her and she remembered her promise.

"Before I go, there's an apple tree . . ."

"Right. That one. It's been waiting for ages for someone to get this far and ask me to lift the spell. Simple. You have to pick every single apple from the tree, even the withered ones from all the past winters. That's all I'll say."

The tree was on the way to Baba Yaga, the third sister, so Kate thought the apple tree might help her.

Frau Holle called after her, "She has a kindly name, but my sister is anything but kind. That's her privilege as the eldest. You know what I mean. Watch out for her iron leg and her sharp fingers."

"But how do I find her? Don't tell me it's at the end of the earth, I've already been there twice."

"No. You go from the lowest to the highest place. Be off!"

The little toad accompanied Kate, showing her a short cut back to the meadow where the apple tree stood, and then went to join all the toad kin who had scattered from Kate's bag a long time ago. She was now an aging woman, and her feet ached, her left knee was bothering her, and she noticed that she wasn't seeing as clearly as she used to. She began to wonder if crones lost their powers in the same way ordinary people did, or if they had ways of compensating.

The apple tree had aged too. Many of its branches were dry and dead, and it seemed to droop dejectedly.

"You came back. I'm amazed. Did you remember to ask?"

"Oh yes, but by the looks of you I'm not sure you're going to like the cure. I have to pick every single apple, including the old dried up ones from all the past winters. Your ancient branches won't take much climbing."

"But you don't have to climb. All you have to do is shake me, as I asked you to do before. You didn't listen then."

This time Kate listened, and began to push and shove the ancient tree with all her strength. Nothing happened.

"Not so hard," the tree complained. "Just touch my bark."

Kate felt the rough bark of the tree in her hands, touched it gently and began to sing a song about sitting under an apple tree that she remembered from childhood. "With nobody else but me," she crooned, as all the apples began to rain down on her.

Then a strange thing happened. The rugged bark began to soften, the tree slowly shrank, and gradually changed into the shape of a tall, white-bearded old man.

"That's what you get for spinning gold for silly girls," he grumbled. "It was the witch's gold, and she didn't like that one bit. And all I wanted was a child to call my own."

Kate had an unfamiliar twinge of compassion, and asked where he would go now that he was free.

"I'm not sure I can go anywhere after standing here for so long, but since I don't have anything better to do maybe I'll come along with you. I've never met the oldest sister, the one with the most power. Maybe she can do something for me."

They set off together, seeking the lowest and the highest place in the world. Neither of them had the slightest idea where that might be, but they had plenty of sour apples to eat along the way. They walked on for seven days and six

305

nights, and on the seventh night they fell asleep in a low valley, under stars so bright that they seemed alive. "Oh," thought Kate as she fell asleep, "I wish those stars were truly alive and could help us."

To make a long story somewhat shorter, that is exactly what happened. Kate passed from the lowest place to the highest place as she slept. When she woke up she found herself in the sky, and there was the chicken-legged hut of Baba Yaga surrounded by a fence of human bones topped with skulls with flaming eyes that watched her as she passed. Baba Yaga tested her with a necklace of crystal beads, which she broke and scattered to the winds.

"Find them and you won't lose your head," she snarled, and all the glowing skulls smiled.

Kate didn't lose her head. She was calm because she knew she had many helpers now, and she could call them because she knew the language of birds. Everyone from the smallest ant to the largest bear helped gather each bead. When the necklace was reassembled it had one extra bead, and no one knew where it had come from.

"Excellent. You have learned well if you have the help of the invisible ones, and now I can teach you the higher wisdoms."

Kate learned about the movements of earth, ocean, air, and the fire below them all. She understood the balancing of sun, moon, and planets, and which stars were truly alive. But in the end she wanted only one thing, to be back in her own realm with the good earth beneath her feet.

"Give up your hair and I'll weave a rope to lower you down," said Baba Yaga, "but you must not open your eyes until you feel the earth under you."

And so it was. Kate was lowered by a rope made from her own strong hair, and managed to keep her eyes closed until she felt her feet strike something solid. Alas, when she opened her eyes she had not reached the earth yet, but was trapped at the top of an immense pine tree. Dark Kate, with all her boldness and all her knowledge, was afraid to climb down by herself. She closed her eyes again and began to call for help from all the creatures she'd met in her long life. It was a bear who climbed to the top and helped her down.

The old man who had been a crab apple tree was waiting.

"Time to move on," he said. And they did. As far as I know, they are traveling still, the old man and the crone, looking for curious girls who wish to learn more than is good for them.

Epilogue

What brought me into fairy tale scholarship in the 1970s was the understanding that fairy tales depicted real people and situations that were personally relevant to many of those whom I interviewed, and to me, much to my surprise. The stories that centered on overcoming great obstacles, and those that treated animal/human transformations, attracted me particularly strongly.

As I continued to explore fairy tale heroines and their adventures and misadventures my appreciation of these women grew, spurred on as I listened to other readers and hearers of tales.

These themes stayed with me as my scholarly career evolved into analyses of how and why stories were still being told by contemporary performers, and, later on, how fairy tales and dreams shared motifs, characters, and even situations. Revisiting my earlier work in this volume gave me a sense of completion. I had overcome my own obstacles (a doctoral degree and university teaching, among others), and I underwent the inevitable transformation that comes with aging and that sometimes seemed almost like the change from human to animal and back again. I developed an intimate and empathic relationship with cronehood, and greater sympathy with the struggles of beautiful young heroines trying to make their way in the world.

Women and fairy tales were very much on my mind as my attention turned to professional storytelling and storytellers, where the variety of female characters opened even more widely as modern tellers brought new life to old tales. Recognizing the deep reality of these stories, tellers were able to connect stories and characters to their own experiences.

When I began to explore dreaming as an expressive art, however, fairy tale heroines did not follow me. Instead, I found much darker figures who threatened and challenged and occasionally even rewarded me, much like the crones of some fairy tales. I have already mentioned Nameless Dread and Selfish Old Bitch among my nightly visitors, each with her own threatening defiance. Perhaps because they managed to speak more fully despite my attempts to silence them, and even to respect my rebelliousness, these dreams suggested other possibilities of finding a balance of light and dark. In my earlier work I had found many heroines too light, and also found myself struggling to understand their dark antagonists. The crone in "Frau Trude" was the catalyst, inviting me to take part in the gradual transformation of a story from dark to light.

I was delighted to discover that I was not alone in this dark journey. Many of those I interviewed for my dissertation had already noted that there was one assertive figure who appeared in both hero and heroine tales, and who was often a source of either transformation or destruction—the hag, the crone, the witch, the wicked stepmother. One man pondered the intriguing possibility that the witch figure, projected onto women by men, might in reverse be a man in women's projected thoughts. A woman was even more positive in considering the witch as a deliberately ambivalent character: "So you get the feeling that there's a good witch and a bad witch in the same person." Like them, I found myself drawn back to the figure of the witch who had frightened yet attracted me as a child. I wanted to carry this line of thought further, so I rechecked the interviews again even more closely to see what people had actually said about the witch figure. Page references here are to Appendix X in my dissertation. Their comments left no doubt that the witch was a powerfully negative figure, often mentioned in connection with the tales of "Snow White," "Hansel and Gretel," and even "Sleeping Beauty," where the vengeful fairy took on the witch archetype for some readers who had not even seen the Disney version. One woman, for example, said, "The active women I remember were like the wicked queen in Snow White" (297), and another agreed, "There's 'Snow White' and 'Hansel and Gretel'—they both had witches that were cruel and vicious. There was *always* somebody old and vicious" (262). But a few, like the woman cited earlier, were perplexed by the deliberately contradictory nature of some crones. Here is her full comment: "But in 'The

Seven Swans' the girl goes to a woman who is misunderstood by the society around her as a witch. But she does help the girl, even though the girl has to pick nettles. So you get the feeling that there's a good witch and a bad witch in the same person (315)." This is a very telling observation, a challenging look at the crone as an intentionally contradictory figure with both dark and light potential, both in the story and perhaps in the reader(s) as well.

Another woman was even more adamant when asked about assertive women: "Aside from witches, I don't remember any strong, controlling women. That's a funny thing, isn't it—the witches control, and they're bad women. The good girls are nice and don't do anything much—that cheeses me off now" (269). Her remark is seconded by another woman who says, "But of course there weren't exactly any strong women in fairy tales, except for the evil ones and the witches" (312). In other words, if you want to be assertive you have to be willing to be "bad."

Two women took this ambivalent power a step further, admitting that they were drawn to stories featuring negatively powerful women. One, discussing Andersen's story of "The Snow Queen," said: "I certainly identified with the women in the stories. The ones I remember are the ones where the woman is the sort of all-powerful figure. She may be meant to be a negative figure, but I didn't see her that way. I thought she was terrible but powerful. I liked her. I liked that story" (319). Later in the interview she tried to recall stories in which the crone was a strong figure. She described such women as interesting, saying, "She would have some power, like Baba Yaga in the Russian ones. She was evil and nasty, but I liked her stories" (322).

The second woman, complaining about "effete princesses," went on to extol "working class girls like Gretel," and by implication, the older and powerful women, whom she connected to her own background: "I didn't feel they [cronish figures] were evil, in general. I identified the strong, older women with those I was brought up with in northern England," and added: "I guess I never considered witches as women, even though we had a woman in our village who was said to be a witch. But I never really identified them by sex. They were just agents, supernatural beings, the same as ogres and giants and dragons. I didn't think of them as male or female, either" (297–98).

These women were willing to ponder the deeper nature of the powerful and usually negative women in fairy tales, but the most surprising observations came from the older man cited earlier, who added a new dimension to female power. He began by seeing witches purely as negative because of their sexual power over men, then seemed to have a vague understanding that they might be projections of male fears, and finally made a leap into possible female projections:

> The only really strong women I remember are the bad ones. You know, I don't remember clearly about the witches, but they were always women, in fairy tales and real life, weren't they? Do you know why? Because women have this power over men because of their sex. They can't help it, but men can't control themselves because of it. I guess for 68 years I've believed it—because of my background—that women weren't interested in sex themselves, but still affected men. Now I hear it's the same with them—so maybe they see men as witches. (338)

Unfortunately it is beyond my present purposes to compare female and male witch/wizard characters, but the added notion of sexual power is an intriguing one that was surely not lost in psychoanalytic approaches.

More to the point, what all these observers agree on is that these older women were powerful and active, capable of transforming themselves and other fairy tale characters. However, it would certainly be a mistake to forget their destructive powers. A friend who read and commented on this epilogue in an e-mail message recalled "a simple fear of witches in childhood" but also a lack of interest in passive heroines like "the Cinderellas or Sleeping Beauties" (Rountree). She went on to speculate on the absence of actual "crones" in her early life that might have fed into this fear of the unknown: "I wonder how many of us were not living near grandmothers in our childhoods? Many of us where I grew up didn't know any aging women at all—the town I lived in was a 'company town' and retirees were required to live elsewhere, as company housing only went to employees. Perhaps this was unusual, but I think older women are still largely unseen and ignored." Even in non-company towns, many older women live in "seniors' centers" where they may not be as active in general society. Perhaps without intention we have become an "ageist" society, where people no longer grow up with grandparents and are mistrustful of, and impatient with, the elderly. This would certainly fuel stereotypes of crones and hags.

Iris went on to ponder the situation and to suggest that perhaps today's crones-to-be will be less negative about their own inevitable aging: "I spoke to a younger friend yesterday about crones, speculating about this, and we thought that the 'babyboomers' are not buying the apparent invisibility, the overlooking, and one way that is meaningful to many of us is celebrating the onset of the crone-state." She felt that such recognition by society was already traditional in many cultures but "might be thought to be new in our own." She noted the numerous "croning" ceremonies that have become more and more familiar in recent years. I underwent my own "croning" with eighteen other folklore women in a tongue-in-cheek ceremony as part of the Women's Section meeting of the American Folklore Society in 1998, and more seriously at a ten-week session in Winnipeg called "Stages of a Woman's Life" that concluded with a croning celebration. Both of these events not only recognized the potential for wisdom and power in older women, but explicitly embraced the witch figures of our childhood fairy tales.

Several books have addressed the power of the crone archetype in the past decade or so, among them Jean Shinoda Bolen's *Goddesses in Older Women*. Bolen concludes this work by underlining the positive power of the dark figure, which would seem to apply equally to men and to women: "The crone archetypes invite us to reflect upon what we know from our own experience. They bring us into the inner realm of meaning, help us to see what matters, to be compassionate, decisive, and, if need be, fierce when change is called for" (206). The archetype is even more boldly developed in each of the thirteen interwoven Grimm and Andersen stories included in *Kissing the Witch* (Donoghue). Here the crones speak for themselves, and the boundaries between the princess and the witch are very deliberately blurred.

Still, the adverse qualities of the witch should not be forgotten. With this in mind, my friend Iris observed, as had the sixty-eight-year old man I mentioned earlier, that "maybe witches were made 'bad' by men telling the stories—women with power were dangerous! We know too much, and won't perpetuate the pretenses." Perhaps, but there are no simple explanations when it comes to crones, hags, and witches because they are often such complex characters. You need to take the bad with the good, and feel what resonates.

To fully consider the witch in all her power is well beyond my intentions here, and in any case she has been thoroughly considered by many other writers. Still, it seems that the time has come for crones, as older women with wisdom and power, to break out of the stereotype so graphically portrayed in Disney's *Snow White and the Seven Dwarfs*. Marvyne Jenoff's re-figuring of the witch in her original story, "Snow White: A Reflection," in chapter 10, offers a strong alternative view of this particular crone. This woman knew when to come to her daughter's rescue, and also when to leave Snow White alone with her prince. This crone comes full circle, becoming a helper rather than a destroyer.

I, too, have come full circle in my own work; this anthology begins with my censure of passive princesses, later I find unexpected strength in their seeming submissiveness, and finally I try to imagine them as the crones they would become if their stories continued. The witch who comes must be your own, if my dream of "Nameless Dread" is any indication. That is, she is looking specifically for you. She cannot be ignored nor destroyed. She has too much to offer anyone, female or male, who can abide her in stories, imagination, dreams, and life. Like Frau Trude, she is waiting to hear a tale that has not yet been told—your own.

Notes

1. In the 1970s a handful of writers interested in children's literature spoke up about the plight of fairy tale heroines. See, for example, Marcia Lieberman (383–95); Lurie ("Fairy Tale Liberation," 42–44). Sporadic references to fairy-tale heroines are also found in de Beauvoir and Friedan.
2. Vengeful heroines are found in abundance in *The Devil's Pretty Daughter:* "What Candy Ashcroft Done," 6; "How Toodie Fixed Old Grunt," 63; and "The Girl and the Road Agent," 139. In the same volume is "The Toad-Frog," 91, an amusing reworking of "The Frog King."
3. See, for example, Dundes's *Study of Folklore,* 107–13, for two examples of phallic interpretation in "Jack and the Beanstalk."
4. See Hays, *Dangerous Sex,* especially chapter 4.
5. For psychological commentary, see: Freud, *General Introduction,* 156–77; Jung, *Collected Works,* vol. 9; Mumford, *City in History,* 15–17.
6. For a provocative interpretation of Cinderella and female sexuality, see Kavablum's *Cinderella,* a short but challenging booklet.
7. See, for example, Berne, *What Do You Say,* especially chapter 3; Bettelheim, *Uses of Enchantment;* Heuscher, *Psychiatric Study;* Hornyansky, "Truth of Fables," 121–32.
8. Interviews were conducted in Miami, Minneapolis, and Winnipeg, from December 1972 to August 1973. Ages ranged from seven to sixty-eight. The full texts are found in Appendix X of my doctoral dissertation ("Romantic Heroines" 261–385).

CHAPTER 2

1. "The Sorcerer's Apprentice" is one of the sequences in the full-length film, *Fantasia*.

2. "*Cinderella* Notes," January 15, 1948. This and subsequent statements by Walt Disney are from the transcripts of film planning sessions available in the archives of Walt Disney Productions in Burbank, California. I am grateful for the assistance provided by David R. Smith and Paula Sigman.

3. Charles Perrault published his *Histoires au contes du temps passé, avec des moralités* in 1697. These heavily sentimentalized reworkings were, at least loosely, based on traditional oral tales.

4. For two years, the planning notes for *Snow White* had the prince captured by the wicked queen, locked in her dungeon, and escaping with the help of his horse and other friendly animals. These sequences were dropped from *Snow White*, but appeared years later, in altered form, in *Sleeping Beauty*.

5. For other examples, see the multiple listings for Vance Randolph and Leonard Roberts in Works Cited.

6. The first is in "White Bear Whittington," from Emelyn Gardner's *Folklore from the Schoharie Hills, New York*; The second is "Bully Bornes," in Leonard Roberts's *South from Hell-fer-sartin*.

7. For a thorough treatment of the subject, see Denis de Rougemont, *Love in the Western World*. His observations are still supported by the continuing popularity of the love story in North America. Witness, for example, the enthusiastic reception of the film *Love Story*, among many others.

8. "Cinderella, or the Little Glass Slipper." While Perrault's version is considerably more romantic than the Grimms', the Disney version exceeds even Perrault's. The animals, so important in the film, are not emphasized by Perrault. In the French version, the sisters are not particularly ugly, nor is their mother domineering—in fact, she hardly appears. There is also scholarly disagreement about the glass slipper, which some think is a mistranslation of the original French word that might mean fur slipper.

9. Page references for this and subsequent quotations are from interviews conducted in 1972 and 1973 for my doctoral dissertation, "Romantic Heroines."

10. There are now a number of treatments of fairy tales as serious literature, expressing a variety of viewpoints. See, among others: Bettelheim, *Uses of Enchantment;* Girardot, "Initiation and Meaning"; Heuscher, *Psychiatric Study;* Lüthi, *European Folktale, Fairy Tale as Art,* and *Once Upon a Time.*

11. For further comments on this topic see Girardot's above-mentioned article, "Initiation and Meaning." Abundant examples of heroes in need of help can be found in the Grimms and other authentic collections of folktales. My own unpublished material from two traditional tellers in Winnipeg has two fine examples: in the first, a French/Métis tale told by Oblate sister Marie Ducharme, a hero keeps losing his magic objects to a greedy witch until he finally heeds advice; in the second, a Polish tale told by university student Sophie Mukoid, a hero is freed from a wizard by a clever girl who does his impossible tasks for him. (He has the good sense to marry her.)

1. The early controversy on fairy tales is discussed in Elizabeth Stone ("Frolicks," n.d.). A more contemporary opponent of fairy tales is Lucy Sprague Mitchell, who felt that their irrational fantasy might "delay a child's rationalizing of the world and leave him longer than desirable without the beginnings of scientific standards" (24). In contrast, an eloquent proponent of fairy tales, Bruno Bettelheim, suggested that "nothing can be as enriching and satisfying to child and adult alike as the folk fairy tale" (*Uses of Enchantment* 5).

2. I should note that not all scholars agree that tale narration is female-dominated. For example, folktale specialist Linda Dégh observes that the reverse is true in Hungary (*Folktales and Society* 92–93), and this seems to be the case in North America as well, judging by narrators listed in Anglo-American collections.

3. Here he also chides me for overemphasizing female passivity in "Things Walt Disney Never Told Us": "In this way Kay Stone's comments on what she considers to be the insipid and uninspiring 'passivity' of female characters in the Grimm tales, while not entirely unfounded, does seem to miss the point that the ultimate initiation is the fortuitous work of the gods, however they are disguised."

4. I conducted interviews in Winnipeg, Minneapolis, and Miami, during 1972–73, with adults and children of both sexes and of differing backgrounds. Twenty-five people were interviewed individually, and nineteen were interviewed in groups sharing the same age. In addition to forty-four formal individual interviews and three group interviews, countless other children and adults responded informally to my general curiosity about what they remembered about fairy tales. I also received material from students and colleagues. Most notably, Linda Dégh showed me the responses to a similar question she asked students in her course in European folktales, taught at the University of California at Berkeley in the spring of 1978. Karen Rowe, of UCLA, sent me a detailed questionnaire on fairy tales handed out to students in a number of classes. Michael Taft also shared student responses from his 1979 classes at the University of Saskatchewan.

5. In my folklore class I asked students to describe in one sentence what they considered to be the main point of the "Cinderella" story. The men overwhelmingly responded that it was a "rags-to-riches" story, emphasizing the heroine's positive actions and her reward. The women characterized it as a "good-over-evil" story, concentrating on the heroine's inherent and unchanging nature and her need to find outside recognition of her goodness.

CHAPTER 4

1. These collections are the ones most often cited by both casual readers and scholarly researchers. The Grimm tales are frequently read in books containing thirty to sixty tales rather than the complete collection. In these selections, heroines in general, and passive heroines in particular, account for a much higher ratio than in the complete collection. The courtly French tales of Charles Perrault, also featuring passive heroines ("Cendrillon" being the best known), have remained popular since they were published in 1697. Hans Christian Andersen's literary tales create even more

downtrodden heroines, including "good" girls, like "The Little Mermaid" and "The Little Matchgirl," who are destroyed despite their virtues. Andrew Lang's several volumes of tales, gleaned largely from other printed collections, also favor helpless heroines, particularly in his earliest volumes in which tales from the Grimms, Andersen, and Perrault and his imitators (Madame D'Aulnoy and Madame de Beaumont) are featured.

2. See references in Marie Campbell, Fauset, Gardener, Randolph, and Robertson in works cited.

3. For two significant folklore studies, see Farrer, *Women and Folklore* and Jordan and Kalčik, *Women's Folklore.*

4. For other examinations of Pandora, see Panofsky and Panofsky (*Pandora's Box*) and Pomeroy (*Goddesses, Whores*). For further examinations of Eve, see Daly (*Beyond God*); Patai (*Hebrew Goddess*); Phillips (*Eve*); and Tribble (*Depatriarchalizing*).

5. For a response to the Jungian approach, see Goldenberg, "Feminist Critique," 443–49.)

6. Of interest are recent and (at the time of this writing) unpublished papers presented at annual meetings of the American Folklore Society. For example: Marta Weigle, "A Mythology of One's Own: Mundus vs. Mythos" (1981); Carol Mitchell, "The Garden of Eden Revisited" (1982); and Carol Edwards, "Feminism and Fairytales Revisited" (1983).

CHAPTER 5

1. See also two other significant critiques of the Grimms: John Ellis, *One Fairy Story Too Many;* and Heinz Rölleke, "Die 'stockhessischen' Märchen."

2. See Richard Shickel's book-length critique, *The Disney Version.*

3. In particular see Umberto Eco, *The Role of the Reader.*

4. For an eloquent exploration of the problem of inter-media translation, see Dennis Tedlock, *The Spoken Word,* and Dell Hymes, *"In Vain I Tried."*

5. See in particular Richard Bauman, *Verbal Art as Performance.*

6. See *Verbal Art as Performance,* 37–46.

7. Two key works are Dundes, *"Nationalistic Inferiority Complexes and the Fabrication of Fakelore,"* and Hobsbawm and Ranger, *The Invention of Tradition.*

8. For complete English texts of both the 1810 and the 1812 variants of "Snow White" see Alfred and Mary Elizabeth David, *The Frog King and Other Tales of the Brothers Grimm,* 303–15.

9. A small grant from the University of Winnipeg allowed me to spend several days in 1978 in the archives of Walt Disney Productions in Burbank, California. I am grateful to archivists Paula Sigman and David R. Smith for their assistance.

10. From a document titled "SNOW WHITE AND THE SEVEN DWARFS, Transcribed from verbatum [*sic*] notes on General Continuity as talked by Walt, 12/22/36."

11. I am grateful to Richard J. Leskosky, assistant professor of Cinema Studies at the University of Illinois, for allowing me to view this 1942 Warner Brothers parody when I was at the university in April 1986.

12. Anthropologist Claude Lévi-Strauss develops this challenging concept in all of his writing. See in particular *Structural Anthropology,* especially chapters 2 and ll.

CHAPTER 6

1. See, for example, Merkel and Nagel's *Erzählen,* Doderer's *Märchen,* and Früh and Wehse's *Frau,* among others.
2. In identifying these contexts I use the concept of "organized storytelling" developed by Richard Alvey in his 1974 doctoral dissertation, "The Historical Development of Organized Storytelling to Children in the United States." Obviously a great deal of oral creativity takes place outside of organized contexts—joke-telling at parties, for example—and in a rich variety of multicultural settings. I confine myself here to organized storytelling in English, as did Alvey. Interestingly, Alvey ends his survey in 1974, almost at the very moment that the "storytelling revival" leaps from schools and libraries onto concert and festival stages for adult audiences.
3. See Marie Campbell, Randolph, and Roberts.
4. A fine example of original composition based on traditional materials is found in Lord (272–75). Here one particularly gifted *guslar* (epic singer), Milovan Vojičić, composed an epic poem dedicated to Milman Parry.
5. For example, Linda Dégh discusses the situation of male and female narrators at great length, particularly with regard to her skilled female narrator who began performing in public only after her male relatives were no longer available (*Hungarian,* esp. 92–93 and 99–102). The dominance of male tellers in Anglo-American tradition is illustrated by the predominance of men in many of the collections cited earlier.
6. Margaret Mills, who conducted field research in Afghanistan, commented to me in a personal note: "Women are in the cultural-educational backwaters, left holding the bag of traditional culture. Dialectologists treat it as a truism that if you want to study archaism in dialects, women often predominate as subjects, because their opportunity to travel and learn to talk to outsiders are limited compared to men's. So their lore tends to be more local or regional—in modern times and, perhaps, always. Men tend to have the floor but women have the lore" (Mills, personal correspondence, 1989).
7. See, for example, Sara Cone Bryant (*How to Tell*) and Ruth Sawyer (*The Way*), both of whom were against forcing tales into narrow pedagogic channels.
8. See, for example, Kotzin's *Dickens and the Fairy Tale.*
9. The interview appeared in *Yarnspinner,* a monthly newsletter published by the National Association for the Preservation and Perpetuation of Storytelling (NAPPS) and available through this organization.
10. In its early years this particular southern-based festival was dominated by tellers from Anglo-American traditions, with the occasional inclusion of Native American tellers. The 1985 festival was more adventurous, featuring performers from Bengal and Ethiopia, as well as established writers and poets who offered their work orally.
11. Ed. note, 2005: In fact, Donald Davis gave up the ministry a few years later and did indeed end up "making storytelling the end of what I do." He now performs and leads workshops throughout North America and beyond, and has written several books.

CHAPTER 7

1. Actually two separate questionnaires were sent out to the 25 selected tellers in the fall of 1987. The first was a fairly complex form with several questions, but when I received only a handful of replies I sent the second, with only three questions, to

those who had not yet responded. Over the next few months I received a dozen more replies, and these form the central portion of this essay. The 17 who responded are: Elisabeth Nash, Mary-Louise Chown-Quanbury, Joyce Birch, Gerri Serrette (all from Winnipeg); Elizabeth Ellis (Texas); Susan Gordon (Maryland); Jane Yolen (Massachusetts); John Harrell and Ruth Stotter (California); Marvyne Jenoff and Marylyn Peringer (Toronto); Renate and Robert Schneider, and Barbara Reed (Connecticut); Lynn Rubright and Ruthilde Kronberg (Missouri); Cathryn Wellner (Washington State).

2. Several of the titles she mentions are from Marie Campbell's collection of Kentucky folktales, *Tales from the Cloud Walking Country.*

3. She lists "The Fisherman and His Wife," "The Frog Prince," "Snow White," "Cinderella," "Sleeping Beauty," "The Wolf and Seven Kids," "Rumpelstiltskin," "Rapunzel," "Hansel and Gretel," "The Goose Girl," "The White Snake."

4. See Bauman, *Verbal Art,* among others.

5. I have made a more thorough description of the story of this story in Radner's *Feminist Messages.*

CHAPTER 8

1. He devotes much of his dissertation to the lifetime development of Mrs. Watanabe, a skilled but illiterate oral narrator who taught herself to read Japanese after she lost her hearing at age 67. She was able to continue learning stories from books in Japanese in her local library. Adams was intrigued to discover that she read world folktales as Japanese tales, and had taken the Grimm tales into her repertoire without distinguishing them as German. These stories were not immediately recognizable as European tales because Mrs. Watanabe adapted them very successfully to her own narrative traditions.

2. In fact, there seem to be only a small percentage of self-supporting tellers from among the hundreds of people who list themselves in the National Storytelling Directory. Sobol estimated about fifty tellers he knew who actually supported themselves through storytelling. In Toronto there are only a handful who draw most of their livelihood from storytelling engagements. Others either tell stories as part of another vocation (still, most notably, teaching and library work) or have another source of income so that they need not rely on performing to support them.

3. Ruth Stotter was the discussant on a panel at the American Speech Communication Association in Atlanta, Georgia, in 1991. Her comments were in response to the four panel papers describing how people assumed their identities as storytellers.

4. The *Canadian Storytelling Directory* had published only two editions as of this writing in 1997, so I supplemented self-descriptions in program write-ups from the Toronto Festival of Storytelling from 1979 to 1995. *The National Storytelling Directory* (published by the National Storytelling Association, formerly NAPPS) printed its first directory in 1984, so this was a good source of comparative information about American tellers for more than a decade.

CHAPTER 9

1. While I am familiar with current attempts to transcribe oral texts from taped tellings using careful ethnopoetic style, I have found that I, and other contemporary tellers, speak in paragraphs rather than in poetic form. Also, since I am recomposing a

printed form of my told story based on a Grimm text, the story will continue to change each time it is told. I respond to the unique character of each audience, in this case, you, the readers.

2. I first read "Mistress Trudy" (also known as "Frau Trude," "Dame Trudy," and "Mother Trudy") in Magoun and Krappe (*Grimms' German Folk Tales,* 157). The text is reprinted here by permission of Southern Illinois University Press. When referring to the Grimm text, I use their title, "Mistress Trudy." When referring to the story in general, it is "Frau Trude," which has a somewhat heavier tone.

3. The suggestions of Susan Gordon and Jo Radner were most helpful in guiding me back to possible influences. I carefully reread Jo's commentary on decoding (Radner and Lanser 412–25) but discovered that decoding in these terms did not apply to the Grimms' "Frau Trude," since it is a male-translated text (Magoun and Krappe) of a male-collected/edited tale (Grimms) based on a male-written poem (as noted in Zipes, *The Complete Fairy Tales,* 407). Still, it was useful to review my own conscious and unconscious retellings in light of decoding feminist messages.

CHAPTER 10

1. See Perrault, *The Fairy Tales of Charles Perrault* and *Perrault's Complete Fairy Tales* for translations.

2. See Grimm, *The Complete Grimm's* [sic] *Fairy Tales* and *The Complete Fairy Tales of the Brothers Grimm* for translations.

3. See Grimm, *The Complete Fairy Tales,* 186–95.

CHAPTER 11

1. See Works Cited for books by Bottigheimer, Dégh, Haase, Holbek, Lüthi, McCarthy, McGlathery, Rohrich, Tatar, Warner, and Zipes, as examples.

2. Marylyn found the published story in *Culture Vivante* (Living Culture, 9:37–43), collected by Luc Lacoursiere from Benoit Benoit in 1955. In his brief commentary Benoit said that he did not recall where or from whom he had learned it, but that "he had known it all of his life." Marylyn noted that Lacoursiere said he knew eleven variants from Acadia and one from Quebec.

3. See the following sources listed in Works Cited: Aarne and Thompson, *Types of the Folktale;* Ashliman, *Guide to Folktales;* MacDonald, *Storyteller's Sourcebook;* Thompson, *Motif Index of Folk-Literature.*

4. Benoit Benoit, the storyteller, was seventy five when he recorded this story for Lacoursiere on July 10, 1955, in Tracadie, New Brunswick ("Chemin des Basques, to be exact," Marylyn added). "L'horoscope" is listed as #2454 in the collection of Luc Lacoursiere in the Archives de Folklore at Laval University, Quebec, Quebec. Marylyn noted that Benoit Benoit had contributed 22 folktales and 185 songs to the archives there. [*Chana Thau and Nathaniel Stone generously checked and corrected the text of the French transcription.*]

CHAPTER 12

1. For another example of a traditional teller adapting to a platform performing context see Mullen, "Traditional Storyteller."

2. This problem is disquietingly familiar to folklorists and ethnographers. Two particularly thoughtful and challenging commentators are Dell Hymes (*"In Vain I Tried"*)
and Dennis Tedlock (*Spoken*).

CHAPTER 14

1. Ed. note 2006: While visiting a friend I noticed a collection of Gypsy folktales on her
bookshelf and opened it to see what it included (Tong, *Gypsy Folk Tales*). The very
first tale was "How the Gypsy Went to Heaven," and since the book was published
in 1989, the year Chris Barsanti took my university class, I am now guessing that this
was his source. His retelling in my folklore class was his own original interpretation.
2. I note here that there are no "authentic" oral texts of stories in the sense of being
original and authoritative, though this is still a controversial topic in folklore scholarship. I suggest that even in fully oral, traditional contexts, there are as many variants of any given story as there are people who have told it (and indeed more, since
tellers vary their tales). With this in mind, both Barsanti's and my variants are only
two of countless others in both oral tradition and contemporary "professional"
telling.
3. This variant was read by a friend, Kira Van Deusen, who has interviewed and gathered stories from women with shamanic backgrounds in the Amur region of Siberia;
she explores what she calls the "crossover" between "normal" and shamanic realities, and the role that traditional narratives play in revealing, expressing, and continuing these points of connection. After reading "The Old Woman and Her Hat,"
Kira commented in a letter that "crossing into the spiritual world is done by using
inner senses. Maybe you can do this by throwing your hat into heaven" (Letter to the
author).

Works Cited

1995/96 Canadian Storytelling Directory. Vancouver: Vancouver Society of Storytelling, 1995/96.

1997/98 Canadian Storytelling Directory. Vancouver: Vancouver Society of Storytelling, 1997/98.

Aarne, Antti, and Stith Thompson. *The Types of the Folktale.* Folklore Fellows Communications No. 184. Helsinki: Academia Scientiarum Fennica, 1973.

Adams, Robert. "Social Identity of a Japanese Storyteller." Diss. Indiana U, 1972.

Alvey, Richard. "The Historical Development of Organized Storytelling to Children in the United States." Diss. U of Pennsylvania, 1974.

Ashliman, D. L. *A Guide to Folktales in the English Language: Based on the Aarne-Thompson Classification System.* New York: Greenwood, 1987.

Azadovskii, Mark. *A Siberian Tale Teller.* Trans. James R. Dow. Monograph Series No. 2, Center for Multicultural Studies in Folklore and Ethnomusicology. Austin: U of Texas P, 1974.

Bacchilega, Cristina. *Postmodern Fairy Tales: Gender and Narrative Strategies.* Philadelphia: U of Pennsylvania P, 1997.

Bauer, George W. *Tales from the Cree.* Cobalt, Ont.: Highway Book Shop, 1973.

Baughman, Ernest W. *The Type and Motif Index of the Folktales of England and North America.* The Hague: Mouton, 1966.

Bauman, Richard. *Story, Performance, and Event.* Cambridge: Cambridge UP, 1986.

———. *Verbal Art as Performance.* Prospect Heights, IL: Waveland, 1977.

Bausinger, Hermann. *Folk Culture in a World of Technology.* Trans. Elke Dettmer. Bloomington: Indiana UP, 1990.

Beauvoir, Simone de. *The Second Sex.* New York: Knopf, 1953.

Benjamin, Walter. *Illuminations.* Trans. Harry Zohn. New York: Harcourt, 1968.

Berne, Eric. *What Do You Say after You Say Hello?* New York: Grove, 1972.

Bettelheim, Bruno. "Bringing Up Children." *Ladies' Home Journal* (Monthly columns in October and November 1973).

———. *The Uses of Enchantment.* New York: Vintage, 1977.

Birch, Carol, and Melissa Heckler. *Who Says? Essays on Pivotal Issues in Contemporary Storytelling.* Little Rock, AR: August House, 1996.

Bly, Robert. *Iron John: A Book about Men.* Reading, Mass.: Addison-Wesley, 1990.

Bolen, Jean Shinoda. *Goddesses in Older Women: Archetypes of Women over Fifty.* New York: Harper, 2002.

Bottigheimer, Ruth. *Fairy Tales and Society: Illusion, Allusion and Paradigm.* Philadelphia: U of Philadelphia P, 1986.

———. *Grimms' Bad Girls and Bold Boys: The Moral and Social Vision of the Tales.* New Haven: Yale UP, 1987.

Briggs, Charles. "Metadiscursive Practices and Scholarly Authority in Folkloristics." *The Journal of American Folklore* 106 (1993): 387–434.

Briggs, Katharine M. *A Dictionary of British Folktales.* Vols. 1 and 2. London: Routledge & Kegan Paul, 1970.

Bronzini, Giovanni Battista. "From the Grimms to Calvino: Folk-tales in the Year Two Thousand." Academic paper presented the 9th Congress of the International Society for Folk Narrative Research, Budapest, 10–17 June 1989.

Brunvand, Jan. *The Study of American Folklore.* New York: Norton, 1968.

Bryant, Sara Cone. *How to Tell Stories to Children.* New York: Houghton, 1924.

Buchanan, Joan. Letter to the author. 10 Dec. 1990.

Bullough, Vern L., and Bonnie Bullough. *The Subordinate Sex: A History of Attitudes toward Women.* Urbana: U of Illinois P, 1973.

Burlakoff, Nikolai, and Carl Lindahl, eds. *Folklore on Two Continents: Essays in Honor of Linda Dégh.* Bloomington, IN: Trickster, 1980.

Cameron, Dianne. Letter to the author. 8 Mar. 1990.

Cameron, Moira. Letter to the author. 6 Feb. 1990.

Cameron, Stewart. Letter to the author. 29 Jan. 1988.

Campbell, Joseph. *The Hero with a Thousand Faces.* New York: Meridian, 1956.

Campbell, Marie. *Tales from the Cloud Walking Country.* Bloomington: Indiana University Press; reprinted by Greenwood, 1976.

Carter, Angela. *The Bloody Chamber.* New York: Harper, 1979.

Chase, Richard. *The Grandfather Tales.* Boston: Houghton, 1948.

———. *The Jack Tales.* Boston: Houghton, 1943.

Cooper, Gerri. "What I Didn't Know That I Knew." Unpublished English honours essay, U of Winnipeg, 1996.

Cooper, Susan. Review of *Womenfolk and Fairytales. New York Times Book Review,* 13 Apr. 1975: 8.

Daly, Mary. *Beyond God the Father: Toward a Philosophy of Women's Liberation.* Boston: Beacon, 1973.

David, Alfred, and Mary Elizabeth David. *The Frog King and Other Tales of the Brothers Grimm.* New York: Signet Classics, New American Library of World Literature, 1964.

Davis, Donald. Conversation with the author. John C. Campbell Folk School, Dec. 1982.

———. "Inside the Oral Medium." *National Storytelling Journal* 1 (1984): 7.

Dégh, Linda. *American Folklore in the Mass Media.* Bloomington: Indiana UP, 1994.

———. "Biology of Storytelling." In *Narratives and Society: A Performer-Centered Study of Narration*. Helsinki: Suomalainen Tiedeakatemia, 1995. 47–61.

———. *Folktales and Society: Storytelling in a Hungarian Community*. Bloomington: Indiana UP, 1969, 1989.

———. *Folktales of Hungary*. Chicago: U of Chicago P, 1965.

———. "Grimms' *Household Tales* and Its Place in the Household: The Social Relevance of a Controversial Classic." *Western Folklore* 38 (April 1979): 83–103.

———. "How Storytellers Interpret the Snakeprince Tale." In *The Telling of Stories: Approaches to a Traditional Craft*. Eds. Morten Nøjgaard, Johan de Mylius, Iørn Pio, Bengt Holbek. Odense, Denmark: Odense UP, 1990. 47–62.

———. *Hungarian Folktales: The Art of Zsuzsanna Palko*. Jackson: U of Mississippi P, 1995.

———. "The Magic Tale and Its Magic." In *Fairy Tales as Ways of Knowing*. Eds. M. Metzger and K. Mommsen. Bern: Peter Lang, 1981. 54–68.

———. *Narratives in Society: A Performer-Centered Study of Narration*. Helsinki: Suomalainen Tiedeakatemia, 1995.

———. "The Variant and the Folklorization Process in *Märchen* and Legend." In *D'un conte . . . a l'autre*. Paris: Editions du CNRS, 1990. 159–170.

Disney, Walt. Film Planning Sessions. "*Cinderella* Notes." Walt Disney Archives, Burbank, CA. 15 Jan. 1948. Transcript.

———. Film Planning Sessions. "*Snow White* Notes." Walt Disney Archives, Burbank, CA. 22 Oct. 1934. Transcript.

Doderer, Klaus. *Über Märchen für Kinder von heute*. Weinheim: Beltz, 1983.

Donoghue, Emma. *Kissing the Witch: Old Tales in New Skins*. New York: Harper, 1997.

Dorson, Richard M. *American Folklore*. Chicago: U of Chicago P, 1959.

———. *Buying the Wind*. Chicago: U of Chicago P, 1964.

Dundes, Alan. "Nationalistic Inferiority Complexes and the Fabrication of Fakelore: A Reconsideration of Ossian, The Kinder- und Hausmärchen, the *Kalevala*, and Paul Bunyan." *Journal of Folklore Research* 22 (1985): 5–18.

———. *The Study of Folklore*. Englewood Cliffs, NJ: Prentice-Hall, 1969.

———. "Text, Texture, and Context." *Southern Folklore Quarterly* 28 (1964): 251–65.

Eco, Umberto. *The Role of the Reader: Explorations in the Semiotics of Texts*. Bloomington: Indiana UP, 1979.

Eliade, Mircea. *The Myth of the Eternal Return*. Princeton: Princeton UP, 1971.

Ellis, John. *One Fairy Story Too Many: The Brothers Grimm and Their Tales*. Chicago: U of Chicago P, 1985.

Fadiman, Clifton. "Afterword." *Fairy Tales by the Brothers Grimm*. New York: MacMillan, 1963. 510.

Farrer, Claire, ed. *Women and Folklore*. Austin: U of Texas P, 1975.

Fauset, Arthur Huff. *Folklore from Nova Scotia*. New York: American Folklore Society, 1931.

Fiedler, Leslie A. *Love and Death in the American Novel*. New York: Criterion, 1960.

Franz, Marie-Louise von. *Individuation in Fairy Tales*. Dallas: Spring, 1977.

———. *Introduction to the Interpretation of Fairy Tales*. New York: Spring, 1970.

———. *Problems of the Feminine in Fairy Tales*. Dallas: Spring, 1972.

———. *Shadow and Evil in Fairy Tales*. Dallas: Spring, 1974.

Freud, Sigmund. *A General Introduction to Psychoanalysis*. New York: Simon and Schuster, 1969.

Friedan, Betty. *The Feminine Mystique.* New York: Dell, 1963.

Früh, Sigrid, and Rainer Wehse, eds. *Die Frau in Märchen.* Kassel: Röth, 1985.

Frye, Northrop. *The Secular Scripture: A Study of the Structure of Romance.* Cambridge, MA: Harvard UP, 1976.

Gans, Herbert J. "The Creator-Audience Relationship in the Mass Media: An Analysis of Movie Making." In *Mass Culture: The Popular Arts in America.* Eds. B. Rosenberg and D. M. White. New York: Free Press of Glencoe, 1957. 315–24.

Gardner, Emelyn. *Folklore from the Schoharie Hills.* Ann Arbor: U of Michigan P, 1937.

Garner, James Finn. *Politically Correct Bedtime Stories: Modern Tales for Our Life and Times.* New York: MacMillan, 1994.

Georges, Robert. "Toward an Understanding of Storytelling Events." *The Journal of American Folklore* 82 (1969): 313–28.

Girardot, N. J. "Initiation and Meaning in the Tale of Snow White and the Seven Dwarfs." *Journal of American Folklore* 90 (1977): 274–300.

Glassie, Henry. *Passing the Time in Ballymenone: Culture and History of an Ulster Community.* Philadelphia: U of Pennsylvania P, 1982.

Goldenberg, Naomi. "A Feminist Critique of Jung." *Signs* 2 (1976): 443–49.

Gordon, Susan. "Invitation and Decision: Storytelling in a Residential Treatment Center for Adolescents." Unpublished masters thesis, Antioch, 1991.

———. "The Powers of the Handless Maiden." In *Feminist Messages: Coding In Women's Folk Culture.* Ed. Joan N. Radner. Urbana: U of Illinois P, 1993. 252–88.

———. Letter to the author. Jan. 1989

———. Letter to the author. May 1989.

———. Tape Recording to the author. "Juniper Tree." 1989.

Gorog-Karady, Veronika. "The New Professional Storyteller in France." Academic paper presented at the 9th Congress of the International Society for Folk Narrative Research. Budapest, Hungary, 10–17 June 1989.

Greenhill, Pauline, and Diane Tye. *Undisciplined Women: Tradition and Culture in Canada.* Montreal: McGill-Queen's UP, 1997.

Grimm, Jacob and Wilhelm. *The Complete Grimm's* [sic] *Fairy Tales.* Trans. Margaret Hunt and James Stern. New York: Pantheon, 1944, 1972.

———. *The Complete Fairy Tales of the Brothers Grimm.* 2 vols. Trans. Jack Zipes. New York: Bantam, 1987.

Haase, Donald, ed. *Fairy Tales and Feminism: New Approaches.* Detroit: Wayne State UP, 2004.

———, ed. *The Reception of Grimms' Fairy Tales: Responses, Reactions, Revisions.* Detroit: Wayne State UP, 1993.

Hallett, Martin, and Barbara Karasek, eds. *Folk and Fairy Tales.* Peterborough, ON: Broadview, 1991.

Harrell, John. *Origins and Early Traditions of Storytelling.* Kensington, CA: York House, 1983.

———. Letter to the author. Nov. 1984.

———. Letter to the author. Undated 1988.

Hays, H. R. *The Dangerous Sex: The Myth of Feminine Evil.* London: Methuen, 1966.

Hesse, Hermann. *Magister Ludi, or The Glass Bead Game.* Trans. Richard and Clara Winston. New York: Bantam, 1986.

Heuscher, Julius. *A Psychiatric Study of Myths and Fairy Tales: Their Origin, Meaning, and Usefulness.* 2nd ed. Springfield, IL: Charles C. Thomas, 1974.

Hobsbawm, Eric, and Terrence Ranger, eds. *The Invention of Tradition.* Cambridge: Cambridge UP, 1984.

Holbek, Bengt. *Interpretation of Fairy Tales: Danish Folklore in a European Perspective.* Helsinki: Academia Scientiarum Fennica, 1987.

Holt, David. Interview with Ken Feit. *Yarnspinner* 6 (Jan. 1982): 2–3.

Hornyansky, Michael. "The Truth of Fables." In *Only Connect.* Ed. Sheila Egoff et al. Toronto: Oxford UP, 1969. 121–32.

Hymes, Dell. *"In Vain I Tried to Tell You": Essays in Native American Ethnopoetics.* Philadelphia: U of Pennsylvania P, 1981.

Jenoff, Marvyne. Letter to the author. Dec. 1987.

———. Letter to the author. 2 Mar. 1989.

———. *The Emperor's Body: A Book of Thirteen Interrelated Adult Fables.* Victoria, BC: Ekstasis Editions, 1995.

———. "Snow White: A Reflection." Unpublished manuscript, 1993.

Jacobs, Joseph. *English Folk and Fairy Tales.* New York: Putnam, n.d.

Jones, Steven Swann. "The Construction of the Folktale: 'Snow White.'" Diss. U of California at Davis, 1979.

Jordan, Rosan, and Susan Kalčik, eds. *Women's Folklore, Women's Culture.* Philadelphia: U of Pennsylvania P, 1985.

Jung, Carl G. *Man and His Symbols.* London: Aldus Books Limited, 1976.

———. *Memories, Dreams, and Reflections.* Ed. Aniela Jaffe. New York: Vintage, 1989.

———. "The Phenomenology of the Spirit in Fairy Tales." In *Collected Works.* Trans. R. F. C. Hull. Vol. 9. Princeton: Princeton UP, 1969. 207–53.

Kane, Alice. "A Most Ingenious Paradox: The Revival of Storytelling." In *Lands of Pleasure.* Eds. Adele M. Fasick, Margaret Johnston, Ruth Osler. Meuchen, NJ: Scarecrow, 1990. 62–70.

Kane, Sean. *Wisdom of the Mythtellers.* Peterborough, Ont.: Broadview, 1995.

Kavablum, Leah. *Cinderella: Radical Feminist, Alchemist.* Guttenberg, NJ: self-published, 1973.

Kiefer, Monica. *American Children through Their Books, 1700–1835.* Philadelphia: U of Pennsylvania P, 1948.

Kolbenschlag, Madonna. *Kiss Sleeping Beauty Good-bye.* Garden City, NY: Doubleday, 1981.

Kotzin, Michael C. *Dickens and the Fairy Tale.* Bowling Green, OH: Bowling Green U Popular P, 1972.

LaBerge, Stephen. *Lucid Dreaming: The Power of Being Awake in Your Dreams.* New York: Ballantine, 1985.

Lang, Andrew. *The Pink Fairy Book.* London: Longman, Green, and Company, 1887. Reprint New York: Dover, 1967.

Leach, Maria. *The Standard Dictionary of Folklore, Mythology and Legend.* New York: Funk & Wagnalls, 1949.

Lee, Tanith. *Red as Blood or Tales from the Sisters Grimmer.* New York: Daws, 1983.

Lévi-Strauss, Claude. *Structual Anthropology.* Trans. C. Jacobson and B. G. Schoepf. London: Allen Lane, 1968.

Lieberman, Marcia. "Some Day My Prince Will Come: Female Acculturation through the Fairy Tales." *College English* 34 (1972): 383–95.

Lord, Albert. *The Singer of Tales.* New York: Atheneum, 1970.

Lottridge, Celia. Taped Interview. June 1993.

Lurie, Alison. "Fairy Tale Liberation." *New York Review of Books* (17 Dec. 1970): 42–44.

——. "Witches and Fairies: Fitzgerald to Updike." *New York Review of Books* (2 Dec. 1971): 2–11.

Lüthi, Max. *The European Folktale: Form and Nature.* Bloomington: Indiana UP, 1986.

——. *The Fairytale As Art Form and Portrait of Man.* Bloomington: Indiana UP, 1985.

——. *Once Upon a Time.* Bloomington: Indiana UP, 1976.

MacDonald, Margaret Read. *The Storyteller's Sourcebook: A Subject, Title, and Motif Index to Folklore Collections for Children.* Detroit: Gale Research Company, 1982.

MacDonald, Tanis. *holding ground.* Toronto: Seraphim Editions, 2000.

MacNeil, Joe Neil. *Tales until Dawn: The World of a Cape Breton Gaelic Story-Teller.* Trans. and ed. John Shaw. Montreal: McGill-Queen's UP, 1987.

Magoun, Francis P., Jr., and Alexander H. Krappe, trans. *The Grimms' German Folk Tales.* Carbondale: Southern Illinois UP, 1960.

Manheim, Ralph. *Grimms' Tales for Young and Old.* Garden City, NY: Anchor Press/Doubleday, 1977.

McCarthy, William. *Jack in Two Worlds.* Chapel Hill: U of North Carolina P, 1994.

McCluhan, Marshall. *Understanding Media: The Extensions of Man.* New York: McGraw, 1964.

McGirr, Carol. Personal Interview. Feb. 1994.

McGlathery, James. *The Brothers Grimm and Folktale.* Urbana: U of Illinois P, 1988.

——. *Fairy Tale Romance: The Grimms, Basile, and Perrault.* Urbana: U of Illinois P, 1991.

Merkel, Johannes, and Michael Nagel, eds. *Erzählen.* Reinbeck bei Hamburg: Rowohlt, 1982.

Mieder, Wolfgang. *Disenchantments: An Anthology of Modern Fairy Tale Poetry.* Hanover, NH: UP of New England, 1985.

Minard, Rosemary. *Tradition and Innovation in Folk Literature.* Hanover, NH: UP of New England, 1987.

——. *Womenfolk and Fairy Tales.* Boston: Houghton Mifflin, 1975.

Mitchell, Lucy Sprague. *Here and Now Story Book.* New York: Dutton, 1948.

Monaghan, Patricia. *The Book of Goddesses and Heroines.* New York: E. P. Dutton, 1981.

Mullen, Patrick. "A Traditional Storyteller in Changing Contexts." In *"And Other Neighborly Names:" Social Process and Cultural Image in Texas Folklore.* Eds. Richard Bauman and Roger D. Abrahams. Austin: U of Texas P, 1991, 266–79.

Mumford, Lewis. *The City in History.* Harmondsworth, Middlesex, England: Kestrel, 1961.

Munsch, Robert. Interview with the CBC. 16 Nov. 1984.

——. Letter to the author. 15 Feb. 1991.

Newsweek 15 Oct. 1973, 101–02.

Oates, Joyce Carol. *Do with Me What You Will.* New York: Vanguard, 1973.

O'Callahan, Jay. Interview. *Yarnspinner* 6 (March 1982): 2–3.

Olrik, Axel. *Principles for Oral Narrative Research.* Trans. Kirsten Wolf and Jody Jensen. Bloomington: Indiana UP, 1992.

Oxford, Cheryl. "Jack in the Next Generation: The Intra-Family Transmission of a Jack Tale." Academic paper presented at the annual meeting of the Speech Communication Association in Atlanta, Georgia, October, 1991.

———. "'They Call Him Lucky Jack': Three Performance-Centered Case Studies of Storytelling in Watauga County, North Carolina." Diss. Northwestern U, 1987.

Panofsky, Dora, and Erwin Panofsky, *Pandora's Box: The Changing Aspects of a Mythological Symbol.* Princeton: Princeton UP, 1962.

Patai, Raphael. *The Hebrew Goddess.* New York: Avon, 1978.

Perrault, Charles. *The Fairy Tales of Charles Perrault.* Trans. Angela Carter. New York: Avon, 1979.

———. *Perrault's Complete Fairy Tales.* Trans. A. E. Johnson et al. New York: Dodd, Mead, 1961.

Phelps, Ethel. *The Maid of the North: Feminist Folktales from around the World.* New York: Holt Rinehart and Winston, 1981.

Phillips, J. A. *Eve: The History of an Idea.* New York: Harper, 1984.

Pomeroy, Sarah. *Goddesses, Whores, Wives, and Slaves.* New York: Schocken, 1975.

Pound, Richard. "Jack at Earl's." Unpublished honours essay, U of Winnipeg, 1996.

Radner, Joan Newlon. *Feminist Messages: Coding in Women's Folk Culture.* Urbana: U of Illinois P, 1993.

———. Letter to the author. Undated 1990.

Radner, Joan Newlon, and Susan S. Lanser. "The Feminist Voice: Strategies of Coding in Folklore and Literature." *Journal of American Folklore* 398 (1987): 412–25.

Raglan, Lord Fitzroy Richard Somerset. *The Hero: A Study in Tradition, Myth, and Drama.* New York: Vintage, 1956.

Randolph, Vance. *The Devil's Pretty Daughter.* New York: Columbia UP, 1955.

———. *Sticks in the Knapsack.* New York: Columbia UP, 1958.

———. *The Talking Turtle.* New York: Columbia UP, 1957.

———. *Who Blowed up the Church House.* New York: Columbia UP, 1953.

Riordan, James. *Tales from Central Russia.* Vol. 1. Harmondsworth, Middlesex, England: Kestrel Books, 1976.

Roberts, Leonard. *Old Greasybeard.* Detroit: Folklore Associates, 1969.

———. *Sang Branch Settlers: Folksongs and Tales of a Kentucky Mountain Family.* Austin: U of Texas P, 1974.

———. *South from Hell-fer-sartin.* 1st ed. 1955; 2nd ed. Berea, KY: Council of the Southern Mountains, 1964.

———. *Up Cutshin and Down Greasy.* Lexington: U of Kentucky P, 1959. Reprint 1964.

Roberts, Warren. *The Tale of the Kind and the Unkind Girls: Aarne-Thompson 480 and Related Tales.* Supplement-Serie zu Fabula, series B: Untersuchungen, vol. 1. Berlin: Walter de Gruyter and Company, 1981.

Rohrich, Lütz. *Folktales and Reality.* Trans. Peter Tokofsky. Bloomington: Indiana UP, 1991.

———. "Introduction." *Fairy Tales and Society: Illusion, Allusion and Paradigm.* Ed. Ruth Bottigheimer. Philadelphia: U of Philadelphia P, 1986. 1–9.

Rölleke, Heinz. "Die 'stockhessischen' Märchen der 'alten Marie': Das Ende eines Mythos um die frühesten KHM-Aufzeichnungen der Brüder Grimm." *Germanisch-Romanische Monatsschrift* 25 (1975): 74–86.

Rougemont, Denis de. *Love in the Western World.* New York: Harcourt, 1940.

Rountree, Iris. E-mail to the author. 11 May 2006.

Rowe, Karen. "Feminism and Fairy Tales." *Women's Studies* 6 (1979): 237–57. Reprinted in *Folk and Fairy Tales*. Eds. Martin Hallett and Barbara Karasek. Peterborough, ON: Broadview, 1991: 346–67.

Sawyer, Ruth. *The Way of the Storyteller*. New York: Viking, 1942. Reprint 1962.

Sexton, Anne. *Transformations*. Boston: Houghton, 1971.

Shaw, John. Letter to the author. Fall 1990.

———. Letter to the author. Undated 1991.

———. Letter to the author. Undated 1993.

———. Letter to the author. Undated 1996.

Shickel, Richard. *The Disney Version: The Life, Times, Art and Commerce of Walt Disney*. New York: Avon, 1968.

Simms, Laura. "The Lamplighters: Storytelling in the Modern World." *National Storytelling Journal* 1 (1984): 8–16.

———. "Storytelling, Children, and Imagination." *Yarnspinner* 6 (June 1982): 2.

Sobol, Joseph. "Everyman and Jack: The Storytelling of Donald Davis." Unpublished master's thesis, U of North Carolina, 1987.

———. "Jack in the Raw." In *Jack in Two Worlds*. Ed. William McCarthy. Chapel Hill: U of North Carolina P, 1994. 3–26.

———. "Jonesborough Days: The National Storytelling Festival and the Contemporary Storytelling Revival Movement in America." PhD dissertation, Northwestern University, 1994.

———. *The Storyteller's Journey: An American Revival*. Urbana: U of Illinois P, 1998.

Spicer, Dorothy. *13 Devils*. New York: Coward-McCann, 1967.

Spiller, Harley. "Cinderella in the Schools." Unpublished student essay, U of Winnipeg, 1979.

Spray, Carol. *Will o' the Wisp: Folktales and Legends of New Brunswick*. Fredericton, NB: Brunswick, 1979.

Stallings, Fran. Letter to the author. 5 Dec. 1990.

Stevens, H. C. *Russian Folktales*. London: Paul Hamlyn, 1967.

Stewart, Polly. "A Response to the Symposium." *Journal of American Folklore* 88 (1975): 101–14.

Stone, Elizabeth. "Frolicks of a Distempered Mind: Early Publications of Fairy Tales in America." Unpublished essay, n.d.

Stone, Kay. "And She Lived Happily Ever After?" *Women and Language* 19.1 (1996): 14–18.

———. "Burning Brightly: New Light on an Old Tale." In *Feminist Messages: Coding in Women's Folk Culture*. Ed. Joan Radner. Urbana: U of Illinois P, 1993. 289–305.

———. *Burning Brightly: New Light on Old Tales Told Today*. Peterborough, Ont.: Broadview, 1998.

———. "The Curious Girl." In *Next Teller: A Book of Canadian Storytelling*. Ed. Dan Yashinsky. Charlottetown, PEI: Ragweed, 1994. 8–14.

———. "Difficult Women in Folktales: Two Women, Two Stories." In *Undisciplined Women: Tradition and Culture in Canada*. Eds. Pauline Greenhill and Diane Tye. Montreal: McGill-Queen's UP, 1997. 250–65.

———. "Fairy Tales for Adults: Walt Disney's Americanization of the *Märchen*." In *Folklore on Two Continents: Essays in Honor of Linda Dégh*. Eds. Nikolai Burlakoff and Carl Lindahl. Bloomington, IN: Trickster, 1980. 40–48.

———. "Fire and Water: A Journey into the Heart of a Story." In *Fairy Tales and Feminism.* Ed. Donald Haase. Detroit: Wayne State UP, 2004. 113–28.

———. *The Golden Woman: Dreaming as Art.* Winnipeg, MB: J. Gordon Shillingford, 2004.

———. "I Never Told This Story to Anyone Before." *National Storytelling Journal* (Fall 1985): 3–7.

———. "Inside Out: Folktale and Personal Story." *Marvels & Tales: Journal of Fairy-Tale Studies* 2.1–2 (1997): 13–23.

———. "Jack's Adventures in Toronto." In *Jack in Two Worlds.* Ed. William McCarthy. Chapel Hill: U of North Carolina P, 1994. 250–71.

———. "Macht mit mir, was ihr wollt" ["Do with me what you will"]. In *Die Frau in Märchen.* Eds. Sigrid Früh and Rainer Wehse. Kassel: Röth, 1985. 164–73.

———. "The Misuses of Enchantment." In *Women's Folklore, Women's Culture.* Eds. Rosan Jordan and Susan Kalčik. Philadelphia: U of Pennsylvania P, 1985. 125–45.

———. "Old Stories/New Listeners." In *Who Says? Essays on Pivotal Issues in Contemporary Storytelling.* Eds. Carol Birch and Melissa Heckler. Little Rock, AK: August House, 1996. 155–76.

———. "Once Upon a Time Today: Grimm Tales for Contemporary Performers." In *The Reception of the Grimms' Fairy Tales: Responses, Reactions, Revisions.* Ed. Donald Haase. Detroit: Wayne State UP, 1993. 250–69.

———. "Oral Narration in Contemporary North America." In *Fairy Tales and Society: Illusion, Allusion and Paradigm.* Ed. Ruth Bottigheimer. Philadelphia: U of Pennsylvania P, 1986. 13–31.

———. "Romantic Heroines in Anglo-American Folk and Popular Literature." Diss. Indiana U, 1975.

———. "Things Walt Disney Never Told Us." In *Women and Folklore.* Ed. Claire Farrer. Austin: U of Texas P, 1975. 42–50.

———. "Three Transformations of Snow White." In *The Brothers Grimm and the Folktale.* Ed. J. M. McGlathery. Urbana: U of Illinois P, 1988. 52–65.

———. "To Ease the Heart: Traditional Storytelling." *The National Storytelling Journal* (Winter 1984): 1–3.

———. "Urban Transformations of Traditional Tales." Academic paper presented the 9th Congress of the International Society for Folk Narrative Research, Budapest, 10–17 June 1989.

———. "The Water of Life." In *At the Edge: A Book of Risky Stories.* Ed. Dan Yashinsky. Charlottetown, PEI: Ragweed, 1998. 211–16.

Stone, Ted. Letter to the author. 14 Jan. 1991.

Storm, Hyemeyohsts. *Seven Arrows.* New York: Ballantine, 1972.

Stotter, Ruth. Letter to the author. Nov. 1984.

Tatar, Maria. *The Hard Facts of the Grimms' Fairy Tales.* Princeton: Princeton UP, 1987.

———. *Off with Their Heads: Fairy Tales and the Culture of Childhood.* Princeton: Princeton UP, 1992.

Tedlock, Dennis. *The Spoken Word and the Work of Interpretation.* Philadelphia: U of Pennsylvania P, 1983.

Thompson, Stith. *The Folktale.* New York: Holt, Rhinehart and Winston, 1946.

———. *Motif Index of Folk-Literature.* Bloomington: Indiana UP, 1955–58.

Tolkien, J. R. R. *Tree and Leaf.* Boston: Houghton, 1964.

Tong, Diane. *Gypsy Folk Tales.* New York: MJF, 1989.

Tribble, Phyllis. "Depatriarchalizing in Biblical Interpretation." In *The Jewish Woman: New Perspectives.* Ed. Elizabeth Koltun. New York: Schocken, 1976. 217–40.

Ueland, Brenda. *If You Want to Write.* St. Paul, MN: Graywolf, 1987.

Van Deusen, Kira. E-mail to the author. June 2000.

———. *The Flying Tiger: Women Shamans and Storytellers of the Amur.* Montreal: McGill-Queen's UP, 2001.

———. Letter to the author. 21 Mar. 1996.

———. *Raven and the Rock: Storytelling in Chukotka.* Seattle: U of Washington P, 1999.

———. *Shyaan am! Tuvan Folk Tales.* Bellingham, Wash.: Udagan Books, 1996.

Voigt, Vilmos. "Modern Storytelling—Stricto Sensu." Academic paper presented at the 9th Congress of the International Society for Folk Narrative Research. Budapest, Hungary, 10–17 June 1989.

Waelti-Walters, Barbara. *Fairy Tales and Female Consciousness.* Montreal: Eden, 1982.

Walker, Barbara. *The Woman's Encyclopedia of Myths and Secrets.* San Francisco: Harper, 1983.

Ward, Donald. "Idionarrating and Social Change." Academic paper presented at the 9th Congress of the International Society for Folk Narrative Research. Budapest, Hungary, 10–17 June 1989.

Weigle, Marta. *Spiders and Spinsters: Women and Mythology.* Albuquerque: U of New Mexico P, 1982.

Weinreich, Beatrice, and Leonard Wolf. *Yiddish Folktales.* New York: Pantheon Books in cooperation with YIVO Institute for Jewish Research, 1988.

Williams, Jay. *Petronella.* New York: Parents, 1973.

———. "The Practical Princess." *Ms. Magazine,* August 1972. 61–64.

Yashinsky, Dan. *At The Edge: A Book of Risky Stories.* Charlottetown, PEI: Ragweed, 1998.

———. *Appleseed Newsletter* (Fall 1989), 5.

———. *Next Teller: A Book of Canadian Storytelling.* Charlottetown, PEI: Ragweed, 1994.

———. *Tales for an Unknown City.* Montreal: McGill-Queen's UP, 1990.

———. Letter to the author. Undated 1991.

Yolen, Jane. Conversation with the author. 20 Mar. 1984.

Zipes, Jack. *The Complete Fairy Tales of the Brothers Grimm.* 2 vols. New York: Bantam, 1987.

———. *Don't Bet on the Prince: Contemporary Feminist Fairy Tales in North America and England.* New York: Methuen, 1986.

———. *Fairy Tales and the Art of Subversion: The Classical Genre for Children and the Process of Civilization.* New York: Wildman, 1983.

Permissions Acknowledgments

All of the chapters in this book have been previously published in the following books and journals:

"Things Walt Disney Never Told Us," *Women and Folklore*, ed. Claire Farrer (1975). Reprinted by permission of the American Folklore Society (www.afsnet.org).

"Fairy Tales for Adults: Walt Disney's Americanization of the *Märchen*," *Folklore on Two Continents: Essays in Honor of Linda Dégh*, ed. Nikolai Burlakoff, Carl Lindahl, et al. (1980). Reprinted by permission of Trickster Press.

"The Misuses of Enchantment: Controversies on the Significance of Fairy Tales," *Women's Folklore, Women's Culture*, ed. Jordan and Kalčik. © 1985 University of Pennsylvania Press. Reprinted by permission of University of Pennsylvania Press.

"Feminist Approaches to the Interpretation of Fairy Tales" and "Oral Narration in North America," *Fairy Tales & Society*, ed. Ruth B. Bottigheimer. © 1986 University of Pennsylvania Press. Reprinted by permission of University of Pennsylvania Press.

"Three Transformations of Snow White," *The Brothers Grimm and Folktale*, ed. James M. McGlathery © 1993 by the Board of Trustees of the University of Illinois. Reprinted by permission of the University of Illinois Press.

"Once Upon a Time Today," *The Reception of the Grimms' Fairy Tales*, ed. Donald Haase (1993). Reprinted by permission of Wayne State University Press.

"Social Indentity in Organized Storytelling," "The Teller in the Tale," and "Old Tales, New Contexts," *Burning Brightly: New Light on Old Tales Told Today*, Kay Stone (1998). Reprinted by permission of Broadview Press.

"Burning Brightly: New Light from an Old Tale," *Feminist Messages: Coding in Women's Folk Culture*, ed. Joan Radner. © 1993 by the Board of Trustees of the University of Illinois. Reprinted by permission of the University of Illinois Press.

"Difficult Women in Folktales: Two Women, Two Stories," *Undisciplined Women,* ed. Pauline Greenhill and Diane Tye (1997). Reprinted by permission of McGill-Queen's University Press.

"Fire and Water: A Journey into the Heart of a Story," *Fairy Tales and Feminism,* ed. Donald Haase (2004). Reprinted by permission of Wayne State University Press.

"In My Mother's Garden," "The Golden Woman: A Dream and a Story," "Follow Your Frog," and "Some Day Your Witch Might Come," *The Golden Woman: Dreaming as Art,* Kay Stone (2004). Reprinted by permission of J. Gordon Shillingford Publishing Inc.

The copyrighted stories in this book have been printed by permission of the following tellers:

"The Horoscope," Marylyn Peringer

"The Juniper Tree," Susan Gordon

"Snow White: A Reflection," Marvyne Jenoff

"The Three Feathers," Stewart Cameron (from his wife Dianne)

"Mistress Trudy" was originally published in *The Grimms' German Folktales,* trans. F. P. Magoun and A. H. Krappe. © 1960 by Southern Illinois University Press.

Joe Neil MacNeil's "The King of Egypt's Daughter," was originally published in *Tales until Dawn,* Joe Neil MacNeil (1987). Reprinted by the permission of McGill-Queen's University Press.

Aarne-Thompson Tale Types

Tale types are italicized, while story texts are in quotation marks.

Index

276, 281, 290, 295, 308; in folktales, 151, 158,
196, 242, 287; lucid dreaming, 255; paralysis
in, 290. *See also* dreams; Pound, Richard
Dundes, Alan, 64, 68
dwarfs: 17, 20, 25, 28, 30, 31, 67, 69; in Jenoff, 151,
152, 159–61. *See also* Snow White

Ellis, Elizabeth, 101, 102, 104, 110
Ellis, John, 64
Ellis, William, 191
epics, 40, 121, 215–16; Yugoslav, 80, 83, 216,
317n4; MacNeil, 208
Eve, 59, 61

Fairbanks, Douglas (as model for Disney
prince), 28, 70
fairies: 18, 39, 153; in Disney, 27–31
fairy tales: disobedience in, 137, 138, 180, 292;
feminist approaches and critiques, 13, 21,
36–38ff, 44, 129, 232–34, 238–40; helpers,
34, 131, 153, 180, 211, 273, 312; interpretations, 19–22, 33–34, 258; popularity of
among tellers, 105; print versions, 44, 63–
66, 72–74, 77–80, 83, 90, 108; readers' responses, 7, 13, 20, 33, 36, 40, 56, 72, 78, 100,
130, 142, 171, 223–24, 307–8, 315n1; reworked, 53–54, 57, 58, 63, 83, 107, 147,
148, 151; romance in, 28, 31, 32, 35, 57, 283;
scholarship, 38, 67, 73, 79, 97, 113, 173, 175,
187 (*see also* Bottigheimer, Dégh, Lüthi,
Rohrich, Tatar); sexuality in, 18; transformation of, 63, 69, 99–100, 109, 142, 157, 242–
43; transformation of characters, 70, 111–12,
131, 133–34, 139–40, 144, 238, 273, 307; violence in, 16, 37, 107, 110, 153, 174. *See also* animals; Disney, Walt; folktales; heroines; interviews; storytelling; *and individual story
titles*
fakelore, 64, 68
fathers: 15, 17–18, 109, 137, 287, 333; in Gordon's
tale text, 163–70; in Jenoff's tale text, 158–
163; Joe Neil MacNeil, 230, 232; Marilyn
Peringer, 178, 180, 183; Maryne Jenoff, 151–
52, 300; Ösküs-ool, 283; in Stewart
Cameron, 201, 205; in Susan Gordon, 154–
56, 161–70, 240
Fauset, Arthur Huff, 5, 17
Feit, Ken, 88
"Fisherman and His Wife, The," 104, 106
Folklore Studies Association of Canada, 142
folktales: British and American, 17, 93; influence

of, 101, 102, 110, 131, 173; personalization of:
153, 156, 172–74, 281, 291; reworked, 130, 148;
scholarship: *See* Dégh; Lüthi. *See also* fairy
tales; interviews; storytelling
"Foolish Jack," 278
Franz, Marie-Louise von, 39, 59
"Frau Trude" (also "Mistress Trudy"): 3, 106,
111, 114, 129, 131–47, 232–41, 294–97, 308,
312, 333; supernatural, 137–38; tale text,
"Mistress Trudy" 133. *See also* "The Curi-
ous Girl"
"Frau Holle, 4, 15, 105, 273, 292, 303–4
French Canada, 67, 124, 176–80, 189–96, 319n2,
319n4
Freud, Sigmund, 13, 19–20, 34, 58
Friedan, Betty, 4, 56, 239
Froebel, Friedrich, 84
"Frog King, The," 106, 234
"Frog Prince, The," 15, 60, 101, 104,
Frye, Northrup, 33

Gaelic language and tradition. *See* MacNeil, Joe
Neil
Gans, Herbert, 71
Garner, Richard, 53–54
Georges, Robert, 115, 117
Germany, 68, 102, 282
giants, 18, 20, 25–26, 33, 45, 67, 236, 237, 271–72,
278, 309; psychological implications, 33, 39,
42, 309
"Gifts of Little Folk," 105
Girardot, N.J., 40, 41, 44, 51–52
"Girl Without Hands, The." *See* "The Handless
Maiden"
Glassie, Henry, 179
goddesses, 58–59, 311
"Godfather Death," 137–38
"Godfather, The," 137
"Golden Feather, The," 282
"Golden Goose, The," 104, 106
"Golden Woman, The." *See* dreams (Kay Stone)
"Goosegirl, The," 105
Gordon, Susan: 104, 108, 110–11, 148–51, 153–
58, 240; tale text, 163–70
Gorog-Karady, Veronika, 149–50, 157
Graham, Morgana, 299
Graham, Paula, 122
Grimm tales: 98–114; crone/witch, 291, 311; Dis-
ney, 28, 31, 45, 62–63, 70–73; 265, 272–73;
heroines, 15, 17, 19, 22, 44, 147–48; oral nar-
ration of, 63–66, 96; popular source, 3, 14,

Grimm tales (*continued*)
25, 147–48, 315n1. *See also* Cinderella; Snow White; villains

Haase, Donald, 98, 232
"Handless Maiden, The," 15, 106, 157, 235; Susan Gordon's comments, 104, 148, 153, 240
"Hansel and Gretel," 14. 15, 16, 38, 101, 103, 104, 105, 107, 147, 308
Harrell, John, 96, 107, 108
Head, George. *See* Aboriginal storytelling
Heaven Can Wait, 32
"Hero Avoids His Predicted Destiny," 189. *See* "The Horoscope"
"The Horoscope," 189–96, 333. *See also* Marylyn Peringer
heroine(s): active, 5, 14–15, 17–19, 44, 57, 138, 236, 273, 277; feminist critiques, 56–59, 239; in Grimms, 14–15, 100; ideal woman, 51, 53; inner strength, 56, 58, 240; passive, 2, 5, 8, 13–14, 17–18, 19, 28, 56, 310; readers' responses, 21–22, 32, 42, 44, 46, 49, 120–31, 278; in scholarship, 8, 14, 36, 38–41, 55; varieties of, 13, 15, 22, 52, 132, 233, 235–36, 240, 242, 307–8; Hesse, Hermann, 113. *See also* Disney, Walt; fairy tales; folktales; interviews
Heuscher, Julius, 20, 50, 54
Hicks family: 83–84, 49, 221; Ray Hicks, 6, 91, 118, 174, 209, 219, 220–21, 225; Stanley Hicks, 83, 221; Hattie Presnell, 83, 84; Marshall Ward, 221
Holt, David, 88
Homo narrans, 122, 150
"Horizon." *See* Tanis MacDonald
Hornyansky, Michael, 20
"Horoscope, The," 176–81, 187; tale text, 189–96. *See also* Marylyn Peringer
Howe, Carol, 122
Hymes, Del, 223

idionarration, 150–52, 154, 157
International Society for Folk-Narrative Research, 146, 148
interviews: "Cinderella," 88, 95, 118; crones, 289; dissertation, 3–8, 15, 19, 21–22, 33, 36, 41, 43, 45, 100, 130, 132, 240, 278; dissident views, 4, 147, 249; dreams, 7; of others, 88, 95, 118; storytellers, 105, 112, 115, 123–24; 146, 172–73, 176–78, 239
Ireland, 179, 256, 282, 295

Jack tales: 5, 83, 103, 277–88; and Disney, 25, 26, 278; and females, 17–20, 39, 43–45, 53; "Jack and the Beanstalk," 20, 42, 101, 278; "Jack and the Devil's Grandmother," 103; and Stewart Cameron, 171, 176, 180, 182–87; tale text, 196–206
Jenoff, Marvyne, 103,106, 110, 148–58, 311; tale text, 158–63
Jewish tales, 282, 283
Jones, Stephen Swann, 62, 67
Jonesborough TN. *See* NAPPS
"Jorinda and Joringel," 105
Journal of American Folklore, The, 178
"Jumping Mouse." *See* Aboriginal storytelling
Jung, Carl, 19; Jungian approach, 39, 59, 143; Jungian "shadow," 143, 266, 293, 295
"Juniper Tree, The": 20, 102, 104, 105, 109–11, 114, 148–49, 153–56, 333; tale text, 163–70. *See also* Gordon, Susan

Kalčik, Susan, 36
Kane, Alice, 110, 124, 128
Karaty-Khan, 283
"Kate Crackernuts," 18
Kavablum, Leah, 45, 58
"Kind and Unkind Girls." *See* "Light Kate and Dark Kate"
King Thrushbeard," 15, 18, 105, 107
King, Stephen, 110
"King of Egypt's Daughter, The," 208, 210, 213, 225, 333; tale text, 225–31
Kolbenschlag, Madonna, 59–60
Kronberg, Ruthilde, 102, 103, 104

LaBrie, Vivian, 141
Lacoursière, Luc, 177, 189, 319n2, 319n4
"Lady Madelaine," 18
Lady Macbeth, 70
Lang, Andrew: feminist critique, 239; and "Misfortune in Youth," 286; as popular source, 4, 14, 56, 148; and "Water of Life," 235, 239, 242
Lasalle, Bruno, 110
Lee, Tanith, 58, 240
Lieberman, Marcia, 4, 21, 38, 41, 57, 239
"Light Kate and Dark Kate," 289–91, 297–98, 333; tale text, 299–306
"Little Red Riding Hood:" in film, 15, 20, 25, 39, 101, 103; as "Little Red Cap," 106
"Little Humpback Horse, The," 282